"Kendrick Norris provides the first comprehensive examination of the symbols, images, texts and traditions of Christmas as seen through the lens of three psychological perspectives. The result is a compelling analysis of its enduring appeal to the human heart, soul, and mind across cultures, across times, in some cases even across religious traditions."

Wayne G. Rollins, PhD, author of *Soul and Psyche,*
Jung and the Bible, and others

"An insightful and informative interpretation of the psychological meaning of Christmas. Christmas will never be the same for anyone who reads it; its meaning will be deepened and the celebration more enthusiastic. I recommend it for everyone, especially those for whom Christmas has become a superficial ritual."

Harville Hendrix, PhD, co-author with Helen LaKelly Hunt of
How to Talk with Anyone About Anything, and co-founder of
Imago Relationship Therapy

"Kendrick Norris retells the Christmas story with the vocabulary of some of our most thoughtful psychologists, and we find its images refreshed and re-empowered."

James Dittes, PhD, Professor Emeritus of Pastoral Theology
and Religious Studies, Yale University

"A brilliant utilization of Kohutian and Jungian hermeneutics to adumbrate the depth of the Christmas myth that may open its meaning to our Post-Modern and Post-secular Age. I would also argue that your volume will become a companion text to Jung's *Aion* in which he argues that the Christ is the symbol of the Self in the Western tradition."

Donald Ferrell, PhD, Jungian Analyst, author of *Logos and*
Existence: The Relationship of Philosophy and Theology in
the Thought of Paul Tillich

Jungian and Psychoanalytic Perspectives on Christmas

By examining its history, traditions, symbols, and representation in the arts through the lens of three major schools of depth psychology, Kendrick L. Norris, a Jungian Analyst and minister, shows how better understanding of the promise of Christmas can allow us to discover what it is that we long for the most.

Why does the winter celebration of Christmas have such a deep-rooted resonance, individually and collectively? This extensively researched book clearly and engagingly articulates the soul reasons why this holiday has such a significant impact on the human psyche. The work begins with an explanation about how depth psychology can be used to understand the Christmas phenomenon, followed by an investigation into the origins and symbols of Christmas. The book closes by delving into the soul meaning of Christmas through the perspectives of Freud, Kohut, and Jung.

This thought-provoking volume will appeal to Jungian Analysts, psychoanalysts, and psychotherapists, as well as those interested in religion and its relation to depth psychology.

Kendrick Lyddon Norris, PhD, NCPsyA, IAAP, is a graduate of the C.G. Jung Institute of New York, past president of the New York Association for Analytical Psychology (NYAAP), and a certified Imago Relationship Therapist. Dr. Norris has worked at the Pastoral Counseling Center of St. Raphael's Hospital and Family Counseling of Greater New Haven, and has been in private practice for more than 30 years. He has three graduate degrees in clinical psychology and pastoral psychology, 40 years of parish experience, and is Minster Emeritus of the First Congregational Church of Guilford, Connecticut.

Jungian and Psychoanalytic Perspectives on Christmas

Origins, Motifs, and Psychological Significances

Kendrick Lyddon Norris

Routledge
Taylor & Francis Group

LONDON AND NEW YORK

Designed cover image: © Virgin and Child, by Dieric Bouts (detail),
Courtesy Metropolitan Museum of Art, New York; Theodore M. Davis
Collection, Bequest of Theodore M. Davis, 1915

First published 2025
by Routledge
4 Park Square, Milton Park, Abingdon, Oxon OX14 4RN

and by Routledge
605 Third Avenue, New York, NY 10158

Routledge is an imprint of the Taylor & Francis Group, an informa business

British Library Cataloguing-in-Publication Data
A catalogue record for this book is available from the British Library

ISBN: 978-1-032-94039-7 (hbk)
ISBN: 978-1-032-94037-3 (pbk)
ISBN: 978-1-003-56862-9 (ebk)

DOI: 10.4324/9781003568629

Typeset in Times New Roman
by Deanta Global Publishing Services, Chennai, India

Contents

Acknowledgments

A book is no easy thing. This one began with an intuitive flash while admiring Dieric Bouts's painting *Virgin and Child* at the Metropolitan Museum of Art in New York. I immediately experienced eureka joy and surety about the prime meaning of Christmas, a subject that had long intrigued me. However, getting to the facts of the insight was no easy task for an intuitive feeling type. Putting bone, sinew, and flesh on notions dancing in my head has been a challenging long-haul endeavor. Fortuitously, ongoing flare-ups of insight kept this project in the land of the living. There were also helpers.

Wondrously, Peter Hawkins, the inaugural professor of religion and literature at Yale Divinity School, was the first to usher me into the august world of symbolism. He removed the cataracts from my eyes so that I could see a more colorful and complex world. Decades later, Jim Dittes, professor of religion and psychology at Yale, heartily encouraged me to pursue this wide-ranging and boundary-breaking exploration of Christmas from a depth psychology perspective and allowed me, against academic protocols, to freely explore the many facets of the topic without requiring a completed thesis. I needed that gypsy freedom.

Jungian analysts Soren Ekstrom, Joe Wagenseller, Don Ferrell, and other colleagues from the New York Association for Analytical Psychology (NYAAP) generously contributed support and suggestions, and made sure that I didn't color too far outside the lines. Most important was meeting the Rev. Wayne Rollins, PhD, professor emeritus of biblical studies at Assumption College, founder and former chair of the Psychology and Biblical Studies Section of the Society of Biblical Literature, and author of *Jung and the Bible* and *Soul and Psyche: The Bible in Psychological Perspective*. Wayne's interests and sensibilities were a head-on match to mine. His enthusiasm for this book was critical to its completion, as were his organizational abilities that helped me keep my thoughts grounded and directed.

I am indebted to my family—my wife, Mary, sons Soren and Evan, and daughter, Lizzie—who endured my absences, strange moods, and the loss of the dining room table. I dedicate this book to Mary, who faithfully stood by me, utilized her expertise as an executive editor, and shared her sustaining love and buoyant smile with me. She is a Jubilee person and my Christmas angel.

Preface

Ernest Jones, psychoanalyst and biographer of Freud, gives warrant to this book: "To ask why we keep Christmas is to ask a good question."[1] Leading Jungian analyst, M. Esther Harding agrees: "There is need for a deeper understanding of the meaning of the birth of Christ."[2] There's much to understand. Why does this winter celebration have such a deep-rooted resonance, individually and collectively? Why, as the cold advances and the year turns, does yuletide alter our moods, skew our behaviors, and shift our priorities? Why do we feel comfort and joy when we hear Burl Ives sing "Have a Holly Jolly Christmas"? Why is our hospitality warmer, even to strangers? Why does this ancient event induce strange rituals, make us dream of home, and privilege children? Why is there always a tinge of disappointment when it's all over? Why Christmas? Remarkably few have published responses to the question. This extensively researched book begins to fill that void with convincing and engaging psychological answers.

C.G. Jung was fond of saying, "If you ask people why they put up a Christmas tree, decorate it and light candles on it, you rarely get a proper answer."[3] Given this prevailing incomprehension, Jung would note that the Christmas tree is a symbol, as are the accompanying ornaments, lights, and presents. Symbols are born from the collective unconscious, which can then invoke their compelling vitality and significance, as it clearly does during the Christmas season. To Jung's point: At Christmas, we are compelled to engage in a card deck of traditions, but we do not understand why.

To answer—why Christmas?—we will use the way of Jung. That is, to be rigorous and relentless. We will look all around, at both the forest and the trees, surveying the wider landscape of Christmas, putting a microscope to each part, identifying and amplifying its symbols, and holding it tight for as long as it takes to reveal its plentiful meanings for the psyche. Christmas, here we come.

Notes

1 Ernest Jones, "The Significance of Christmas," in *Essays in Applied Psycho-Analysis,* 2 (Hogarth Press, 1951), 212.

2 M. Esther Harding, "The Christmas Message from the Point of View of Analytical Psychology," *Concern,* December 1970, 20.

3 Aniela Jaffe. *Reflections on the Life and Dreams of C.G. Jung* (Daimon, 2023), 142; William McGuire and R.F.C. Hull, *C.G. Jung Speaking: Interviews and Encounters* (Princeton University Press, 1977), 353-58. Astute religious leader Fulton J. Sheen, in *From the Angel's Blackboard: The Best of Fulton J. Sheen* (Triumph Books, 1995), 207, posits a similar ignorance: "Once a year, at Christmas time, everyone is happy and loving, kind and generous, but one wonders if they know why they are happy."

Introduction

Throughout the Western world, no other holiday exerts as much influence over us as that of Christmas. Christmastime is so attractive and compelling that even the measured or dour describe it as "magical." It is not just that the retail economy is oriented to and dependent upon Christmas gift-giving or that throngs quest after the perfect evergreen tree with the passion of Parsifal seeking the Holy Grail. Moods are elevated for the majority; expectations run high—for most. Churches burst their pews, everyone comes home or wants to be home, and largesse is the rule as lavish preparations are made for what has become the day of all days. December becomes a month-long high tide of good cheer and hospitality. Hope brims. Why? How do we account for this day's power of engagement? Or, as poet Carl Sandburg ponders: "Why does the story never wear out?"[1]

Historian Clement Miles understands that "Christmas is the most human and lovable of the Church's feasts."[2] Writer Brenda Ueland speaks for many when she pens, "Christmas evokes the brightest memories."[3] But some agree with humorist Ogden Nash that "Roses are things which Christmas is not a bed of them."[4] Indeed, John Updike sardonically penned *The Twelve Terrors of Christmas*.[5] And many churches offer "Blue Christmas" worship as Christmas approaches. Yet those who find Christmas a month-long headache or heartache only further reveal how impactful Christmas remains in contemporary life and our psyches.

As a pastor of one congregation for 38 years, I can attest to the palpable qualitative difference in affect among parishioners on Easter Sunday and Christmas Eve. Easter is impressive, majestic, larger than life, but it feels simply like a more intense Sunday. This makes sense because, for Christians, every Sunday is a little Easter, and Easter is Sunday *grande*. Christmas Eve is something altogether different, a magnitude greater. The joy is deeper, the embraces longer, the smiles broader. Given the outward meaning of each celebration—Easter with its ultimate promise of eternal life and Christmas with its "Infant Holy, Infant Lowly" birth narrative— this is failed logic. Although Easter, the monarch of hope, should win our hearts hands down, just the opposite is true. Somehow the babe born in a manger wields a more potent promise. Perhaps Shakespeare can help us understand this:

DOI: 10.4324/9781003568629-1

Some say that ever 'gainst that season comes
Wherein our Savior's birth is celebrated,
This bird of dawning singeth all night long;
And then, they say, no spirit dare stir abroad;
The nights are wholesome, then no planets strike,
No fairy takes, nor witch hath power to charm,
So hallow'd and so gracious is the time.[6]

Well said, but far-fetched? Here are two testimonies revealing that people can find these lofty words remarkably real. An intelligent and accomplished young Chinese woman raised in Hong Kong by a "Tiger Mom" entered therapy for depression. This December psychotherapy session with me, however, her mood was entirely different. For the first time in our meetings, she had a gleam in her eye and a broad smile on her face. She radiated joy. When I inquired about this remarkable shift in her mood, she enthusiastically explained. Though not from a Christian family, she had been enrolled in a Catholic school to get the most important thing to ensure her future: a high-quality education. Not wanting anything to get in the way of learning, the nuns saw it as their task to squash and prohibit other interests. This was experienced as oppressive cruelty. The Christmas season was the one time of year when her nun-teachers softened their countenances and loosened the shackles on their charges. Their culture's most propitious time, Chinese New Year, followed Christmas and required of each celebrant a gracious spirit to others if they hoped for happiness and prosperity themselves. Marching to collective requisites, her mother, as well as the nuns, briefly replaced scoldings with smiles. The current multitude of nighttime Christmas lights thus evoked for her past times of blessed reprieve from being relentlessly controlled and belittled. At Christmas, her witches became impotent, and she a prisoner freed.

In 1906, Rainer Maria Rilke wrote a letter to his wife, Clara, to be read on Christmas Eve. He shared a similar Christmas story as my analysand:

You know … what Christmas was to me in my early childhood; even when the military academy made a hard, unbelievably malicious life, devoid of wonders, appear so real that no other reality seemed possible to me beside that undeserved one; even then Christmas was still real and was that which approached with a fulfillment that went out beyond all wishes, and when it was out beyond the very last, never even wished ones, then only did it really begin, then what had hitherto walked, unfolded wings and flew, flew till it was no longer to be seen and one knew only its direction, in the great flowing light.[7]

As frosty winter arrives, an auspicious spirit warms many with heightened expectations.

Unlike other high holy days, Christmas is more self-driven than church-directed. Christmas belongs to the people: They engage with it, uphold its customs, and take responsibility for celebrating it. In December, most Christian homes become a

Christmas chapel with a crèche (a tradition from Italy), a Christmas tree (a custom from Germany), and perhaps even mistletoe (a practice from England). Giving and receiving presents alternatively makes each person a Magi and then a Christ Child. Christmas cards cross vast distances, and even yards are festooned with bright lights and bold figures. Christmas is a pursuit of the people.

I live in a small New England community where churched and unchurched folks, shivering and joy-filled, gather on the town green to sing carols and light the town Christmas tree on the Friday closest to the start of December. No clergy lead the group. Town residents place single candles in their windows. All is bright and gay, even on the dark eve of a cold winter night. Here, as in villages and cities across America, the Christmas spirit is good for a whole month. Of course, this is not liturgically correct—devout Christians understand the season of Advent as solemn preparation for the holy day—but this town-wide "good cheer" reveals how Christmas has taken on a life of its own. For centuries, families and communities have celebrated Christmas quite independent of ecclesiastical correctness or approval. That may be part of the joy.

Something else astonishes about this holiday. Christmas magnetism transcends the usually rigid boundaries, making it the only Christian festival that appeals to non-Christians. Its symbols and rituals collectively attract, delivering believers and non-believers into a different psychological sphere. A 2013 Pew Research poll found that 87 percent of American non-Christians celebrate Christmas.[8] While two-thirds of Americans identify as Christian, a 2017 Pew Research poll reported that 90 percent of Americans celebrate Christmas.[9] A 2019 Gallup poll established that "more than 80 percent of people (Americans) with no religious affiliation celebrate Christmas, with about two in 10 ascribing at least some religious significance to it."[10]

Ernest Jones, Freud's biographer, writes:

> I remember when crossing to America a couple of years ago in December finding that nearly half of the passengers were American Jews rushing through in order to be "home for Christmas"; and no doubt the same observation could be made in any other year.[11]

My childhood Jewish friends in New York City would ably and happily decorate what they euphemistically called "Hanukkah bushes." Stephen Nissenbaum, the Jewish author of a book about Christmas, admits to putting his toys in a sack and distributing them to other children living in his Jersey City apartment building:

> For me, growing up as I did in an Orthodox Jewish household, this ("The Night Before Christmas") was surely part of my fascination for Christmas itself, that magical season which was always beckoning. [12]

According to Freud's letters to his children, Christmas celebrations were part of his family holiday tradition. He even had separate bank accounts for Christmas presents.[13]

The New York Times reports that "Istanbul's largely Muslim population has embraced Christmas as a secular holiday."[14] Amy Yadev, a Sikh, describes celebrating Christmas in her family, signing December emails with "Merry Christmas," and feeling the "aura of festivity, positive spirit and joy around me."[15] In Japan, where only 1 percent of the population is Christian and where Christianity is looked upon with great suspicion, Christmas has become a thriving holiday. "In 2020, All Nippon Airways delivered more than 80,000 letters to Santa from children all over the country."[16] Hotei, the jolly and rotund Japanese god, is now conflated with Santa Claus. Every year in December, "revelers put a Santa hat and beard on the Hotei statue in Tokyo's Maitreya Temple."[17] Something universal about Christmas sweeps people into its prevailing current.

Joyce Sequichie Hifler, a Cherokee whose ancestors were marched to Oklahoma on the Trail of Tears, brings Native American wisdom to people of all faiths. Here she writes about her childhood:

> My memories are filled with special people and the things they said, beautiful Christmas trees and the smells of delicious food. … I loved my grandmother's hot biscuits and the love she baked into each one. But perhaps what I loved the best was that Christmas was about the birth of a child—and I loved being part of that child every day of my life.[18]

On the momentous occasion of orbiting space, James Irwin noted, "The Earth reminded us of a Christmas tree ornament hanging in the blackness of space."[19] A remarkable view so few see, a free-floating environment physically and psychically, emotions robust—and the astronauts' first association is with Christmas.

Grace Lynne Haynes, a young African American artist with paintings on two *New Yorker* covers in 2020, states: "I consider art a spiritual practice. I remember when I wasn't making art. It was like my senses weren't alive. [When I resumed] it was like I felt Christmas again."[20] So many meanings for so many. No wonder 19th-century history of religions scholar Hermann Usener proclaimed Christmas to be "the mother of all festivals."[21] Something about the mystery and magic of Christmas enchants so many at a very deep level.

In 1971, the same year John Lennon hopefully imagined world peace with no religions, he released a song ("Happy Xmas (War Is Over)") earnestly wishing everyone a merry, merry Christmas. How does this make sense? Howard Thurman, theologian and civil rights leader, proposes that "Christmas is a mood, a quality, a symbol."[22] This is our approach as well. Therefore, this book makes no claims about the person of Jesus or the theological Christ, topics irrelevant to our purposes. Through the disciplines of history and psychology, we work toward understanding why the Christmas cast of characters, particularly the symbol of the baby Jesus, causes the axis of the Western psyche to tilt in December.

The first chapter carefully explains why depth psychology is our best means to understand this brimming over at Christmas. With that understanding in full grasp, we note that Christmas is kaleidoscopic, with many colorful pieces making up the complex whole. Each fragment requires exploration. In this pursuit, we next investigate the origins of Christmas—the onset, syncretistic development, and ever-widening manifestations of the celebration of Jesus' birth. We continue our circumambulation by elucidating the prominent motifs of Christmas in hope of giving readers confidence that the answers to our question "Why Christmas?" are well grounded in the phenomenology of Christmas.

In the book's last three chapters, depth psychology is our guide to comprehending how Christmas stirs and answers our constitutive longings. The perennial, powerful, and manifold resonance of Christmas is explained through the insights of Psychoanalysis (Sigmund Freud), Self psychology (Heinz Kohut), and Analytical psychology (C.G. Jung). By its conclusion, this book conveys the strongest psychological meanings operational at Christmas. This will be an expedition, bringing you to familiar landscapes as well as vistas not yet imagined. Welcome.

Notes

1 Carl Sandburg, "Star Silver," *The Complete Poems of Carl Sandburg* (Harcourt Brace Jovanovich, 1970), 685. From the poem "Star Silver," by Carl Sandburg, © 1970 HarperCollins Publishers, used with permission.
2 Clement A. Miles, *Christmas in Ritual and Tradition: Christian and Pagan*, 2nd ed. (T. Fisher Unwin, 1913), 157.
3 Brenda Ueland, *Me* (The Schubert Club), 1983.
4 Ogden Nash quote found in *Elizabeth David's Christmas* (David R. Godine, 2008) 1.
5 John Updike, *The Twelve Terrors of Christmas* (Pomegranate, 1999).
6 William Shakespeare, *The Tragedy of Hamlet, Prince of Denmark* (Washington Square Press, 1992), 19.
7 Rainer Maria Rilke, *Letters of Rainer Maria Rilke: 1892–1910* (Norton, 1945), 249.
8 Besheer Mohamed, "Christmas Also Celebrated by Many Non-Christians," Pew Research Center, 2013. Accessed November 15, 2024, pewresearch.org/short-reads/20 13/12/23/christmas-also-celebrated-by-many-non-christians. This includes 76 percent of Asian American Buddhists and 76 percent of Hindus; 32 percent of Jews had a Christmas tree in their homes.
9 Pew Research. "Americans Say Religious Aspects of Christmas Are Declining in Public Life," December 12, 2017. pewresearch.org/religion/2017/12/12/americans -say-religious-aspects-of-christmas-are-declining-in-public-life. Accessed November 15, 2024.
10 Gallup. "More Americans Celebrating a Secular Christmas," by Zach Hrynowski, December 20, 2019. Accessed November 15, 2024, news.gallup.com/poll/272378/am ericans-celebrating-secular-christmas.aspx.
11 Ernest Jones, "The Significance of Christmas," in *Essays in Applied Psycho-Analysis*, Vol. 2, ed. Ernest Jones, *The International Psycho-Analytical Library*, no. 41 (The Hogarth Press, 1951), 213.
12 Stephen Nissenbaum, *The Battle for Christmas: A Social and Cultural History of Christmas That Shows How It Was Transformed from an Unruly Carnival Season into the Quintessential American Family Holiday* (Alfred A. Knopf, 1996), ix.
13 Rita Teusch, "Selections from Two German Journals," *The Psychoanalytic Quarterly* 83, no. 3 (2014), 757.
14 Stephen Kinzer, "Strange, That's Santa in the Seat of the Sultans!" *The New York Times*, December 21, 1996, 4.

15 Amy Yadev, "Celebrating Christmas as a Non-Christian Sikh," Center for Interfaith Dialogue, December 17, 2020. Interfaith.wisc.edu/2020/celebrating-Christmas-as-a -non-christian-sikh-amy-yadev.

16 Gaijin Pot, "Ho, Ho, Hotei: The Japanese Santa Claus," *Japan Today*, December 7, 2021, 1–4.

17 Megan Bryson, "Japan's Laughing Buddha Hotei Is Merging into Santa Claus," The Conversation.com, published December 12, 2022. theconversation.com/japans-lau ghing-buddha-hotei-is-merging-into-santa-claus-both-are-roly-poly-sacred-figures-wi th-a-bag-of-gifts-195090, accessed May 11, 2025.

18 Joyce Sequichie Hifler, *A Cherokee Feast of Days*, Vol. 3 (Council Oak Books, 2002), 387.

19 Michael Reagan, ed. *The Hand of God* (Andrews McMeel, 2011), 158.

20 Grace Lynne Haynes, *State of the Art*, Season 39, Episode 4. PBS, aired April 24, 2021.

21 Ludwig Jekels, "The Psychology of the Festival of Christmas," in *Selected Papers* (International Universities Press, 1952), 143. On December 24, 1859, the *Chicago Times* called Christmas "this Monarch of the Holidays."

22 Howard Thurman, *The Mood of Christmas & Other Celebrations* (Friends United, 1985), ii.

Chapter 1

Approaching Christmas from a Depth Psychology Perspective

The enduring impact of Christmas on Western culture is as remarkable as it is taken for granted. What lies behind this Christmas commotion? Understanding what Christmas means for the psyche requires that we probe the bounteous human substrata. We ask, why did the Nativity narrative strike such a deep root, perennially bursting forth so wildly? Why the profusion of Christmas motifs? What gives them life? What do they symbolize? The field of depth psychology provides an array of understandings to forage for answers.

This chapter's three sections take up the task. The first section, "The Bible as a Book about the Soul," explains that although a literary/historical critical approach to Scripture is vital, it is insufficient. The contemporary emergence (some would say reawakening) of a psychological reading of Scripture is essential for a richer comprehension of the text and what it has led to, including the celebration of Jesus' birth. The second section, "Soulless Psychology," provides abstracts of empirical psychology's recent research about Christmas, proving it also inadequate to address our questions. Finally, "A Depth Psychological Approach" considers how the transpersonal world of symbols, stories, and archetypes helps us to understand our attachment to, fascination with, and enthusiasm for Christmas. This aligns us with the discerning assessment of Jungian analyst Aniela Jaffé: "The hypothesis of an unconscious underlying consciousness is the hallmark of psychological research in this century."[1]

The Bible as a Book about the Soul

The New Testament, consisting of the 27 books we know today, was not canonized until the late fourth century. In 382 CE, Pope Damasus, faced with a plethora of diverse Latin translations, commissioned his secretary and biblical scholar, Jerome, to produce a "uniform and dependable" edition.[2] The Western church relied upon this text until the Protestant Reformation of the 16th century. For more than a thousand years, only those who knew Latin—preaching priests and church scholars heavily influenced by sanctioned tradition and established doctrine—could access the Bible. For the Reformers, Scripture was central ("*sola scriptura*" or "prima

DOI: 10.4324/9781003568629-2

scriptura" were their ardent cries), a focus that compelled new vernacular translations so that any literate person could study the Bible.

With the coming Enlightenment, the critical analysis of Scripture ascended. Objectivity, neutrality, and rationality increasingly became the norm. It was a sea change, with readers moving beyond dogma-based assumptions to investigating how the books of the Bible developed, as well as uncovering the historical events that led to the texts. The historical–critical method developed into four methodologies: Textual, source, form, and redaction, with the addition of literary criticism in the 20th century. This approach continues to have a strong hold on seminaries and religious studies programs around the world.

Biblical criticism has capably grounded us with ever-widening perspectives of Scripture, as well as finer analyses of individual texts. However, just as biblical criticism was a giant leap forward in biblical insight, some stakeholders have taken a further leap. In 1983, New Testament professor Gerd Theissen asked, "Can the life context of religious texts be clarified without consideration of psychic forces and aspects?"[3] An excellent query. Historical biblical criticism cannot answer for us why the stories of Christ's Nativity have profoundly affected the masses for millennia, why such an image as the crèche scene arose to reside in so many homes, or as Carl Sandburg asked, "Why does the story never wear out?"[4]

To interpret a section of Scripture—what it has meant and motivated—without relating it to the psyche makes for a heartless horseman approach, which explains why biblical criticism has never preached well. Its dispassionate objectivity fails to connect with those who seek to understand their engaged relatedness to certain portions of holy texts. A psychological interpretation of the Bible is needed. Frederick Grant gives us our method and our mandate: "beyond the historical and exegetical interpretation of the Bible lies the whole new field of depth psychology and psychoanalysis."[5]

Traditional biblical scholars have been suspicious of those who examine the holy book with a psychological eye. Their position: "psychological exegesis is poor exegesis."[6] Such antipathy is perplexing to those who find it natural to analyze psychologically the things that matter most. Yet, the traditionalist's protest is more than trash talk. There have been problems with a psychological approach to Scripture, some self-inflicted and some inherent. D. Andrew Kille explains:

> Much of the skepticism about psychological approaches, I believe, is based on experiences with earlier attempts to apply psychological categories and insights to the text that were not appropriate to the dimensions of the text that the interpreter sought to unfold. Some of the earliest efforts at psychological interpretation took the form of psychoanalyzing biblical characters, thus delineating, sometimes with a perverse glee, the pathological aspects of Paul, the prophets, or even Jesus. Indeed, the proliferation of studies which sought to explain Jesus as an ecstatic personality, an epileptic, a paranoiac or a "case of nerves" finally drove Albert Schweitzer to submit as his M.D. thesis *The Psychiatric Study of Jesus: Exposition and Criticism*.[7]

Misplaced efforts and poor analysis blemished early attempts in this nascent field. Furthermore, the best that the psychological interpretation of the Bible can realize are multiple, subjective possibilities. Multiple because there are so many psychological schools, each addressing the text with their own assumptions and approaches. They are subjective because we are the subject. Although gifted with the ability for self-reflection,[8] we cannot entirely transcend ourselves to be completely objective scientists of the soul. However, the limits of the methodology do not negate the potent understandings to be reaped.

Some contemporary biblical scholars call for a joint enterprise. John Dominic Crossan suggests that efficacious Bible study is best conducted by a "multitude of disciples interacting mutually."[9] Gerd Theissen agrees:

Anyone who thinks that this religion can be illuminated historically and factually without psychological reflection is just as much in error as one who pretends that everything about this religion can be said in this fashion.[10]

The essential truth, as Jeffrey Staley notes, is that we need "an exegesis of souls that parallels our exegesis of texts."[11] J. Harold Ellens, founding editor of *The Journal of Psychology and Christianity,* points out:

Psychology is another lens through which it is possible to see any text and understand dimensions of it and the ways it reflects the living human document behind it which could not be understood if one did not employ this lens.[12]

Let's delve deeper.

Psyche/Soul

Etymologically, the word *psychology* proclaims itself indispensable for investigating the soul. *Psyche,* a Greek word and hence a New Testament word, is translated into English as "soul."[13] By definition, psychology is the science of the soul, giving a basis for Freud's reference to psychoanalysts as "soul healers."[14]

In October 2023, NASA launched its mission to the asteroid Psyche, named in the 16th century for the Greek goddess of the soul. Scientists cannot study Earth's core because it is too deep and too hot. Thus, they can learn much about our planet by exploring this asteroid, which appears to be another planet literally stripped to its metal-rich core. Being so elemental, it is hard for us to say what the soul is, but the fortuitous naming of this asteroid Psyche (soul), which is only core, offers analogous images.

The soul is the human core: A centered unity, whose magma warms, enflames, and fertilizes. The soul may also be regarded as the fecund fount, the immanent nebula, the vigorous central rhizome of human life. Merriam-Webster defines soul as "the immaterial essence, animating principle, or actuating cause of an individual life."[15] Philosopher G.B. Kerferd points out that such thinking is quite ancient, being pre-Platonic. As early as the sixth century BCE in Greece, the soul was seen as the "epitome of the individual," as the epicenter of thought, will, and emotion, as the "quintessence of human life."[16] Biblical scholar Wayne Rollins agrees:

> [The soul] is the center of emotions, longings, intentions, both spiritual and physical, constituting that spiritual-emotional-mental complex that more than any other ingredient identifies an individual's special personality and uniqueness and demonstrates the distinctive qualities of humanness.[17]

Jesus Portrayed as Soul Sage

Religious people of the West believe the soul comes from God and returns to God.[18] Genesis 2:7 reports that God "breathed into his nostrils the breath of life" and Adam became a "living soul."[19] The soul has tribulations and triumphs. Thus, mother-to-be Mary, filled with joy, declares, "My soul [psyche] magnifies the Lord" (Luke 1:46). The psyche/soul can be stirred up (Acts 14:2), unsettled (Acts 15:24), subjected to temptation (2 Peter 2:14), and besieged by passions (1 Peter 2:11).[20] And, as John writes (3 John 1:2), all can be "well with your soul."

There is much debate about Jesus' nature, purpose, and significance. This is not our concern. However, according to those who knew Jesus best, he was gifted with soul wisdom and ardent about soul work. This supports our claim that the Bible is a soul book. Jesus taught that the soul is a person's most precious possession. He warned, "For what will it profit them to gain the whole world and forfeit their soul?" (Mark 8:36).[21] He urged people to love both God and neighbor with their "whole souls" (Matthew 22:37, 39). Like the prophet Jeremiah, Jesus invited the weary to find rest for their souls.[22]

The human heart is often used as a synonym for soul.[23] Jesus cared less about what came from a person through their mouths than what proceeded from their hearts (Mark 7:18–20). He saw hypocrisy, the disconnect between avowals and actions, as most pernicious, leaving the soul a "whitewashed sepulcher" (Matthew 23:27). Jesus counseled that "where your treasure is, there will your heart be also" (Matthew 6:21). Delving deep into the heart, he warned that those who are angry are murderous, and those who lust are adulterers (Matthew 5:22, 28). Outwardly, objectively, this is madness; but inwardly, subjectively, according to the soul, it rings true.

As a master storyteller of the inner life, Jesus showed the conceit, struggle, and transformation of a prodigal younger son who finally "came to himself" (Luke 15:17). Yet, this was only part one of Jesus' parabolic soul study. He then surprised his audience by focusing on the elder child, the one with whom most identify. He, who seemed so solid, Jesus revealed as also lost. This firstborn son always did what was righteous, but his soul was resentful. Physically, he never left his father's side. Yet for him to feel inwardly at home, to finally rest in the bed of integrity and with a comforter of joy, he too would have to embark on an adjusting soul journey.

Jesus' soul insights were so penetrating that, 19 centuries before the advent of depth psychology, he was pointedly showing his followers the dangerous dynamics of projection:

> Why do you see the speck that is in your brother's eye, but do not notice the log that is in your own eye? Or how can you say to your brother, "Let me take the speck out of your eye," when there is the log in your own eye? You hypocrite, first take the log out of your own eye, and then you will see clearly to take the speck out of your brother's eye. (Matthew 7:3–5)

Augustine and Psyche/Soul

Augustine of Hippo (354–430 CE) is widely accepted as the most important theologian of early Christianity.[24] He wrote frequently and significantly about the soul in his treatises *Concerning the Soul and Its Origin*, *Concerning the Two Souls*, *Concerning the Immortality of the Soul*, *Concerning the Greatness of the Soul*, and *The Soliloquies*. He is best known for *The Confessions*, which are penetrating self-reflections. Here he talks about such things as "the roarings and groanings of my heart" and that the "light of my eyes … was within" (VII:7); "I was admonished by all this to return to my own self, and, with you to guide me, I entered into the inner-most part of myself … and I saw with my soul's eye" (VII:10); he graphically tells of the effectiveness of his "inner ear" and of the "pilgrimage" of the soul (XII:11).[25]

Wayne Rollins, in his seminal volume, *Soul and Psyche: The Bible in Psychological Perspective,* points out this revealing section of Augustine's *The Soliloquies* (1:7):

> *Reason:* What, then do you want to know?
> *Augustine:* The very things for which I have prayed.
> *Reason:* Summarize them concisely.
> *Augustine:* I want to know God and the soul.
> *Reason:* Nothing else?
> *Augustine:* Nothing else at all.[26]

To Augustine, these were the two most crucial things: The knowledge of God and the knowledge of his own soul.[27] How was this to be achieved? Not by reason or empirical observation but by self-investigation. For Augustine, interiority is sacred; it provides a means to self-understanding at the soul level and access to the knowledge of God.[28] It is interesting to note that it was a theologian, Philipp Melanchthon (1497–1560), protégé of Martin Luther, who was the first to use the term "psychologia" in his treatises on the soul.[29]

We leapfrog from Augustine to modern times, casting our gaze on Franz Delitzsch, who in 1856 wrote *A System of Biblical Psychology*.[30] He offended almost everyone. The materialists, evangelicals, and biblical scholars all assailed him. Undeterred, he staunchly defended his new "science" and soon published a second edition. His book was comprehensive, addressing the classical and patristic understanding of the psyche, as well as the newly developing fields of biblical criticism and modern psychology. Delitzsch was convinced that "biblical psychology" was a premier means to understanding the "psychical constitution" of the individual.[31] For him, the Bible devotes itself to the task of psychology, spelling out the origin, nature, habits, destiny, and welfare of the soul.

Arguing that the New Testament is "the most important book in the world" and one that "finds men where they live," Frederick C. Grant in 1950 called for a greater range of research:

> New Testament theology, in brief, must be based upon a thorough study of history and exegesis, literary criticism and analysis, and sound textual criticism as well. It cannot stop with these ... The student of New Testament theology must also understand religious psychology.[32]

Increasingly, scholars in the last two generations have acknowledged and fleshed out Delitzsch's and Grant's claims that "the Bible is a book with a vested interest in the human soul/psyche."[33]

In the last decade of the 20th century, the psychological study of Scripture gained new adherents and was granted new credentials. In 1991, the prestigious Society of Biblical Literature added a division on "Psychology and Biblical Studies." Rollins notes further felicitous developments:

> In its 1993 inaugural issue, *Biblical Interpretation: A Journal of Contemporary Approaches* announced the need for "the field of biblical studies to become more public and more pluralistic," inviting the submission of "articles that discuss specific biblical texts in the light of fresh insights that derive from the diversity of relevant disciplines," including sociology, anthropology, archaeology, philosophy, history, linguistics, literary theory, and psychology. Similarly the Pontifical Biblical Commission in its 1993 document on "The Interpretation of the Bible in the Church" devoted two columns in its survey of contemporary biblical scholarship to "Psychological and psychoanalytical approaches" as part of a "methodological spectrum of exegetical work ... which could not have been envisioned thirty years ago."[34]

In addition, highly respected mainline biblical scholar Joseph Fitzmyer wrote:

> The psychological and psychoanalytical analyses of human experience have proven their worth in the area of religion and enable one to detect multidimensional aspects of the biblical message ... The aid that can come from this approach cannot be underestimated.[35]

What then is more appropriate than to study the story of Jesus' birth via psychology, the study of the soul? Rollins elucidates:

In the end, the goal of psychological biblical criticism is to look at the Bible and its interpretation with an eye to what James Dittes has called the "habits of the soul." ... From a psychological biblical-critical perspective, the Bible is preeminently a demonstration of the "habits of the soul." It is a book of the soul, written to the soul, about the soul, for the soul's care and cure.[36]

As we will come to see, the motifs found in the Nativity narratives, as well as the whole culture of Christmas they have produced, reflect primal "habits of the soul." An ultrasound of the psyche is required to explain the gravitational pull of Christmas, the ineluctable power of its collective and individual engagement.

Soulless Psychology

How ironic then, that as the scholarly investigation of Scripture has begun to embrace psychology—the study of the soul—much of contemporary psychology has lost its taste for its namesake, the soul (*psyche*). Some years ago, while taking a PhD-level course on personality from the psychology department at Yale University, I was startled by the pure glee of students as they dismissed the notion of a "human mind" as primitive superstition. For them, there was just a brain. No wonder one wag observed: "Pity poor psychology. First it lost its soul, then its mind, then consciousness, and now it's having trouble with behavior."[37] How did this happen?

Historically, psychology has been divided into two camps. Philosopher Christian von Wolff authored two volumes that described each standpoint. *Psychologia Empirica* (1732) described empirical psychology, which focuses on observable and measurable sense experience. Present-day manifestations of this approach are found in experimental and behavioral psychology. M. Sherif describes this in part:

The brave new world of scientism was represented by the models of Wundt and Titchener and by the behaviorism of Watson. The first asserted that the prime task of scientific psychology was the discovery of mental elements and then the laws of their compounding; the second, that the scientific task was a search for elemental reflexes and principles of their linkages. Each model, in is own terminology, advocated its approach as the only way to lay solid foundations for the ultimate explanation of more complicated forms of behavior.[38]

In his second book, *Psychologia Rationalis* (1734), von Wolff presents rational psychology, also known as philosophical or metaphysical psychology, which is based on a Platonic model that reflects upon the nature of the self.[39] While also relying on clinical experience, the various schools of depth psychologies aptly fit here.[40] Thus, there are two psychological ways to read the Christmas story: The empirical and the depth psychological.

Empiricists, who find no scientific evidence for the soul, dismiss it as a false construct.[41] If we look to empirical psychological research about Christmas, we find multiple studies researching the rates of mortality, suicide, and depression around the Christmas season and investigations of Christmas shopping, gift-giving, and gift-wanting. For instance, one analyzed 300,000 deaths from natural causes in Ohio from 1979 to 1981. They found evidence of a death rise after Christmas, but not the expected death drop prior to Christmas.[42] A 2004 study found cardiac mortality highest on Christmas Day and next highest the day after Christmas and New Year's Day.[43]

Other studies revealed, contrary to popular assumptions, lower rates of suicides before, during, and after Memorial Day, Thanksgiving, and Christmas.[44] A comprehensive analysis of attempted suicides vis-à-vis major holidays examined 24,388 cases between 1989 and 1996 from 11 European countries and found fewer than expected suicides before Christmas but 40 percent more attempts than expected after Christmas. They concluded that their findings supported the theory of the "broken promise effect,"[45] when reality falls short of expectations. In another study, researchers reviewed all cases (17 to 78 years of age) of nonfatal deliberate self-harm at three London hospitals on Valentine's Day, Christmas Day, and two control dates between 1983 and 1989 inclusive. There were significantly fewer cases on Christmas.[46] In the 2018 *Nordic Journal of Psychiatry*, researchers reported that although there was a nonsignificant decrease in suicides on Christmas and New Year's Eve, there was a significant increase on New Year's Day.[47]

In a paper discussing the difference between "holiday blues syndrome" and clinical depression, psychiatric nurse Marjorie Baier suggests the former may be caused by elevated social demands, unmet expectations, and physical stress, such as lack of sleep. She proposes intervention to reduce stress and promote coping mechanisms.[48] In a similar vein, psychologist Robert Friedberg, after reviewing other studies, reports no significant increase in psychopathology during major holidays. However, there is a rise in dysphoria following the holidays, especially after Christmas.[49] Velamoor, Voruganti, and Nadkarni et al. studied 55 psychiatric patients and found that most reported feeling lonely, stressed, and depressed during the Christmas season.[50]

On the other hand, another team examined the number of emergency psychiatric admissions for each month between 1991 and 1997. They equated the Christmas season with the whole month of December and found that none of the months differed significantly for admissions.[51] A 2023 review of studies around the globe in various sociocultural settings found no increased use of emergency psychiatric services in December at Christmastime. In fact, they were lower.[52]

Christmas eating, gifts, and cards are also common areas for research. A 2023 study found that unhealthy eating during the Christmas season did not diminish the individual's sense of well-being because of the buffering effect of social norms for unhealthy eating at this time of the year.[53] Most do gain weight over Christmas, an average of 1.3 pounds (600g) in the United States, 1.8 pounds (800g) in Germany, and 1.1 pounds (500g) in Japan.[54] Another study looking at the Christmas card network of 87 adults discovered half the cards received were from those not considered family or close friends, or from those not seen for more than a year.

Recipients likewise described having an emotional reaction to half of the cards. Young adults saw holiday greeting cards as a way of maintaining social ties, while older adults viewed them as a link to their personal past. Receiving a greater number of cards from close social contacts increased feelings of social embeddedness.[55] Probing the "reciprocity norm" in 1976, Kunz and Woolcott found that 20 percent of people reciprocated a Christmas card received from a stranger; a study 40 years later found that only 2 percent did.[56] Hill and Dunbar report:

> Total network sizes estimated from Christmas card lists are remarkably close to the value of 150 predicted for human social group size based on the relationship between group size and brain size across primates.[57]

Fischer and Arnold explored the effects of gender on Christmas gift shopping. They found that women were more involved than men. This was less true when men held "egalitarian gender-role attitudes."[58] Dyble, van Leeuwen, and Dunbar also studied gender differences in Christmas gift-giving. They found men and women spend similar amounts for family and those dear, but women spend significantly more on the "most distant network layer."[59]

Ferrari, in a study of procrastination at Christmas, determined that people who started shopping at the last possible minute could be divided into two groups: Those whose lack of diligence was due to perceived business commitments and work responsibilities, and those for whom Christmas shopping was a threat to self-esteem and therefore put off as long as possible.[60] O'Cass and Clarke examined 422 letters to Santa to determine brand awareness and preference and request styles. The not-so-startling discovery was that children adopt meaningful strategies (including graphics) to secure their requested gift and the specific brand. Furthermore, manufacturers who heavily promoted their toy and also linked it with the Christmas myth and the symbolism of giving were more likely to get the lion's share of the particular market.[61]

The title of one paper, "The Psychology of Christmas," purports to answer our question: "What are the psychological meanings of Christmas?"[62] However, the paper's inquiry only points to three obvious responses: Gift-giving maintains important relationships; Christmas is a time of celebration, especially with our families; and Christmas is a complex festival because of the "uneasy 'marriage' of secular and Christian content."[63] Kasser and Sheldon's research found that people who engage in the spiritual and family rituals of Christmas are happier (increased positive feelings of well-being) than those who focus on the material aspects.[64] Another study concluded that spending money on gifts for others makes one more satisfied than spending it on yourself.[65]

There is little doubt that a mix of the hormones cortisol, serotonin, and dopamine spikes throughout the Christmas season.[66] Christmas brings a bagful of responsibilities. Still, a survey by Greenberg Quinlan Rosner Research found that less than 38 percent felt increased stress; 80 percent of respondents "looked forward to the holidays as a time of good cheer," which included the positive emotions of happiness, love, high spirits, and connectedness.[67] Danish neurologists noted that "The Christmas spirit has been a widespread phenomenon for centuries, commonly described as feelings of joy and nostalgia mixed with associations to merriment, gifts, delightful smells, and copious amounts of good food." These researchers utilized functional MRI brain imaging to explore where the "Christmas spirit" resides:

> We identified a functional Christmas network comprising several cortical areas, including the parietal lobules, the premotor cortex, and the somatosensory cortex. Activation in these areas coincided well with our hypothesis that images with a Christmas theme would stimulate centers associated with the Christmas spirit. The left and right parietal lobules have been shown in earlier fMRI studies to play a determining role in self transcendence, the personality trait regarding predisposition to spirituality. Furthermore, the frontal premotor cortex is important for experiencing emotions shared with other individuals by mirroring or copying their body state, and premotor cortical mirror neurons even respond to observation of ingestion mouth actions. Recall of joyful emotions and pleasant ingestion behavior shared with loved ones would be likely to elicit activation here. There is growing evidence that the somatosensory cortex plays an important role in recognition of facial emotion and retrieving social relevant information from faces. Collectively, these cortical areas possibly constitute the neuronal correlate of the Christmas spirit in the human brain.[68]

While these empirical studies are interesting and sometimes yield important, if unsurprising, results, they are not helpful to our task of uncovering the psychological meanings of Christmas. They tell us what *is,* but not *why*. Such studies are unable to address, much less elucidate, the soul meanings of Christmas. Delitzsch explains the problem:

> It has been a fundamental error of most psychologists hitherto, to make the soul only extend so far as its consciousness extends; it embraces, as is now always acknowledged, a far greater abundance of powers and relations than can commonly appear in its consciousness.[69]

To grapple with the mysterious sweep and power of Christmas, we turn to the kind of psychology that has not deserted psyche—depth psychology, "soulful" psychology.

A Depth Psychological Approach

The watershed discoveries of Sigmund Freud (1856–1939), C.G. Jung (1875–1961), and Heinz Kohut (1913–1981) about the psyche led to the development of three influential psychological schools: Psychoanalytical, analytical, and self psychology, respectively. Jung and Kohut were faithful disciples of Freud. Yet both were dogged prospectors who discovered additional veins of the psyche from their own clinical work. What all three have in common—what is the primary tenet of depth psychology—is the belief that beneath human consciousness lies a lively and influential unconscious that affects human life every bit as much as consciousness. While the unconscious cannot be directly known, it reveals itself in feelings and actions that are contrary or surprising to our ego position: Slips of the tongue, powerful repulsions, and strange affections, to name but a few. The unconscious also causes affect to be magnified, behaviors to become compulsive, and images to become compelling. These are all found in the celebration of Christmas, making us quick to think that the unconscious has a major share in its importance.

Freud wrote: "I believe that a large part of the mythological view of the world, which extends a long way into the most modern religions, is nothing but psychology projected onto the external world."[70] In other words, the fascinating myths, narratives, and images we find in Scripture have direct links to our psyche, our soul, our unconscious. Erwin Goodenough, history of religion scholar, argues that just as important as the historical facts and scientific discernments we consciously unearth and order are the "pictures, images, forms, all the stuff that parades before us in our nightly dreams" that engage us and move us.[71] What connects ego and soul, what relates consciousness to unconsciousness are these—what we call symbols. As Jung discovered, "The unconscious can be reached and expressed only by symbols."[72]

Symbols, then, convey and draw us to potent inner dynamisms. "Symbols," writes Oskar Doering in *Christliche Symbole* (1933), "are metaphors for the eternal in the form of the transient; in them the two are 'thrown together,' fused in a unity of meaning."[73] In line with this understanding, Paul Tillich, one of the premier theologians of modern times, suggests six characteristics of a symbol:

1. Symbols point beyond themselves to something else.
2. Symbols participate in that to which they point.
3. Symbols open up levels of reality that otherwise are closed to us.
4. Symbols unlock dimensions and elements of our soul that correspond to the dimensions and elements of reality.
5. Symbols cannot be produced intentionally. They grow out of the individual or collective unconscious and cannot function without being accepted by the unconscious dimension of our being.
6. Like living beings, they grow and die (for example, the symbol of the king).[74]

Symbols, therefore, are pregnant with meaning and are fascinating because they possess the uncanny ability to touch the fullness of our being—the rational and the irrational. Or as Jolande Jacobi puts it: "the symbol always addresses the whole psyche."[75] This helps explain why Christmas images are so potent and charming.

The scriptures of all religions are dripping with symbols. The living symbols found in the myths, parables, and stories of sacred texts reverberate within the vast recesses of the psyche—its haunts, habits, and hopes. When I preached to my congregation and interpreted the text psychologically—exploring symbols, inner dynamics, and unconscious depths—it was amazing how many people expressed the same sentiment: "It seemed like you were preaching just to me." This is because, despite all our particularities and idiosyncrasies as individual egos, we all share the common humanity of a soul.[76]

The Collective Unconscious

Fundamental to grasping the role of stories and symbols on the psyche/soul is Jung's theory of the collective unconscious, a brilliant conception that appreciably enlarged Freud's understanding. In *Structure and Dynamics of the Psyche,* Jung describes a bi-level unconscious:

> According to my view the unconscious falls into two parts which should be sharply distinguished from one another. One of them is the personal unconscious; it includes all those psychic contents which have been forgotten during the course of the individual's life. Traces of them are still preserved in the unconscious, even if all conscious memory of them has been lost. In addition, it contains all subliminal impressions or perceptions which have too little energy to reach consciousness. To these we must add unconscious combinations of ideas that are still too feeble and too indistinct to cross over the threshold. Finally, the personal unconscious contains all psychic contents that are incompatible with the conscious attitude. This comprises a whole group of contents, chiefly those which appear morally, aesthetically, or intellectually inadmissible and are repressed on account of their incompatibility.[77]

Deeper still, the transpersonal layer of the psyche is global and constitutional:[78]

> The other part of the unconscious is what I call the impersonal or collective unconscious. As the name indicates, its contents are not personal but collective, that is, they do not belong to one individual alone but to a whole group of individuals, and generally to a whole nation, or even to the whole of mankind. These contents are not acquired during the individual's lifetime but are products of innate forms and instincts, mythological and primordial images.[79]

So, although the personal unconscious is individualistic, the collective unconscious is universal. We all partake in "a sphere of unconscious mythology whose primordial images are the common heritage of mankind."[80] This means there is an entrenched deep-level intimacy among humans. Furthermore, while the personal unconscious is time-bound, "the collective unconscious comprises in itself the psychic life of our ancestors right back to the earliest beginnings."[81]

Jung frequently employed the image of the sea to symbolize this collective unconscious because its "unfathomable depths lie concealed beneath the reflecting surface," and it signifies a "collecting-place where all psychic life originates."[82] He imagined the collective unconscious as "the sea upon which the ego rides like a ship."[83] What dwells in these depths? The "most ancient" and "most universal" images of humanity are "deposits of thousands of years of experience of the struggle for existence and for adaptation."[84] Jung calls them *archetypes* because they are typical forms that appear spontaneously and perpetually all over the world in myths, fairy tales, fantasies, and dreams.[85] They are "the most important mythological motifs … common to all times and races."[86]

Comparative mythologist Joseph Campbell describes these a priori forms as:

> a cast of inevitable stock characters that have played through all time, through the dreams and myths of all mankind, in ever-changing situations, confrontations, and costumes, yet, for all that, are as predictable in their company as the characters of a *Punch and Judy* stage.[87]

Archetypes are congenital, numinous, and autonomous. Jung moves us a step closer to our agenda when he concludes that these mighty images "are the avowal and recognition of the soul, and at the same time the revelation of the soul's nature."[88] Johannes Turrius, 16th-century Swedish Bishop, says this in an interesting way: The soul "has within herself the 'selfness' of all mankind."[89]

All this applies to Scripture. Jungian analyst Edward Edinger states:

> The events of the Bible, although presented as history, psychologically understood are archetypal images, that is, pleromatic events that repeatedly erupt into spatio-temporal manifestation and require an ego to live them out. As we read these stories with an openness to their unconscious reverberations, we recognized them to be relevant to our most private experience.[90]

These "unconscious reverberations," fascinations, and larger-than-personal emotions are telltale signs of an activated archetype. The widespread, mysterious, and gripping attraction of Christmas imagery indicates that some of the most basic human needs and desires—universal and timeless—inhabit the capacious Christmas landscape.

Because the archetypes are universal, biblical scholars J. Cheryl Exum and David Clines are correct in suggesting that a psychoanalytic approach to Scripture enables us to "ask what it is about the human condition in general that these texts reflect."[91] And because the archetypes are timeless, Phillips Brooks (1835–1893), who penned "O Little Town of Bethlehem," could declare: "The summons of Christ to anxious humanity is not a memory of something which happened years ago; it is something which is actually happening now, to-day."[92] For many people on Christmas Eve, mother and child, shepherds and Magi become as numinous as the star was 2,000 years ago: The "silent night," lowing cattle, and announcing angels still warm the soul and still bring a "heavenly peace."

In his 1995 article, "Jesus Before He Could Talk," Jack Miles, a former Jesuit with a Harvard doctorate in biblical studies, speaks assuredly about Christmas and the Nativity narrative. He contends that "for most of the hundreds of millions who

... will hear the story again on Christmas Eve, what counts in it is neither theologi-cal nor historical but psychological."[93] In suggesting that the Christmas story is a *story*, he leads us forward:

> Jesus was born in Palestine sometime near the turn of the era. That much is his-torical. The rest—the census, "no room in the inn," the manger, the shepherds, the wise men, the slaughter of the innocents and the flight into Egypt—is not historical. Conservative scholars like Raymond E. Brown and John P. Meier agree with radicals like John Dominic Crossan and Burton Mack that these leg-ends are theology in narrative form, stories told to convey and inspire religious belief rather than establish historical fact. Arguments continue to rage about the historicity of the Gospels as a whole, but about the historicity of the "infancy narratives"—prologues added to the Gospels of Matthew and Luke long after the core passion and resurrection narrative in each was written—there is at this point virtually no debate ... The Christmas story is Jesus' baby picture ... an "artist's impression" rather than a photograph.[94]

This is the salient takeaway. Although the Nativity stories may have been consciously constructed for theological purposes, they arose from the collective unconscious of the authors and speak to the collective unconscious of the readers.[95] This is what priest, friend, and collaborator with Jung, Victor White understood: "It is precisely in the psyche, and with the aid of psychology, that they have discovered the personal significance to themselves ... of the Incarnation."[96] Miles's conclusion is profound: "The Christmas story ... need not be believed, but it still matters, and it still works."[97]

Notes

1 Aniela Jaffé, *The Myth of Meaning in the Work of C.G. Jung* (Daimon, 1984), 29.
2 Bruce M. Metzger, *The Bible in Translation: Ancient and English Versions* (Baker Academic, 2001), 32. Jerome was not eager to take on the task. He wrote, "You urge me to revise the Old Latin version, and, as it were, to sit in judgment on the copies of the Scriptures that are now scattered throughout the world; and, inasmuch as they differ from one another, you would have me decide which of them agree with the original. The labor is one of love, but at the same time it is both perilous and presumptuous—for in judging others I must be content to be judged by all."
3 Gerd Theissen, *Psychological Aspects of Pauline Theology*, trans. John P. Galvin (Fortress Press, 1987), 28.
4 Carl Sandburg, *The Complete Poems of Carl Sandburg* (Harcourt Brace Jovanovich, 1970), 695.
5 Frederick C. Grant, "Psychological Study of the Bible," in *Religions in Antiquity: Essays in Memory of Erwin Ramsdell Goodenough,* ed. Jacob Neusner, Studies in the History of Religion Vol. XIV (E.J. Brill, 1968), 113.
6 Gerd Theissen, *Psychological Aspects of Pauline Theology,* 1.
7 D. Andrew Kille, "Psychology and the Bible: Three Worlds of the Text," *Pastoral Psychology* 51, no. 2 (2002), 128.
8 "The Creator of all things ... has granted to the human soul the capacity of raising itself above itself by self-investigation," Franz Delitzsch, *A System of Biblical Psychology*, trans. Robert Ernest Wallis (Baker Book House, 1977), xiv.

9 John Dominic Crossan, "Perspectives and Methods in Contemporary Biblical Criticism," *Biblical Research* 22 (1977), 41.

10 Theissen, *Psychological Aspects of Pauline Theology*, 398.

11 Jeffrey L. Staley, *Reading with a Passion: Rhetoric, Autobiography, and the American West in the Gospel of John* (Continuum, 1995), 37.

12 J. Harold Ellens, "The Bible and Psychology: An Interdisciplinary Pilgrimage," *Pastoral Psychology* 45, no. 3 (1997), 207.

13 Compare to *nephesh* in Hebrew, *anima* in Latin, and *Seele* in German.

14 Sigmund Freud and Oskar Pfister, *Psychoanalysis and Faith: The Letters of Sigmund Freud and Oskar Pfister*, ed. Heinrich Meng and Ernst L. Freud, trans. Eric Mosbacher (Basic Books, 1963), 126. Based on his 1950 Terry Lecture (Yale), Erich Fromm spends a whole chapter on "Psychoanalyst—Physician of the Soul," in *Psychoanalysis and Religion* (Yale University Press, 1950), 65–98.

15 *Webster's Ninth New Collegiate Dictionary*, ed. Frederick C. Mish (Merriam-Webster, 1988), 1126–1127.

16 G.B. Kerferd, "Psyche," in *The Encyclopedia of Philosophy*, ed. Paul Edwards (MacMillan, 1967), 513.

17 Wayne Rollins, *Jung and the Bible* (John Knox Press, 1983), 45. Similarly, Rollins says that the soul "appears to constitute the self and its interrelated faculties of perception, sensation, mind, memory, emotion, will, and imagination, among others," in *Soul and Psyche: The Bible in Psychological Perspective* (Fortress Press, 1999), 6, 105.

18 Additionally, from a Christian point of view, the soul not only derives from God but also must give account to God. Jesus, in the Parable of the Rich Fool, warns that one night God will say to us: "Your soul [psyche] is required of you" (Luke 12:20).

19 P.J. Achtemeier, *Harper's Bible Dictionary* (Harper & Row, 1985), 982; R.B. Girdlestone, *Synonyms of the Old Testament: Their Bearing on Christian Doctrine* (Logos Research Systems, 1998), 56.

20 Rollins, *Jung and the Bible*, 45.

21 Jesus is quite clear that the soul/psyche is even more important than physical life: "Do not fear those who kill the body but cannot kill the soul" (Matthew 10:28).

22 Matthew 11:29; (Jer. 6:16).

23 "The first extant work by a Christian expressly devoted to the subject of the soul is *De Anima* of Tertullian, written between AD 208 and 211." White, *Soul and Psyche: An Enquiry into the Relationship of Psychiatry and Religion*, 25. G. De Vries calls it "the first Christian psychology." In Chapter 15, using texts from the Hebrew Bible and the Christian Scriptures, Tertullian argues that the soul resides (is "enshrined") in the heart.

24 For a comprehensive examination of classical and medieval philosophers and patristic theologians who write about the psyche/soul/anima, see the first chapter of Wayne G. Rollins, *Soul and Psyche*.

25 Augustine, *The Confessions of Saint Augustine*, trans. Rex Warner (Mentor, 1963), 49, 92, 146, 291. In this, Augustine follows Plotinus (205–270 CE), one of his most important teachers. See also R.S. Peters and C.A. Mace, "Psychology," in *The Encyclopedia of Philosophy*, ed. Paul Edwards (Macmillan, 1967), 5.

26 Rollins, *Soul and Psyche*, 15.

27 T. Kermit Scott, *Augustine: His Thought in Context* (Paulist Press, 1995), 230.

28 Phillip Cary, *Augustine's Invention of the Inner Self: The Legacy of a Christian Platonist* (Oxford University Press, 2000).

29 François H. Lapointe, "Origin and Evolution of the Term 'Psychology'" in *American Psychologist* 25, no. 7 (1970), 640.

30 Delitzsch, *A System of Biblical Psychology*.

31 Delitzsch, *A System of Biblical Psychology*, x, 16, 19.

32 Frederick C. Grant, *An Introduction to New Testament Thought* (Abingdon-Cokesbury Press, 1950), 26, 27.

33 Rollins, "Lecture Psychologique" (unpublished manuscript), 7. It is interesting to note that Paul Tillich formed the "New York Psychology Group" in 1941. William A. Rogers, "Tillich and Depth Psychology," in *The Thought of Paul Tillich*, ed. James Luther Adams, Wilhelm Pauck, and Roger Lincoln Shinn (Harper & Row, 1985), 105.

34 Wayne G. Rollins, "Psychology, Hermeneutics, and the Bible," in *Jung and the Interpretation of the Bible*, ed. David L. Miller (Continuum, 1995), 11–12.

35 Joseph A. Fitzmyer, *Scripture, the Soul of Theology* (Paulist Press, 1994), 51–52.

36 Rollins, *Soul and Psyche,* vii.

37 *Rollins, Soul and Psyche,* 6.

38 M. Sherif, "Self Concept," *International Encyclopedia of the Social Sciences*, Vol. 14, ed. D.L. Sills (Collier/Macmillan, 1968), 150.

39 Rollins, *Soul and Psyche,* 5.

40 In many of his essays, Jung is quick to point out that factual evidence garnered from his own introspection and consultations with analysands was the first step in developing his theories: "First I made the observation, and only then did I hammer out my views." C.G. Jung, "On the Nature of the Psyche," *Structure and Dynamics of the Psyche*, ed. and trans. Gerhard Adler and R.F.C. Hull, Vol. 8, *The Collected Works of C.G. Jung* (Princeton University Press, 1975), 204.

41 "Already in the mid-1600s, British Empiricist Thomas Hobbes had dismissed the notion of soul as at best a metaphor for life and at worst 'pernicious Aristotelian nonsense,' tracing all psychological events to material causes in the nervous system and brain." Wayne Rollins, *Soul and Psyche*, 5.

42 Bryand Byers and Richard A. Zeller, "Christmas and Mortality: Death Dip, No; Death Rise, Yes," *Professional Psychology: Research and Practice* 18, no. 4 (1987).

43 David P. Phillips et al., "Cardiac Mortality Is Higher Around Christmas and New Year's Than at Any Other Time: The Holidays as a Risk Factor for Death," *Circulation* 110, no. 25 (2004).

44 David P. Phillips and John S. Wills, "A Drop in Suicides Around Major National Holidays," *Suicide and Life-Threatening Behavior* 17, no. 1 (1987); Thomas G. Sparhawk, "Traditional Holidays and Suicide," *Psychological Reports* 60, no. 1 (1987).

45 G. Jessen et al., "Attempted Suicide and Major Public Holidays in Europe: Findings from the WHO/EURO Multicentre Study on Parasuicide," *ACTA Psychiatrica Scandinavica* 99, no. 6 (1999).

46 Sarah J. Cullum et al., "Deliberate Self-Harm and Public Holidays: Is There a Link?" *Crisis: Journal of Crisis Intervention and Suicide* 14, no. 1 (1993).

47 Gergö Hadlaczky and Sebastian Hökby, "Increased Suicides During New Year, but Not During Christmas in Sweden: Analysis of Cause of Death Data 2006–2015," *Nordic Journal of Psychiatry* 72, no. 1 (2018), 72–74.

48 Marjorie Baier, "The 'Holiday Blues' as a Stress Reaction," *Perspectives in Psychiatric Care* 24, no. 2 (1987), 64–68.

49 Robert D. Friedberg, "Holidays and Emotional Distress: Not the Villains They Are Perceived to Be," *Psychology: A Quarterly Journal of Human Behavior* 27, no. 1 (1990).

50 Varadaraj R. Velamoor et al., "Feelings About Christmas, as Reported by Psychiatric Emergency Patients," *Social Behavior and Personality* 27, no. 3 (1999), 303–308.

51 Varadaraj R. Velamoor et al., "Psychiatric Emergency Rates During the Christmas Season in the Years 1991–1997," *Psychological Reports* 85, no. 2 (1999), 403–404.

52 Else Schneider et al., "Who Is Afraid of Christmas? The Effect of Christmas and Easter Holidays on Psychiatric Hospitalizations and Emergencies—Systematic Review and Single Center Experience from 2012 to 2021," *Front Psychiatry* 11, no. 13 (2023).

53 Nada Kadhim et al., "The Buffering Role of Social Norms for Unhealthy Eating Before, During and After the Christmas Holidays: A Longitudinal Study," *Group Dynamics: Theory, Research, and Practice* 27, no. 2 (2023), 133–150.

54 E.E. Helander et al., "Weight Gain over the Holidays in Three Countries," *New England Journal of Medicine* 375, no. 12 (2016), 1200–1202.

55 Karen L. Fingerman and Patricia C. Griffiths, "Season's Greetings: Adults' Social Contacts at the Holiday Season," *Psychology and Aging* 14, no. 2 (1999), 192–205.

56 Brian Meier, "Bah Humbug: Unexpected Christmas Cards and the Reciprocity Norm," *The Journal of Social Psychology* 156, no. 4 (2016), 449. "The reciprocity norm refers to an expectation that people will help those who helped them."

57 R.A. Hill and R.I.M. Dunbar, "Social Network Size in Humans," *Human Nature: An Interdisciplinary Biosocial Perspective* 14, no. 1 (2003), 53–72.

58 Eileen Fischer and Stephen J. Arnold, "More Than a Labor of Love: Gender Roles and Christmas Gift Shopping," *Journal of Consumer Research* 17, no. 3 (1990).

59 Mark Dyble et al., "Gender Difference in Christmas Gift Giving," *Evolutionary Behavioral Sciences* 9, no. 2 (2014), 140.

60 Joseph R. Ferrari, "Christmas and Procrastination: Explaining Lack of Diligence at a 'Real-World' Task Deadline," *Personality and Individual Differences* 14, no. 1 (1993).

61 Aron O'Cass and Peter Clarke, "Dear Santa, Do You Have My Brand?: A Study of the Brand Requests, Awareness and Request Styles at Christmas Time," *Journal of Consumer Behavior* 2, no. 1 (2002).

62 Carole B. Burgoyne and Stephen E.G. Lea, "The Psychology of Christmas," *The Psychologist*, December (1995), 552.

63 Burgoyne and Lea, "The Psychology of Christmas," 549–552. They do explore the rules of reciprocity and size of gifts.

64 Tim Kasser and Kennon M. Sheddon, "What Makes for a Merry Christmas?" *Journal of Happiness Studies* 3, no. 4 (2002), 313–329.

65 E.W. Dunn et al., "Spending Money on Others Promotes Happiness," *Science* 319 (2008), 1687–1688.

66 For a tongue-in-cheek editorial posing as serious medical findings, see M. Ludwig, "Christmas: An Event Driven by Our Hormones?" *Journal of Neuroendocrinology* 23, no. 12 (2011), 1191–1193.

67 "Holiday Stress Survey," Greenberg Quinlan Rosner Research, December 12, 2006, apa.org/news/press/releases/2006/12/holiday-stress.pdf, accessed May 11, 2025.

68 A. Hougaard et al., "Evidence of a Christmas Spirit Network in the Brain: Functional MRI Study," *BMJ* 351 (2015), h6266. Japanese researchers used structural MRIs and questionnaires to study subjective happiness in 50 subjects. Their findings suggest that the precuneus area of the brain "mediates subjective happiness by integrating the emotional and cognitive components of happiness." See also Wataru Sato et al., "The Structural Neural Substrate of Subjective Happiness," *Scientific Reports* 5, no. 1 (2015), 15891.

69 Delitzsch, *A System of Biblical Psychology*, 330.

70 Sigmund Freud, *The Psychopathology of Everyday Life* (1901), ed. J. Strachey, Vol. 6, *The Standard Edition of the Complete Psychological Works of Sigmund Freud* (Hogarth Press, 1960), 259.

71 Erwin R. Goodenough, *Toward a Mature Faith* (Prentice-Hall, 1955), 51.

72 C.G. Jung, "Commentary on 'The Secret of the Golden Flower,'" *Alchemical Studies*, Vol. 13, *The Collected Works* (Princeton University Press, 1976), 28.

73 Jolande Jacobi, *Complex/Archetype/Symbol in the Psychology of C.G. Jung* (Princeton University Press, 1974), 77.

74 Paul Tillich, *Dynamics of Faith* (Harper Torchbooks, 1957), 41–43.

75 Jolande Jacobi, *The Psychology of C.G. Jung* (Yale University Press, 1973), 97.

76 The Judeo-Christian perspective ascribes this fact to the belief that each and every one is created in the image of God.

77 C.G. Jung, "The Psychological Foundations of Belief in Spirits" (1948), in *Structure and Dynamics of the Psyche*, 310; see parallel statement in C.G. Jung, "On the Psychology of the Unconscious" (1917), in *Two Essays in Analytical* Psychology, Vol. 7, *Collected Works*, 66.

78 C.G. Jung, "Analytical Psychology and Education" (1946), in *The Development of Personality*, Vol. 17, *Collected Works*, 117.

79 C.G. Jung, "The Psychological Foundations of Belief in Spirits," 310; see a parallel statement in Vol. 7, 66.

80 C.G. Jung, "On the Relation of Analytical Psychology to Poetry" (1931), *The Spirit in Man, Art, and Literature*, Vol. 15, *Collected Works*, 80.

81 C.G. Jung, "The Significance of Constitution and Heredity in Psychology" (1929), *Structure and Dynamics of the Psyche*, Vol. 8, *Collected Works*, 112.

82 C.G. Jung, *Psychology and Alchemy* (1943), Vol. 12, *Collected Works*, 48; "Principles of Practical Psychotherapy" (1935), in *The Practice of Psychotherapy*, Vol. 16, *Collected Works*, 12.

83 C.G. Jung, "The Meaning of Psychology for Modern Man" (1934), *Civilization in Transition*, Vol. 10, *Collected Works*, 138. "Just as the sea stretches its broad tongues between the continents and laps them round like islands, so our original unconsciousness presses round our individual consciousness."

84 C.G. Jung, "On the Psychology of the Unconscious," 66. See also *Psychological Types (1921)*, Vol. 6, *Collected Works*, 221.

85 C.G. Jung, "Schizophrenia" (1958), *The Psychogenesis of Mental Disease*, Vol. 3, *Collected Works*, 261. Jung was not the first to note the archetypes, but more than any other, he described their fundamental nature in the human psyche. Jung writes: "The term 'archetype' occurs as early as Philo Judaeus, with reference to the *Imago Dei* (God-image) in man. It can also be found in Irenaeus, who says: 'The creator of the world did not fashion these things directly from himself but copied them from archetypes outside himself.'" In the *Corpus Hermeticum*, God is called archetypal light. The term occurs several times in Dionysius the Areopagite, as for instance in *De coelesti hierarchia*, II, 4: "immaterial Archetypes" ... The term *archetype* is not found in St Augustine, but the idea of it is. Thus, in *De diversis quaestionibus* LXXXIII, he speaks of "*ideae principales*, 'which are themselves not formed ... but are contained in the divine understanding.'" "'Archetype' is an explanatory paraphrase of the Platonic *eidos*. For our purpose this term is opposite and helpful, because it tells us that so far as the collective unconscious contents are concerned, we are dealing with archaic or—I would say—primordial types, that is, with universal images that have existed since the remotest times." See also C.G. Jung, "Archetypes of the Collective Unconscious" (1954), *The Archetypes and the Collective Unconscious*, Vol. 9, *Collected Works*, 4–5.

86 C.G. Jung, *Psychological Types* (1921), Vol. 6, *Collected Works*, 443. Psychologically, we could equate this with what Apostle Paul called "principalities and powers" (Romans 8:38). See also C.G. Jung, "On the Psychology of the Unconscious," 65.

87 Joseph Campbell, "Editor's Introduction," *The Portable Jung* (Viking, 1973), xxxi.

88 C.G. Jung, "The State of Psychotherapy Today" (1934), *Civilization in Transition*, Vol. 10, *Collected Works*, 172.

89 C.G. Jung, *Mysterium Coniunctionis* (1954), Vol. 14, *Collected Works*, 83. Letter from 1567.

90 Edward Edinger, *The Bible and the Psyche: Individuation Symbolism in the Old Testament* (Inner City Books, 1986), 13.

91 *The New Literary Criticism and the Hebrew Bible*, ed. J. Cheryl Exum and David J.A. Clines (Sheffield Academic Press, 1993), 18.

92 Phillips Brooks, *Christmas Carols* (E.P. Dutton, 1877), 29. After the Civil War, Brooks went to the Holy Land, spending Christmas Eve in Bethlehem.

93 Jack Miles, "Jesus Before He Could Talk," *New York Times Magazine* (December 24, 1995), 28.

94 Miles, "Jesus Before He Could Talk," 30.

95 Rollins, *Soul and Psyche*, 156–157. "Unlike the historical-critical approach which sees the text as a historical artifact, the psychological-critical approach sees the text as a product of, and participant in, a complex psychic event, riddled with conscious and unconscious factors. As such, the text appears as an autonomous literary, historical, and psychic entity, whose meaning can no longer be reduced simply to what the author intended. Rather, it participates in the galaxy of meaning that gave birth to the author as author (of which the author as person is only partially conscious), and can change the lives of readers, extending as far as conscious and unconscious reckoning can reach."

96 Victor White, *Soul and Psyche, An Enquiry into the Relationship of Psychiatry and Religion* (Collins and Havill Press, 1960), 13.

97 Jack Miles, "Jesus Before He Could Talk," 33.

Chapter 2

Origins of the Feast of the Nativity

As people are drawn to a mountain or stand uniquely satisfied before the crashing surf of the open sea, so too does Christmas rouse a sweeping, visceral response. The mystery of Christmas is compounded, the enigma greater when we realize that Christmas was not originally a centerpiece of Christian life, liturgy, or theology. It did not occur to the earliest Christians to observe Jesus' birthday. As biblical scholar Herman Hendrickx affirms: "The stories about Jesus' birth and childhood were not part of the earliest Christian preaching."[1]

Nativity Narratives

The Apostle Paul is the earliest and most prolific New Testament author. His first letter to the Thessalonians was written in 49 CE, just 20 years after Jesus' death. More than half of the 27 books of the New Testament are "directly or indirectly related to Paul."[2] Yet in his grand corpus of epistles, there is no mention of the Nativity, except for a single passing note in his letter to in Galatians 4:4: "In the fullness of time God sent his Son, born of a woman."[3] Amazingly, that is all that Paul, the dominant New Testament chronicler, has to say about Jesus' birth—no shepherds, no angels, no swaddling clothes, not even a mention of the mother's name. Either Paul had not heard the Nativity accounts or he did not think they warranted attention.

Paul had other things to tell:

> For I handed on to you as of first importance … that Christ died for our sins in accordance with the scriptures, and that he was buried, and that he was raised on the third day in accordance with the scripture.
>
> (1 Corinthians 15:3–4)

Above all, and time after time, Paul (Philippians 3:10) proclaims, "Christ and the power of his resurrection." Although Paul barely and only once alludes to the Nativity, over and over he reminds his readers: "God raised the Lord and will also raise us by his power."[4] New Testament scholar Joseph Fitzmyer clearly sums up the Pauline kerygma: "Through the passion, death, and resurrection Christ has

DOI: 10.4324/9781003568629-3

become a 'power' (*dynamis*) producing a new life in the Christian believer, which eventually ensures his resurrection and life 'with Christ.'"[5] At Christianity's commencement, there is no talk about Jesus' birth.

We discover the same lack of interest in the earliest Gospel, written by Mark in Rome about 65 CE.[6] It is the *prima materia* upon which the Gospels of Matthew and Luke are based.[7] In this original and foundational Gospel, the curtain opens with Jesus at thirty years old.

Biblical scholar Paul Minear reminds us that the "full title of Mark's document as it left his hands was 'The beginning of the gospel of Jesus Christ, the son of God.'"[8] However, this "beginning" is silent about Mary's pregnancy and Jesus' birth. Even though "Mark is concerned with presenting the story of a life in the conviction that this life is the life of the Son of God,"[9] virgin birth, rustling angels, and weary, wary Magi are not known or of concern to him. In this, Mark and Paul—the two earliest reporters—align.

Like Paul, Mark fixes his readers' focus on the Passion/Resurrection drama:

Jesus began to teach them that the Son of Man must undergo great suffering, and be rejected by the elders, the chief priests, and the scribes, and be killed, and after three days rise again. He said this all quite openly.

(8:31–32a)

Mark spends eight chapters (half the book) on the Passion/Resurrection of Jesus but records not one word about his Nativity. As such, Mark confirms the core kerygma found in Paul (1 Corinthians 15) and the insignificance of Jesus' birth.[10]

The Gospels of Matthew and Luke do include Nativity narratives, but they were written a generation or more after the Gospel of Mark. "Thus it seems that the Gospel of Matthew was composed in the period 80–100, for which 90 may serve as a good symbolic figure," and "a date for Luke in the mid-80s appears likely."[11] Remarkably, it is some 25 years after Mark, some 60 years after Jesus' death, that the Gospels of Luke and Matthew tell the first stories about the birth of Jesus.[12]

Adding to the obvious tardiness of the foremost Nativity accounts is a second glaring fact: In the four Gospels (Matthew, Mark, Luke, and John), we find a consistent account of Jesus' Passion and Resurrection. Just the opposite is true with the infancy narratives. If we compare the lengthy and complicated infancy narrative of Luke (1:5–2:38) with the brief but ominous infancy narrative of Matthew (1:18–2:23), it becomes immediately clear that they have but seven things in common: (1) An angel tells of a miraculous, holy birth (Luke 1:35; Matthew 1:20); (2) Mary is the virgin mother (Luke 1:26; Matthew 1:18); (3) the child is to be named Jesus (Luke 1:31; Matthew 1:21); (4) the child will be a "savior" (Luke 2:11; Matthew 1:21); (5) the child is born in Bethlehem (Luke 2:4–7; Matthew 2:11); (6) the child comes during the time of Herod the Great (Luke 1:5; Matthew 2:1)[13]; and (7) Jesus is revealed in a nighttime experience of a bright light—angels in Luke 2:8, a star in Matthew 2:2–9. The remainder of the dramatic reporting of Matthew and Luke are quite disparate.

In their imaginations, Christians have been quick to conflate the two accounts into a single story, and this composite is magnificently concretized in the beloved crèche. This is possible because, while Luke's and Matthew's accounts are substantially different, they do not contradict each other. Luke recounts the story from Mary's point of view, disclosing the parallel pregnancy of her cousin Elizabeth with John the Baptist, the Annunciation, the Magnificat, awful hospitality ("no room, no room!"), a firstborn child lying in a manger, and a host of proclaiming angels suddenly appearing before scared, then jubilant, shepherds, who go in haste to visit the holy family and "make known to them what had been told to them about this child" (Luke 2:17). In Matthew, Joseph is central to the story and the details are dissimilar, including a prophetic star and Magi from the east who bear precious gifts of gold, frankincense, and myrrh; Herod's jealous fear; and an escape in the nick of time for a marked baby.

While it is true that Luke and Matthew composed their Gospels with different faith communities in mind, this alone does not explain the divergent facts they offer. These inconsistent testimonies of Jesus' birth call into question their reliability.

In *The Birth of the Messiah,* a comprehensive book on the infancy narratives of Matthew and Luke, biblical scholar Raymond Brown suggests that the birth stories were afterthoughts. For many who today find Christmas foundational, Brown makes an eye-widening statement: "paradoxically, one may speak of the Gospels as developing backwards."[14] That is, from the death and Resurrection of Jesus— which gave the primary understanding of who Jesus was—back to the other stories about his ministry and finally to his birth. The birth narratives simply gave added witness "for those who had already come to faith through the proclamation of the death and resurrection."[15] According to Brown, the infancy narratives were a later canonical development created to answer specific problems of a maturing and growing faith community. This would, of course, explain why the earliest Gospel is devoid of a birth story:

Why were the infancy narratives composed? ... *Curiosity* certainly plays a role in both the canonical and apocryphal infancy stories. Christians wanted to know more about their master: his family, his ancestors, his birthplace. ... *Apologetics* may explain certain aspects of the infancy stories. Some would see an apologetic against non-Christian followers of JBap in the Lucan stories of JBap's birth, e.g., in order to protect the superiority of Jesus ... ; Luke describes JBap as acknowledging Jesus even before birth (1:41, 44). Others would see an anti-Docetist aspect in the emphasis on the birth of Jesus. More plausible is the suggestion that the story of Jesus' birth in Bethlehem was intended as a response to a Judaism skeptical about the Messiah who came from Galilee (John 7:41, 52). If Judaism was already beginning to charge that Jesus was illegitimate, the virginal conception offered an explanation that allowed for an irregularity in the birth, but at the same time, defended the purity of the mother and the sanctity of the child. Partly apologetic and partly *theological* factors may have been involved in the development of a pre-Matthean story that drew a parallel between Joseph the legal father of Jesus and Joseph the patriarch who dreamed dreams and went to Egypt. ... Thus, many factors, some no longer to be detected with certitude, went into the development of infancy stories—besides the most obvious possible factor: A Christian memory of events that happened.[16]

Whatever the motive, the accounts were belated. Minear puts it succinctly: "These preparatory stories did not arouse public attention at the time. Those who first responded to the messages of John and Jesus showed no signs of having known these stories."[17]

Early Christian Liturgy

The Nativity stories came late to the canon and later still to the church's liturgy. Ralph P. Martin, in his book *Worship in the Early Church,* does not even mention the Feast of the Nativity (Christmas).[18] The Book of Acts gives us our earliest glimpse of Christian worship and what was central to the first Christians:

> They devoted themselves to the apostle's teaching and fellowship, to the breaking of bread and the prayers.
>
> (2:42)

> With great power the apostles gave their testimony to the resurrection of the Lord Jesus, and great grace was upon them all.
>
> (4:33)

Marcel Metzger, in his *History of the Liturgy*, shows how these two elements were inextricably linked in the worship experiences of the primitive church. The "breaking of bread," also known as the "Lord's Supper" (1 Corinthians 11:20) or Eucharist, draws its power and meaning from the post-Resurrection experiences of Jesus, where he shares his resurrection spirit:

> In these meetings, the risen Christ sets down the essential elements that constitute his Church: he converses with his disciples, he convinces them of his resurrection, he shares with them his Spirit and his word, he "breaks bread" and eats with them (Mark 16:14–20; Luke 24:13; John 20:19–29; Acts 1:3–8). Each manifestation of the Risen One ends with the sending ... disciples to proclaim the good news of the resurrection to the whole universe.[19]

The original emphasis of worship that attracted increasing numbers to those first house churches was the renewing ("Behold, I make all things new," Revelations 21:05) and uniting ("that all may be one," John 17:21; see also Acts 2:44–46) power of Christ. In Section 9:4 of the Didache, one of the most important liturgical orders of the early church, we see the Eucharist as a drawing together of followers in the power of the risen Christ:

As the bread broken was once scattered on the hills, and after it had been brought together became one, so may thy Church be gathered together from the ends of the earth unto thy kingdom; for thine is the glory, and the power, through Jesus Christ, for ever.[20]

Even a modern sociologist looking back on this primitive scene underlines the relational nature of early Christian worship: "It maintained a relationship with Jesus as 'risen Christ.'"[21] The central focus on the Resurrection is further demonstrated by the new day Christians selected for worship. It was no longer the seventh day of the week—the Jewish Sabbath—but "on the first day of the week of every week" (1 Corinthians 16:2), the day that Jesus rose from the dead. Justin Martyr, in his *First Apology* (ca. 153 CE), describes weekly worship and its absolute focus on Sunday:

And on the day called Sunday there is an assembly of all who live in cities or in the country together in one place, and the memoirs of the Apostles or the writings of the prophets are read, as long as time permits. Then when the reader has finished, the ruler in a discourse instructs and exhorts to the imitation of these good things. Then we all stand together and offer prayers; and, as we said before, when we have finished the prayer, bread is brought and wine and water, and the ruler likewise offers up prayers and thanksgivings to the best of his ability. ... But we all hold this common gathering on Sunday, since it is the first day, on which God transforming darkness and matter made the Universe, and Jesus Christ our savior on the same day rose from the dead.[22]

The first generation of Christians purposefully chose Sunday, the first day, as their primary day of worship because it was the first day of creation and the day Christ rose from the dead.[23] Every Sunday was a "little Easter."[24] Easter was paramount; Christmas, yet to be born.

Christmas and the Fourth-Century Liturgy

When did the Feast of the Nativity (Christmas) make its debut as part of the Christian liturgical year? Astonishingly, it was centuries after Jesus' birth. Paul Bradshaw in his book *Early Christian Worship* states this categorically:

There is no firm evidence for the Christian observance of either 25 December or 6 January before the fourth century. Of course, it is always possible that one or both of these festivals was in existence at an earlier date, but if so, we have no knowledge of it.[25]

In his sermon, *In diem natalem*, delivered at Antioch in 386 CE, John Chrysostom, Archbishop of Constantinople, reveals, "It is not yet the tenth year since this day [the Feast of the Nativity] has become clearly known to us."[26] We also have the diary of Egeria, a female pilgrim who traveled from western Europe to the holy lands between 381 and 384 CE. She gives us a comprehensive look at the Jerusalem liturgy for the year 383 when Cyril was bishop of Jerusalem.[27] She mentions four great feasts: Easter, Pentecost, Epiphany, and the Dedication. Historian John Wilkinson explains that Epiphany was celebrated as the Feast of the Nativity. Although Egeria's description of the Epiphany is mostly missing, the blanks are filled in by the Armenian Lectionary, which provides readings and rubrics for fifth-century liturgies in Jerusalem.[28] The scripture lessons are what we would today consider Christmas texts: Luke 2:1–20 and Matthew 1:18–25, 2:1–12.[29] In explanation, Wilkinson writes:

> From the same source [Armenian Lectionary] we learn that the proceedings in Bethlehem began in the afternoon with a synaxis at the Shepherds', and continued with a Gospel in the Cave of the Nativity, and Lucernare in the church, which formed in the beginning of the vigil. The vigil culminated, like that of Easter, with a midnight celebration of the Eucharist, and, when it was over, the bishop and the Jerusalem monks left for Jerusalem in order to celebrate the feast there.[30]

Finally, a Christmas liturgy developed, including one of the earliest known Christmas carols, a fourth-century hymn:

> He was born at Bethlehem,
> He was raised at Nazareth,
> He lived in Galilee.
>
> We saw a sign in heaven,
> A star that showed itself.
> The watching shepherds
> Were filled with wonder,
> Falling to their knees, they sang:
> Glory to the Father,
> Alleluia!
> Glory to the Son,
> Alleluia!
> And glory to the Holy Spirit,
> Alleluia, Alleluia, Alleluia![31]

The Apostolic Constitutions were written between 375 and 380 CE in Syria.[32] Here we find an admonition to celebrate: "Brethren, observe the festival days, and first of all the Nativity, which you are to celebrate on the twenty-fifth of the ninth month" (V, 13:1).[33] The year began in spring, with the equivalent of our month of April being the first month, so the ninth month was December.

While the celebration of the birth of Jesus had no part in the beginnings of Christian worship, it did come to stand on its own as an engaging and formidable subject of worship generations later. Louis Duchesne (1843–1922) in *Christian Worship: Its Origin and Evolution*—the book that became the standard for understanding early Christian worship for much of the 20th century[34]—writes:

> It is thus clear that towards the end of the third century the custom of celebrating the birthday of Christ had spread throughout the whole church, but that it was not observed everywhere on the same day. In the West the 25th of December was selected, and in the East the 6th of January.[35]

The Feast of the Nativity now marked the beginning of the liturgical year.[36]

Syncretism

J.S. Bach borrowed the music of a highly popular love song of 1601, "*Mein G'müt ist mir verwirret, das macht ein Jungfrau zart*" ("My peace is shattered by a young maiden's charms"), for some of his greatest religious works. "Albert Schweitzer calls this the most important melody of Bach's *St. Matthew Passion* (1727) in which its use, five times, is central to and casts its mood over the whole work."[37] We know it today as "O Sacred Head, Now Wounded," describing the pain and shame of Jesus' Crucifixion. Bach also used it for the first and last chorales of his *Christmas Oratorio* (1735).[38] Paul Simon continued the practice of appropriation by using "Bach's" melody for his 1973 hit, "An American Tune." Ironic since it is a German tune but now restored back to a secular lament.

It seems part of human nature to use the established and cherished to create a fresh but equally attractive analog. Such metamorphoses can be immensely fertile. Up-and-coming religions frequently pirate the well-loved celebrations of settled religions into their own rituals. This long-lived strategy of amalgamation is called syncretism. It's *possible* because the two are analogous enough; it's *profitable* because high-energy engagement is rapidly achieved.

Feminist scholar Judith S. Antonelli, in her commentary on the Torah, argues that Jews co-opted pagan harvest rites for their own festivals:

> Although the Jewish festivals were given national historical meaning—the Exodus (Pesach), the Revelation at Sinai (Shavuot), and living in the wilderness (Sukkoth)—they are essentially nature festivals, which are rooted in the seasonal cycles of the Land itself. Because of this, their structure and symbols are found among the Canaanites. The Torah retained the basic format of the festivals but changed their mode of worship, in order to eliminate the bloodshed and the orgies.[39]

Similarly, the melding of Christian worship and symbols with those of Indigenous cultures has been common wherever missionaries traveled. In Ireland, during their Iron Age (600 BCE to 550 CE), all roads led to the Hill of Tara—the sacred seat of the High Kings. St. Patrick (387–461) built his church there, co-opting its spiritual power in the hearts of the people and incorporating Druidic religion into Christianity.

Another striking example is found in the Mission Chapel of the Taos Pueblo. There, large and bold above the altar, is a statue of Mother Mary. Far to stage right is a diminutive figure of Jesus. For an Anglo-American Christian, especially a Protestant, the disconnect is immediate. Without waiting for the question to be asked, our Pueblo guide explained: "our primary native god is a fertility god; therefore, it was natural for us to focus on Mary, as the fertile one."[40]

In Assisi, Italy, one finds the remarkable first-century BCE Temple of Minerva (counterpart to Greek Athena) with its six Corinthian columns and pediment. Rushing past this remarkably well-preserved facade to explore deeper, one discovers, all too abruptly, a 16th-century Christian sanctuary that in the 18th century was renovated in High Baroque.[41] The discrepancy between outer and inner is a vibrant example of Christian arrogation. Similarly, the sanctuary of Święty Krzyż in southern Poland was constructed over a temple to the triple deity Swist, Poswist, and Pogoda, quickly replaced by the concept of a Holy Trinity.[42]

Many are the instances where one thing indelibly written on the heart of a particular culture has been used with the facility and felicity of intravenous valium, to pleasantly introduce Christian sensibilities. Charles Squire, in his book on Celtic mythology, makes this very point:

> What concerns us is that we are face to face in Britain with living forms of the oldest, lowest, most primitive religion in the world—one which would seem to have been once universal, and which, crouching close to the earth, lets other creeds blow over it without effacing it, and outlives one and all of them.
>
> It underlies the three great world-religions, and still forms the real belief of perhaps the majority of their titular adherents. It is characteristic of the wisdom of the Christian Church that, knowing its power, she sought rather to sanctify than to extirpate it. What once were the Celtic equivalents of the Greek "fountains of the nymphs" were consecrated as "holy wells." The process of so adopting them began early. St. Columba, when he went in the sixth century to convert the Picts ... sanctified no less than three hundred such springs. Sacred stones were equally taken under the aegis of Christianity. Some were placed on the altars of cathedrals, others built into consecrated walls.[43]

Saint Gregory (later to be Pope Gregory I), when confronting the unconverted peoples of Britain, told his missionaries not to "throw out 'that which is good, but adapt it.' If they decorate their temples to the Sun god, let them continue to do it in honour of the Son of God."[44]

As Constantine co-opted Christianity to advance the Roman Empire, Christianity co-opted pagan feasts for its own gain. In particular, the celebration of Christmas became a natural vehicle for subsuming the numinously charged objects and popular rituals of polytheists and nature worshippers. We cite just a few examples.

It was the wisdom of Ephraim the Syrian in the fourth century to have the Christmas celebration last until January 6, which then included the well-loved Roman Kalends (New Year's) that was celebrated throughout Europe and to the furthest limits of the empire. The Synod of Tours (567) declared these 12 days to be a festive tide of the church, and the Twelve Nights of Christmas became immensely popular.[45]

The Venerable Bede (*De temp. rat.,* xiii), writing in the early part of the eighth century, speaks about the pagan English prior to 500 CE:

> The ancient people of the Anglican nations began the year on December 25th, when we now celebrate the birthday of our Lord ... which is the very night now so holy to us, was called in their tongue *Modranecht*, that is to says, 'Mothers' Night,' by reason of the ceremonies which in that night-long vigil they performed.[46]

It was the practice of the Bohemians at the beginning of each month to carry about the image of their god Bel, singing a Czechic song, and bringing gifts in tribute. The hope of this real-life liturgy was for Bel to grant them good fortune for the ensuing month. But then along came Saint Adalbert (c. 956-997). Historian Tille writes:

> In order that Christians might not also celebrate the beginning of the months according to heathen custom, (St. Adalbert) changed this celebration of the beginnings of months into a celebration of Christ's Nativity and of the week following it, thinking that it would be better to exercise that habit in the time in which Christ was born, than at the beginning of months, at which honour had once been bestowed upon Bel. He also is said to have altered the name and sense of that celebration, making of *kalensiare colendisare* (from *colere,* to revere), because through that usage Christ is revered at his birthday, and not the Calends.[47]

Like a new Roman emperor stealing the marble from his predecessor's monuments to make his own, Christmas over the centuries has subsumed Persian, Roman, Germanic, Celtic, and many other religious celebrations and practices. The tactic of syncretism, conflating and interchanging old and new to produce freshly energized and appealing symbols, has been extraordinarily successful.

Conclusion

Although absent in the earliest New Testament writings and absent in the first centuries of worship, once initiated the Feast of the Nativity was ardently celebrated. It spread widely and wildly, indicating not just the efficacy of syncretism but a deep-rooted soul connection—one that still reawakens each December. This brimming correlation will be mapped in our final three chapters. But first there is much to tell about the why and wherefore of December 25 becoming the centerpoint—the birthdate known round the world.

Notes

1 Herman Hendrickx, *The Infancy Narratives: Studies in the Synoptic Gospels* (Geoffrey Chapman, 1984), 1.

2 Bart D. Ehrman, *The New Testament: A Historical Introduction to the Early Christian Writings*, 2nd ed. (Oxford University Press, 2000), 260, 4.

3 It could be argued that Paul's kenotic passages in Philippians 2:6–7 and 2 Corinthians 8:9 make a loose reference.

4 See 1 Corinthians 6:14. See also Romans 1:4, 4:24–25, 6:4–9, 7:4, 8:11, 8:34, 9:17, 10:9; 1 Corinthians 15; 2 Corinthians 1:9, 4:14, 5:15, 10:5; Galatians 1:1; Ephesians 1:20, 2:6, Philippians 3:10–11; Colossians. 2:12, 3:1; 1 Thessalonians 1:10.

5 Joseph A. Fitzmyer, *Pauline Theology: A Brief Sketch* (Prentice Hall, 1967), 4. See also, C.H. Dodd, *The Apostolic Preaching and Its Development* (Harper and Row, 1964), 13.

6 W.D. Davies, *Invitation to the New Testament: A Guide to Its Main Witnesses* (Doubleday, 1969), 198.

7 Ehrman, *The New Testament: A Historical Introduction*, 76–84.

8 Paul S. Minear, *Mark*, ed. Balmer H. Kelly, 25 vols., Vol. 17, *The Layman's Bible Commentary* (John Knox Press, 1962), 31.

9 Davies, *Invitation to the New Testament*, 200.

10 Furthermore, in Dodd, *The Apostolic Preaching and Its Development*, 52: "We must remember that when Mark was complete, its resurrection narrative was certainly a good deal longer."

11 M. Eugene Boring, *New Testament Articles, Matthew, Mark*, ed. Leander E. Keck, Vol. 8, The New Interpreter's Bible, 12 vols. (Abingdon Press, 1995), 106; R. Alan Culpepper, *Luke, John*, Vol. 9, *The New Interpreter's Bible*, ed. Leander E. Keck, 12 vols. (Abingdon Press, 1995), 8.

12 Joseph Fitzmyer argues for the possibility that when Luke originally composed his Gospel, it began with what is now the third chapter, "to which he subsequently prefixed the prologue and the infancy narrative" in *Luke the Theologian: Aspects of His Teaching* (Paulist Press, 1989), 29.

13 Also in common (Matthew 1:1–16; Luke 3:28–38) is the seemingly illogical fact that Jesus' genealogy is traced through Joseph, his father who is not really his father. Though even here there is an interesting and important difference. Matthew traces Jesus back to the great patriarch Abraham and great King David, while Luke traces Jesus' lineage all the way back to Adam. This makes sense as Luke is reaching out to Gentiles and wants a wider inclusiveness.

14 Raymond E. Brown, *The Birth of the Messiah: A Commentary on the Infancy Narratives in the Gospels of Matthew and Luke* (Doubleday & Company, 1977), 26.

15 Brown, *The Birth of the Messiah*, 27.

16 Brown, *The Birth of the Messiah*, 28–29.

17 Paul S. Minear, *The Bible and the Historian: Breaking the Silence About God in Biblical Studies* (Abingdon Press, 2002), 89. For an interesting perspective on the infancy narratives, Professor Zacharias P. Thundy has provided two chapters on "infancy parallels" in his book, *Buddha and Christ: Nativity Stories and Indian Traditions* (E.J. Brill, 1993).

18 Ralph P. Martin, *Worship in the Early Church* (William B. Eerdmans, 1974).

19 Marcel Metzger, *History of the Liturgy: The Major Stages,* trans. Madeleine M. Beaumont (Liturgical Press, 1997), 18. (Luke 24:30–35; see also Acts 2:42; 20:7–22).

20 Charles H. Hoole, trans. *The Didache* (Athenaeum of Christian Antiquity, 1994), 5.

21 Thomas F. O'Dea, *The Sociology of Religion,* Foundations of Modern Sociology, ed. Alex Inkeles (Prentice Hall, 1966), 38.

22 St. Justin Martyr, *The First and Second Apologies*, ed. Walter J. Burghardt, trans. Leslie William Barnard, Vol. 56, *Ancient Christian Writers: The Works of the Fathers in*

Translation (Paulist Press, 1997), 71. Similarly, in Acts 20:7 we find: "On the first day of the week, when we meet to break bread." And ·in VII 30 of the Apostolic Constitutions, we read: "On the day of the resurrection of the Lord, that is to say Sunday (which we call 'the Lord's Day'), assemble yourselves together without fail, giving thanks (*eucharistein*) to God, and praising him for all those mercies he has bestowed on you through Christ, delivering you from ignorance, error and bondage." See also, W. Jardine Grisbrooke, *The Liturgical Portions of the Apostolic Constitution* (Grove Books, 1990), 50.

23 Eberhard Arnold, *The Early Christians after the Death of the Apostles* (Plough Publishing House, 1972), 389. Paul Bradshaw, *Early Christian Worship: A Basic Introduction to Ideas and Practice* (Liturgical Press, 1996), 75. Metzger, *History of the Liturgy,* 27. It is interesting to note that the Russian word for Sunday is *Voskresenye* meaning "resurrection"; see Calendars from the Sky, webexhibits.org/calendars/week (accessed August 20, 2003).

24 Thomas Talley, *The Origins of the Liturgical Year* (Liturgical Press, 1986), 16.

25 Bradshaw, *Early Christian Worship,* 86. "Origen, writing in about the year 245, says that it is most improper to keep the birthday of Jesus Christ, as though He were a mere king or Pharaoh." Arthur Weigall, *The Paganism in Our Christianity* (G.P. Putnam's Sons, 1928), 240.

26 James F. White, *Documents of Christian Worship: Descriptive and Interpretive Sources* (Westminster John Knox Press, 1992), 31.

27 John Wilkinson, *Egeria's Travels to the Holy Land*, rev. ed. (Ariel Publishing House, 1981), 54, 71, 80, 262, 283.

28 Wilkinson, *Egeria's Travels to the Holy Land,* 253.

29 Wilkinson, *Egeria's Travels to the Holy Land,* 262.

30 Wilkinson, *Egeria's Travels to the Holy Land,* 80.

31 Lucien Deiss, *Springtime of the Liturgy: Liturgical Texts of the First Four Centuries* (Liturgical Press, 1967), 257.

32 Paul F. Bradshaw, *The Search for the Origins of Christian Worship: Sources and Methods for the Study of Early Liturgy* (Oxford University Press, 1992), 93

33 Grisbrooke, *The Liturgical Portions of the Apostolic Constitutions,* 46. In Chapter VIII 33:6 we read, "Let them [the slaves] rest on the festival of his birth, because on it unexpected grace was granted to men that the Word of God, Jesus the Christ, should be born of the virgin Mary for the salvation of the world," 51.

34 Bradshaw, *The Search for the Origins of Christian Worship,* 134.

35 L. Duchesne, *Christian Worship: Its Origin and Evolution: A Study of the Latin Liturgy up to the Time of Charlemagne*, 5th ed. (Society for Promoting Christian Knowledge, 1923), 260.

36 Thomas J. Talley, *The Origins of the Liturgical Year,* (Pueblo Publishing Company, 1986), 85.

37 Albert C. Ronander and Ethel K. Porter, *Guide to the Pilgrim Hymnal* (United Church Press, 1966), 136.

38 Ronander and Porter, *Guide to the Pilgrim Hymnal.*

39 Judith S. Antonelli, *In the Image of God: A Feminist Commentary on the Torah* (Jason Aronson, 1997), 472.

40 Taos Pueblo guide, NM, April 23, 2003.

41 The transformation took place in 1539 by order of the pope.

42 Malgorzata Oleszkiewicz, "Mother of God and Mother Earth: Religion, Gender, and Transformation in East-Central Europe," Hawaii International Conference on Arts and Humanities (San Antonio, 2003), 11–12.

43 Charles Squire, *The Mythology of the British Islands* (Blackie and Son, 1905), 416–417.

44 Maria Hubert, *Christmas in Shakespeare's England* (Sutton Publishing, 1998), 92.

45 Susan K. Roll, *Toward the Origins of Christmas* (Kok Pharos Publishing House, 1995), 122.
46 Arthur Weigall, *The Paganism in Our Christianity* (G.P. Putnam's Sons, 1928), 258.
47 Alexander Tille, *Yule and Christmas: Their Place in the Germanic Year* (David Nutt, 1899), 102–103.

Chapter 3

Pagan Synergy

There are two dates that everyone in the Western world knows: Their own birthday and December 25, the birthday of Jesus. Historian Paul Bradshaw writes: "The earliest evidence for the existence of a feast of the Nativity of Jesus on this date (December 25) is its inclusion in what is known as the Roman Chronograph of 354."[1]

Is this the actual day of Jesus' birth? Priest and scholar Vernon Staley confirms what we suspect: "There is no authoritative tradition bearing on the date of our Lord's birth."[2] The date is neither noted in scripture nor found in early Christian documents. Interestingly, only in modernity has there been social concern for actual birthdays, with Germans given credit for first celebrating children's birthdays (*kinderfeste*) with cake and candles in the 1700s. That we do not know Jesus' birth date is hardly surprising.

Historian Clement Miles speaks plainly: "No one now imagines that the date [of Jesus' birth] is supported by a reliable tradition."[3] Most likely December 25 was chosen because it served a purpose or held a meaning. There are two cogent theories about why this date was assigned to Jesus' birth. Both may be true. The first is known as the "computation" hypothesis and the second as the "history of religion" hypothesis.

Louis Duchesne, a French priest and historian, first presented the idea that ancient Christians arrived at December 25 by trying to calculate the exact date from information already supposed to be true. He wrote, "The date of the birth of Christ was fixed by taking as a starting point that which was believed to be the date of his death."[4] Though this logic seems inexplicable to the modern mind, it made perfectly good sense to early Christians and has even been widely accepted as part of the proof of the date of Shakespeare's birth.

Rabbinic tradition indicates that "Time is thought of as a series of integral years so that the day of creation and the day of final redemption are the same, and on that same basis the births and deaths of the patriarchs are placed on the same day."[5] In a fourth-century Christian document known as *de solstitiis,* the rabbinic habit of equating birth and death dates is slightly altered. This ancient anonymous author links the date of conception with the date of death: "for on the day that he was conceived on the same day he suffered."[6] Many early Christians believed that Jesus

DOI: 10.4324/9781003568629-4

was conceived on the same date as his death, including Augustine (354–430) who wrote: "For he [Jesus] is believed to have been conceived on the 25th of March, upon which day also he suffered."[7]

In the early part of the third century, Hippolytus of Rome concluded that Jesus was crucified in the year 29 CE. In that particular year, Passover fell on March 25; hence, a conception date of March 25.[8] Adding nine months, they arrived at December 25. This became the accepted day in Rome. However, in the Christian East, where April 6 was taken as the date of Jesus' death, the Nativity celebration was held on January 6.[9] Duchesne's theory has the advantage of explaining both the December 25 and January 6 dates.

While the computation theory is based on Judeo-Christian "in-house" under-standings, the "history of religions" approach proposes that Christians co-opted a popular pagan celebration date for their own. Johann Karl Ludwig Gieseler first suggested this view in his 1831 history of the origins of Christmas, *Lehrbuch der Kirchengeschichte*, a work dependent upon Egyptologist Paul Ernst Jablonski's *De origine festi nativitatis Christi* (1757). Hermann Usener's wide-ranging work, *Das Weihnachtsfest*, published in 1889, led the way for scholars to energetically research and debate this hypothesis.[10] Today, this argument is widely accepted. In a nutshell:

> December 25th was chosen at Rome because it was also the date of the winter Solstice in the Julian calendar and a popular pagan feast, the *dies natalis Solis invicti*, the birthday of the invincible sun, established by the emperor Aurelian in 274.[11]

Sol Invictus

Packaging the pagan god Sol with the Feast of the Nativity helps explain the lat-ter's abrupt adoption across the Roman Empire. The timing of their engagement yielded maximum impact: At the onset of the celebration of Jesus' birth, Sol was at the apogee of his influence, making their marriage most auspicious for newcomers. Mapping Sol's remarkable increase of prestige, power, and function is instructive to discovering some of the bedrock meanings of Christmas.

Sol had early beginnings. According to the first known Roman calendars, Sol was worshipped in the fourth century BCE.[12] Roman Republic (509–27 BCE) coins (see Figure 3.1 A and B) depicting Sol with a radiate crown date back at least as far as 200 BCE.[13] Sol had humble beginnings. Originally, he was the Roman equivalent of the minor Greek god Helios, just one fledgling in a brood of cultic divinities.[14] Roman historian Georges Dumezil notes that this anthro-pomorphized star's (*autochthonous Sol*) role was simply as regulator of the sea-sons.[15] For a god, this was a modest portfolio, but he began moving up the ladder. Historian Galston Halsberghe points to Sol's growing responsibilities: "a minor but independent place was taken by Sol, the sun god, protector of fertility, health and honesty."[16]

A

B

C

D

Figure 3.1 [A] Sol, radiate and draped, 42 BCE. [B] Sol in quadriga, second century BCE. [C] Radiate bust of Nero, r. 54–68 CE. [D] Colossus statue of Nero as Sol, 64–65 CE. Courtesy George Votsis.

From the first century CE, Sol began a steady two-century ascendancy, culminating in his becoming the god in chief of the Roman Empire. Four emperors, with their own motives in mind, were like sherpas who helped Sol achieve the summit.

Long before Ralph Waldo Emerson, Emperor Nero (r. 54–68 CE) cynically hitched his wagon to a star: Sol. Nero's palace tells the tale. His residence took "nearly four hundred acres of what had formerly been the most thickly inhabited zone in the city—the largest piece of land that any European monarch has ever carved out of his capital to make a residence for himself."[17] While we could talk about the architectural genius—the ivory, jewels, mother-of-pearl, carved marble, painted ceilings, exquisitely tiled floors, or pipes that sprayed perfume on guests[18]—the palace's constant references to Sol are the most meaningful. Frescoes of Helios and son Phaëthon were prominent.[19] According to mythology, Helios rested in a golden mansion.[20] Overlaid with gold leaf, Nero's palace was called the *Domus Aurea* (Golden House).[21] Its central room, the octagonal hall, was dramatically designed with domed rotunda and oculus to showcase the sun.

To leave no doubt that Nero, demagogue that he was, sought to affiliate himself with Sol's omnipotence, he commissioned a ten-story-high statue of himself as Sol (see Figure 3.1D). His marketing worked. "When the conspiracy against Nero was discovered, the sun god was considered to have saved the emperor."[22] The symbiosis is further displayed as Nero is frequently portrayed on his coins wearing the rayed crown of the sun god (see Figure 3.1C).[23] Many emperors continued this numismatic public relations practice, which increased the esteem of both parties.

The next giant step forward for the sun cult happened when Varius Avitus Bassianus became emperor in 218 CE at age 14. He was from Emesa, a critical outpost of the Roman Empire, where the local sun god Elah-Gabal was worshipped. Bassianus was not only a follower of this sun god of Emesa, but also the great-grandson of the high priest, and thus a hereditary priest himself.

Upon becoming emperor, Bassianus took the name of Elagabalus, after Sol Elah-Gabal.[24] He ardently championed his namesake deity, building two magnificent temples to Sol Elagabalus in Rome. David Van Meter writes:

> Most of the emperor's concerns were given over to the cult of Baal, and he lavished embarrassingly devout attentions on a sacred black monolith he had shipped to Rome from Emesa.[25]

His coins (see Figure 3.2) frequently show him sacrificing to Sol, and the supernatural stone of Emesa. Elagabalus's grand ambition was to elevate his provincial Sol (Elah-Gabal) as the supreme deity of the empire. He might have been successful, if he were not an unmitigated rogue. Elagabalus did not adhere to the senate's laws, was given to excess, and shocked everyone by marrying a vestal virgin, Aquilia Severa. Behaving "with all the parochialism of a small town mayor," he forced the Roman senators, much to their dismay, to wear Phoenician dress during his sacrifices to the sun.

> The offense was aggravated by Elagabalus' claim of supremacy for the provincial cult of which he was priest, and his placing in the shrine of his god, as tokens of sovereignty, the symbols of other deities. ... Among the mass of Solar devotees the recognition of an affinity between their cults did not diminish mutual jealousy or local exclusiveness. Not even a priest who was also a Roman emperor could identify the solar religion with one of its local forms. Still less could he make his Ba'al ruler of the Roman pantheon.[26]

His reign was brief. After a well-placed bribe, there was "general satisfaction when, on March 6th, 222 CE, Elagabalus and his mother Julia Soaemeias were murdered in the praetorian camp. Their bodies were dragged through the streets of

Figure 3.2 [A] Laureate bust of Elagabalus (r. 218–222 CE). Courtesy Heritage Auctions/ HA.com [B] Stone of Emesa (black conical meteorite) in quadriga, four parasols around. Courtesy Heritage Auctions/HA.com [C] Bust of Aurelian, radiate and cuirassed (r. 270–275 CE). [D] Aurelian standing right, holding spear and receiving victory wreath from woman, left. Legend reads "Restorer of the World."

Rome and thrown into the Tiber."[27] With his demise, the waxing cult of Sol was held in abeyance. But not for long.

From the reign of Elagabalus, the empire was disintegrating. It was a time of darkness and chaos. Pretenders and usurpers took their toll, as did a consuming plague and the invasion of the Germans and Persians.[28] Anarchy raged. It was left to the distinguished general Aurelian to reestablish order and unify the empire by winning campaigns throughout the Roman world.

Under Aurelian's reign (270–275 CE), the empire was returned to its former extent, and he was hailed as *restitutor orbis* (restorer of the world; see Figure 3.2D). Importantly, "Aurelian managed the ensuing peace as vigorously as he has prosecuted his wars."[29] He provided economic reforms, expanded welfare programs, and built a heavily fortified wall around Rome, 12 miles long and 20 feet high.[30] But perhaps his most effective peace initiative was promoting the cult of Sol Invictus.

Aurelian came from Illyria, where his mother was a priestess of the sun, and the dominant part of his army came from the Balkan Peninsula as well.[31] Not only was this deity close to his own heart, but he also envisioned Sol as a means of unifying the empire:

> To Aurelian the way to accomplish this unity lay in the cult of Sol Invictus ... which he intended to make the official national cult for the citizens of his empire. This cult would—he was convinced—form the mortar with which to cement his political system into a solid structure destined successfully to eliminate all resistance for a long time to come.[32] Since many gods were worshipped in the empire, often on a region-to-region or family-to-family basis, establishing a primary state god would ensure basic concord.[33] The sun god seemed particularly promising because he was worshipped, albeit by many different names, throughout the Roman realm. With a longing for order and peace after fifty years of turmoil and anguish, amalgamating these analog gods was sage. It would even appeal to the troops for whom sun worship was the prevalent religion.[34]

In his campaign to the east, Aurelian visited Elagabalus's Emesa and restored the Temple of the Sun at Palmyra. In his campaigns to the west, he acknowledged the Celtic and Germanic gods of light and healing.[35] He was successful because, unlike Elagabalus who tried to elevate a "petty provincial cult" above all others, Aurelian incorporated sun cults from the east and west of the empire into a centralized and supreme Roman deity.

In 274, Emperor Aurelian established the state cult of Sol Invictus, "making it the universal religion of the empire."[36] It was the right vehicle at the right time. To this end, Aurelian "established a college of senators as *pontifices dei Solices* (priests of the sun god)," and built a lavish temple dedicated to Sol known as Templum Solis Aureliani. The legends on his coins declared SOL DOMINUS IMPERI ROMANI (Sol, lord of the Roman Empire) and often pictured Sol holding a globe and victorious over the enemies of Rome.[37] "To the Roman, state and religion were not separable entities,"[38] so stability and solidarity prevailed. The cohesion around Sol was a thrust toward monotheism for social harmony. When was the *Dies natalis Solis invicti*? "The god's birthday was naturally the winter Solstice, identified as 25 December."[39]

Constantine the Great (r. 306–337) further solidified the place of Sol, and like Nero and Aurelian, emphasized his relationship with Sol, as evidenced in his coinage (see Figure 3.3). One of the most telling is a jugate bust where Constantine holds the world, with Sol in the secondary position (see Figure 3.3A).[40] Constantine's coins bear a legend similar to Aurelian's: SOLI INVICTO COMITI (To the unconquerable sun, companion).[41] And, in the tradition of Nero, at the very center of Constantinople—the new Rome—he placed a statue of himself as Sol, "with rayed

A

B

C

D

Figure 3.3 [A] Jugate bust of Constantine (r. 307–337) with shield; Sol in the secondary position. Courtesy British Museum, 1863.0713.1. [B] Sol, radiate and draped, holding a globe with raised hand. The legend reads "To the Unconquered Sun, Companion." [C] Laureate head of Saturn (106 BCE). [D] Saturn, veiled and holding a scythe, symbol of agriculture (230–260 CE).

head and thunderbolt in hand, atop a huge red stone column, there receiving sacrifices and prayers."[42]

Pressing further, on March 7, 321, Constantine instituted the first day of the week, the Day of the Sun, "as a recognized civil holiday, significant both for the Christians as the day of resurrection and for sun-cult adherents."[43] Linking the Christian day with a holiday enhanced the prestige of the church. The genius of this cross-fertilization continued as "popular pagan festivals and feasts were slowly absorbed into the Christian calendar, with 'holy days' in memory of local martyrs providing other welcome breaks from drudgery."[44]

From the latter part of the third century, Sol Invictus became the supreme god of the Roman world.[45] And, as detailed by author John Ferguson, soon after "the Christians arrogated to themselves the celebration of Sol for the birthday of Christ as counter blast to its popularity":

> The reason why the fathers transferred the celebration of 6 January to 25 December was this. It was the custom of the heathen to celebrate on the same 25 December the Sun's birthday, and to kindle lights in token of festivity. In these Solemnities and festivities the Christians also took part. So when the doctors of the Church perceived that the Christians had a leaning to this festival, they took counsel and resolved that the true Nativity should be celebrated on that day.[46]

What did Sol mean to the people? To some, Sol Invictus was literally the physical sun; to others, the real Sol lay behind the material sun.[47] Either way, this meant an orderly cosmos under the direction of Sol. In addition, Sol represented new life, light, and peace—three central motifs of Christmas.

A Ripe Time

This formidable association was the result of a convergence of sociocultural dynamics and pagan/Christian concerns. In the 313 CE Edict of Milan, the Emperors Licinius and Constantine put an end to the bloody persecutions of Christians.[48] Enjoying a more favored status and with existential threats from the government gone, the church no longer huddled to survive but poised to advance. They attempted to draw pagans away from their popular festival Sol Invictus (unconquered sun) to see Christ as the true sun of righteousness.[49] Such a link was also expedient because many of the new converts to Christianity could not do without their traditional festivals, and Christians were inclined to this celebration of lighting lights.[50]

However, the popularity of the festival of Sol Invictus alone would not have cemented this birth date without significant symbolism in common with the birth of Jesus. Susan K. Roll, in her comprehensive study, *Toward the Origins of Christmas*, quotes from the calendar of Canopus of 239 CE: "Birthday of the Sun. Light will increase." This, she concludes, indicates the "notion of the sun dying and being reborn as a child."[51] Macrobius (ca. 400 CE), chronicler of ancient Roman religious practices, concurs:

> These differences in age have reference to the sun, for at the winter Solstice the sun would seem like a little child, like that which the Egyptians bring forth from a shrine on an appointed day, since the day is then at its shortest and the god is accordingly shown as a tiny infant.[52]

Therefore, on December 25, both Sol and Jesus are infant gods. Furthermore, both are gods of light. The 243 CE Christian treatise, *De pascha computus*, already associates the birth of Jesus with the Hebrew text of Malachi 4:2:

> O how admirable and divine is the providence of the Lord, that on that day on which the sun was made on the same day was Christ born … and so rightly did the prophet Malachi say to the people: "the sun of righteousness shall rise upon you, with healing in his wings."[53]

Patristic writers and preachers used this text and others to "bolster a parallelism between Christ and the sun which would fit the theoretical pattern of a conscious replacement of the earlier Natalis Invicti by Christmas."[54]

> To be clear: In the beginning, the solar symbolism of Christ was prior to and independent of association with Sol. In the New Testament, Jesus is spoken of as a redeeming light. Matthew, alluding to Isaiah 9:2, explicitly declares that Jesus is "the great light" that has been seen by "those who sit in darkness" (Matthew 4:14–16).[55] John, in his prologue, heralds Jesus as the "true light, which enlightens everyone" (John 1:9): "What has come into being in him was life, and the life was the light of all people. The light shines in the darkness, and the darkness did not overcome it."[56]

Repeatedly, Jesus claims to be this light that shines in the darkness. In John 9:5, his declaration is remarkably strong: "I am the light of the world."[57] How this took over in the imagination of the populace is clearly seen in a painting by Correggio (1489–1534). In his "Holy Night" (also known as "Adoration of the Shepherds" or "Nativity," see Figure 3.4), the Christ child is the sole source of light that enlightens his onlookers.[58]

Clement of Alexandria (150–215 CE) referred to Christ as the "Helios (sun-god) that transverses the universe," and in the mausoleum of the Julius family discovered in excavations under St. Peter's Basilica is a dramatic mosaic of Christ as the sun god driving his chariot across the skies (see Figure 3.5). Many added Balaam's prophecy from Numbers 24:17: "A star shall come forth out of Jacob." This very connection of Jesus to light is explicitly made in the earliest known representation of the Virgin and Child. In a fresco from the first half of the second century in the Roman Catacomb of Priscilla, Prophet Balaam points to the star above a veiled Mary and a frightened, clinging Jesus.[59]

Augustine's intriguing remark from *Quaestionum* in *Heptateuchum* VII.90 (PL 34.629) gives additional credence to the Sol connection:

> But also they call it (the nativity) the birthday of the unconquered. Who, surely, is so unconquered as our Lord who triumphed over conquered death? Assuredly, what they dedicate to be the birthday of the sun is himself the sun of

Figure 3.4 Holy Night (1522), by Correggio. Incamerastock/Alamy Stock Photo

Figure 3.5 Christ is represented as the sun god in this early Christian mosaic (3rd–4th century CE), found on the ceiling of the Vatican Necropolis beneath the Basilica of Saint Peter, Rome. Sonia Halliday Photo Library/Alamy Stock Photo

righteousness of whom the prophet Malachi said: "To you who fear his name the sun of righteousness shall rise and healing is in his wings."[60]

Who could be more invincible than the one resurrected. These previous associations of Christ with the sun made the Sol festival even more attractive as a vehicle to achieve large numbers of converts. In other words, it may have been a natural co-opting rather than an outright hijacking, demonstrating an early means of evangelism and clearly revealing the deep human attraction to the infant God who brings new life, light, and peace.

Mithraism

Another dominant cult of worship of the time, the Mithraic mysteries, is closely associated with Sol Invictus,[61] probably adding to the vigor of both (see Figure 3.6). It can also be related to the flourishing celebration of the Feast of the Nativity.

Figure 3.6 Mithras (right, in Phrygian cap), with Sol (left, in crown and mantle) clasping hands. Flavius Aper's Altar, Eastern European (PTUJ) Relief, c. 260 CE. Courtesy © Aleš Chalupa

First, Mithras was seen as the "ruler of the cosmos" and was explicitly named "the unconquerable sun" (Sol Invictus).[62] The great Persian *yast* (hymn) to Mithras, dated to the fourth or even fifth century BCE, vigorously declares that he is the sun god who sees all: "has ten thousand spies, is strong, all-knowing, undeceivable" and "in the morning brings into evidence the many shapes ... as he lights up his body."[63] Just like Sol, Mithras was often depicted holding the cosmic sphere.[64] He was called *invictus*.[65] And Mithras's birthday, the Mithrakana, was December 25.[66]

Furthermore, Mithraism, being "widespread and popular in the third and fourth centuries," was a sister religion to Christianity.[67] There was baptism, a sacramental meal, observance on Sunday, a solstitial birth date, a teacher with 12 disciples, and many similarities in doctrine:[68]

> Mithraism resembled Christianity in its monotheistic tendencies, its sacraments, its comparatively high morality, its doctrine of an intercessor and redeemer, and its vivid belief in a future life and judgment to come. Moreover Sunday was its holy-day dedicated to the Sun.[69]

The parallels to Jesus' story are intriguing: Mithras was not only born in a cave, but adoring shepherds attended his birth, and he had a last supper with his followers before returning to the supreme god of light.[70]

"Arising at the same time and spreading in roughly the same geographical area, Mithraism and Christianity embodied two responses to the same set of cultural forces."[71] Mithraic temples, which were built underground, often in caves, are found "from Britain to the Black Sea, from the Rhine to the Nile," from Spain to Dura-Europos.[72] In other words, allegiance to Mithras was as broad as the entire Roman Empire and, many argue, Christianity's most dangerous rival. Kenneth Scott Latourette, Yale professor of Oriental History, goes so far as to suggest that the birthday of Mithras may have been "appropriated by Christians to compete with that faith."[73]

It is probable that the Magi described in the New Testament were followers of Mithras. Magi were the priests of Persia where Mithras took center stage.[74] In 614, Persian invaders did not destroy the Church of the Nativity in Bethlehem because on the facade they saw representations of the Magi wearing typical Persian dress. "The invaders mistook the magi for worshipers of Mithras, bringing gifts to the altar."[75]

Finally, Mithraism, as an empire-wide religion, mysteriously came to an end in the fourth century,[76] at the very time when Christ's birthday was being roundly celebrated. Was this just a coincidence, or was Christianity the leviathan that swallowed up Mithras's followers with the promise of an even more powerful sun god ("the true light") who also had the same birth date?[77] The connection between the insurgence of the Feast of the Nativity and the decline of Mithraism is plausible. Historian Manfred Clauss goes this far:

> the similarities between the two religions ... must have encouraged Mithraists in particular to become Christians. They had no need in their new faith to give

up the ritual meal, their Sun-imagery, or even their candles, incense and bells. Some elements of Mithraism may well have been carried over into Christianity, which partly explains why even in the sixth century the church authorities had to struggle against those *stulti hominess*, those simple clowns, who continued on the very church-steps to do obeisance to the Sun early in the morning, as they always had done, and pray to him.[78]

The interconnections between the Mithraic mysteries, Sol Invictus, and the Feast of the Nativity dramatically reveal how deep-seated the desire for an omnipotent sovereign of light and order is in the human psyche.

The Satunalia

The Saturnalia, held in honor of the god Saturnus, was a grand Roman festival joyously celebrated from December 17 through 24, immediately preceding the sun's birthday.[79] In Greece, Saturn was known as Cronus (Time), a monster who devoured his own children. However, in Rome, Cronus/Saturn was an entirely different sort of god. Dethroned by Zeus, who hurled him from Mount Olympus, Saturn came by boat to the site of what would be Rome and founded Saturnia, a fortified village.[80] This storyline was commemorated in the coinage of early Romans, often showing the face of Saturn on the obverse and the prow of a ship on the reverse.

Saturn was the *numen* of agriculture.[81] Roman coins associate him with the harvest (see Figure 3.3D). Macroblus, in his early fifth-century CE book, *The Saturnalia*, writes:

> Saturn is credited with the invention of the art of grafting, with the cultivation of fruit trees, and with instructing men in everything that belongs to the fertilizing of the fields. Furthermore, at Cyrene his worshipers, when they offer sacrifice to him, crown themselves with fresh figs and present each other with cakes, for they hold that he discovered honey and fruits. Moreover, at Rome men called him "Sterculius," as having been the first to fertilize the field with dung (*stercus*).[82]

Additionally, Saturn's reign was described as the golden age of innocence and purity.[83] Universal peace and plenty were the orders of the day. "There was neither want, nor weariness, nor war, in his golden age."[84] It was also an egalitarian time, for "as yet there was no division into bond and free."[85] Writing in the eighth century BCE, Hesiod portrays this golden age in *The Work and Days*:

> In the beginning, the immortals
> who have their homes on Olympos
> created the golden generation of mortal people.
> These lived in Kronos' time, when he
> was the king of heaven.

They lived as if they were gods,
their hearts free from all sorrow,
by themselves, and without hard work or pain;
no miserable
old age came their way; their hands, their feet,
did not alter.
They took their pleasure in festivals,
and lived without troubles.
When they died, it was as if they fell asleep.
All goods
were theirs. The fruitful grainland
yielded its harvest to them
of its own accord; this was great and abundant,
while they at their pleasure
quietly looked after their works, in the midst of good things
[prosperous in flocks, on friendly terms with the blessed immortals].[86]

No wonder then that the Temple of Saturn took a prominent place on the Roman Forum from as early as 501 BCE.[87]

In honor of Saturn's beneficent reign, the festival of Saturnalia was instituted. It began with a great sacrifice at the Temple of Saturn followed by a public feast open to all. At first, this was a single day of celebration on December 17, but its robust appeal to the masses necessitated an increase, first to three days and finally to a full week of "general excitement and religious rejoicing."[88] At this point, Saturnalia abutted the celebration of Sol's birthday. As the years passed, this annual mid-December celebration of Saturn and his golden age grew into the most popular and "merriest festival of the year, 'optimus delirium.'"[89]

> "Io! Saturnalia! Io! Io! Io!" that was the greeting that echoed through the holiday season. For it was in honor of Saturn—this day carnival of thanksgiving—good, old generous Saturn, kindest and most provident of gods.[90]

Saturnalia was glorious. Friends gathered to feast, make merry, and wish one another good fortune. Pointed red hats were worn, wax tapers (*cerei*) were lit and exchanged, holly branches and wreathes were hung, and laughter abounded.[91] A generous spirit awoke and presents of all description, including terra-cotta dolls (*sigillaria*) and good luck gifts called *strenae* (lucky fruits or cakes) were given and received.[92] Sound familiar?

Saturnalia was also wild, sometimes hilarious, sometimes vicious. A mock king—the Lord of Misrule—was appointed to preside over the unbridled revelries. His commands might be ridiculous but still binding. As Lucian (126–80 CE) describes: "One must shout out a libel on himself, another dance naked, or pick up the flute-girl and carry her thrice round the house."[93] The Lord of Misrule instigated chaos, the direct counterpoint to the strict order of the Roman rule. Wild abandon—drinking and gambling, riot and license—became normative for the populace.[94]

Saturnalia inverted social order. The most astonishing yet recognizable feature of Saturnalia was the temporary reversal of class structure: The rich would wait on their own slaves. Macrobius describes this: "For in houses where religious usages are observed it is the practice at Saturnalia to compliment the slaves by first providing for them a dinner as though prepared by the master."[95] According to Lucian, this is because Cronosolon, the priest of Cronus (Saturn), laid down the law:

All men shall be equal, slave and free, rich and poor, one with another ... dignities and birth and wealth shall give no precedence. All shall be served the same wine ... every man's portion of meat shall be alike. When the rich man shall feast his slaves, let his friends serve with him.[96]

Saturnalia was also a time of peace. Macrobius explains that "it was held to be an offense against religion to begin a war at the time of the Saturnalia, and to punish a criminal during the days of the festival called for an act of atonement."[97] Cronosolon pronounced that at Saturnalia "anger, resentment, threats, are contrary to law."[98] Millennia later, this same seasonal spirit blessed my analysand with a joy-filled reprieve (see Introduction).

Those days, absent of want, inequality, weariness or war, were long past. The Iron Age of social dysfunction, cruelty, and enmity was now the brutal reality. Bulfinch notes this telling conversation between King Evander and Aeneas about Saturn's rule:

Such peace and plenty ensured that men ever since have called his reign the golden age; but, by degrees, four other times succeeded, and the thirst of gold and the thirst of blood prevailed, the land was prey to successive tyrants.[99]

For the Romans, there was keen yearning to regain this Garden of Eden. Professor Stringfellow Barr writes: "Virgil's *Aeneid* and Horace's *Jubilee Hymn*, and indeed Augustan poetry in general, reflected the belief or hope that the Golden Age of Saturn was about to return."[100] Saturnalia, then, like the Christian Advent/Christmas season, was not just a time of looking back, but an eschatological hope, a looking forward to a second coming.

Virgil (70–19 BCE) in "Fourth Eclogue" of his *Bucolics* sounds like a Hebrew prophet when he imagines the "regeneration of the world with the birth of a child, at a date only forty years before the Christian era."[101]

We have reached the last Era in Sibylline song, time has conceived and the great Sequence of the Ages starts afresh. Justice, the virgin, comes back to dwell with us, and the rule of Saturn is restored. The Firstborn of the New Age is already on his way from high heaven down to earth.

With him, the Iron race shall end and golden Man inherit all the world.

Smile on the Baby's birth, immaculate Lucina your own Apollo is enthroned at last.[102]

Not only does Saturnalia come immediately before Sol's (and, eventually what is identified as Christ's) birthday, but there are other connections as well. In explaining the origin of the custom of exchanging round wax tapers during Saturnalia, Macrobius points out that many believed "in the reign of Saturn that we made our way, as though to the light, from a rude and gloomy existence."[103] He then makes the identification clear: Saturn "must assuredly be understood to be the sun."[104] One other interesting connection: According to David Ulansey, Mithras (directly connected with Sol Invictus who is directly connected with Christ) was the ruler of the cosmos (*kosmokrator*) from the moment of his birth and had the power to advance the world ages.[105]

Before concluding this chapter, we must make one brief but essential diversion into the philosophical underpinnings of the original unity symbolized by the sun. According to Neoplatonic philosopher Plotinus (204–270 CE), before essence, there is the One: "The One, therefore, transcendent to all differentiation and form, is the source of all."[106] The soul descends from the heavens into the multiplicity of existence. Incarnated, it always yearns and strives to return to the One—to celestial paradise. As noted by Plotinus (III, 8, 7), this unitive origination point becomes the soul's goal.[107]

It is not hard to imagine that Plotinus's thought contributed to the cultural milieu that spawned the beginnings of the Feast of the Nativity. The connections are many. Plotinus's popular philosophy was current during the beginning and subsequent explosion of the celebration of Christ's Nativity. Plotinus's thought strongly influenced Augustine, was congenial with monotheism, easily linked to the sun god that Jesus replaced, and looked to the final peace of restoration with the One—in other words, as the return to the Golden Age in final fashion. Susan Roll concludes:

> Late Platonism was occasionally cited by twentieth century scholars as the last gasp of pre-Christian solar monotheism, of which the institution of the feast of Christmas (if one grants the premise that Christmas "replaced" Natalis Solis Invicti) provided a clear paradigm.[108]

This spiderweb of connections—with Saturn, Mithras, and Christ being identified with Sol Invictus; the hope of return to the Golden Age/the One through Saturn, Mithras, and Christ; and the date of the advent and rise of the celebration of Christ's Nativity near the decline and fall of Mithraism, among others—helps us to understand the immense weight that Christmas unconsciously carries.

We return now to our primary line of thought. A preponderance of scholars conclude that somewhere in the late third to fourth century, Saturnalia became absorbed into the Christian festival of Christmas.[109] Clearly, that is what Increase Mather (1639–1723), president of Harvard and Puritan clergyperson, believed when he wrote critically in 1687 that early Christians observing the Nativity on December 25 did not do so "thinking that Christ was born in that Month, but because the Heathen's Saturnalia was at that time kept in Rome, and they were willing to have those Pagan Holidays metamorphosed into Christian [ones]."[110]

Whether to recruit converts or to keep the members they had from slipping away, church leadership had every reason to conflate Saturnalia with the Feast of the Nativity. Eventually all the expectations of the Golden Age, as well as the spirit and customs of Saturnalia, became assimilated into the worship of Christ's birth. "The Church finally succeeded in taking the merriment, the greenery, the lights, and the gifts of Saturn and giving them to the Babe of Bethlehem."[111] The Saturnalia supplemented the Feast of the Nativity to become the Christmas we know that celebrates evergreens, lights, gift-giving, revelry, social inversion, a deep desire for joy, equality, and peace and an eschatological hope for the Golden Age.

The Stage Is Set

Here are the broad-stroke findings of our historical-critical examination. Scriptural comments about Jesus' birth are later and minimal. We find a similar story in the development of the Christian liturgy. Easter was the first and foremost feast day. All evidence points to the fact that the Feast of the Nativity did not come into the liturgy until the beginning of the fourth century.

The date of December 25 was selected as Jesus' birthday, likely for one of two reasons: First, according to ancient tradition, Jesus was conceived on the same day that he died. Since he died on either March 25 or April 6, the date of his birth was set as December 25 in the West, and January 6 in the East. A second theory notes that the birth date of the popular Roman god Sol Invictus was December 25, winter solstice according to the Roman calendar. Christians co-opted this as Jesus' birth date because they could not suppress Sol's worship and saw this as a natural way to attract new converts to one who was also "the light of the world." This correlation was intensified by another god, Mithras, also worshipped throughout the empire as a sun god born on December 25. And though the celebration of the Nativity of Christ suddenly flourished, the worship of Mithras floundered. Adding more power to the pagan punch, the immensely popular weeklong holiday of Saturnalia, immediately preceding the birthday of Sol—with its longing for the Golden Age when all were equal, good, and happy—was eventually incorporated as well.[112] Thus we can conclude the *Dies natalis solis invicti*, the Mithraic mysteries, and Saturnalia all fortified the inherent significance of, and added fresh meanings to, the celebration of Jesus' birth.

By the end of the fourth century, the Feast of the Nativity was securely established and was burgeoning in the hearts of the populace of the Roman Empire, whose state religion was now Christianity. In 1038, it would become known as

Cristes maesse (Christ's mass), and in 1131 was written for the first time as one word: *Cristemesse*—our Christmas.[113]

Notes

1   Paul Bradshaw, *Early Christian Worship: A Basic Introduction to Ideas and Practice* (Liturgical Press, 1998), 86. "In Constantinople the first festival of Christ's birth on December 25 was celebrated in 379, in Nyssa of Cappadocia in 382, in Antioch in 388." Alexander Tille, *Yule and Christmas: Their Place in the Germanic Year* (David Nutt, 1899), 121.
2   Vernon Staley, *The Liturgical Year: An Explanation of the Origin, History and Significance of the Festival Days and Fasting Days of the English Church* (A.R. Molwbray & Co., 1907), 23.
3   Clement Miles, *Christmas in Ritual and Tradition, Christian and Pagan* (T. Fisher Unwin, 1912), 23.
4   Louis Duchesne, *Christian Worship: Its Origin and Evolution: A Study of Latin Liturgy up to the Time of Charlemagne*, 5th ed. (Society for Promoting Christian Knowledge, 1923), 261.
5   Thomas J. Talley, *The Origins of the Liturgical Year* (Pueblo Publishing Company, 1986), 82.
6   Talley, *The Origins of the Liturgical Year*, 93–94.
7   *Augustin: On the Holy Trinity, Doctrinal Treatise, Moral Treatises*, ed. Philip Schaff, Vol. 3. *Nicene and Post-Nicene Fathers* (T&T Clark, 1993), 74.
8   Staley, *The Liturgical Year*, 24.
9   In the end, most churches settled on the December 25 date for Christ's Nativity. Some have seen this as a shift in theology. January 6 was also the date of Jesus' baptism and the festival of Epiphany that commemorated the deification of Christ. God's voice was heard: "this is my beloved child, with whom I am well pleased." Many early Christians did not believe that Jesus was God at his birth, but used this text to argue that he was adopted by God at his baptism. Hence, giving a special birth date to Christ, December 25, was tantamount to a major change in Christology: Jesus is the natural son of God. The Church of Rome, where Christmas was first celebrated on December 25, was the major advocate of this position. See also Tille, *Yule and Christmas*, 119–20.
10   Susan Roll, *Toward the Origins of Christmas* (Kok Pharos Publishing House, 1995), 130–132.
11   Paul F. Bradshaw, *The Search for the Origins of Christian Worship: Sources and Methods for the Study of Early Liturgy* (Oxford University Press, 1992), 202.
12   Bradshaw, *The Search for the Origins of Christian Worship*, 27.
13   R.A.G. Carson, *Principal Coins of the Romans: The Republic c. 290–31 BC*, Vol. 1 (British Museum Publications, 1978), 23.
14   Herbert Spencer Robinson and Knox Wilson, *Myths and Legends of All Nations* (Bantam Books, 1961), 173. See also Pierre Grimal, ed., *The Dictionary of Classical Mythology*, trans. A.R. Maxwell-Hyslop (Basil Blackwell, 1986), 424.
15   Georges Dumezil, *Archaic Roman Religion*, Vol. 1 (University of Chicago Press, 1970), 169, 170, 389.
16   Gaston H. Halsberghe, *The Cult of Sol Invictus* (E.J. Brill, 1972), 26.
17   Michael Grant, *History of Rome* (Prentice Hall, 1978), 314.
18   Grant, *History of Rome*, 308, 15.
19   John Ferguson, *The Religions of the Roman Empire* (Cornell University Press, 1982), 46.

20 Grimal, *The Dictionary of Classical Mythology*, 190.

21 Michael Jordan, *Encyclopedia of Gods* (Facts on File, 1993), 241.

22 Halsberghe, *The Cult of Sol Invictus,* 35.

23 Ferguson, *The Religions of the Roman Empire*, 61.

24 N.G.L. Hammond and H.H. Scullard, eds., *The Oxford Classical Dictionary* (Oxford University Press, 1970), 377.

25 David Van Meter, *Handbook of Roman Imperial Coins: A Complete Guide to the History, Types and Values of Roman Imperial Coinage* (Laurion Press, 1991), 180.

26 Ferguson, *The Religions of the Roman Empire*, 52–53.

27 David R. Sear, *Roman Coins and Their Values* (Audley House, 1974), 200.

28 Grant, *History of Rome*, 363–64.

29 Van Meter, *Handbook of Roman Imperial Coins*, 256–257.

30 Eusebius, *The Church History: A New Translation with Commentary*, trans. Paul L. Maier (Kregel Publications, 1999), 287.

31 Ferguson, *The Religions of the Roman Empire*, 54.

32 Halsberghe, *The Cult of Sol Invictus*, 136. In the 14th century BCE, Pharoah Amenhotep IV tried to reform the Egyptian pantheon into a monotheistic religion with Aton, god of the sun, the supreme god. See Erik Hornung, *Akhenaten and the Religion of Light*, trans. David Lorton (Cornell University Press, 1999), 87–89.

33 Georges Dumezil, *Archaic Roman Religion*, Vol. 2. (University of Chicago Press, 1966), 432.

34 Jacob Burckhardt, *The Age of Constantine the Great*, trans. Moses Hadas (Doubleday, 1949), 24.

35 Ferguson, *The Religions of the Roman Empire*, 54.

36 *The Oxford Classical Dictionary*, 152. Here we note similarities to Louis XIV (1638–1715) of France who inherited a country internally divided, militarily exhausted, and nearly bankrupt. He deified himself as the radiate image of the sun and brought his country back to health and vigor. See also Andrew Lossky, *Louis XIV and the French Monarchy* (Rutgers University Press, 1994), 15, 86.

37 Lesley Adkins and Roy A. Adkins, *Dictionary of Roman Religion* (Oxford University Press, 1996), 209–210.

38 Halsberghe, *The Cult of Sol Invictus*, IX.

39 Ferguson, *The Religions of the Roman Empire*, 54.

40 E. Togo Salmon, *Roman Coins and Public Life Under the Empire* (University of Michigan Press, 1999), 134.

41 Grant, *History of Rome*, 392.

42 Ramsay MacMullen, *Christianity & Paganism in the Fourth to Eighth Centuries* (Yale University Press, 1997), 34.

43 Roll, *Toward the Origins of Christmas*, 115.

44 Brian Moynahan, *The Faith: A History of Christianity* (Doubleday, 2002), 94.

45 Erwin R. Goodenough, *Jewish Symbols in the Greco-Roman Period*, Jacob Neusner, ed. (Princeton University Press, 1988), 168.

46 Ferguson, *The Religions of the Roman Empire*, 54, 239.

47 Goodenough, *Jewish Symbols in the Greco-Roman Period*, 168.

48 Marcel Metzger, *History of the Liturgy: The Major Stages* (Liturgical Press, 1997), 64. In 380, Emperor Theodosius recognized Christianity as the state religion.

49 Paul L. Maier, *In the Fullness of Time: A Historian Looks at Christmas, Easter, and the Early Church* (Kregel Publications, 1997), 29.

50 MacMullen, *Christianity & Paganism in the Fourth to Eighth Centuries*, 155.

51 Roll, *Toward the Origins of Christmas*, 33.

52 Macrobius, *The Saturnalia*, trans. Percival Vaughan Davies (Columbia University Press, 1969), 129. The quote continues: "Afterward, however, as the days go on and

lengthen, the sun at the spring equinox acquires strength in a way comparable to growth in adolescence, and so the god is given the appearance of a young man. Subsequently, he is represented in full maturity, with a beard, at the summer solstice, when the sun's growth is completed. After that the days shorten, as though with the approach of his old age—hence the fourth of the figures by which the god is portrayed."

53 Talley, *The Origins of the Liturgical Year*, 90–91.

54 Roll, *Toward the Origins of Christmas*, 157, 23.

55 Professor Sigmund Mowinckel points out that mythical elements appear frequently in Isaiah. He believes that Isaiah 9:1–6 makes direct allusion to "the birth of a new sun god" who signifies the end of chaos, winter, and death. The prophet begins by giving a picture of the national situation as night and darkness and then announces the dawning of the light.

56 Also, in "Saying 50" of the Gospel of Thomas, we read: "Jesus said: If some say to you, 'Where have you come from?' say to them, 'We have come from the light, where the light came into being by itself, established itself, and appeared in an image of light.' If they say to you, 'Are you the light?' say, 'We are its children.'" Marvin W. Meyer, *The Secret Teachings of Jesus: Four Gnostic Gospels* (Random House, 1984), 28.

57 "Arise, shine; for your light has come," exhorts Isaiah 60:1. In Ephesians 5:14, Paul identifies Jesus as this light: "Awake, O sleeper, / And arise from the dead, / And Christ shall give you light."

58 Mario Di Giampaolo and Andrea Muzzi, *Correggio: Catalogo Completo Dei Dipinti* (Cantini, 1993), 123. This painting from 1522 was "the first picture in the history of painting in which the light is represented as shining forth from an object within the picture." Cynthia Pearl Maus, *The World's Great Madonnas: An Anthology of Pictures, Poetry, Music and Stories Centering in the Life of the Madonna and Her Son* (Harper & Bros., 1947), 31.

59 Matthew Powell, *The Christmas Creche: Treasure of Faith, Art & Theater* (Pauline Books & Media, 1997), 30. Susan Roll points out that there are, at least, several explanations for such an occurrence: (1) it may be "an early indication that Christians did not disdain from appropriating a non-Christian Solar deity and reinterpreting it as Christ; (2) it may "represent Christ in the traditional role of the sun-god who guides souls of the dead to their eternal rest"; (3) the combination of symbolism could have been pragmatic, "intended to disguise a Christian tomb at a time when Christians still risked deadly persecution, not dissimilar to the use of letter-signals such as Alpha and Omega, the Chi Rho, and the Ichthus," 125.

60 Talley, *The Origins of the Liturgical Year*, 95.

61 Adkins and Adkins, *Dictionary of Roman Religion*, 209.

62 David Ulansey, *The Origins of the Mithraic Mysteries: Cosmology and Salvation in the Ancient World* (Oxford University Press, 1989), 103–122.

63 Manfred Clauss, *The Roman Cult of Mithras: The God and His Mysteries*, trans. Richard Gordon (Routledge, 2000), 3.

64 Ulansey, *The Origins of the Mithraic Mysteries*, 95–99.

65 Clauss, *The Roman Cult of Mithras*, 25.

66 Ferguson, *The Religions of the Roman Empire*, 239.

67 Duchesne, *Christian Worship: Its Origin and Evolution*, 261.

68 William Sansom, *A Book of Christmas* (McGraw-Hill, 1968), 30–33.

69 Miles, *Christmas in Ritual and Tradition, Christian and Pagan*, 23.

70 John Matthews, *The Winter Solstice: The Sacred Traditions of Christmas* (Quest Books, 1998), 53. Apollo and Attis were also born in a cave during the midwinter solstice; the wonder child Osiris is restored to life on December 25. "In Celtic myth, Culhwch's quest to release the child god Mabon from his dark prison is symbolic of the release of light at the Solstice," 57.

71 Ulansey, *The Origins of the Mithraic Mysteries*, 4.
72 Clauss, *The Roman Cult of Mithras*, 16, 26–27.
73 Kenneth Scott Latourette, *The First Five Centuries: A History of the Expansion of Christianity*, Vol. 1 (Harper & Bros., 1937), 326.
74 Arthur Weigal, *The Paganism in Our Christianity*, 247–248.
75 Powell, *The Christmas Creche*, 21–22. In the Gnostic text, *The Book of the Bee*, the Magi are 12 in number: four bringing gold, four myrrh, and four frankincense. See also Matthews, *The Winter Solstice*, 60.
76 Clauss, *The Roman Cult of Mithras*, 32.
77 Ernest Jones believed it was because Christianity offered something that Mithraism could not: a feminine element in the form of Mary, who, in the fourth century, went from being the Mother of God to the "Queen of Heaven." Ernest Jones, "The Significance of Christmas," in *Essays in Applied Psycho-Analysis*, Vol. 2 (Hogarth Press, 1951), 217.
78 Clauss, *The Roman Cult of Mithras*, 172.
79 Adkins and Adkins, *Dictionary of Roman Religion*, 210.
80 Grimal, *The Dictionary of Classical Mythology*, 412.
81 Ferguson, *The Religions of the Roman Empire*, 69, 211.
82 Macrobius, *The Saturnalia*, 59.
83 Thomas Bulfinch, *Myths of Greece and Rome* (Penguin Books, 1983), 21.
84 Genevieve Foster, *Augustus Caesar's World: A Story of Ideas and Events from BC 44 to 14 AD* (Charles Scribner's Sons, 1947), 56.
85 Macrobius, *The Saturnalia*, 59.
86 Hesiod, *The Works and Days, Theology, the Shield of Herakles,* trans. Richmond Lattimore (University of Michigan Press, 1959), 31–33.
87 Adkins and Adkins, *Dictionary of Roman Religion*, 200.
88 Macrobius, *The Saturnalia*, 70–73.
89 *The Oxford Classical Dictionary*, 955.
90 Foster, *Augustus Caesar's World*, 56.
91 *The Oxford Classical Dictionary*, 955. Some scholars believe that the little clay figures of the holy family—Mary, Joseph, and Jesus—traditionally sold in Rome's Piazza Navona at Christmastime are "the modern-day counterparts of the *sigillaria* exchanged as gifts during the pagan Saturnalia." See also Thompson, *Holiday Symbols*, 534.
92 Tille, *Yule and Christmas*, 85. Earl W. Count and Alice Lawson Count, *4000 Years of Christmas: A Gift from the Ages* (Seastone, 2000), 34.
93 Miles, *Christmas in Ritual and Tradition, Christian and Pagan*, 166.
94 Collins, *Stories Behind the Great Traditions of Christmas*, 23.
95 Macrobius, *The Saturnalia*, 158.
96 Miles, *Christmas in Ritual and Tradition, Christian and Pagan*, 166–167.
97 Macrobius, *The Saturnalia*, 70.
98 Miles, *Christmas in Ritual and Tradition, Christian and Pagan*, 166.
99 Bulfinch, *Myths of Greece and Rome*, 300–301.
100 Stringfellow Barr, *The Mask of Jove: A History of the Graeco-Roman Civilization from the Death of Alexander to the Death of Constantine* (J.B. Lippincott, 1966), 231.
101 Benjamin Hall Kennedy, *P. Vergili Maronis Bucolica, Georgica, Aeneis: The Works of Virgil with Commentary and Appendix* (Longmans, Green, and Co., 1876), 306, xxv.
102 Virgil, *The Pastoral Poems: A Translation of the Eclogues*, trans. E.V. Rieu (Penguin Books, 1949), 41.
103 Macrobius, *The Saturnalia*, 61.
104 Macrobius, *The Saturnalia*, 148.
105 Ulansey, *The Origins of the Mithraic Mysteries*, 95–124.
106 Plotinus, *The Essential Plotinus*, trans. Elmer O'Brien (Hackett Publishing, 1964), 20.

107 Plotinus, *The Six Enneads*, trans. Stephen MacKenna and B.S. Page (William Benton, 1952), 132.
108 Roll, *Toward the Origins of Christmas*, 119.
109 Adkins and Adkins, *Dictionary of Roman Religion*, 210; *The Oxford Classical Dictionary*, 955.
110 "A Testimony against Several Prophane and Superstitious Customs, Now Practiced by Some in New-England," (London, 1687), 35, found in Stephen Nissenbaum, *The Battle for Christmas* (Knopf, 1996), 4. We also need to note that the Romans' Kalends, the celebration of the New Year that lasted three days and was filled with license, banqueting, and games, may also have played a part in the development of Christmas. It has many similarities to Saturnalia: Gifts were generously exchanged, toasts of strong drink common, extravagant meals consumed, slaves "breathe the air of freedom," houses were again decorated with lights and greenery and the new consuls were inducted into office. Miles, *Christmas in Ritual and Tradition, Christian and Pagan*, 24, 168.
111 Count and Count, *4000 Years of Christmas*, 37–38.
112 Duchesne, *Christian Worship: Its Origin and Evolution*, 261.
113 Tille, *Yule and Christmas*, 159.

Chapter 4

The 12 Motifs of Christmas

According to comparative religion scholar Wilfred Cantwell Smith, to get the full sense of a scriptural account, one must explore the text's background as well as observe its foreground. What scripture produced is every bit as important as where it came from. We now consider the bountiful *Nachleben*—the "afterlife," the "continuing history," or "forward history"—of the Nativity texts.[1]

Every December, certain thoughts and feelings, moods and behaviors reliably arise like a Dutch garden. As dormant flower bulbs of every kind, the multiplicity of Christmas now explodes in awaited forms and robust hues. These Christmas motifs are both sacred and profane, often with no clear line of demarcation. Spiritual practices and elegant customs sometimes reign. But Christmas, like Garth Brooks in his song, also has "Friends in Low Places." Christmas Midnight Mass and the office Christmas party celebrate two types of spirits altogether, both attractive. And in December, they mingle comfortably.

The conflation of the birthday of the Son of God with the yearly rebirth of Sol happened naturally. But its success in adding a major holiday to the Christian ranks revealed the expediency of such mergers. This syncretism—sometimes ecclesiastically calculated, sometimes advanced by people—continued through centuries as Christians courted farther reaches of Europe. Many of the rituals and symbols associated with Christmas have mixed pedigrees from repeated intermarriages of Christianity with ancient religions. These assimilated traditions were pagan, or better put, universally symbolic. Eschewing purely pious practices, they embraced human wholeness. In addition to holy hopes, humanity's shadow side is warmly welcomed—notably our lust for material life, penchant for greediness, requirement for periodic revelry, and even occasional aches for subversion. Christmas traditions are as manifold as humans are complex. Some customs are sacred, some secular, some have twin roots. But all hold an authentic, life-affirming attraction. As a conglomerate festival, Christmas champions the indivisibility of the psyche, fueling the generalized feeling of gladness during the darkest time of the year.

We now delve into the 12 motifs of Christmas: Merriment, light, evergreens, Saint Nicholas/Santa Claus, homecoming/family, extravagant welcome, radical inversion, excess, the Child, the crèche, gifts/benevolence, and peace.

DOI: 10.4324/9781003568629-5

"Merry Christmas"/Yule

From the last centuries BCE to the early centuries CE, "Io Saturnalia" was the jubilant December greeting heard across the Roman Empire. It reflected the mounting mood of the populace. As Christianity burgeoned and bound itself to indigenous traditions, "Merry Christmas" became a hope-filled greeting. When the English were converted to Christianity in the sixth and seventh centuries, Christmas became identified with the joyous pagan celebration of Yule (*Jol*), meaning "jollification."[2] Yule, as Saturnalia before it, enlarged the Christmas spirit, adding even more merriment to the solemnity. Historian Clement Miles expounds:

> The heathen folk-festivals absorbed by the Nativity feast were essentially life-affirming, they expressed the mind of men who said "yes" to this life, who valued earthly good things. On the other hand, Christianity ... was at bottom pessimistic as regards this earth, and valued it only as a place of discipline for the life to come; it was essentially a religion of renunciation that said "no" to the world.

> The struggle between the ascetic principle of self-mortification, world-renunciation, absorption in a transcendent ideal, and the natural human striving towards earthly joy and well-being, is perhaps the most interesting aspect of the history of Christianity; it is certainly shown in an absorbingly interesting way in the development of the Christian feast of the Nativity. The conflict is keen at first; the Church authorities fight tooth and nail against these relics of heathenism, these devilish rites; but mankind's instinctive paganism is insuppressible.

> The Church's Christmas, as the Middle Ages pass on, becomes increasing "merry"—warm and homely, suited to the instincts of ordinary humanity, filled with a joy that is of this earth, and not only a mystical rapture at a transcendental redemption.[3]

Debates about Yule's original meaning smolder, but not about its intensity and mirth.[4] During the reign of Norway's King Hacon the Good (r. 946–61), it became law that Yule celebrations would occur while the Christians kept Christmas.[5] Yule was so fundamental to northern cultures that it became another word for Christmastide. English poet George Wither (1588–1667) conveys the good cheer:

> *So, now is come our joyful'st feast;*
> *Let every man be jolly ...*
> *Drown a sorrow in a cup of wine,*
> *And let us all be merry.*[6]

Frédéric Mistral (1830–1914), Nobel laureate in literature, revealed how centuries later the heart of Yule joy still beats robustly as he recalled Yule celebrations with family in France. "As members gathered, 'Merry Christmas!' was the deep-felt greeting and when the Yule log was lit all would cry out: '*Allegresse! Allegresse! Allegresse!* (Happiness! Happiness! Happiness!).'"[7] Likewise, sixty-plus years after its release, hearts are still stirred by the warm resonant voice of Burl Ives singing, "Have a Holly Jolly Christmas."

Light

Light is an elemental and aboriginal symbol of both Nativity narratives. For Matthew, the guiding star leads searching strangers to a distant land and an obscure manger. According to Luke and in line with the Law of Moses, 40 days after his birth, Jesus was presented to God at the Temple where Simeon, an aged, single-minded holy man, was inspired at just that moment to enter. Holding the baby in his arms, he declared Jesus "a light to lighten the Gentiles" (Luke 2:32). Rembrandt's painting *Simeon in the Temple* (1631) conveys the tenebrous sacred space with the baby as the sole source of light, revealing heaven-bound ecstasy on Simeon's face. John, in his theological prologue, represents the preexistent but now incarnating Jesus as the light of life, the antidote to darkness. In John's Gospel (8:12, 9:5), Jesus twice affirms "I am the light of the world."

Christmas was called the Feast of Lights in the Latin Church.[8] There were precursors, most obviously the eight-day, nine-candle midwinter Jewish celebration of Hanukkah. This older Feast of Lights is one of the happiest Jewish holidays.[9] Likewise, Saturnalia celebrants made wide use of candles. The foreboding darkness was a prime enemy of premodern people who struggled for protection against unseen enemies, especially malevolent spirits. Most ancient cultures celebrated winter solstice by lighting fires and candles as a sign that the sun would now regain its strength and burn longer each day. This helps explain how Santa Lucia (283–304), the martyred saint of Italy, whose name means luminance and is represented carrying a lamp, became so beloved in Scandinavia.[10] She thus naturally belongs, not to her country of origin, but to a land whose midwinter witching hours nearly overshadow the entire day. On December 13 (the shortest day of the year according to the historic Julian calendar), a young woman—the oldest girl in the family or one chosen by the community for the town-wide celebration—comes in a white dress and red sash with candles burning in her evergreen crown. This beloved tradition of at least 400 years has spread to Germany, Latvia, Russia, and even China. As a living symbol of hope that long nights will wax no more, she and her entourage of star boys and candle maids, all dressed in white and holding single tapers, inaugurate the Christmas season (see Figure 4.1).[11] The Swedish version of "Santa Lucia" is sung with joyful abandon, emphasizing the winter solstice theme:

> The night goes with weighty step
> Round yard and hearth,
> As the sun departs from earth,
> Shadows are brooding
> There in our dark house,

Figure 4.1 Candlelight procession of the Swedish choir at the Santa Lucia Festival, York Minster, England. Alternative Occasions/Alamy Stock Photo

> Walking with lighted candles
> Santa Lucia, Santa Lucia.[12]

Oxford scholar H.F. Tozer concludes Dante Alighieri's (1265–1321) inclusion of Santa Lucia in each volume of *The Divine Comedy* symbolizes "illuminative grace,"[13] a more Christian interpretation. Swede Helge Åkerhielm merges the two views: "The torch in the darkness, the unafraid offensive of light and good in the devouring blackness and the winter storm: it is that which in the final analysis are the innermost core of the Swedish Christmas."[14]

Just as the Santa Lucia Festival was a natural admixture of Christmas ideals and winter solstice hope, ancient torches were uninhibitedly passed on to Christmas rituals in so many other ways. Throughout the Middle Ages, in both church and home, it was customary to light one large candle on Christmas Eve until Twelfth Night, to commemorate the Star of Bethlehem.[15] Charles Reade in his 1870 novel, *Put Yourself in His Place*, presents a vivid picture of Christmas customs of the times. On Christmas Eve, the squire's house was gloriously decorated.

> The materials were simple—wax-candles and holly; the effect was produced by a magnificent use of these materials. There were eighty candles of the largest size sold … and twelve wax pillars, five feet high, and the size of a man's

calf. ... The holly was not in sprigs, but in enormous branches, that filled the eye with glistening green and red; and in the embrasure of the front window stood a young holly-tree, entire, eighteen feet high, and gorgeous with five hundred branches of red berries. ... The wax pillars lighted, and their flame shone through the leaves and berries magically. ... With the first stroke of midnight, out burst the full organ and fifty voices, with the "Gloria in excelsis Deo" and the lighters ran along the walls and lighted the eighty candles, and, for the first time, the twelve waxen pillars, so that, as the hymn concluded, the room was ablaze, and it was Christmas Day.[16]

To the present day, light, in every form imaginable, is an essential element of the Christmas celebration around the globe (see Figure 4.2). There is the centuries-old New England tradition of placing a single candle in each window of the home during Advent and Christmastide. An important symbol of Christmas in Mexico and the American Southwest are *farolitos* (little lanterns), votive candles set on sand inside brown paper bags, their golden glow outlining buildings, patios, walkways, and even plazas. "Luminarias"—small bonfires stacked in log cabin form about three feet high—are also often used at churches, homes, and public squares.[17] Similarly, in Cajun towns along the Mississippi River, hundreds of huge bonfires, *feux de joie* ("fires of joy," also lit on Epiphany in France), often as tall as 30 feet, are ignited on Christmas Eve so that Papa Nöel can find his way.[18]

A corollary midwinter tradition is the massive, crackling Yule log or Christmas block. Best known as a Germanic/Scandinavian custom, it relates to a Celtic fire ritual.[19] From ancient to nearly modern times, burning bonfires and Yule logs at the winter solstice, the darkest time of the year, was believed to ward off demons and encourage the sun to regain its full strength. Of course, it was also highly practical, giving the comfort of warmth and the advantages of illumination. M. Fertiault reveals the transformation to Christian practice:

This is a huge log, which is placed on the fire on Christmas Eve, and which in Burgundy is called, on this account, la Souche de Noel. Then the father of the family ... sings solemnly Christmas carols with his wife and children, the smallest of whom he sends into the corner to pray that the Yule-log may bear him some sugar-plums. Meanwhile, little parcels of them are placed under each end of the log, and the children come and pick them up, believing, in good faith, that the great log has borne them.[20]

So fundamental was this Yule log that Tille notes a document from 1184 that gives the pastor of the Ahlen Church in Westphalia the right to have a whole tree delivered each year to the parsonage for his festive fire on Christmas Eve.[21] The meaning of candles and fires is clear: Warmth in cold, light in darkness, life in a time of death—or as the poet Richard Crashaw (1613–1649) wrote, "Summer in winter, day in night."[22]

Figure 4.2 Madonna and Child, by The Reverend Sawai Chinnawong, Thailand, 20th century; used with permission of the artist.

The centrality of light continues to be found in winter celebrations across the continents. The five-day Diwali festival of lights is as paramount to Hindus as Christmas is to Christians. Diwali means "row of lights," referring to clay lamps placed outside homes symbolizing the victory of light over darkness. Kwanzaa ("first fruits"), another midwinter celebration, is likewise focused on light. Each night, from December 26 to January 1, a candle is lit to observe Nguzo Saba (seven principles) of Kwanzaa: *Umoja* (unity), *kujichagulia* (self-determination), *ujima* (collective work and responsibility), *ujamaa* (cooperative economics), *nia* (purpose), *kuumba* (creativity), and *imani* (faith). The Quran (24:35) affirms this: "Allah is the light of the heavens and the earth." Light is a universal symbol of illumination, protection, and gnosis. It transcends particularistic faith and, for Christians, has been forever bonded to the Holy Child in a manger.

Evergreens

Tightly woven into the fabric of Christmas celebrations, the significance of evergreens is timeless, long predating Jesus' birth. During winter solstice in ancient Rome, an evergreen shrub called the "herb of the sun" was especially favored.[23] Evergreen wreaths played a prominent part in the celebration of Saturnalia. Holly and ivy, two plants synonymous with Christmas, were equally associated with Saturn: "Saturn's club was made of holly wood, and his sacred bird, the gold-crested wren, made its nest in the ivy."[24]

Druids believed the "Oak King" and "Holly King" had a mighty struggle for control of the forest. In the end, Holly King always won in winter because it remained green while the seemingly mightier oak lost its leaves and stood naked.

> Because of the "magical" power of the holly to survive and prosper in even the darkest and cruelest winters, Druids instructed the Celts that this plant was the most powerful plant in the woods. Thus, people picked boughs of holly and brought them into their houses. They believed the tree's magic would help protect them from the evil they believed infused the season of night.[25]

Looking for even earlier roots, some scholars see a similarity with the Egyptian midwinter festival honoring the sun god Horus, who—like Jesus—was understood to have had a miraculous birth.[26] The symbol for this Egyptian solstitial celebration was a palm tree, another evergreen.[27] Sir George Birdswood, in the first volume of the *Asiatic Quarterly Review* (1886), argues that the Christmas tree may well have come from the land where Hebrew slaves were used to build its monuments:

> [T]he ancient Egyptian practice of decking houses at the time of the winter solstice with branches of the date-palms, the symbol of life triumphant over death, and therefore of perennial life in the renewal of each bounteous year and the supporters of these suggestions point to the fact that pyramids of green paper,

covered all over with wreaths and festoons of flowers and strings of sweetmeats, are often substituted in Germany for the Christmas-tree.[28]

The evergreen's symbolism is ancient, pervasive, and clear.

Evergreens have been paired with Jesus' birth for at least half a millennium. "Bring home Christmas" has long meant gathering and displaying the family evergreens. In what appears to be material from John Stow's *1598 Survey of London* (1598), we find the following:

> Against the Feast of Christmas every man's house, as also their parish churches, were decked with holly, ivy, bay and whatsoever the season of the year afforded to be green, the conduits and standards in the streets were likewise garnished.[29]

Box, bay, ivy, holly, yew, juniper, spruce, and fir were apotropaic, seen as shields against demons who became more aggressive as the nights grew longer.[30] Evergreens thrive—retaining their color and bearing fruit (ivy, holly, and mistletoe)—in the "dead of winter"; therefore, they are potent symbols of eternal life.[31] Wreathes' circular shape, without beginning or end, made them doubly persuasive as symbols of triumphant perpetuity. In Britain, long before Christmas trees, a holy bough consisting of a "double hoop of willow or hazel, around which were garlanded and plaited evergreens—ivy, bay, rosemary, holly, and mistletoe" was hung on the front door.[32] Encouraged by the church, consecrated by the priest, it bestowed a special blessing on all who practiced the custom.

> Anyone who visited the house during the Christmas season, which was the season of peace and goodwill to all men, had to show his or her goodwill with an embrace under this bough, something like the Kiss of Peace in Churches today.[33]

This tradition eventually transmuted into our custom of kissing under the mistletoe, an ageless symbol of bringing beauty from dung, life from death.[34]

Now to the Christmas tree.[35] Fyodor Dostoevsky begins one of his short stories with these words: "The other day I saw a wedding. But no! I'd better tell you about the Christmas tree. The Wedding was all right! I liked it very much, but the other affair was much better."[36] When someone as substantial as Dostoevsky writes this, we know that the Christmas tree represents something extraordinary.

According to a 2023 Christmas Tree Association survey, "94 percent of consumers plan to display at least one Christmas tree in their home."[37] How did this all come about? In a legend of unknown origin, the Holy Family hid one night in an old pine tree, which lowered its branches to conceal them from Herod's soldiers. Awakening safely in the morning, Baby Jesus raised his arms and blessed the tree. It is said that cutting a pine cone lengthwise reveals the imprint of Christ's hand.[38] The helpfulness of evergreens to those in need remains a frequent theme.

The most direct precursor to the Christmas tree seems to be European Druids' winter worship practices:

During the winter solstice they tied apples to the branches of oaks and firs to thank Odin for blessing them with fruitfulness. They also made offerings of cakes shaped like fish, birds and other animals. Lighted candles, honoring the sun god Balder, were placed in the boughs.[39]

This Druidic practice calls to mind the German legend of the "Thunder Oak," a giant tree sacred to Thor, god of thunder, with huge limbs arching toward the heavens. Thor's priests sacrificed man and beast at an altar beneath the tree, with blood watering its roots. One Christmas Eve, as townsfolk gathered around the Thunder Oak and Thor's priests raised their knives to slay their victims, the Christian missionary Boniface hurried to the altar. He swiftly drew an axe and swung again and again at the monstrous tree. As he concluded his strokes, a mighty rush of wind blew the tree over in an enormous crash, splitting it into four pieces. Just behind there stood a tiny young fir tree completely unhurt. Saint Winifred then spoke to the horrified worshippers:

This little tree shall be your holy tree tonight. It is the tree of peace and salvation, a tree of life, a tree of hope. Behold, how it points toward heaven! Let this tree be called the Tree of the Christ Child. Gather about it, not in the wildwood, but in your homes. There it will shelter no bloody deeds, just loving gifts and acts of kindness. Let the peace of Christ reign in your heart! [40]

The people were so impressed by the happenings that they took the little fir to the house of their chief. Boniface used the wood of the Thunder Oak to build the chapel of Saint Peter, where the people were taught the rites of Christmas.

In perhaps the most famous legend about a Christmas tree, Martin Luther travels alone over the snow-covered countryside on Christmas Eve. Moved by the beauty of thousands of glittering stars above, he cut a little fir tree, brought it into the house, and placed lighted candles upon it as a way to share the experience with his wife and young son.[41] However pleasing this tale, one connecting the Christmas tree with the Reformation, it cannot be substantiated.

Notwithstanding, the tradition of placing trees inside took hold in Germany. Some say as early as 1492, but no later than 1570 a market for Christmas trees began to prosper in Strasbourg.[42] A forest ordinance from Ammerschweier in Alsace, dated 1561, says that no burgher "shall have for Christmas more than one bush of more than eight shoe's length."[43] The first record of evergreen trees decorated for Christmas is in a 1605 travel book about Alsace: "At Christmas time in Strasburg they set up fir trees in the rooms, and they hung on them roses cut of many-colored paper, apples, wafers, gilt, sugar and so on."[44] Mention is also made in 1743 of a Christmas tree set up in a castle in the Swedish province of Södermanland.[45]

Prussian mercenaries introduced the Christmas tree to America during the Revolutionary War, but it failed to catch on. Similarly, in the early 1800s, when

Germans settled in Pennsylvania, it remained of small interest. However, all this dramatically changed on February 10, 1840, when German Prince Albert wed England's Queen Victoria and the venerated German tradition was brought to Windsor Castle, popularizing it for their subjects (see Figure 4.3).[46] It was not long before an engraving of the royal couple's tree appeared in American newspapers and the new tradition swept across the continent. By the 1880s, many worried that the seasonal demand might just wipe out fir trees altogether.[47]

Claude Lévi-Strauss sums up the tradition of the Christmas tree for us:

> If in prehistoric times there had never been a cult of tree worship that continued in a variety of folklore customs, modern Europe would no doubt have invented the Christmas tree. ... Other medieval practices testify to this perfectly: the yule log (turned into cakes in Paris) made from a log big enough to burn through the night; Christmas candles, large enough to achieve the same result; the decoration of buildings (a custom in existence since the Roman Saturnalia ...) with green branches of ivy, holly, pine. Finally, and with no relation to Christmas, stories from the Round Table refer to a supernatural tree all covered in lights. In this context the Christmas tree seems to be a syncretic response, that is to say, it focuses on one object previously scattered attributes of others: magic tree, fire, long-lasting light, enduring greenness.[48]

It is interesting to note that Chinese people have long used evergreen kumquat and mandarin trees during their New Year celebration. A central ritual of the Japanese New Year is placing *kadomatsu*, arrangements of pine and bamboo (also an evergreen), at the entrances of homes and temples.[49] Some Native American tribes make use of cedar, pine, and juniper for their winter ceremonies. Without a doubt, humans have for millennia been deeply moved by that which remains green despite the season, a blatantly manifest and compelling symbol of good fortune, hope, and enduring life.

Saint Nicholas/Santa Claus

For children, the word *Christmas* brings an immediate and singular thought: Santa Claus. Also known as Father Christmas, Kris Kringle, Sinter Klass, Peiznichel, or some 120 other names, he has long been exuberantly worshiped as the god of gifts. *The Ottawa Free Trader* of December 14, 1847, includes this depiction:

> Christmas ... is again with us bringing to the "young'uns" high expectations of visits from that saintly goblin of youthful fancy, old Santa Claus, who, generous-hearted, jolly old hombre, comes stealthily, with well stocked pack and furred feet, to fill the stockings duly suspended by chimney corner, with brightly painted toys and gaily decorated sweet-meats."[50]

Figure 4.3 Queen Victoria, Prince Albert, and family at Windsor Castle; from *The Illustrated London News*, December 23, 1848. World History Archive/Alamy Stock Photo

Figure 4.4 Saint Nicholas Providing Dowries, by Bicci di Lorenzo (1373–1452); the start of Christmas giving. Courtesy Metropolitan Museum of Art, New York; Gift of Coudert Brothers, 1888; 88.3.89

We know him well! But do we? He has had a most remarkable transformation. The real-life Saint Nicholas was born around 270 CE in the town of Patara, Lycia, present-day Turkey.[51] Like Francis of Assisi who would follow him into the hearts of so many, Nicholas was the son of a wealthy merchant and an especially compassionate young man. The following account became the center of his legend:

> A widowed nobleman had fallen on hard times. Penniless, he could not take care of his three teenage daughters. Desperate, he considered selling the eldest into prostitution. In the middle of the night, Nicolaos threw a bag of gold through the father's window; this provided a dowry for the girl and she was saved.
>
> Later, again under cover of darkness, Nicolaos did this twice more, for the other two girls (see Figure 4.4.). The third time, the father caught him in the act. Embarrassed, and to escape the resulting notoriety, Nicolaos left home to join a religious group.[52]

Becoming a priest, and later the bishop of Myra, he continued helping those in distress. Charles Jones, in his scholarly work on Saint Nicholas, notes a sixth-century story that describes him as a modern Joseph who saved Egypt from starvation:

> Once when a famine spread over the whole of Lycia … Then to a certain seaman who had dealt in grain, the great Nicholas appeared in the night. After giving him three measures of gold in pledge, Nicholas ordered him to approach the city of Myra and sell the grain to the citizens there. The merchant, astonished at

finding the gold in his hand ... went to Myra, where he sold his grain to the city. Those who live in the city ascribe the relief of famine in that instance to God and the great Nicholas (as they do much else).[53]

Three loaves of bread became the first iconographic symbol for Nicholas. He became famous for saving sailors, fishermen, and travelers, and Mediterranean mariners would not leave shore without a supply of "Saint Nicholas loaves" that they would throw into the sea at the first sight of a storm.[54] Hence, this led to the oft-recited Nicholas prayer for present and future protection:

> God, who didst grace the blessed Nicholas as protector of imperiled innocence whilst he lived, and after his death by countless miracles, grant that by his merits we may be freed from perversion of justice while alive and from the fire of hell after death.[55]

Nicholas, like his colleagues, was deadly serious about sin and its repercussions.

Nicholas died on December 6, 326.[56] Holy and heroic, compassionate and caring, he was so popular with the people that they immediately proclaimed him a saint (see Figure 4.5). For a while, more "churches were dedicated in his name than in the name of any other apostles."[57] In France and Germany, more than 2,000 churches were built in his honor; in Greece, England, Russia, and Italy, 400 more.[58] By the end of the 11th century, the reliquary of Nicholas had been transported from East to West; his reputation as the great helper of those in jeopardy preceded his remains. According to one Russian religious chronicler, "Saint Nicholas heals everyone, as much in Lycia as in the Latin land, and he extends his benevolence to the confines of Russia."[59] When Saint Anselm came to England in 1092, he found an active Nicholas cult. Anselm's effusive prayer shows the magnitude of Nicholas's appeal.

> I will call upon Nicholas, that great confessor, whose name is glorified throughout the globe. ... Why wouldst thou, my Lord, be invoked by everyone throughout the world unless thou art advocate for every postulant?[60]

In the West, the name Nikolaos and its variants (80 in France alone) became immensely popular. "Nicholas" made up 1.6 percent of Christian names in London between 1540 and 1549, and likewise between 1640 and 1649.[61] While we say "every Tom, Dick, and Harry" in the United States, it's every "Jan, Piet, en Klaas" in the Netherlands.[62] Between the ninth and 15th centuries, no fewer than five popes took the name.[63]

Then came the Reformation and the Renaissance. Saint Nicholas's days as a religious superstar, as an efficacious saint to whom the multitudes prayed, waned dramatically. Historian Roland Bainton explains that now reason mitigated against legend, old understandings became superstition, new learning and new theology

Figure 4.5 Saint Nicholas of Bari, by Carlo Crivelli (1472). Courtesy of the Cleveland Museum of Art; Gift of the Hanna Fund 1952.111

meant that "holy wells became mineral baths" and invoking the intercession of Saint Nicholas waned dramatically.[64]

However, in such places as Russia, Germany, and Holland, Nicholas survived the Reformation's onslaught against the veneration of the saints, becoming a folklore icon. In Holland, Nicholas brought presents to children on December 6, often leaving the gifts in their shoes that they had filled with hay to feed his horse.[65] This gift-giving tradition, inspired by tales of his unselfish sharing, was immensely popular.[66] As art historian Dmitri Tselos suggests, it may also be related to the common Nativity celebration (which sounds a lot like Saturnalia) of a fourth-century eastern Roman city.

> The celebrants wore festive clothes with colourfully embroidered tunics and they decorated the doors and windows with fresh greenery and candles. They prepared sweets, such as figs, dates and honey, or fashioned handmade gifts, such as decorative candles, clay figures and dolls, or set aside medallions and coins, all of which they gave their friends and families in imitation of the Magi who bestowed gifts upon Jesus, Mary and Joseph.[67]

How did Saint Nicholas come to North America? Most likely he made the Atlantic crossing with the first Dutch families coming to New Amsterdam in 1623. While the Dutch Reformed Church shared the Puritans' disdain for nonbiblical figures and practices, we know that—despite severe fines—Saint Nicholas Eve continued to be celebrated in 17th-century Amsterdam.[68] As psychoanalyst Adriaan de Groot remarked, "St. Nicholas has demonstrated remarkable toughness against his adversaries."[69] The beloved custom was smuggled in and clandestinely practiced in New Amsterdam. John Pintard (1759–1844), cofounder of the Massachusetts and New York Historical Societies, wrote to his daughter Mary in 1819:

> In old times St. Class used to cross the Atlantic and brought immense supplies of cookies etc. from Amsterdam, ship loads for every house and family was visited, not only in this city but in Albany and all the intermediate towns.[70]

The earliest surviving mention of Nicholas in New York is in the December 23, 1771, edition of *Rivington's New-York Gazetteer*, reporting on an earlier gathering: "a great number of Sons of that ancient Saint celebrated the day with great joy and festivity."[71] Further suggesting an early and elevated position of Saint Nicholas is Washington Irving's *A History of New York*, published as a satirical guidebook to New York in 1809 under the pseudonym Diedrich Knickerbocker.[72] Here, Saint Nicholas is alluded to some 30 times: As a figurehead, his long pipe reaching to the end of the bowsprit on the first ship from the Netherlands to the New World; as responsible for the exact location of the first settlement; as the immediate patron saint of New York, bringing great prosperity; and called upon frequently for protection.[73]

The United States in the early 19th century proved fertile ground for further metamorphoses of Saint Nicholas to Santa Claus. From its inception in 1804, the New York Historical Society annually celebrated Saint Nicholas Day. By 1810, this became an annual dinner. "Amidst hilarity, jocundity, and to crown all, fraternity," glasses were raised to toast, "*Sancte Claus, goed heylig man!*"[74] This tradition still continues.

Other changes can be gleaned from Pintard's letters to his daughter. By 1819, he references Saint Class with Saint Nicholas in parentheses.[75] On December 26, 1827, he reports: "we had St. Class in high snuff yesterday."[76] In 1828, he relates the details and the joy:

> All due preparations having been made by the children, the preceding evening by placing hay for his horses & invoking St. Class, Gude Heylig Man, He came accordingly, during the night, with most elegant Toys, Bon bons, Oranges, etc., all which after filling the stocking suspended at the sides of Mothers Chimney, were displayed in goodly order on the mantle to the extatic (sic) joy of Pintard & Boudy in the morning, whose exultations resounded thro' the house.[77]

As the generosity of Saint Nicholas merged with Christmas, three publishing events created an even larger persona of Santa Claus. First, in 1821, a new edition of Washington Irving's *A History of New York* appeared. Added were some engaging flourishes:

> Riding over the tops of trees, in that self same wagon wherein he brings his yearly presents to children … the smoke from his pipe spread like a cloud overhead … when he had smoked his pipe, he twisted it in his hatband, and laying his finger beside his nose, gave a very significant look then mounting his wagon, he returned over the tree tops and disappeared.[78]

Less saint and more mythical gift giver, he brings good cheer and can touch his nose to translocate. Second, in New York in 1821, an anonymous illustrated book, *The Children's Friend*, was released with this poem:

> Old Sante Claus with much delight
> His reindeer drives this frosty night,
> O'er chimneytops, and tracks of snow,
> To bring his yearly gifts to you. [79]

Santa Claus now arrives on Christmas Eve, reindeer replacing horses. A year later, Clement Moore, while on a Christmas Eve sleigh ride, composed "A Visit from St. Nicholas" for his children. Orville Holley, editor of the *Troy Sentinel*, published it on December 23, 1823, with this foreword:

We know not to whom we are indebted for the following description of that unwearied patron of Children—that homely but delightful personification of parental kindness—Santa Claus, in costume and equipage, as he hops about visiting the firesides of this happy land with Christmas bounties; but from whomsoever it may have come, we give thanks for it.[80]

Moore did much more than transform one reindeer into eight and a wagon into a sleigh. He pictured in words the modern Santa and captured the magic of Christmas Eve. The gaunt saint in clerical garb is now a jolly elf (fitting for Yuletide). His eyes twinkle, he laughs, his belly shakes as he bestows his longed-for gifts, and takes his leave saying, "Merry Christmas to *all,* and to *all* a good night!" By 1840, says Christmas historian Jock Elliott, "there could hardly have been a family in the country that was not familiar with the visit of St. Nicholas."[81]

The final touch goes to illustrator Thomas Nast, who bestowed the image of Santa. In 1863, he started drawing his conceptions of Moore's kindly present-giver for *Harper's Weekly.*[82] Each year, until 1886, Nast provided another Christmas illustration, usually of Santa.[83] In 1881, he drew his most famous Santa Claus picture, the one that we know even today as the "real" Santa Claus (see Figure 4.6).[84]

Moore added engaging personal touches and tapped into a deep well of older motifs. Whether he knew these from his studies as a professor of religion or whether they emerged from his own unconscious, we will never know. For instance, the German myth of the great god Wotan (Odin), who on the night of winter solstice, "rode through the skies on a white stallion, showering reward on the good folk and punishment on the bad." Likewise, in Scandinavia, the god Thor traveled by night in a chariot drawn by two large goats, Cracker and Gnasher. In Germany, Freya, a fertility sprite, "livened things up at Christmas time, entering people's houses on the smoke from the hearth's fire."[85] The ancient Norse winter solstice festival honored Herthe, goddess of the home. Before the holiday feast, a fire of fir boughs was laid on the altar of flat stones in the belief that Herthe would appear in the smoke to bring the family good fortune. "The Norse altar stones became our modern hearth stones, and Santa's trip down the chimney was an updated version of Herthe's appearance in the smoke."[86] Moore and Nast's combined vision flourished immediately.

As gracious and magical as Santa Claus became, vestiges of his cleric past remained. The moral agenda attached to Saint Nicholas could not be shaken loose. He was, after all, a saint who upheld holy behavior, and he did not distribute his treasures indiscriminately. His visit also brought judgment. Good children were rewarded; troublesome tykes had reason to fear. This manifested differently in mainland Europe than in the United Kingdom and the United States.

On the continent, jovial gift-giving Santa was paired with cruel, punishing henchmen. In French-speaking parts of Europe, Pére Fouettard ("Father Whipper") accompanies Saint Nicholas, checking and judging a list of approved behaviors for each child. To well-behaved youngsters, Nicholas brings gifts. To hellions, Pére Fouettard gives coal as a symbol of shame, or a whipping, or carries them away in

MERRY OLD SANTA CLAUS

Figure 4.6 Perhaps the best known of Thomas Nast's annual drawings of Santa Claus, created for *Harper's Weekly* (1881)

his wicker backpack. In France's Alsace-Lorraine, the sinister boogeyman Hans Trapp—dressed in a bearskin, with blackened face, long beard, and threatening rod—accompanies Santa, threatening to carry off problem children to the dark forest where they will remain.

"Until quite recently, Nicholas and Satan visited together in parts of Hungary."[87] In the Saint Nicholas play in Oberammergau, he orders his company to carry off a delinquent child for punishment: "The terror and shrieks thus caused have created a vast misery among children."[88] Equally terrifying is Krampus (German for "claw"), son of Norse underworld god, Hel, who after suppression by the church arose as a consort of Saint Nicholas. Krampus would beat naughty children with birch branches, eat them, or take them to hell. Central European children did not know if they would awaken on Christmas to injury or gifts.[89] A deep part of Dutch culture is Zwarte Piet (Black Pete), who scares, punishes, and might even carry off children in his burlap sack (see Figure 4.7).[90] As years have gone by, Zwarte Piet has become more beloved than feared, and is now also amusing children and giving treats.

In America and the United Kingdom, Santa had no dark helpers. But the grand gift giver's side job was a coercive nudge to good behavior. This is clear from the time of a Christmas book from 1785, *Christmas Tales for the Amusement and Instruction of Young Ladies and Gentlemen in Winter Evening*, by Solomon

Figure 4.7 Saint Nicholas arrives at a Dutch village accompanied by Zwarte Piet, who will punish children who have behaved badly. Pictorial Press Ltd/Alamy Stock Photo

Sobersides.[91] This tome was continually reissued for 13 years as parents looked for help in the moral education of their children.

In his essay "A Merry Christmas to You," highly esteemed minister of the mid-19th century, Theodore Ledyard Cuyler, calls Santa Claus "the patron saint of good boys and girls."[92] Yes, even for children, even with jolly Santa, there was the separation into sheep and goats. In 1821, an anonymous book, *The Children's Friend*, put these words into Santa's mouth:

> But where I found children naughty,
> In manner rude, in temper haughty,
> Thankless to parents, liars, swearers,
> Boxers, or cheats, or base tale-bearers.

> I left a long, black, birchen rod,
> Such, as the dread command of God
> Directs a Parent's hand to use
> When virtue's path his sons refuse.[93]

The 1834 annual edition of *The Pearl*, called a "Christmas book," included an elegant conceit by Elizabeth Dwight Sedgwick, granddaughter of the American prophet Jonathan Edwards. "The Game of Jackstraws and the Christmas Box" concerns a father who uses the expectation of Christmas presents to advance each of his four children's characters. On Christmas morning, much to their chagrin, each child discovered not presents in their stockings but a personalized poem from Saint Nicholas citing their major character flaw: Hal needed to control his passion. Fanny needed perseverance, Robert to be more scrupulous, Mary to refrain from straying off course. With the stick came a carrot. If the identified vice was improved upon, Saint Nicholas would resume his usual role and bring a treasured gift the following year. Ingeniously, each child must demonstrate that a corresponding virtue has replaced the vice before any gift can be truly owned.[94] For instance, the easily frustrated Fanny must solve a complicated lock to get to her gift. Robert must honestly assess his siblings' strengths in certain areas as superior to his own before he can rightly possess his presents, and so on.

Charles Dickens's *A Christmas Carol*, published in 1843, eventually found its way into almost every English-speaking heart and home. If any Christmas book has pierced the human soul, this is it. Scrooge, Bob Cratchit, and Tiny Tim are characters for the ages. Not only does the story describe Christmas customs of the time—and include ghosts—but it is also a story of transformation, hope, love, family, charity, and goodwill: A morality tale where the scales on Scrooge's eyes fall and the hardness of his heart breaks.

My childhood best friend had four sisters, and his parents had a stern Christmas custom of putting a lump of coal in each child's stocking. The largest piece, of impressive size, was in the stocking of the child deemed the worst behaved that year, the smallest for the best deportment. This inescapable parental judgment caused my pal considerable anxiety in December.

Our childhood friends were appalled and grateful their parents did not know of this tradition. But no child escapes the explicit and repetitive December warning of "Santa Claus Is Coming to Town": no rascality, no pouting—Santa is watching and making a list.

Moore presented a Santa who bestows gifts without judgment. As the spirit of the time mitigates stern judgments, as modern psychological understanding shows that we all are an admixture of the best and worst, we come to a Christmastime where dread is gone for most children and only "visions of sugarplums danced in their heads." Modern Santa, who like many of our Christmas traditions has a long and complicated arc of development, yearly provokes a magical, liminal time of joy and expectation with just a pinch of angst.

Homecoming/Family

Hestia, goddess of hearth and home, presides at Christmastime. As Charles Dickens expressed, "I *do* come home at Christmas. We all do, or we all should."[95] Writing in 1898, William Walsh tells us that on Christmas Eve in Germany: "Family and guests begin to gather at five o'clock."[96] Ecuadorian Michael Alvear observes that a Latino Christmas is a "wonder to behold" because of the huge extended family that gathers.[97] Irish psychologists noted a trend toward more vacant beds in a hospital psychiatric unit before Christmas, suggesting that attempts were made to allow patients to get home for the holiday.[98] If Christmas is about anything, it is about being home or wanting to be home. If exigencies make the trip impossible, one inevitably thinks of home, feels it in one's heart, and likely looks to momentarily adopt another family for the occasion.

Historian Stephen Nissenbaum argues that this poignant connection between home and Christmas did not take place until the middle third of the 19th century. He believes this "religion of domesticity" at Christmastime swept across American society with the advent of a new deity—Santa Claus.[99] While this assertion may hold some truth, in that the degree of connectivity intensified from this time on, the relationship of home, family, and Christmas is considerably older than he suggests.

As we have seen, family meals were part of the Saturnalia celebration that merged with the Feast of the Nativity. Thus from the fourth century, gaining force with the Yule connection circa 900, it is easy to believe this partnership persisted. A December 24, 1666 diary entry affirms this Christmas/home tradition.

I to church, where our Parson made a ... good sermon. ... Then home and dined well on some good ribs of Beef roasted and mince pies; only my wife, brother, and Barker and plenty of good wine of my own, and my heart full of true joy and thanks to almighty God for the goodness of my condition at this day.[100]

Similarly, two diary entries from a woman of the 1780s mention Christmas family gatherings.

> Dec. ye 19. It be but 6 days to Christmas, and I do hope the mud will be all gone for then, for John's cusson Tom be cumming, and Emma and her ladd and his sweetheart.
>
> Dec. ye 23. We have bin verrie bussie with sum goodlie things to eat. Boiled hams and great big mince pies and roast geese and hens and boiled and roasted beef, all reddie for eating. ... Carters wife be cumming early to get ready for our visitors who be cumming tomorrow.[101]

Once again New York chronicler John Pintard gives important information in an 1825 letter to his daughter.

> Mr. Marston had written to Capt. Partridge asking a furlough for his son to come home at Xmas, in which case Pintard was to accompany him. But Capt. has answered that the applications for similar favours are so numerous that he is constrained to adhere to his rules & to refuse them all.[102]

And when the *Daily Pantagraph* of Bloomington, Illinois, printed on December 25, 1865, "A Merry Christmas to all our readers and all our friends. This day they are nearly all situated in the bosom of their families,"[103] we assume they are not reporting on a new phenomenon. Clearly, home and Christmas were popular partners long before the 19th century.

One final illustration. In December 1940, Jan Sliwinski published a book of Polish Christmas carols. He wrote the following in his dedication:

> I remember such a December in 1915 when we Polish legionnaires in the Volhynian forests were standing under the starry sky for the midnight mass. The soldiers' voices singing carols filled the air with heavenly warmth and sweetness.
>
> For six long war winters the Polish soldier has sung these carols in many foreign lands and found comfort in them. The Polish carol has become the unacknowledged symbol of the exile's yearning for home.[104]

At Christmas, feelings for family are charged and focused. Freya Stark strikes root: "Christmas, in fact, is not an external event at all, but a piece of one's home that one carries in one's heart."[105] At Christmas, many experience the deep call-and-response between soul and home. It is not just the intensity of the desire but also the drive to broaden our notion of family.

Extravagant Welcome

At Christmas, our concept of family is enlarged. Washington Irving reveals how Christmas moves us:

> Now Christmas is come,
> Let us beat up the drum,
> And call all our neighbors together;
> And when they appear,
> Let us make them such cheer,
> As will keep out the wind and the weather, etc.[106]

Eighteenth-century historian Brand notes that the whole 12 days of Christmas is a jovial time of visiting friends.[107] Yule hospitality is extended beyond family and a wider coterie of acquaintances. In *A Christmas Carol*, heart-hardened Scrooge is confronted by his nephew.

> I am sure that I have always thought of Christmas time … the only time I know of, in the long calendar of the year, when men and women seem by one consent to open their shut-up hearts freely, and to think of people below them as if they really were fellow-passengers to the grave, and not another race of creatures bound on other journeys. And therefore, Uncle, though it has never put a scrap of gold or silver in my pocket, I believe that it *has* done me good, and *will* do me good; and I say, God bless it![108]

At Christmas, extravagant hospitality becomes common. Lillian Smith, in her book *Memory of a Large Christmas,* shares a wonderful example of this Christmas welcome. Her family was prosperous until World War I, when the family fortune was lost. They retreated from town to a farm they worked together, often bartering for goods. It had always been important to have a "large Christmas," and deprivation would not change that. So, "In that year of austerity," her father "invited the chain gang to have Christmas with us":

> Close to noon on Christmas Day we saw them coming down the road: forty-eight men in stripes, with their guards … a few laughing, talking, others grim and suspicious. All had come, white and Negro. We had helped Mother make two caramel cakes and twelve sweet potato pies and a wonderful backbone-and-rice dish … and there were hot rolls and Brunswick stew, and a washtub full of apples which our father had polished in front of the fire on Christmas Eve. It would be a splendid dinner, he told Mother who looked a bit wan, probably wondering what we would eat in January. … our father went from man to man shaking hands, and soon they were talking freely with him, and everybody was laughing at his funny—and sometimes on the rare side—stories. And then there was a hush, and we in the kitchen heard Dad's voice lifted up: "And it came to pass in those days."

Dad was standing there, reading from St. Luke. ... all were listening to the old old words. ... When my father closed the bible, he gravely said he hoped their families were having a good Christmas, he hoped all was well "back home." Then he smiled and grew hearty. "Now boys," he said, "eat plenty and have a good time. We're proud to have you today. We would have been a little lonely if you hadn't come. Now let's have a Merry Christmas.[109]

Generations later, this foundational aspect of Christmas celebration remains, as is elegantly stated in *The New York Times* editorial entitled "The Magic Circle":

All over America, families will soon be sitting down for Christmas dinner. Some of them could have modeled for Norman Rockwell. Others will include family members not of the same blood, the same creed, the same color. Never mind. On this day, they are all related. Even those who are connected may not have seen one another all year. They live in different towns, maybe even different worlds, and most of the time they walk disparate paths. Not today. To know where you're going to be at Christmas is to have a still point in a turning world.

The dinner is more than a meal. It is a bonding. This table at which we are seated, whether it be a long mahogany oval or a card table masked by a linen square, is enclosed by a magic circle, one in which we are invited to be merry.

Very often we succeed; the circle does its magic. Outside it lies everything we have come from and to which we will return, and all the journeys we are forced to take alone. But here, for a few hours, we are safe, companioned, with our own kind. Humankind. How fitting it is to celebrate this day, honoring the birth of a child to loving parents, by acquiring brothers and sisters, aunts and uncles and cousins. By tomorrow we'll have dispersed; today we are family.[110]

The Christmas season brings us together. Nuclear families return home. Extended families gather. Friends join in and often strangers as well. The Yule spirit opens our hearts to see all humanity as our true, larger family. Extravagant welcome brings us joy because it's a fundamental human need to be together and to belong, to engage the outsider and to know them.

Radical Inversion

Christmas is a topsy-turvy time. One of the most gripping aspects of Saturnalia was the prescribed inversion of class structure: Masters served slaves. This radical elevation of those deemed least and lowest to power and prominence fits naturally with the celebration of Christ's Nativity. "Nobody" Mary becomes the mother of God. Luke, and by extension the early church, did not miss this holy irony as he records in Mary's Magnificat:

My soul magnifies the Lord,
And my spirit rejoices in God my Savior,

For he had looked with favor
On the lowliness of his servant ...
He has brought down the powerful from their thrones,
And lifted up the lowly.

(Luke 1:46b–48a, 52)

During Saturnalia, this social inversion reminded participants what they yearned for: The golden age of Saturn, with no class distinctions and equality among all. During the season of the Nativity this was a reminder that social rank was ephemeral, while all souls in Christ are equally valuable and eternally so. Polydore Vergil (1470–1555) reflects on this Christian midwinter tradition:

> For then servants have authority over their masters and one of the domestics, being made on that occasion a Lord, all the heads of families and their children willingly yield obedience to him. We do this to prove that all should be as free as brothers in Christ.[111]

Francis Grose, in *A Provincial Glossary* (18th century), tells of a customary Christmas privilege for servants in farmhouses of northern England to drink their master's ale with a meal as long as the Yule log burned.[112] Likewise, in the antebellum South, masters commonly gave special privileges to those enslaved on Christmas or the week of Christmas. One American enslaver wrote in his diary of December 25, 1858, "Spent the day waiting on the Negroes, and making them as comfortable as possible." While enslaved people normally could not enter the main house or even pass the white picket fence, they had unprecedented familiarity on Christmas: "Here all authority and distinction of colour ceases, black and white, overseer and book-keeper mingle together in the dance." One planter said that during Christmas, "it is difficult to say who is the master."[113] When Christmas spirit took hold, the death grip of racism and classism was loosened, and even those considered chattel were seen with human faces.

Saturnalia's tradition of social inversion also played out on the streets of Rome with coronation of the "Lord of Misrule." This mock monarch, much to the populace's pleasure, commanded them to behave rudely and indecently. Bizarre behavior and revelry were literally ordered. This was a necessary venting of those repressed and oppressed and a ridiculing of authority.

Particularly interesting is how these twin rituals of Saturnalia merged with Christianity and then gave way to very colorful, if not outrageous, Christian expressions. In 1898, William S. Walsh in his *Curiosities of Popular Customs and of Rites, Ceremonies, Observations, and Miscellaneous Antiquities* wrote:

> It has always been the aim of the early church to reconcile heathen converts to the new faith by the adoption of all the more harmless features of their festivities and ceremonials. With Christmas the church had a hard task. Though it aimed only to retain the pagan forms, it found it could not restrain the pagan spirit. In spite of clerical protest and papal anathemas, in spite of the condemnation from the wise and the sane, Christmas in the early days frequently reproduced

all the worst orgies, the debaucheries and indecencies, of the Bacchanalia and the Saturnalia. ... The Council of Auxerre was moved to inquire into the matter (Feast of Fools). A Flemish divine rose and declared that the festival was an excellent thing and quite as acceptable to God as that of the Immaculate Conception, there was great applause of his like-minded brethren. Then Gerson, the most noted theologian of day, made a counter-sensation by retorting that "if all the devils in hell had put their heads together to devise a feast that should utterly scandalize Christianity, they could not have improved upon this one."[114]

We turn now to manifestations—both boisterous and even belligerent—of the upside-down Christmas rituals.

Feast of Fools

The "Feast of Fools" was celebrated into the 18th century in Germany, Bohemia, the United Kingdom, and, especially, France.[115] It began as a feast of the subdeacons, the lowest rank of clergy. As distinguished from canons and bishops, these were the priestly rabble of poor, ill-educated peasants. They wanted their special day and they got it—right after Christmas. Burlesques of the liturgy were performed, including miming and mimicking senior clergy and profane singing.[116] In 1445, the Paris Faculty of Theology described the Feast of Fools this way:

> Priests and clerks may be seen wearing masks and monstrous visages at the hours of office. They dance in the choir dressed as women, panders, or minstrels. They sing wanton songs. They eat black puddings at the horn of the altar while the celebrant is saying Mass. They play dice there. They cense with stinking smoke from the soles of old shoes. They run and leap through the church, without a blush at their own shame. Finally they drive about the town and its theatres in shabby traps and carts and rouse the laughter of their fellows and the bystanders in infamous performances, with indecent gesture and verses scurrilous and unchaste.[117]

It is impossible to miss the intent: Mighty clerics are put down from their thrones, and priests of low degree are exalted. Inferior clergy are given ecclesiastical dignity. While sitting on the bishop's throne acting like a fool still made one just a fool, this was a time of dramatic relaxation from excessive control and a mockery of those who enforced it. The symbols of the office were turned over to the Bishop of Fools as the Magnificat was sung: *Deposuit potentes de sede, et exaltavit humiles* (He has put down the mighty from their thrones and lifted up the lowly).[118]

An associated tradition that touched the general populace was the Feast of the Ass. This crude reenactment of the flight of Mary, Joseph, and Jesus into Egypt featured a young girl holding a baby riding a richly garbed donkey into church, with the bishop and his clergy following behind.[119] The archbishop of Sens, who died in 1222, recorded the ceremony. The service lasted the whole night, hymns praised the ass in a most discordant manner as wine was "unsparingly distributed" to thirsty choristers, and the clergy danced around the ass and imitated his braying. The officiating priest, instead of saying "*Ite Missa est—*Go, you are sent" at the end of Mass, concluded by braying three times—*Hin-Han, Hin-Han, Hin-Han.* The people responded in kind.[120] In identifying with this humblest beast of burden, those lowly could feel how in the Nativity story they also are valued, seen, and loved—all deep-seated psychological needs. They also could laugh at the expense of the normative stiffness of worship, what Sansom calls the "solsticial excuse for carousal."[121] The psyche needs periodic reprieves from social demarcations and release from the corsets of propriety.

Boy Bishop/King of the Bean

Two less mischievous traditions sprang from overturning status. The first, the boy bishop, was practiced all over Europe, tracing back to the early 10th century[122] or earlier: Brand says it is mentioned at the Constantinopolitan synod of 867.[123] On November 13, 1554, the bishop of London ordered each parish to have a boy bishop,[124] with a choirboy chosen by peers to have authority of the bishop. The chosen one wore rich Episcopal robes with a miter on his head, and held the pastoral staff while the rest of the choir dressed and acted like priests, yielding canonical obedience to the boy bishop. He directed the "cathedral dignitaries act as taper and incense bearers, thus reversing matters so that the great performed the functions of the lowly."[125]

The boy bishop—sometimes known as the "Nicholas Bishop" to honor the patron saint of youth—was selected on December 5, eve of Saint Nicholas Day. In some traditions, this was a single-day affair; in others, the term ran through December 28, Innocents' Day of Childermas.[126] On December 7, 1229, the boy bishop in the chapel of Heon near Newcastle-upon-Tyne said vespers before Edward I. His majesty gave considerable presents to him and the other boys who sang with him. This tradition was substantially dignified compared to the clergy's unrestrained mimicry at the Feast of Fools. As in the Christmas text from Isaiah, a child was lifted up to lead them.

A similar tradition on Twelfth Night—popular in England, Germany, and Holland, and still practiced in Italy, France, and Spain—features an obvious derivative of the king of Saturnalia who presided over the fun and feast. It involves selecting the "Epiphany King" or "King of the Bean"[127] using a bean—a sacred vegetable of ancient times—placed into a cake.[128] The 16th-century writer Étienne Pasquier describes it well.

When the cake has been cut into as many portions as there are guests a small child is put under the table, and is interrogated by the master under the name of Phebe [Phoebus], as if he were a child who in the innocence of his age represented a kind of Apollo's oracle. To this questioning the child answers with the word: *Domine.* Thereupon the master calls on him to say to whom he shall give the piece of cake which he has in his hand: the child names whoever comes into his head, without respect of persons, until the one with the bean is given out.

Figure 4.8 *The Feast of the Bean King*, by Jacob Jordaens (1593–1678) depicts a Flemish folk custom for Epiphany: Whomever finds the bean hidden in the cake becomes king of the feast. Peter Horree/Alamy Stock Photo

He who gets it is reckoned king of the company, although he may be a person of the least importance. This done, everyone eats, drinks, and dances heartily[129] (see Figure 4.8).

Becoming king was always a matter of luck, not station. In places whenever the "King imbibed, shots were fired," or as an account in *A World of Wonders* (1607) reports, the whole company would shout, "The King drinketh, the King drinketh!"[130] He might be dressed in full kingly regalia, choose a queen, or be given a fool to amuse him. A tradition in Lorraine, as noted in a 19th-century account, reserves the first two slices of cake for *le bon Dieu* and the Blessed Virgin, to be later given to the first poor person who appeared.[131] Today, king cake continues to be served, notably in Louisiana at Mardi Gras (the start of Lent), but elsewhere at New Year's.[132]

Mumming/Caroling/Wassailing

Over the centuries, those living on the edge have been profoundly touched and emboldened by the story of Jesus, a king born in poverty, surrounded by beasts, and attended by lowly shepherds. As we have seen, there is a long Christmas tradition to entitle those of lesser means to special treatment, with those well-to-do feeling obligated to respond favorably to their less fortunate brothers and sisters. In some cases, poor people actually stormed the houses of the elite, pounding on doors and windows, demanding the best food and the finest drink. Mumming, caroling, and wassailing all fall into this category, and sometimes overlap.

Throughout eastern and western Europe, the tradition of "mumming" was quite common up to the 20th century. Brand describes it:

> Mumming is a sport of this festive season which consists in changing clothes between men and women, who, when dressed in each other's habits, go from one neighbour's house to another, partaking of Christmas cheer, and making merry with them in disguise. It is supposed to have been originally instituted in imitation of the Sigillaria, or festival days added to the ancient Saturnalia.[133]

"Mummers," "tipperers," or "guisers" (because of their outlandish costumes, masks, or faces disguised with burnt cork) visited the wealthy. Because of the perquisites they collected as by Christmas right, they would enter houses uninvited. Once inside, they might sing or dance, but most usually they would perform a Christmas drama.[134] For this unsolicited entertainment, mummers expected a substantial gratuity.

In Russia, mummers found a not so subtle means of maximizing their gain. They came "disguised as Lazaruses, that is blind beggars,"[135] reminding their hosts of the parable of the rich man condemned to eternal torment for not giving generously to Lazarus (Luke 16:18–25). Mumming also took place in New England, as wealthy Bostonian Samuel Breck recalls (ca. 1780):

> I have seen them at my father's, when his assembled friends were at cards, take possession of a table, seat themselves on rich furniture and proceed to handle the cards, to the great annoyance of the company. The only way to get rid of them was to give them money, and listen patiently to a foolish dialogue between two or more of them. One of them would cry out, "Ladies and gentlemen sitting by the fire, put your hands in your pockets and give us our desire." When this was done and they had received some money, a kind of acting took place.[136]

Then there were the carolers who sung at wealthier homes expecting to be rewarded. Today small groups of selfless choristers might stroll after dark, singing "Joy to the World" or "Silent Night." But carolers of yesteryear were boisterous and tended toward extortion. Even the ever popular "We Wish You a Merry Christmas" that begins with well-wishes soon turns to insistent demand.

> Now give us some figgy pudding
> And bring it us here!
> We won't leave until we get some ...[137]

Likewise, this chant leaves no doubt about the demand and the threat:

> We've come here to claim our right ...
> And if you don't open up your door,
> We will lay you flat upon the floor.[138]

With these traditions, the lowly joyously transgressed social constraints of every type while the mighty acquiesced. Colorful costumes, eerie masks, manic performances, and gender exchange were all part of the wild abandon. But most central of all: Those powerless were not ordered about but instead unapologetically demanded from those powerful. Underlying the show was the real meaning: The turning upside down of status, a reversal of class, as Mary proclaimed in her Magnificat. A sense of fairness was briefly entertained—equanimity, even if for a day.

A peasant girl advances over the greatest queen. Lowly shepherds are the first to get the important news. Kings bow to a boy born in a rude cave. It is Magnificat time. With the coming of the child there was a reversal: The high are made low, and the low made high. From Saturnalia to European and American traditions, masters serve slaves, elders serve young, rich serve poor. This whole section of various Christmas traditions can be summed up as "formalization of the essential topsy-turveydom of Christmas."[139]

Excess

Christmas is a time of excess. Overindulgence has long been and continues as part of the Christmas spirit. In Europe and the Eastern Christian Empire, commemorating Christ's Nativity was yoked to the immoderation of Saturnalia and Kalends. "All through the Middle Ages the dual rivers of riot and religion, from which many, high and low, rich and poor, contrived to drink deeply at Christmas, flowed together."[140] More recently, H.L. Mencken in his *Christmas Story* writes, the police officer was dyspeptic at Christmas but "not because he objected to its orgies as such."[141]

In the United States and probably most of the West, alcohol consumption is highest on the nights before Christmas and New Year's. Long remembered in the church where I served as a student minister was the Christmas Eve service when the pastor leaned over the high pulpit, pointed his finger to the congregation, and in full throat exclaimed: "If I lit a match, this church would blow up!" Christmas is a time of drinking.

Libanius (314–93 CE) writes about Roman winter festivals: "The impulse to spend seizes everyone. He who the whole year has taken pleasure in saving and piling up his pence, becomes suddenly extravagant."[142] This human propensity to occasionally open the dam of restraint easily transfers to the celebration of Jesus' birth. Intemperate buying seems sine qua non of Christmas.

In pre-Christian times, December was known as *geola*, Old English for "feast month."[143] Aside from any other welling up of the psyche, feasting was a matter of utmost practicality for northern Europeans. The herds and flocks needed to be thinned before winter takes its toll. This was the perfect season to slaughter, and prior to refrigeration, December was naturally a month of mighty meat eating.

Saint Gregory Nazianzus (ca. 330–389) warned his flock "not to feast to excess" and urged "the celebration of the festival after a heavenly and not after an earthly manner."[144] But pagan currents ran too strong, so that eventually, "The Church tried to make it a real day of worldly joy, excluding from it all fasting as early as AD 561."[145] Theodore's Penitential (668–690 CE) "regarded it an excuse if a man ate too freely at Christmas."[146] In other words: Unapologetic feasting. This Yule overindulgence continued unabated despite legislation against it in Scotland, England, and America.[147]

> The rich magnificence of Henry V opened Westminster Hall to a banquet for his Queen whose astounding list of foodstuffs runs into paragraphs ... Edward IV fed more than two thousand people each day over the Christmastide of 1482 at Eltham. Henry VII sat down to a Christmas court dinner of a hundred and twenty dishes.[148]

Christmas largesse was not just for royalty. At Christmas, everyone who could played king or queen. In France, on Christmas Eve of 1896, "half a million dozen oysters" were sold as appetizers at Les Halles (Paris), where "the thoroughly up-to-date Parisian divides his Christmas up into many courses, taking each at a different place."[149] Such sophisticates were more than equaled by the miners in the Rockies in 1858 who "began with oysters and pork and then moved on to elk, antelope, buffalo 'smothers' and grizzly bear a la mode, followed by swans, crane and quails, wines and whiskeys brought by wagon train for the Christmas event."[150] Actor Norman Beaton remembers well:

> Christmas for me as a child in Guyana was a time of scents. Ginger and other spices would have been drying outside for some time. The quality of light changed, and we would sense a thrill in the air. ... It really was a festival of food. ... Everybody would be cooking both sweet and savoury dishes with a variety of spices and the smell was everywhere. We all used to be very excited.[151]

Our own experiences confirm that part of Christmas joy is grandiose repast. In a letter published in *The Gentleman's Magazine* of 1802, Matthew Meanwell misquotes Shakespeare and writes of another type of overdose:

Christmas comes but once a year,

Therefore we'll be merry.—Shakespeare

Certain of my friends, too, men of business, have prevailed upon me to run into some degree of extravagance, by joining them in a few parties of pleasure, as they are called and which I never do at other times, without a prospect of increasing my own trade, and making profitable connections; but there was no resisting this argument that *Christmas comes but once a year*, which they strongly enforce by another, *It is a poor heart that never rejoices*. And what man would be supposed to have so poor a heart as not to rejoice once a year … reconciling myself to myself, as well as I can, I think how lucky it is, that Christmas comes but once a year!"[152]

Clergy in the 1700s worried that the Feast of the Nativity had become "some Heathenish feast of Ceres or Bacchus."[153] One midnight Christmas Eve service, some parishioners told me they had just come from a Bacchanalia. They were simply following a long tradition. At Christmas, Saturnalia revelry is widely embraced. Yule excess is a major joy, albeit one that often leads merrimakers to physical and financial hangovers.

The Child

John Grisham's *Skipping Christmas* is the story of Luther and Nora Krank.[154] Their daughter, Blair, a member of the Peace Corps, will for the first time be away for Christmas. Luther and Nora decide not to celebrate Christmas at all—no parties, no gifts, and no decorations. This is not as easy as they imagine, as it goes against every expectation of their small community. The neighbors, at first incredulous, become indignant and then mean-spirited, but Luther and Nora stand firm. Yet one person can change their minds in an instant—their child. On Christmas Eve, Blair calls from the local airport—she *will* be home for Christmas. With the help of the community they had forsaken, Luther and Nora pull it together, just in time, for Blair to have the Christmas she had always had. Because Christmas is for children, whatever their age.

This makes sense because Christmas is about the birth of a child. But it is more complicated than that. The real question is when did "ordinary" children become the focus of Christmas? Psychoanalyst Ernest Jones says, "It is hard to determine how and when Christmas became so predominantly the children's festival that it now is."[155] Consider a few things: In 1960, French historian Philippe Aries created controversy by advocating that our current concept of the child is modern, and that children in the past were not considered much more than miniature adults.[156] Prior to the 16th century, family life was about survival. For most of history, "approximately 27% of infants failed to survive their first year of life, while approximately 47.5% of children failed to survive to puberty."[157] Their labor was required by the family. And for centuries the church thought the devil had to be removed from them.[158] No wonder that shortly after Saint Nicholas's death in 343 CE, he became the patron saint of children based on several accounts of him saving young people from terrible fates.[159]

For the last 600 years, children's fortunes have enjoyed a steady upward trajectory. Jan Steen's 1666 painting shows children receiving gifts and being the center of Christmas Day (see Figure 4.9). In 1690, John Locke proposed that humans were

Figure 4.9 The Feast of Saint Nicholas, by Jan Steen (1665–1668). Ian Dagnall Computing/ Alamy Stock Photo

born a tabula rasa (blank slate), meaning that the devil did not have to be educated out of the young.[160] Jean-Jacques Rousseau in 1762 warned against overeducation: "Why fill with bitterness the fleeting early days of childhood, days which will no more return for them than for you?"[161] William Wordsworth's 1804 "Ode on Intimations of Immortality from Recollections of Early Childhood" significantly increased the worth of every child.

Not in entire forgetfulness,
And not in utter nakedness,
But trailing clouds of glory do we come
From God who is our home.
Heaven lies about us in our infancy![162]

In 1822, Davies Gilbert published a collection of carols because of the delight they gave him as a child.[163] Elliott argues that Clement Moore's poem that same year, "A Visit from St. Nicholas (The Night Before Christmas)," changed forever the fortunes of children: "I do not think it is much of an exaggeration to say that it liberated childhood. … Christmas was for children."[164] In the *Ottawa Free Trader* of 1847, we read: "Christmas, dear delightful Christmas, with its crowd of youthful recollections and joyous associations, is again with us bringing to the 'young'uns' high expectations."[165]

In her 1900 book, Swedish feminist Ellen Key suggested that the 20th century would be the century of the child.[166] She was correct: Children fare better now than ever before. A variety of writers chronicled this shift and its relationship to Christmas: Every year, from 1920 to 1939, a letter bearing a stamp from the North Pole, penned and signed by Father Christmas, arrived for J.R.R. Tolkien's children.[167] For poet Dylan Thomas in 1952, it was *A Child's Christmas in Wales*.[168] Reporter Harrison Salisbury, winner of the Pulitzer Prize in 1955, recorded with bold certainty, "Yes, Christmas was *the* day of my childhood."[169] Theologian Hisako Kinukawa noted that "while the Christmas celebration in Japan is mostly consumerism/commercialism, the exception is for Christian churches and families with younger children. Then crèches are displayed."[170] Even Jewish historian Nissenbaum cannot help but assert the obvious: "Christmas made children the center of attention and affection."[171]

At Christmastime today, children reign supreme, superseding adults in value and power as most thoughts and gifts are directed their way. At Christmas, the grown-ups vicariously participate in a sense of wonder through the delighted anticipation of children. As Clement Miles concludes, today's Christmas is "above all things a children's feast and the elders who join in it put themselves upon their children's level."

Most men are ready at Christmas to put themselves into an instinctive rather than a rational attitude, to drink of the springs of wonder, and return in some degree to an earlier, less intellectual stage of development—to become in fact children again.[172]

Christmas is a remarkable occasion when many experience their inner child, remembering, if not grasping for, the experiences of past Christmases. "The earth has grown old with its burden of care," as Phillips Brooks writes, "but at Christmas it always is young."[173]

The Crèche

Whether an inexpensive manger from the dollar store or a hand-carved work of art, *presepios* (Italian), *Krippen* (German), or *crèches* (French) are ubiquitous at Christmas. What Christian household does not have one that is taken out with the rest of the ornaments and set up as background scenery? For many, the figures of the Holy Family and friends are a central part of their Christmas tradition and an irresistible inducement to enter that Bethlehem night.

According to tradition, Francis of Assisi initiated a custom that eventually led to the Nativity sets of today. The Franciscan brothers and townspeople of Assisi usually celebrated Christmas Eve in the local church, but the year 1223 was different. To increase accessibility to the Gospel text and portray its message as powerfully as possible, Francis had a fresh plan. Fellow brother and first biographer, Thomas of Celano, says Francis had a keen sense of "the humility of the incarnation."[174] He quotes Francis:

> For I wish to do something that will recall to memory the little Child who was born in Bethlehem and set before our bodily eyes in some way the inconveniences of his infant needs, how he lay in a manger, how, with an ox and an ass standing by, he lay upon the hay where he had been placed.[175]

To make the Christmas liturgy more tangible and comprehensible for ordinary people, the nearby forest of Greccio became a new Bethlehem, as part of Francis's dramatic living pantomime.[176] The people came with "candles and torches to light up that night that has lighted up all the days and years with its gleaming star," and "were filled with new joy over the new mystery."[177] Francis's novel approach more than succeeded—"the near was blended with the old and far"[178]—and in one form or another, it has been reproduced ever since.

Because live Nativity plays were not always possible, a tradition spread of placing triptychs showing the Nativity story on altars or of setting up large fixed figures of stone, terra-cotta, or naturalistically painted wood in special devotional rooms[179] (see Figure 4.10).

> One particular play *Kindlwiegen* (rocking the infant), was performed in the High Middle Ages and was intended to focus people's thought on the infant Jesus as the Savior of the world. In the course of time, this play made its way into private homes where small figures of the infant Jesus in a cradle were rocked and sung to sleep.[180]

Historian Clement Miles says that "Lasst uns das Kindlein wiegen" was beautifully sung by vast 14th-century German congregations gathering around Christ's cradle (*Krippe*). Solemnity, festive joy, and tender sentiments were mingled.

> Let us rock the Child and bow our hearts before the crib!
> Let us delight our spirits and bless the child:
> Sweet little Jesu! Sweet little Jesu!

Figure 4.10 Nativity scene sculptures (ca. 1291) thought to be the oldest in existence, created by Arnolfo di Cambio for Pope Nicholas IV; Santa Maria Maggiore church, Rome. Janet Horton/Alamy Stock Photo

Let us greet His little hands and feet, His little heart of fire,
And reverence Him humbly as our Lord and God!
Sweet little Jesu! Sweet little Jesu![181]

The humanness, warmth, and joy of such a "liturgy" not surprisingly won over the hearts of the masses.

The popular desire to visually reconstruct events of the Nativity eventually led to artists creating small, detailed depictions of the Holy Family and the story's larger cast. The personal crèche was born (see Figure 4.11). Rudolf Berliner in *Die Weihnachtskrippe* wrote that the *Krippen* were intended "to help the pious to have the feeling that they were entering the scene of the holy event, so as to inspire them to as deep a form of meditation as possible on the path of salvation."[182]

Not surprisingly, the crèche became an effective tool for missionaries. Jesuits in the 17th century brought their crèches to Asia, India, Africa, and South America. Those in Canada (1642) "vividly describe the unexpected success their crèches had with the Hurons, the Mohawks, and other Native Americans."[183] When Saint Jean de Brébeuf (1593–1649) penned the first Christmas carol in a Native American language (Huron), "*Jesous Ahatonnia*—Jesus is born" was sung in front of the manger scene.[184] "The angel choir appeared to the braves, the stable became a bark

Figure 4.11 Nativity Carving, Tanzania, 20th century.

lodge, and chiefs from afar worshiped at the manger of the Infant King, who was dressed in rabbit skins."[185]

So while the first crèches were Italian, German, and French, it was not long before they were enjoyed and made in almost every country in the world. The custom began to take hold in North America in 1741, when Moravians from Germany settled in Bethlehem, Pennsylvania. Having a special fondness for Christmas, their Nativity scenes, called *putzes*, were remarkably detailed and extensive, including bridges, houses, fences, fountains, and even waterfalls.[186] South America is likewise known for its remarkably elaborate crèches, where a whole room may be dedicated to reconstructing the Bethlehem landscape with mountains, plains, valleys, and desert to put the shepherds and Magi in context.[187] While church attendance declines precipitously, crèches remain highly popular, and collections are often publicly displayed.

The crèche, as other artwork, allows the viewer to "forget the distance of time and space that separates him from Bethlehem."[188] The original awe of the holy night becomes present awe. Or as Jesuit priest Philip de Berlaymont wrote in 1609: "The function of the crèche is to recreate the events of the nativity so that all who view the scene may personally experience the wonder of those who originally beheld it."[189]

Gifts/Benevolence

The impulse to give at the anniversary of Jesus' birth strikes all but the most hardened scrooge. We give gifts, without any thought that this might be optional. Our list runs long as part of a social expectation that runs as deep as any we can imagine. The origin of Christmas gift-giving is unambiguous. Matthew reports that the weary Magi from the East fell to their knees and offered the babe in a manger their presents: Gold, frankincense, and myrrh. Flesh was soon put on the bare-bones biblical account. Three gifts gave reason to assume three kings. Then they were given names—Caspar, Melchior, and Balthasar—and a story. Prominent church historian Owen Chadwick explains:

> They were shown as men of each age of life, so that every human soul from child to dotard might feel that they could bring gifts. Later still, they were shown as men of various races, so that everyone in the world could feel that they were bringing their gifts to the lap of Mary.[190]

When it comes to Christmas, traditions of Saturnalia are often never far behind. During this happiest time of the year, dolls (*signillaria*), fruits, and cakes (*strenae*) were exchanged as gifts of good luck. Tille shares an interesting development:

> It was an old institute for the landlord to give his tenant a cart-load or wheelbarrow load of wood at the birth of a child. Christ being regarded, in the fourteenth and fifteenth centuries, as a kind of universal brother to mankind, the occasion

of his birth was taken as an opportunity for gifts similar to those which children received at the birth of a baby brother or sister. In the beginning of the sixteenth century such gifts to children were called in North Germany *kindsvot*, or child's foot, the same name being given to the present of straw which the cattle, swine, geese, and ducks receive that day, in order to take part in the rejoicing over Christ's birth.[191]

There are numerous Yuletide manifestations of this archetype of generosity. In Spain, the Three Kings (*Tres Reyes Magos*) themselves make the gift-giving trek. Italy has a woman figure called Befana (a corruption of Epiphania), and Russia has Babushka or the white-robed girl Kolyada. In Germany, the Christ Child is imagined as a girl who appears on behalf of newly born Jesus. In France, depending on locale, it is Saint Nicholas or Père Nöel. In Sweden, gifts are distributed by a gnomish Father Christmas figure, Jultomten, whose gifts, *julklapp*, are disguised in multiple wrappings and boxes and sometimes thrown through an open window. In 1968, Sansom reported some of the variety of seasonal ways of giving:

In Syria the camel of Jesus brings the gifts to children; in Harlem, New York, a black Santa Claus has been seen distributing white golliwogs; in Finland the present-giver has been known as the great Ukko, an old man in a cap and furs but uniquely with no beard, only a long white moustache—possibly a Mongolian influence; in Poland a traditional mother star brings gifts, and in Hungary children look to the angels; in Mexico, and for instance, in parts of Arizona, where earthenware is cheap, a *piñata* or large decorated vessel is hung up and blindfolded children beat it with sticks until it breaks, showering them with nuts and sweetmeats. Nevertheless in recent times the technical advance of image-communication and the international nature of commerce has seen the jovial, generous figure of Santa Claus appearing in many of these countries where he was never known before.[192]

All this reveals a picture of how idiosyncratic practices grow from the same human instinct as our imagination makes fresh connections. We are hardly surprised then that Santa Claus and his reindeer evolved from kings on camels.

Though children relish it most of all, we are all glad to be put in the position of the Christ Child. Receiving the perfect gift that honors us is just as wonderful as giving the perfect gift to another. Who has not been moved by O. Henry's *The Gift of the Magi*, where intimate partners Della and Jim sacrifice their most precious possession to purchase what the other wants most? The story concludes with these words: "Of all who give and receive gifts such as they are wisest ... They are the magi."[193]

When it comes to giving gifts, our first thoughts are of family and friends, but our circle quickly becomes significantly broader. In the second ring are tradespeople who have skillfully helped us throughout the year. Christmas tips are common and expected, and this is not new. In *Wuthering Heights*, Nell says, "and then I remember how old Earnshaw used to come in when all was tidied, and call me a cant lass, and slip a shilling into my hands as a Christmas box."[194] She is referencing a tradition, known in nearly every English-speaking country except the United States, celebrated as Boxing Day.

As Christmas mobs of commoners demanded food and drink, well-to-do people used their own servants to dispense "gifts" and to clean up the house and grounds after the onslaught. For this work, the masters gave their servants boxes filled with extra necessities and goodies. Brand writes:

> The Christmas-box ... was formerly the bounty of well-disposed people, who were willing to contribute something towards rewarding the industrious, and supply them with necessities. But the gift is now almost demanded as a right.[195]

Eventually, English servants began bringing their own boxes to work on the day after Christmas. Employers would put coins into these boxes. Maids, for instance, carried their "Milly's Box," a corruption of "Milady's Box," referring to the Virgin Mary. The outside was covered with a "sacred cloth" and the inside held a small figure of Baby Jesus. The maids, carrying their boxes, sang Christmas carols, and for an offering would open the box so that the Holy Child could be seen.[196] Soon it became standard practice for those with disposable income to give year-end monetary bonuses to "bakers, blacksmiths, newspaper boys, butchers, and everyone else who provided services for the household."[197] Under Queen Victoria, Boxing Day became a fully recognized holiday, with the royal family leading the way. In America, the tradition of tipping lives without an official name, but gives a little extra joy at Christmas to those who live paycheck to paycheck.

The third field of giving is made up of unknown constituents of the human family in dire need, where the perfect gift may be an essential item for their physical well-being. As Louisa May Alcott writes in *Little Women*, Christmas is a time for "givin' way vittles and drinks, clothes and firin'."[198] Not only was it usual to invite several lonely or less fortunate people into one's house for Christmas dinner, but great suppers were provided for those most in need in English hospitals.[199] On January 3, 1891, the *Chepstow Weekly Advertiser* reported:

> Christmas Day at Chepstow workhouse was befittingly opened by Divine Service in the morning at which the chaplain officiated. But the Christmas dinner was, no doubt, to the inmates, the chief business of the day. The Master and Matron, Mr. T.V. and Miss Steel, had tastefully decorated the dining hall.

> Each able bodied person was supplied with ½ lb prime beef and their platters piled up with potatoes and parsnips, which was followed by a supply of plum pudding of excellent quality, washed down, by the adults who were not teetotal, with an allowance of ale. ... it was a gratifying sight to see the way in which the poor people ... enjoyed their Christmas fare.[200]

Henry Van Dyke's *The Story of the Other Wise Man* elegantly displays the spirit behind such altruism. When the star appears, Artaban is pledged to meet his three fellow Magi at the Temple of the Seven Spheres. Yet he is waylaid multiple times, unable to pass strangers in need. Thus he loses time and all but one of the gifts meant for Jesus. After 33 years, now an old man, he finally arrives in Jerusalem, where he is compelled to use his perfect pearl to ransom a young girl about to be sold into slavery. Dying at the same time that Jesus is dying on the cross, Artaban's head rests upon the saved girl's lap, and she hears a faint sweet voice respond to his dying murmurs: "Verily I say unto thee, inasmuch as thou hast done it unto one of the least of these my brethren, thou hast done it unto me." The other wise man had found the King.[201] In this story, Van Dyke shows that Nativity gifts are just as surely given to the Christ Child when they are given to those in need.

Washington Irving likewise wrote: "Christmas is the season for kindling ... the genial flame of charity in the heart."[202] And so at Yule, the spirit of unrequited generosity is prominent and unabashed. This is well noted in perhaps the most famous newspaper editorial, in the 1897 *New York Sun*, when editor Francis Pharcellus Church responded to a query about the existence of Santa: "Yes, Virginia, there is a Santa Claus. He exists as certainly as love and generosity and devotion exist."[203] In the novel *Les Misérables*, Valjean plays the part of Father Christmas to Cinderella-esque Cosette. Though her stepmother has placed a sparkling 10-sous piece in her own children's shoes, Cosette's broken, ash-covered clog is tragically empty—until Valjean drops in a gold Louis on Christmas Eve.[204]

Today, gifts to those needy flow most freely at Christmastime, whether via Salvation Army pots with their bell-ringing Santas, church offering plates, or gifts to local charities. Most religious and many secular groups provide those less fortunate with special meals and seasonal food staples, as well as donations of gifts of clothes and toys.

Peace

Saturnalia looked longingly back to the golden age. During its celebration, war was proscribed, execution forbidden, peace the mainline hope. This segment of the Roman holiday naturally coupled with Christ's Nativity, the biblical justification demonstrably evident. When the multitude of heavenly host shared good news with scared shepherds about the holy birth, their benediction was clear: "On earth peace" (Luke 2:14). And, Isaiah's prophecy of shalom is the hope of so many during Christmastide: "For unto us a child is born ... The Prince of Peace." (Isaiah 9:6)

In his journal from 1404, Adam of Usk writes about attending the Papal Mass on Christmas Day: "In the same Mass, double Gospel and Epistle are read, in Latin by two Latins, and then in Greek by two Greeks, for their satisfaction, for they say they were driven from the Church."[205] At Christmas, the olive branch is extended even to rivals of the worst sort—siblings of faith.

At Christmas, the indelible longing for amiable kinship bursts forth full strength. In Slavonic churches, a "Peace of God" rite takes place among the congregation at the end of Christmas morning Mass, with a kiss bestowed on each cheek, one to another, saying, "Christ is born!" and answered "Of a truth he is born!" with kisses returned. This goes on until each person has kissed and been kissed by all present.[206]

This balm of Christmas harmony affects not just ecclesiastical discord, neighborhood spats, or personal grievances, but also civil society. In England, the law of King Ethelred (r. ca. 968–1016) ordained the period from Advent through Epiphany as a time of concord and peace, when all strife would cease. Later, Edward the Confessor (r. 1042–1066) and King Henry I (r. 1110–1135) declared that strict peace be kept for Christ's Nativity till a week after Epiphany.[207] The decree evolved into everyday language, as seen in the 1955 Christmas issue of *Tatler*, where an article entitled "The Royal Christmases of Queen Victoria" declared "Christmas was coming: the Feast of the Prince of Peace."[208]

An ancient Scandinavian custom dictates that if enemies encounter each other under a tree with mistletoe, they must lay down their arms and maintain a truce for one day.[209] The Celts also thought that holly, a plant that could tame the bitter wind, had the power to bring peace and understanding. So during disputes, angry parties would work out their differences under a holly tree.[210]

Folklore and the history of war note many cases where the Christmas spirit overcame deadly hostilities, if but briefly, with informal truces that combatants courageously initiated, accepted, and enjoyed. In many stories of European hostilities, as well as during the American Civil War, Christmastime brought cessation of conflict and fraternization with the enemy. William Sansom, in *A Book of Christmas*, powerfully and poignantly describes the 1914 truce in the trenches:

> And then, at midnight on Christmas Eve, allied soldiers in various sectors of the freezing trenches heard a new, less congruous sound—a brass band in the German trenches playing carols … emblematic of Christmas itself, a simple sound of human goodwill against thunderous voices of ancient gods receding.

> The music went through the night; early next morning there came from the German trenches cries of "Merry Christmas, Tommy," heads popped above the parapets, and soon there began the tentative approach to each other … men for a time shook hands and exchanged presents. Goldflake cigarettes went to Fritz, and Tommy tasted a German cigar, plum pudding went east and German sausage west. A halfway line was agreed on, and on this a football match was played … No man's land for a time was everyman's.[211]

Historians Malcolm Brown and Shirley Seaton in their book, *Christmas Truce: The Western Front, December 1914*, are resolute: "the truce *did* take place, and on a far greater scale than has generally been realized"[212] (see Figure 4.12). On this occasion, as others before, Christmas prompted a momentary return to a golden

Figure 4.12 Illustrated London News, January 23, 1915, with a caption reading "The Light of Peace in the trenches on Christmas Eve: a German soldier opens the spontaneous truce by approaching the British line with a small Christmas tree."

age. Truly, even if only episodically, the Christ Child is the Prince of Peace. It will always be the case, as poet John Greenleaf Whittier penned, that "our heart's desire the angels' midnight psalm, / Peace, and good-will to men!"[213]

Conclusion

Walsh, in *Curiosities of Popular Customs*, tells of a Christmas Eve ritual among rural Russians that combines many of these motifs:

> At sunset young and old assemble in the principal street of the village, and, forming a procession, visit the houses of the resident nobleman, the mayor, and other village dignitaries, where they sing carols and receive coppers in return. This part of the ceremonies is called *Kolenda*, which means begging for money or presents. A masquerade follows which the adults transform themselves into imitation cows, pigs, goats, and other animals in remembrance of the nativity of the manger.

> As soon as the evening star appears above the horizon, a colatzia, or supper, is served. A long table is covered with straw. Over this cloth laid, on which the samovar is placed, together with fish prepared in various ways, and different kinds of cake. The feast begins by dividing the blessed wafer, a small portion of which is given to each person present. This is a sacred rite in which none dare refuse to participate.

> At the conclusion of the evening-star celebration, a majority of the peasants proceed to the house of the nobleman whom they first visited, where an immense tree has been prepared for them. This tree is laden with inexpensive presents of various kinds.[214]

Much energy, extravagance, and license merge with holy awe, humility, and giving. From medieval times—and probably well before—until today, Christmas (also known as the Feast of the Nativity) has long maintained its composite nature. Two strong strands, the secular and the profane, originate with the very invention of the celebration, which purposefully yoked the birth of Christ to the birthday of Sol as well as to the already highly charged celebrations of Saturnalia and Kalends. Part of the force of Christmas is that the highest ideals and meanest indulgences coexist. Christmas has always been a time to celebrate a holy birth, a time for friends and family, a time to reverse social order, a time for excess and even decadence. Chadwick sums it up for us:

> So Christmas in our age is a harmony of three elements: the junketing of the Roman crowd trying to relieve the gloom of winter, the Roman cult of the sun and of its light, and, at the heart, the memory of a birth in a manger in the Palestinian town of Bethlehem.[215]

Like trying to drink from a fire hydrant, no psyche can take on the expansive force of Christmas at any one moment. It is a jingle jangle jumble of secular and sacred. It reveals the highest and lowest of humanity's behaviors and hopes. At Christmas, the theological and the cultural are equal partners and, as we shall now see, both take turns dancing with the psychological.

Notes

1 Wilfred Cantwell Smith, "The Study of Religion and the Study of the Bible," *Journal of the American Academy of Religion* 39, no. 2 (1971), 131–140.
2 Arthur Weigall, *The Paganism in Our Christianity* (G.P. Putnam's Sons, 1928), 259.
3 Clement A. Miles, *Christmas in Ritual and Tradition, Christian and Pagan*, 2nd ed. (T. Fisher Unwin, 1913), 25–26.
4 Was Yule a Norse New Year? Was it a time to sacrifice animals to the gods and pledge allegiance to one's Lord? Was this pre-Christian Germanic/Scandinavian festival originally related to one-eyed, long-bearded, All-Father Odin? One of his names was Jólnir ("Yule one"). Odin took all Vikings who died in battle to himself. He was also the leader of the terrifying Wild Hunt, where a troop of spirits rode the stormy winter night. Prudence Jones and Nigel Pennick, *A History of Pagan Europe* (Routledge, 1995), 160. People in Scandinavian countries also believed that the dead return home at this time. If so, was Yule something like a Mexican Day of the Dead? Rudolph Simek, *A Dictionary of Northern Mythology*, trans. Angela Hall (D.S. Brewer, 2007), 180–181, 379–380. Some scholars translate the early Germanic word as "wheel," in the sense of the forward movement of the year. This argues that Yule was initially a fire ritual—not just for warmth and illumination—performed at the winter solstice. Alexander Tille, *Yule and Christmas: Their Place in the Germanic Year* (David Nutt, 1899), 91; Sue Ellen Thompson, *Holiday Symbols: A Guide to the Legend and Lore*, 2nd ed. (Omnigraphics, 2000), 450. From ancient to nearly modern times, burning bonfires and Yule logs at winter solstice was believed to scare off demons as well as to welcome and encourage the waxing of the light. Other scholars argue that Yule derives from the early Germanic word for "feast"—a time to brew beer and butcher livestock that would not be needed in spring. Consequently, ample food was available for familial and communal banquets. Gerry Bowler, *The World Encyclopedia of Christmas* (McClellan & Steward, 2000), 254. See also Kathleen Stokker, *Keeping Christmas: Yuletide Traditions in Norway and the New Land* (Minnesota Historical Society Press, 2000), 5–10; and Christopher Nichols, "From Jól to Yule," *Scandinavian Archaeology*, December 23, 2021 (scandinavianarchaeology.com).
5 Snorri Sturlson, *Heimskringla or The Lives of the Norse Kings* (Dover, 2018), 86.
6 George Wither, "A Christmas Carol," *Poems by George Wither* (George Routledge & Sons, 1891), 121.
7 Bowler, *The World Encyclopedia of Christmas*, 255.
8 John Brand, *Observations on the Popular Antiquities of Great Britain* (1795), ed. Sir Henry Ellis (Henry G. Bohn, 1849), 471.
9 Rabbi Joseph Telushkin, *Jewish Literacy: The Most Important Things to Know About the Jewish Religion, Its People, and Its History* (William Morrow, 1991), 575. For an in-depth description of the origins of Hanukkah and its parallels with Christmas, see Benjamin Beit-Hallahmi, "Sacrifice, Fire, and the Victory of the Sun: A Search for the Origins of Hanukkah," *Psychoanalytic Review* 63, no. 4 (1976), 497–509.
10 Rosa Giorgi, *Saints in Art*, trans. Thomas Michael Hartmann, Stefano Zuffi, ed. (J. Paul Getty Museum, 2003), 230.

11 Ewert Cagner, ed. *Swedish Christmas* (Tre Tryckare, 1955), 180–184.
12 "Songs and Rhymes from Sweden," Mama Lisa's World of International Music & Culture, accessed November 10, 2024, mamalisa.com/?t=es&p=1302.
13 H.F. Tozer, *Dante: La Divina Commedia: Notes on Inferno* (Clarendon Press, 1902), 14.
14 Cagner, *Swedish Christmas*, 89.
15 Thompson, *Holiday Symbols*, 86.
16 Charles Reade, *Put Yourself in His Place* (1870), (Chatto & Windus, 1885), 143, 46, 50.
17 Thompson, *Holiday Symbols*, 80, 86.
18 Rick Bragg, "A Cajun Christmas Tradition Won't Die Down," *The New York Times*, December 24, 1995.
19 Thompson, *Holiday Symbols*, 450.
20 M. Fertiault, "Christmas in Burgundy," trans. Henry W. Longfellow, in Hamilton W. Mabie, ed., *The Book of Christmas* (Macmillan, 1909), 222.
21 Tille, *Yule and Christmas*, 91.
22 Richard Crashaw, *The Poems English Latin and Greek of Richard Crashaw* (Oxford University Press, 1957).
23 Thompson, *Holiday Symbols*, 451.
24 Thompson, *Holiday Symbols*, 534.
25 Ace Collins, *Stories Behind the Great Traditions of Christmas*, (Zondervan, 2003), 113–114.
26 Pierre Grimal, ed., *Larousse World Mythology*, trans. Patricia Beardsworth (Chartwell Books, 1976), 31, 36.
27 Thompson, *Holiday Symbols*, 77.
28 William S. Walsh, *Curiosities of Popular Customs and of Rites, Ceremonies, Observations, and Miscellaneous Antiquities* (Gibbings & Co., 1898), 242. In "The Christmas of 1888," John Greenleaf Whittier writes: "Our homestead pine-tree was the Syrian palm." From *The Complete Poetical Works of John Greenleaf Whittier* (Houghton Mifflin Company, 1894), 467.
29 Earl W. and Alice Lawson Count, *4000 Years of Christmas: A Gift from the Ages* (Seastone, 2000), 77.
30 "The spines of the holly leaves became thickets to catch and hold the hags; juniper-smoke is a demon-chasing incense." Count, *4000 Years of Christmas,* 76.
31 Thompson, *Holiday Symbols*, 82. Especially in climates where most trees are deciduous, evergreens evidence permanence.
32 Maria Hubert, *Christmas in Shakespeare's England* (Sutton Publishing, 1998), 92.
33 Hubert, *Christmas in Shakespeare's England*, 93.
34 Collins, *Stories Behind the Great Traditions of Christmas*, 25–26.
35 For a comprehensive look at the meaning of the Christmas tree, see Frank S. Deming, Jr., "Christmas Tree-Cosmic Tree: Archetypal Dimensions in Contemporary Interviews on the Tree at Christmas" (Doctor of Ministry Dissertation, Princeton Theological Seminary, 1990.)
36 Fyodor Dostoevsky, "The Christmas Tree and a Wedding," in *The Best Short Stories of Dostoevsky*, trans. David Magarshack (Modern Library, 1992), 95.
37 "Deck the Halls and Embrace Christmas Tree Care and Maintenance This Holiday Season," Christmas Tree Association, November 27, 2023, christmastreeassociation.org/press-releases/deck-the-halls-and-embrace-christmas-tree-care-and-maintenance-this-holiday-season, accessed May 13, 2025.
38 Sheryl Ann Karas, *The Solstice Evergreen: The History, Folklore and Origins of the Christmas Tree* (Aslan Publishing, 1991), 95.
39 Karas, *The Solstice Evergreen*, 24.

40 Karas, *The Solstice Evergreen*, 94.
41 Mabie, *The Book of Christmas*, 66.
42 "The Great Christmas Tree of Strasbourg's Christmas Market," Enjoy Strasbourg, October 18, 2023, enjoystrasbourg.com/great-christmas-tree-strasbourg/, accessed May 13, 2025.
43 Count, *4000 Years of Christmas*, 86.
44 Sansom, *A Book of Christmas*, 121.
45 Cagner, *Swedish Christmas*, 51.
46 For a detailed look at the cultural transfer of the Christmas tree and other German Christmas customs to England see Neil Armstrong's "England and German Christmas Festlichkeit, c. 1800–1914," *German History* 26, no. 4 (2008), 486–503.
47 Collins, *Stories Behind the Great Traditions of Christmas*, 74–75.
48 Claude Lévi-Strauss, "Father Christmas Executed," in *Unwrapping Christmas*, Daniel Miller, ed. (Clarendon Press, 1993), 42.
49 Reiko Mochinaga Brandon and Barbara B. Stephan, *Spirit and Symbol: The Japanese New Year* (Honolulu Academy of the Arts, 1994), 64–68.
50 Stephen E. Engels and Theresa Rice, *An Illinois Christmas Anthology* (Partridge Press, 1991), 1.
51 D.L. Cann, *Saint Nicholas, Bishop of Myra: The Life and Times of the Original Father Christmas* (Ottawa: Novalis, 2002), 23.
52 Jock Elliott, *Inventing Christmas: How Our Holiday Came to Be* (Abrams, 2001), 33–34.
53 Charles W. Jones, *Saint Nicholas of Myra, Bari, and Manhattan: Biography of a Legend* (University of Chicago Press, 1978), 27.
54 Jones, *Saint Nicholas of Myra, Bari, and Manhattan*, 24.
55 Jones, *Saint Nicholas of Myra, Bari, and Manhattan*, 41.
56 Count, *4000 Years of Christmas*, 65.
57 Elliott, *Inventing Christmas*, 36.
58 Catholic University of America, ed., *New Catholic Encyclopedia*, Vol. 10 (McGraw Hill, 1967), 455. The Byzantine princess Theophano, wife of Otto (973–83), brought his cult to Germany.
59 Jones, *Saint Nicholas of Myra, Bari, and Manhattan*, 199.
60 Jones, *Saint Nicholas of Myra, Bari, and Manhattan*, 217.
61 Jones, *Saint Nicholas of Myra, Bari, and Manhattan*, 331. On the other hand, the name Nicholas, as well as names of other nonbiblical saints, are quite rare in New England.
62 Jones, *Saint Nicholas of Myra, Bari, and Manhattan*, 265.
63 *New Catholic Encyclopedia*, 275–276. St. Nicholas I (858–867); Nicholas II (1058–1061); Nicholas III (1277–1280); Nicholas IV (1288–1292); Nicholas V (1447–1455). And, of course, there were the Russian tsars Nicholas I and II.
64 Jones, *Saint Nicholas of Myra, Bari, and Manhattan*, 282.
65 Elliott, *Inventing Christmas*, 36.
66 Brand, *Observations on the Popular Antiquities of Great Britain*, 420.
67 *Greek Star*, December 22, 1988. Found in Cann, *Saint Nicholas*, 159.
68 Jones, *Saint Nicholas of Myra, Bari, and Manhattan*, 330–331. He was the tutelar saint of the Dutch.
69 Adriaan D. de Groot, *Saint Nicholas: A Psychoanalytic Study of His History and Myth* (Mouton & Co., 1965), 22.
70 John Pintard, *Letters from John Pintard to His Daughter, Eliza Noel Pintard Davidson 1816–1820*, Vol. 1 (New York Historical Society, 1940), 164.
71 Jones, *Saint Nicholas of Myra, Bari, and Manhattan*, 333.
72 Lewis Leary, *Washington Irving* (University of Minnesota Press, 1963), 16–18.

73   Diedrich Knickerbocker, *A History of New York: From the Beginning of the World to the End of the Dutch Dynasty* (1809) (John R. Alden, 1884), 63, 84, 89, and throughout.
74   Knickerbocker, *A History of New York*.
75   Pintard, *Letters from John Pintard to His Daughter, 1816–1820*, Vol. 1, 38, 156, 64, 354.
76   Pintard, *Letters from John Pintard to His Daughter, Eliza Noel Pintard Davidson 1821–1827*, Vol. 2, 384.
77   Pintard, *Letters from John Pintard to His Daughter, Eliza Noel Pintard Davidson 1828–1831*, Vol. 3, 53.
78   Stephen Nissenbaum, *The Battle for Christmas* (Knopf, 1996), 86
79   Nissenbaum, *The Battle for Christmas*, 73.
80   Jones, *Saint Nicholas of Myra, Bari, and Manhattan*, 347.
81   Elliott, *Inventing Christmas*, 47.
82   Sansom, *A Book of Christmas*, 109.
83   Elliott, *Inventing Christmas*, 57.
84   Nissenbaum, *The Battle for Christmas*, 87.
85   De Groot, *Saint Nicholas*, 24–7. Ernest Jones, "The Significance of Christmas," in *Essays in Applied Psychoanalysis*, Vol. 2. *Essays in Folklore, Anthropology and Religion* (Hogarth Press, 1951), 49–50.
86   Thompson, *Holiday Symbols: A Guide to the Legend and Lore*, 89. In his book *Breaking Open the Head: A Psychedelic Journey into the Heart of Contemporary Shamanism* (Broadway Books, 2002), Daniel Pinchbeck claims that the famous psychedelic fly agaric mushroom—whose red cap with white spots Siberian shamans used to bring gifts from the other world and to attract reindeer—"was incorporated, consciously or not, into the story of Santa Claus," 220.
87   Miles, *Christmas in Ritual and Tradition*, 230.
88   Miles, *Christmas in Ritual and Tradition*, 312.
89   Charles Rivers Editors, *Saint Nicholas and Krampus: The History of the Popular Companions Who Reward and Punish Children During the Christmas Season* (pub. by author, 2024; three chapters on Krampus).
90   Jones, *Saint Nicholas of Myra, Bari, and Manhattan*, 310.
91   Solomon Sobersides, *Christmas Tales for the Amusement and Instruction of Young Ladies and Gentlemen in Winter Evening* (Isaiah Thomas, 1786).
92   Allison C. Putala, *Christmas in Prose and Verse: Its Origin, Celebration and Significance* (Platinum Press, 2000), 143.
93   Nissenbaum, *The Battle for Christmas*, 73.
94   Elizabeth Sedgwick, "The Game of Jackstraws and The Christmas Box," in *The Pearl; or, Affection's Gift* (Thomas T. Ash, 1834), 17–52.
95   Charles Dickens, *A Christmas Tree (1850) & What Christmas Is as We Grow Older (1851)* (Rimington and Hooper, 1927), 22.
96   Walsh, *Curiosities of Popular Customs*, 234.
97   Michael Alvear, "The Christmas That Comes to the Door" (op-ed), *The New York Times,* December 25, 2000.
98   Clive G. Ballard Carol Bannister; Rachel Davis, Sumithra Handy, et al., "Christmas Census at a District General Hospital Psychiatric Unit," *Irish Journal of Psychological Medicine* 8, no. 1 (1991), 46–47.
99   Nissenbaum, *The Battle for Christmas*, 48.
100 Maria Hubert, *The Great British Christmas* (Sutton Publishing, 1999), 40.
101 Maria Hubert and Andrew Hubert, *A Monmouthshire Christmas* (Alan Sutton Publishing Limited, 1995), 20–21.
102 Pintard, *Letters from John Pintard to His Daughter, 1821–1827*, Vol. 2, 205.
103 Engels, *An Illinois Christmas Anthology*, 1.

104 Maria Hubert and Andrew Hubert, *A Wartime Christmas* (Sutton Publishing, 1999), 10.

105 Freya Stark, *The Zodiac Arch* (Tauris Parke Paperbacks, 1968), 60.

106 Washington Irving, *Old Christmas in Merrie England* (Peter Pauper Press, n.d.), 38.

107 Brand, *Observations on the Popular Antiquities of Great Britain*, 21.

108 Charles Dickens, *A Christmas Carol* (1843) (Stewart, Tabori & Chang, 1990), 12–13.

109 Lillian Smith, *Memory of a Large Christmas* (Norton, 1961), 60–62.

110 "The Magic Circle," editorial, *The New York Times,* December 25, 1989, 30. From The New York Times. © 1989 The New York Times. All rights reserved. Used under license.

111 Jones, *Saint Nicholas of Myra, Bari, and Manhattan,* 300.

112 Brand, *Observations on the Popular Antiquities of Great Britain*, 468.

113 Nissenbaum, *The Battle for Christmas,* 275–277, 279. In a bit of cynical realism, Nissenbaum suggests a hidden, sinister motive: "The Lord of the Manor let the peasant in and feasted them. In return, the peasant offered something of true value in a paternalistic society—their goodwill."

114 Walsh, *Curiosities of Popular Customs,* 228.

115 In the Cathedral of Amiens, France, the Feast of Fools was still observed as late as 1721. Thompson, *Holiday Symbols,* 158.

116 Sansom, *A Book of Christmas,* 97.

117 Burgo Partridge, *A History of Orgies* (Bonanza Books, 1960), 95.

118 Miles, *Christmas in Ritual and Tradition,* 303.

119 Thompson, *Holiday Symbols,* 159; William Hone, *Ancient Mysteries Described* (Spring Tree Press, reissue 1969 from 1823), 161.

120 Thompson, *Holiday Symbols,* 162; also in Miles, *Christmas in Ritual and Tradition,* 305.

121 Sansom, *A Book of Christmas,* 46.

122 Miles, *Christmas in Ritual and Tradition,* 306.

123 Brand, *Observations on the Popular Antiquities of Great Britain*, 427.

124 Hone, *Ancient Mysteries Described,* 198; Jones, *Saint Nicholas of Myra, Bari, and Manhattan,* 305.

125 Miles, *Christmas in Ritual and Tradition,* 306.

126 Hone, *Ancient Mysteries Described,* 195.

127 Sansom, *A Book of Christmas,* 78.

128 William Hone, *Everyday Book,* found in Mabie, *The Book of Christmas,* 387.

129 Miles, *Christmas in Ritual and Tradition,* 339–340.

130 Brand, *Observations on the Popular Antiquities of Great Britain*, 23.

131 Miles, *Christmas in Ritual and Tradition,* 320.

132 Dana Hatic and Hillary Dixler Canavan, "The King Cake Tradition, Explained," Eater.com, February 2, 2024; Clément Thiery, "King Cake: A French Tradition Little Known in the U.S.," *France-Amérique,* January 2, 2020.

133 Brand, *Observations on the Popular Antiquities of Great Britain*, 461–462.

134 Miles, *Christmas in Ritual and Tradition,* 298–303.

135 Miles, *Christmas in Ritual and Tradition,* 302.

136 Nissenbaum, *The Battle for Christmas,* 39.

137 Hugh Keyte and Andrew Parrott, eds., *The Shorter New Oxford Book of Carols* (Oxford University Press, 1993), 255.

138 Nissenbaum, *The Battle for Christmas,* 10.

139 J.M. Golby and A.W. Purdue, *The Making of the Modern Christmas* (University of Georgia Press, 1986), 26.

140 William Muir Auld, *Christmas Traditions* (MacMillan, 1931), 126–127.

141 H.L. Mencken, *Christmas Story* (Knopf, 1946), 10.

142 Sansom, *A Book of Christmas,* 33.

143 Thompson, *Holiday Symbols*, 89.
144 Brand, *Observations on the Popular Antiquities of Great Britain*, 520. Golby and Purdue, *The Making of the Modern Christmas*, 24.
145 Tille, *Yule and Christmas*, 121.
146 Tille, *Yule and Christmas*, 131.
147 "That all days that heretofore have been kept holy, besides Sabbath days, such as Yule [Christ-mass] day, Saint's days, and such others, may be abolished, and, and a civil penalty against the keepers therefore by ceremonies, banqueting, fasting, and other such vanities." General Assembly of the Church of Scotland, Articles to Be Presented to my Lord Regent's Grace (1575). Margo Todd, *The Culture of Protestantism in Early Modern Scotland* (Yale University Press, 2002), 183. Under the leadership of Oliver Cromwell and much to the horror of the majority of the nation's citizens, the Parliament forbade the observance of Christmas in 1647. New England theocracy agreed and from 1659 to 1681, Christmas observances were banned. *Records of the Governor and Company of Massachusetts Bay*, Vol. 4, part 1 (1853), 336–337.
148 Sansom, *A Book of Christmas*, 47–48.
149 Walsh, *Curiosities of Popular Customs*, 235.
150 Sansom, *A Book of Christmas*, 18.
151 Hubert, *Christmas Around the World*, 145.
152 Sansom, *A Book of Christmas*, 213.
153 Nissenbaum, *The Battle for Christmas*, 7, 13.
154 John Grisham, *Skipping Christmas* (Doubleday, 2001), 40.
155 Jones, "The Significance of Christmas," 223.
156 Philippe Aries, *Centuries of Childhood: A Social History of Family Life*, trans. Robert Baldick (Vintage Books, 1962).
157 A.A. Volk and J.A. Atkinson, "Infant and Child Death in the Human Environment of Evolutionary Adaptation," *Evolution and Human Behavior* 34, no. 3 (2013), 182–192.
158 Margaret Reeves, "'A Prospect of Flowers': Concepts of Childhood and Female Youth in Seventeenth-Century British Culture," in E.S. Cohen and M. Reeves, eds., *The Youth of Early Modern Women* (Amsterdam University Press, 2018), 36–37.
159 Brand, *Observations on the Popular Antiquities of Great Britain*, 417–418.
160 Hugh Cunningham, *Children and Childhood in Western Society Since 1500*, 3rd ed. (Routledge, 2020), 46.
161 Cunningham, *Children and Childhood in Western Society Since 1500*, 49.
162 Reeves, "'A Prospect of Flowers,'" 39–41.
163 Elliott, *Inventing Christmas*, 95.
164 Elliott, *Inventing Christmas*, 54.
165 Engels, *An Illinois Christmas Anthology*, 1.
166 Cunningham, *Children and Childhood in Western Society Since 1500*, 137.
167 J.R.R. Tolkien, *The Father Christmas Letters* (Houghton Mifflin, 1976).
168 Dylan Thomas, *A Child's Christmas in Wales* (New Direction Books, 1954).
169 Chester G. Anderson, ed., *Growing up in Minnesota: Ten Writers Remember Their Childhoods* (University of Minneapolis Press, 1976), 69.
170 Hisako Kinukawa, "The Christian Church in Japan" (seminar at First Congregational Church, Guilford, CT, November 30, 2003).
171 Nissenbaum, *The Battle for Christmas*, xii.
172 Miles, *Christmas in Ritual and Tradition*, 358–360.
173 Jones, "The Significance of Christmas," 223.
174 Thomas of Celano, *St. Francis of Assisi: First and Second Life of St. Francis*, trans. Placid Hermann (Franciscan Herald Press, 1988), 75.
175 Thomas of Celano, *St. Francis of Assisi*, 76.
176 Nina Gockerell, *Nativity Scenes* (Taschen, 1998), 6.

177 Celano, *St. Francis of Assisi*, 76.
178 John Greenleaf Whittier, *The Complete Poetical Works of Whittier* (Houghton Mifflin, 1894), 267.
179 Hanns Swarzenski, *An 18th Century Creche* (Museum of Fine Arts, 1967), 7.
180 Gockerell, *Nativity Scenes*, 9.
181 Miles, *Christmas in Ritual and Tradition*, 109.
182 Gockerell, *Nativity Scenes*, 10.
183 Swarzenski, *An 18th Century Creche*, 9.
184 Matthew Powell, *The Christmas Crèche: Treasure of Faith, Art & Theater* (Pauline Books & Media, 1997), 102.
185 Maria Hubert, *Christmas Around the World* (Sutton Publishing, 1998), 74.
186 Cuyler, *The All-Around Christmas Book*, 22.
187 Thompson, *Holiday Symbols*, 79.
188 Swarzenski, *An 18th Century Creche*, 6.
189 Swarzenski, *An 18th Century Creche*, 9.
190 Owen Chadwick, *A History of Christianity* (St. Martin's Press, 1995), 25.
191 Tille, *Yule and Christmas*, 95–96.
192 Sansom, *A Book of Christmas*, 106–107.
193 O. Henry, *The Gift of the Magi* (Hawthorn Books, 1972).
194 Emily Brontë, *Wuthering Heights* (1847) (Bantam Books, 1981), 49.
195 Brand, *Observations on the Popular Antiquities of Great Britain*, 494.
196 Hubert, *Christmas in Shakespeare's England*, 93.
197 Collins, *Stories Behind the Great Traditions of Christmas*, 39.
198 Louisa May Alcott, *Little Women* (1868) (Running Press, 1995), 12.
199 Hubert, *The Great British Christmas*, 39.
200 Hubert and Hubert, *A Monmouthshire Christmas*, 102–103.
201 Henry Van Dyke, *The Story of the Other Wise Man* (Harper & Brothers, 1906), 73–75.
202 Phyllis Hobe, ed., *The Meaning of Christmas* (A.J. Holman, 1975), 15.
203 Francis Pharcellus Church, "Yes Virginia, There Is a Santa Claus," editorial, *New York Sun*, September 21, 1897.
204 Victor Hugo, *Les Misérables*, trans. Lee Fahnestock and Norman MacAfee (New American Library, 1987), 413–414.
205 Hubert and Hubert, *A Monmouthshire Christmas*, 73–75.
206 Miles, *Christmas in Ritual and Tradition*, 101.
207 Tille, *Yule and Christmas*, 164–167.
208 Hubert, *The Great British Christmas*, 89.
209 Thompson, *Holiday Symbols*, 83.
210 Collins, *Stories Behind the Great Traditions of Christmas*, 113–114.
211 Sansom, *A Book of Christmas*, 227–229.
212 Malcolm Brown and Shirley Seaton, *Christmas Truce: The Western Front December 1914* (Papermac, 1984), xxi.
213 Whittier, *The Complete Poetical Works of Whittier*, 467.
214 Walsh, *Curiosities of Popular Customs*, 235–236.
215 Chadwick, *A History of Christianity*, 24.

Chapter 5

Christmas and the Oedipal

Freud

For some, the previous accounting of historical facts and objective manifestations is enough to comprehend Christmas. Not for us. Like Jung, we want to know what primordial dynamics lie beneath; in all the Nativity images, objects, and commotion.[1] In these concluding three chapters, we move beyond the conscious cultural experiences of Christmas to the subterranean wonders of the psyche that annually alter our gaze and stir us up. The insights of Sigmund Freud, Heinz Kohut, and C.G. Jung plunge us into our collective depths to expose some of the sedimentary layers that invigorate this primal soul story. Our threefold exploration via Psychoanalytic, Self, and Analytic psychologies yields multiple truths about the psychological meaning of Christmas. This is as it should be because "symbols are polyvalent rather than univocal."[2]

Sigmund Freud (1856–1939) was the progenitor of depth psychology. Accordingly, this chapter introduces the psychodynamic insights made by the Freudian camp concerning the Christmas phenomenon.

Freud and Religion

Regrettably, Freud made no direct observations about Christmas. This had less to do with the fact that Freud was Jewish than that he held religion in contempt and attacked it with a broad blade. He was "glad" that he had "no religion," and described himself as "a completely godless Jew" and "an infidel Jew."[3] Religion, according to Freud, is infantile dependency, "wish fulfillment," "universal neurosis," "blissful hallucinatory confusion,"[4] mass delusion,[5] analogous to the dynamics of paranoia,[6] an obsessive-compulsive disorder,[7] and a fumbled attempt to deal with Oedipal issues.[8]

Freud's contention in *The Future of an Illusion* (1927) was that, just as individuals move from childhood to adulthood, so must they turn away from religion to gain maturity.[9] In *Civilization and Its Discontents* (1930), Freud made this accusation:

> The whole thing is so patently infantile, so foreign to reality, that to anyone with a friendly attitude to humanity it is painful to think that the great majority of mortals will never be able to rise above this view of life.[10]

DOI: 10.4324/9781003568629-6

Freud's scorched-earth policy against religion reveals he viewed religious convic-tion as an irredeemable enemy to psychic health. Of course, the fact that Freud had the psychic energy to write so many books vehemently alleging the pathol-ogy of religion indicates the possibility that his own personal issues were at play. Psychoanalyst Edwin Wallace claims that Freud had a hidden agenda to psycho-pathologize religion.[11]

> My thesis is that because psychoanalysis for Freud (largely unconsciously) partook of the character of "positive community" with its own therapeutic and reintegrative symbolism, he had to oppose it to all the more traditional "posi-tive communities" and commitment therapies—foremost among which was religion.[12]

This would help explain Freud's discriminatory comment that psychoanalysts "need not be doctors and should not be priests."[13]

C.G. Jung recalls a conversation in which Freud told him:

> My dear Jung, promise me never to abandon the sexual theory. That is the most essential thing of all. You see we must make a dogma of it, an unshakable bul-wark ... against the black tide of mud—of occultism.[14]

According to Jung, occultism to Freud meant "everything that philosophy and reli-gion ... had learned about the psyche."[15] Given the subsequent breakup between Jung and Freud, simply trusting Jung's assessment would be naive. However, in this case, we have good corroborating evidence. For almost 30 years (1909–37), Freud carried on correspondence with Oskar Pfister, a Swiss pastor and psycho-analyst who believed that Freud's insights could be a divine vehicle for healing. Freud called Pfister his "old friend," and often closed his letters to him, "your devoted, Freud."[16] While generally enthusiastic, Pfister resisted Freud's atheism and authored academic articles taking issue with such books as *Civilization and Its Discontents*. On November 24, 1927, Pfister wrote to Freud:

> I do not properly understand your outlook on life. It is impossible that what you reject as the end of an illusion and value as the sole truth can be all. A world without temples, the fine arts, poetry, religion, would in my view be a devil's island to which men could have been banished, not by blind chance, but only by Satan. In that case your pessimism about the wickedness of mankind would be much too mild. You would have to follow it through to its logical conclusion. If it were part of psycho-analytic treatment to present that despoiled universe to our patients as the truth, I should well understand it if the poor devils preferred remaining shut up in their illness to entering that dreadful icy desolation.[17]

This exchange indicates that Jung's report of Freud's comprehensive dismissal of *religion* in the broadest sense was on the mark.

Freud himself knew there was at least some truth to Jung's and Pfister's complaint. In a remarkable comment, Freud notes the "extraordinary increase in the neuroses since the power of religion has waned."[18] He reaffirmed this observation a decade later:

> Even those who do not regret the disappearance of religious illusion from the civilized world of to-day will admit that so long as they were in force they offered those who were bound by them the most powerful protection against the danger of neurosis.[19]

Nonetheless, Freud saw "poetry, religion, and philosophy" as a "binding force for the majority" and not a healthy thing.

> Even the highest achievements of the human spirit must bear a demonstrable relation to the factors found in pathology—to repression, to the efforts at mastering the unconscious and to the possibilities of satisfying the primitive instincts. ... For it was obvious that the forms assumed by the different neuroses echoed the most highly admired production of our culture.[20]

According to Freud, nowhere was this truer than with religion, which has "been able to effect absolute renunciation of pleasure in this life by means of the promise of compensation in a future life."[21]

Freud's meta-attacks on faith in general left no time, much less interest, for a discussion of such an apparently particularistic issue as Christmas. How ironic then that "the most important of all Freud's case histories"[22] would center around Christmas, and how regrettable that Freud, because of his antipathy for religion and his need to fiercely shepherd his theories, missed this focus, depriving us of his thoughts on its meaning.

A Missed Opportunity: The Case of the Wolf-Man

"I was born on Christmas Eve, 1886."[23] So begins the memoir of Sergei Pankejeff, Freud's analysand better known as the Wolf-Man. In "From the History of an Infantile Neurosis," Pankejeff's case is explicated with constant reference to psychoanalytic theory. Freud writes:

> It is concerned with a young man whose health had broken down in his eighteenth year after a gonorrheal infection, and who was entirely incapacitated and completely dependent upon other people when he began his psycho-analytic treatment several years later. He had lived an approximately normal life during the ten years of his boyhood that preceded that date of his illness, and got through his studies at his secondary school without much trouble. But his earlier years were dominated by a severe neurotic disturbance, which began immediately before his fourth birthday as an anxiety-hysteria (in the shape of an animal

phobia), then changed into an obsessional neurosis with a religious content, and lasted with its offshoots as far as into his tenth year.[24]

According to Pankejeff's recollections, his life took a dramatic turn for the worse during the Christmas of 1890.[25] Before the Wolf-Man's fourth Christmas/birthday, he was a "good natured, tractable, and even a quiet child."[26] Following his fourth Christmas/birthday, he became "discontented, irritable and violent, took offence on every possible occasion, and then flew into a rage and screamed like a savage."[27] What happened? Two things.

First, the Wolf-Man had a dream with a "lasting sense of reality" that distressed him deeply.[28] This dream became the central feature of Freud's case study, convincing him that the "causes of [Pankejeff's] infantile neurosis lay concealed behind [the dream]."[29] The Wolf-Man described it as follows:

> I dreamt that it was night and that I was lying in my bed. … Suddenly the window opened of its own accord, and I was terrified to see that some white wolves were sitting on the big walnut tree in front of the window. There were six or seven of them. The wolves were quite white, and looked more like foxes or sheepdogs, for they had big tails like foxes and they have their ears pricked like dogs when they pay attention to something. In great terror, evidently of being eaten up by the wolves, I screamed and woke up. … The only piece of action in the dream was the opening of the window; for the wolves sat quite still and without making any movement on the branches of the tree, to the right and left of the trunk and looked at me. It seemed as though they had riveted their whole attention upon me.[30]

The Wolf-Man drew a picture, and later painted the scene (see Figure 5.1).[31] His association to the tree was that of a Christmas tree.[32] Freud noted:

> He had gone to sleep, then, in tense expectation of the day which ought to bring him a double quantity of presents. We know that in such circumstances a child may easily anticipate the fulfillment of his wishes. So it was already Christmas in his dream; the content of the dream showed him his Christmas box, the presents which were to be his were hanging on the tree, but instead of presents they had turned into—wolves.[33]

The second occurrence, from his fourth Christmas/birthday, was that he was not given a double quantity of presents, which he thought he was due, being both Christmas and his birthday. This began, according to him, his "naughty period."[34] Again, Freud noted:

> The importance of this date of Christmas day had been preserved in his supposed recollection of having had his first fit of rage because he was dissatisfied

Figure 5.1 Painting of his Christmas Eve dream by "The Wolf Man," Sergei Pankejeff. ©
Freud Museum London

with his Christmas presents. ... [H]e had preserved the essential connection
between his unsatisfied love, his rage, and Christmas.[35]

The dream and the incident of dissatisfaction both relate to Christmas. Freud
interpreted that the wolves "replace the Christmas presents hanging on the tree."[36]
Therefore, according to Freud's description and the Wolf-Man's associations, we
have a man born on Christmas who experiences a wolves/Christmas gifts/Christmas
tree dream immediately preceding a Christmas/birthday, where his expectations
were dashed and he, therefore, experienced the dual occasion as woefully inadequate. Christmas is underlined again and again. In the language of depth psychology, Christmas is here "over-determined"—a sure sign that the unconscious
wants diligent attention to be paid. Undoubtedly, for the Wolf-Man, the meaning
of Christmas was a critical area for in-depth investigation.

However in his description of the case, Freud gives Christmas no consideration.
He ignores this unmistakable focal point and hastily moves to what he judges as the
heart of the matter: "the reversals of the latent material to be found in the content of
the dream."[37] Aided, if not limited, by the assumptions of his sexual theory, Freud

penetrates the dream's distortions, interchanges, and oppositional transformations as follows:

1. That the dream had a lasting sense of reality means that some part of the dream's latent material "relates to an occurrence that really took place and was not merely imagined."[38]
2. "The attentive looking, which in the dream was ascribed to the wolves, should rather be shifted on to him."[39]
3. The motionlessness of the wolves meant "the most violent motion."[40]
4. That "the wolves were quite white" represents, for Freud, "the white of his [the Wolf-Man's] parents' bedclothes and underwear."[41]

Freud comes to a firm interpretation. The dream was a screen memory for the Wolf-Man, at age one and a half years, witnessing the "primal scene" of his parents having "coitus *a tergo* [from behind], three times repeated."[42] The fact that there were six or seven wolves instead of two representing mother and father is, according to Freud, "welcomed by the resistance as a means of distortion."[43]

Not only does this interpretation surprise readers, for it is neither self-evident nor commonsensical, but there is much to argue against it. The Wolf-Man never remembered the primal incident and strongly suggested it was most unlikely. According to Karin Obholzer, the Wolf-Man told her: "The whole matter is improbable, because children in Russia slept with the nurse in her room and not with the parents in their room."[44]

Furthermore, according to Strachey, the translator of *The Complete Psychological Works*, the Wolf-Man case study served two complementary agendas for Freud. In his mind, this case provided "conclusive evidence ... of infantile sexuality," and therefore, provided support for "his criticisms of Adler and more especially Jung."[45] Freud writes in his "Introductory Remarks" about the current "battle which is raging round psycho-analysis":

This case history was written down shortly after the termination of the treatment, in the winter of 1914–15. At that time I was still freshly under the impression of the twisted reinterpretations which C.G. Jung and Alfred Adler were endeavouring to give to the findings of psychoanalysis.[46]

We begin to suspect an obsession on Freud's part when he alludes to the "obstinate" Jung five times, including this barely veiled reference:

But during the last few years there has grown up another kind of opposition as well, among people who, in their own opinion at all events, take their stand upon the ground of analysis, who do not dispute its technique or results, but who merely think themselves justified in drawing other conclusions from the same material and in submitting it to other interpretations. ... one runs the risk of becoming intoxicated with one's own assertions and, in the end, of supporting opinions which any observation would have contradicted. For this reason it seems to me to be incomparably more useful to combat dissentient interpretations by testing them upon particular cases and problems.[47]

This whole case was put under the massive burden of this secondary agenda. Freud further opens the door to critique when he writes the following about the Wolf-Man's case: "Our knowledge of his sexual development before the dream makes it possible for us to fill in the gaps in the dream."[48] That seems an understatement. Freud's sexual theories became the very template by which the dream was interpreted, shoehorning his diagnosis. Barry Magid, in "Self-Psychology Meets the Wolf Man," speaks for many when he concludes that Freud "forced the facts of this difficult case to conform to his expectations about the centrality of infantile sexuality in neurogenesis."[49]

The Wolf-Man's dream, its timing, and associations, dangled the silvery lure of Christmas dynamics before Freud, but he did not bite. Perhaps the anti-Semitic environment of late 19th-century Viennese culture made Christmas too dangerous a subject. Perhaps his inflamed prejudice against religion closed his eyes to the most obvious subject for investigation. Most likely, however, Freud was blinded to the obvious by his dogma of infantile sexuality and his need for proof to reproach Jung.[50] For whatever reason, this case was a squandered occasion to have the pioneer of depth psychology address the meaning of Christmas. Given what we presently know about the Wolf-Man's early life from his own autobiography, it seems that the Self psychology of Heinz Kohut would have been the best way to understand the Wolf-Man's problems and dream. For that, we must wait to the next chapter. We turn now to other psychoanalysts' assessments of Christmas, observations that Freud might have made himself had he focused on it.

A Survey of the Psychoanalytic Literature on Christmas

Given the conspicuous effects of Christmas on human emotions and behavior, some psychoanalysts have written thoughtfully about its significance. As with us, their concern is not about the reliability of the Jesus story but how those narratives impact the psyche.

Ernest Jones

Writing in the early 1930s, Ernest Jones—founder of the British Psychoanalytic Society—began his essay, "The Significance of Christmas," with this declaration: "To ask why we keep Christmas is to ask a good question."[51] He points to Christmas as a holiday unique among all the Christian religious festivals because only it appeals to non-Christians as well. Jones spends time on the "history of religions" approach to Christmas established in the first chapter. His argument is not as comprehensive as ours, but his evidence includes analogs from even more cultures. For instance, he observes:

The fact remains that the date had already been established in innumerable pagan religions in just this sense. The 25th December was the birthday of many a Persian, Phoenician, Egyptian and even Teutonic Sun-God. And the decision [to choose December 25th as the date of Christ's birth] was in line with the general syncretizing activities of the church in the early centuries when it was combating paganism.[52]

From the beginning of human history, the success of crops has been attributed to the power of the sun. The sun preserved life, yielding abundance. Jones notes that the Egyptians represented the newborn sun with the image of an infant, which on the winter solstice—his birthday—the priests displayed to worshippers.[53]

Jones abruptly jumps to his conclusion, reminding us of the Freudian axiom that religions are an attempt to solve on a cosmic stage the "loves and hatreds that take their source in the complicated relations of children and parents."[54] With an apparent link missing between the body of his argument, he concludes:

Historically expressed, the festival of Christmas is thus a fusion of many strains of pagan customs and beliefs, but one which Christianity has inspired with a fresh spiritual significance. Psychologically it represents the ideal of resolving all family discord in a happy reunion, and to this it owes its perennial attraction.[55]

For Jones, this hope of dissolving, resolving, or at least momentarily denying, family discord generates gaiety and explains the gravitational force of Christmas.

If we can set aside the large gap in his logic, Jones's paper underlines the fundamental Christmas desires for homecoming and peace (as described in Chapter Four). He underscores that something about Christmas heightens the possibility of "resolving all family discord in a happy reunion." [56] And even if such a calm is only short-lived or partially present, it makes for a refreshing interlude. When family members sheath their porcupine quills for Christmas, it echoes in the heart's chambers, soothes the adrenal glands, and gladdens the mind.

Eisenbud and Sterba

During World War II, a mini debate about the meaning of Christmas broke out between two psychoanalysts. Jule Eisenbud, in the paper "Negative Reactions to Christmas," brings two notions to the table. First, Christmas is like any other significant festival, secular or religious. Holidays, he asserts, are meant for unbridling the id, a time socially sanctioned to be immoderate or exhibitionist.[57] According to Eisenbud, Christmas is set apart simply by the larger degree of authorized indulgence. He writes:

Of all festivals, that marking the Christmas and New Year season is characterized by the greatest relaxation on the part of the superego society, so to speak. This is the season when governments grant amnesties and penal institutions distribute pardons. It is a season when the solid citizen becomes liquid and "the devil is raised." When all is over, repression resumes and the air is disinfected with good resolutions.[58]

From what we have already established about the Christmas motif of excess, Eisenbud's argument makes sense. No doubt, moral license has always been characteristic of midwinter in the West. These adopted revelries became well-loved parts of the celebration of Christ's Nativity. Given all we know about the Lord of Misrule, the Bishop of Fools, the mummers and guisers, the Christmas office parties and overindulgent feasting, drinking, spending, and other behaviors, it is impossible to deny Eisenbud's claim. As historian Clement Miles puts it, "the severest moralist utters no blame on this occasion."[59]

Yet, because our laxity is robust, in the corner of our psyche lurks the ambivalent Saint Nicholas, who is both generous gift giver and harsh judge. He is after all "the patron saint of good boys and girls."[60] Eisenbud notes that some people, suffering inner conflict, cannot avail themselves of the freedom offered at the holidays and "must never for any reason discard their sackcloth."[61]

This leads Eisenbud to the second and lengthier part of his paper. He describes two women analysands who annually found Christmas particularly distressing. One woman usually got fired from her job around Christmas, and the second became particularly harsh and unyielding in December. According to psychoanalytic theory of the time, Eisenbud provided this interpretation: As young girls, both perceived their mothers as loving their brothers more, and giving them more or better-quality presents. One claimed, "He always had 'more to play with' than she had."[62] Both had infantile wishes for a penis to equally compete with their brothers for parental affection and presents. Both expected Santa Claus would magically provide a desired gift. One mother had promised: "If you're a good little girl, Santa Claus will bring you anything you desire."[63] Both had hopes dashed when Christmas morning brought no physical change. This, according to Eisenbud, led to chronic masculine (phallic) strivings in the women and the miserable (highly symptomatic) Christmases they endured year after year.

These two cases cause us to wonder: Is Christmas such an emotionally charged day that it makes a particularly good time for traumatic experiences to occur and do psychic damage, or does the neon-light focus on Christmas make it a handy occasion on which to constellate chronic feelings of disappointment? And, more to the point, does something about Christmas—the birth of a special child—remind us of our perceived specialness or lack thereof? The next section and following chapter address this.

But first we turn to Richard Sterba's paper, "On Christmas." Published three years after Eisenbud, it took issue with Eisenbud's notion that festivals do not have particularistic meanings but rather are generic occasions for the id to run wild. Sterba writes:

Simple and easily accessible observations, not of patients but of one's own family, friends and acquaintances, as well as the general universal Christmas behavior, present convincing proof that our emotional experience of Christmas is much more determined by the religious and archaic content of the Christmas festival than is recognized by Eisenbud.[64]

Sterba argues that the "general display of mangers" and "other religious Christmas symbols" leaves no doubt that Christmas is demonstrably about the legendary birth of the Christ Child. This leads Sterba to his main point, alluding to the motif of home, that our "own behavior at Christmas is also an acting out of childbirth in the family."[65] The remainder of his paper elucidates the "astonishing" similarities of customs surrounding pregnancy/childbirth and family Christmas rituals. To appreciate his analogies, we must remember that this reflects the birth traditions of the 1940s:

1. "There is a long preparatory period of growing excitement and impatient secret anticipation which corresponds to the period of pregnancy. Everyone is expecting."
2. "The typical Christmas rush is filled with the same hasty preparation and excitements which goes on in the family when a woman is in labor."
3. "Presents are secretly bought and hidden" and "persons shout at one another if they enter the forbidden room or look at the prohibited object, exactly as if a birth were taking place and the children were anxiously kept away from any possibility of observing or finding out about it."
4. "On Christmas Day friends and relatives visit each other to exhibit their presents and they love to have them admired just as if they were the happy presents of a newborn baby."
5. "The relaxation of the superego which Eisenbud mentions accompanies the joy reaction to the arrival of a child. On such occasions fathers often get drunk and kings give amnesties to prisoners."
6. "The presents come down the chimney since the fireplace and chimney signify vulva and vagina in the unconscious and the child-present thus comes out of the birth canal."
7. "Thus Santa Claus with his fat belly is a pregnant woman and he acts in a most natural way when he drops his presents down the chimney *per viam naturalem*." (We can add that the Christmas gift giver in Russia is an old woman called Babushka.[66])
8. "Santa's bag full of presents is another symbol of the pregnant abdomen and corresponds to the doctor's bag in which the child is supposed to arrive."[67]

Sterba abruptly concludes his essay with the following claim:

Such an interpretation of the emotions engendered by the Christmas festival seems to be a much more accurate picture of the underlying unconscious fantasies than that offered by Eisenbud. At the same time it is more fruitful because it leads to a better understanding of those emotional disturbances of patients which are centered around the complex of feelings, wishes, magical fulfillments or frustrations of childbirth.[68]

Sterba neither explains how this is so, nor gives any case studies to support his thesis. Fortunately, other psychoanalysts took on the task.

Boyer, Volkan, and Ast

A decade later, psychoanalyst L. Bryce Boyer coined the term "Christmas neurosis."[69] Surmising that the psychodynamics of depressive reactions at Christmastime had been insufficiently considered, Boyer studied from a psychoanalytic perspective 17 patients who chronically suffered Christmas depression. In 1985, he published a follow-up study of an additional 50 patients who regressed and exhibited depressive reactions during the Christmas season.[70] Boyer concluded that Christmas depression was "primarily the result of reawakened conflicts related to unresolved sibling rivalries."[71]

The analysands in the case studies shared this in common: They valiantly attempted to be the favored child but felt they had failed. For instance, Mrs. W., a 30-year-old, childless housewife, annually suffered severe anxious depression around Christmas. Though an only child, she felt unwanted. She perceived her mother's and father's affections as directed to a paternal nephew who had lived with her parents before she was born and who she believed to be her actual brother. "She attributed her undesirability to her being female. ... In her quest for a penis, she had pursued various masculine avocations and engineering as a profession."[72] Again, we remember that this was written in 1955, before modern understandings broke down rigid boundaries of masculine/feminine roles and enabled the fluidity for natural affinities to be engaged without the automatic and demeaning charge of "penis envy."[73] Boyer diagnosed her as suffering from intense sibling rivalry:

> Her basic wish was to be her parents' only child, a child so beautiful that the entire world would love her and give her whatever she wanted without expecting anything in return.[74]

For Boyer, Christmas constellates unconscious turmoil around the jealousies and competition with one's siblings because Christmas celebrates the birth of the Christ Child, the special one so favored that any competition with him is futile. We must only view some of the multitude of Holy Family paintings to see the absolute adoration and near oneness that he, and he alone, enjoys with his parents (see Figure 5.2). According to Roman Catholic tradition, Jesus does not even have siblings. Boyer notes that "during one Christmas depression, she [Mrs. W.] consciously considered Christ to be her rival."[75] The Christ Child then becomes an analog for and reminder of the rival sibling one can never supplant. Eventually, unconscious hostility toward siblings or their substitutes (such as a boss or coworker) causes

Figure 5.2 The Nativity, by Zanobi Strozzi (1412–1468). Courtesy Metropolitan Museum of
    Art, New York; Rogers Fund, 1924

outward conflict that often turns inward. This aggression toward the self leads to
lowered self-esteem and depression.

It also must be admitted that many cultures for centuries have preferred male
children. Even today, infertile American couples find it easiest to adopt girls from

places like China, Korea, and Colombia. "Favorite sons" is not just a political expression, for women often express resigned disappointment that their mother feels that way about their oldest brother. A recent graduate of a prestigious women's college quipped when her only brother drove up, "God's home!" No wonder a popular shirt among feminists of all genders shows a Nativity scene with the caption: "It's a girl!"

Vamik D. Volkan and Gabriele Ast add a fascinating case of their own in *Siblings in the Unconscious and Psychopathology*. Mira was the firstborn child. Her father wanted a son. A brother, Bernd, was born with Down syndrome and was hospitalized for a year before "coming home for good on December 24th when Mira was celebrating her third Christmas."[76] The new baby's handicap only compounded her sense of "losing" her parents to him. Shortly after her brother's arrival, she injured her head severely, continued to have accidents, and further identified with him by acting as if she had a mental disability. She was also overly aggressive with younger children and nearly killed her baby sister by fracturing her skull. As a child, "she perceived a picture of Jesus in her room as someone consisting of 'scary eyes.'"[77] Throughout her high school years, she was involved in an admixture of generous caring for others and dangerously aggressive acts against others and herself. The beginning of her cure was the following recollection:

> As Mira's third Christmas in analysis approached she was busy unearthing her past memories and feeling that she had a cancerous lesion (a "bad baby") in her abdomen. Now she recalled Bernd's arrival to their home the day before Christmas. Mira could see in her mind's eye a big cradle. At Christmas time the family would take this cradle out of storage and place it under the Christmas tree. A baby Jesus doll would be placed in it along with dolls of Joseph, Mary and some animals surrounding them. … When Bernd was first brought to the house on December 24th, *he* was put into this cradle and under the Christmas tree. Bernd was the baby Jesus![78]

Mira's case clearly illustrates Boyer's concept of the "Christmas neurosis." At Christmastime, the sibling rival and Christ Child merge in the unconscious fantasy as the primary target and recipient of the parents' love, and therefore both become an insurmountable, unmovable, and hated obstacle. The bottom line is that the "extravagant welcome" that Christmas promises was actually lacking or not experienced.

We might suppose that those able to unconsciously identify with the Christ Child as the privileged one during the Christmas season would unconsciously feel the victor over their siblings and not suffer anxiety and depression. And we could argue that those able to unconsciously indulge this positive fantasy are free to let peace reign, even if only for Christmas Day.

Boyer dismisses the notion that Christmas depression might be the result of physiological changes due to the dark and cold of the season.[79] He notes that depression increases at Christmastime even in Hawaii and Argentina. He also denies that Christmas neurosis is a distinct clinical entity.

> The depressive reactions which occur at this time of the year are phenomenologically and dynamically the same as those observed at other times. The constellation surrounding Christmas makes it a more important holiday and a more powerful trigger for reactions in the predisposed.[80]

In other words, depression and anxiety due to unconscious sibling rivalry can afflict those so injured in any season. Yet, in those sufferers, the occasion of Christmas—the birthday of the uniquely beloved child—soundly strikes the minor chord of their failure to achieve what they so vehemently desire: To be number one in the hearts of their parents. One cannot compete with the Christ/sibling rival. Christmas, though not the progenitor of the conflict, can instigate a yearly eruption of unconscious futility and rage.

Ludwig Jekels: "The Psychology of the Festival of Christmas"

The most substantial paper with a psychoanalytical approach to the meaning of Christmas comes from Ludwig Jekels. On December 13, 1934, he presented "The Psychology of the Festival of Christmas,"[81] arguing that the Feast of the Nativity was unconsciously instituted in an attempt to deal with the Oedipal complex, the overcoming of the father by the son.[82] Although Christmas neurosis, as noted by Eisenbud, Boyer, as well as Volkan and Ast, can be devastatingly real, even afflicting many in minimal ways, Jekels's analysis has a broader collective resonance.

Jekels begins with a historical investigation, noting what we now know well, that the actual birth date of Christ was neither known nor even celebrated until the fourth century. He ponders, "What motives had the Church in instituting this festival and by what tendencies was she probably influenced?"[83] He posits that the celebration of Christmas established itself throughout the Roman Empire within a ten-year period. Though this may be an exaggeration, his point is well taken. There was a rapid and widespread grassroots embrace of the Feast of the Nativity, a remarkable triumph that calls for understanding. Jekels's first conclusion: Christmas was giving "expression to a popular craving."[84] But what was this universal yearning that Christmas assuaged?

Jekels believes that the choice of the date, December 25, holds the answer. It is the winter solstice, the birthday of the Unconquered Son—*Natalis Solis Invicti*. This is the turning of the year. The longest night is past, and the days pleasantly lengthen. Today we talk of a "new moon," but for the ancients, the expression was attached to the sun. Jekels goes on to credit someone named Meyer (not further identified) as pointing out that the sun after the solstice was "called in vigorous popular phrase 'the new' or 'young' sun. Poets, astronomers, and orators have made use of this idea."[85]

The weary sun is replaced by a burgeoning one. The winter solstice then symbolizes a transfer of power. And this astrological event abuts the New Year, where
it is auld lang syne for the old. He offers corroboration from ancient Rome:

> The principal ceremony—and this has a special bearing on the hypothesis I am
> submitting to you—was the entering of the new, annually elected consuls upon
> their office in place of the retiring consuls of the previous year.[86]

This was a solemn state festival where the incoming magistrates, with great pomp
and circumstance, made their way to the Capitol and were installed before the
assembled Senate. Not only is Christmas celebrated on the solstice, but it is literally
and emotionally connected to the turn of the New Year.

With Freudian orthodoxy, Jekels has no doubt that this ousting by the young
represents the universal struggle: The son's rivalry with his father.

> The attitude of the son to the father that is termed ambivalent by psychoanaly-
> sis, that inescapable psychological fate which decrees that, side by side with
> his love and respect for his father, there are in the son's mind powerful hostile
> tendencies which impel him to enter into rivalry with his father, to dispute his
> superiority, shake off his authority and, if not actually supplant him, at least to
> rank himself as his father's equal.[87]

This clash is seen repeatedly, clothed in the symbolism of myths, fairy tales, and
legends. Here Jekels discovers the desire to be equal with the father barely disguised beneath the outer cloak of Christmas pageantry.

He calls our attention to the first great theological controversy of the Church,
one that began raging shortly before the Feast of the Nativity was commonly
observed. The debate between Arius, an intellectual parish priest in Alexandria,
and Athanasius, the first deacon and later bishop of Alexandria, centered on the
nature of Christ.[88] The Christian community engaged the dispute with amazing
enthusiasm. Theological slogans were shouted, demonstrations were held, heated
arguments were commonplace.[89] This, according to Jekels, was the fertile ground
out of which the celebration of Christ's Nativity established itself.

Without going into the details surrounding the controversy, Jaroslav Pelikan,
Sterling Professor of History at Yale, presents the issue succinctly:

> The fundamental question creating discord was the relation between the
> Godhead and Jesus as the son of God: in the formulation of one modern scholar,
> "Is the divine that has appeared in earth and reunited man with God identical
> with the supreme divine, which rules heaven and earth, or is it a demigod?"[90]

The first great Church Council took up the matter. Emperor Constantine and 318
bishops, many still bearing the scars of Roman persecution but now enjoying

imperial patronage, gathered in Nicea in 325 CE to settle the issue.[91] Saint Nicholas, bishop of Myra, who became the beloved Santa Claus, was present.[92] Jesus was declared to be "God of God, Light of Light, very God of very God; begotten not made, being of one substance [*homoousios*] with the father."[93] Apparently Constantine himself suggested the word *homoousios*, "used to indicate that the Son was 'consubstantial' with the father ... and implied no division or separation of the Son from the Father."[94]

With the council's pronouncement of the consubstantiality of Father and Son and assigning a special date for Christ's Nativity, the popular notion that Jesus was a human exalted by God and adopted as the Son of God at his baptism was crushed. A high Christology won the day. The Son is God not simply by an indwelling of the Spirit of God, but because of his own essential divinity, Christ is neither inferior nor subordinate to God the Father. Jekels makes this conclusion:

> In my view the introduction of the festival of Christ's nativity indicates a grow-
> ing tendency to regard the son as wholly co-equal with the Father ... this is the
> fundamental dogma implied in the inauguration of the Christmas feast.[95]

The prescribed annual Christmas Scriptures support the contention that the Son (Christ) is co-regent with the Father (God). In grand poetry, John 1:2–3 declares: "He was in the beginning with God. All things came into being through him, and without him not one thing came into being." Luke reports that at the Annunciation, the angel Gabriel says to Mary of the child she will bear: "Of his kingdom there shall be no end" (1:33b). In Matthew's version (2:1–4) of the Nativity, the holy child is born a king, is worshipped by kings, and once grown claims: "The Father and I are one" (John 10:30).

It is not easy for us to conceive from our secular-world bleachers, but this doctrinal debate was fiercely engaged and decidedly charged. As in our political protests of today, affect flooded over and slogans became battle cries. "We read, for instance, that in the streets of Alexandria and Constantinople heads were broken over the formula of the *homoousia*."[96] Why would the consubstantiality of Father and Son have been so important to the Christian populace of the fourth century? What was the large-scale, heartfelt—albeit unconscious—need to have the Son be coequal to the Father? According to Jekels, it has to do with freeing Christians from intense feelings of sin and guilt. The connection between the ascendancy of the Son with the release from moral blame becomes apparent when we turn to the foundational Freudian concept of the superego.

The superego functions much like God the Father does for Christians. Little children need, admire, and fear their parents. Eventually, they identify with them and introject their standards into a powerful psychic dynamic that Freud called the superego. This internal process continues to enlarge by incorporating the principles and prohibitions of important authority figures in one's life. This superego has two aspects: The ego ideal and the conscience. The ego ideal is a positive force that encourages us to behave in certain ways. It whispers—"You ought to be like this," and encourages—"You should do that!" The conscience has a negative cast. It warns—"You may not be like this," and thunders—"You shouldn't do that."

This moral organ of the personality carries enormous clout as it judges with unweary vigilance the actions and even the thoughts of the ego. Freud explains: "As the child was once under compulsion to obey its parents, so the ego submits to the categorical imperatives of its super-ego."[97] Like parents, the superego embodies power and enforces its standards by physical and psychological rewards or punishments. When one behaves correctly, refraining from the prohibited and engaging the prescribed, the ego is rewarded by physical feelings of well-being and psychological feelings of pride. But when one crosses the superego, there is punishment. Physically, one may get sick, injure themselves, or lose something. Psychologically, one is besieged with anxiety, shame, or feelings of inferiority. Freud wrote: "The tension between the demands of the conscience and the actual performance of the ego is experienced as a sense of guilt."[98] In some cases, the superego becomes extraordinarily harsh and punishing, leading to severe depression.[99] Jekels writes:

> It can be no wonder that the super-ego, derived from such sources as these, is invariably felt by the ego to be a vastly superior institution whose authority and rules are absolute, and which exercises over the ego itself a perpetual supervision, criticism and censorship.[100]

Psychologically, the superego calls the ego to account. Theologically, it is God who (in Christianity) sets the boundaries and judges violations. On behalf of God the Father, the Church engaged in stifling moral oppression and punishment.[101] Early Christians were subjected to exacting standards of behavior, and transgressions required embarrassing and self-abasing *exomologesis*—public confession and public penance. James Dallen describes the rigorous and humiliating gauntlet:

> *Exomologesis* went beyond inner feeling and verbal statement. Internal conversion was presupposed, at least to the extent of wanting to be converted, but a holistic view of conversion required that it be shown more through deeds than words in order to gauge its sincerity and depth. Wearing penitential garb, the sinner begged for pardon and peace through the community's intercession. Seeking the Church's prayer, they knelt in sackcloth and ashes at the entrance to the place of assembly. Each Sunday at the time of worship they approached those who were gathered and plead for recognition as penitents and eventual reconciliation to the Church.[102]

In the first centuries, reconciliation for grave offenses was not repeatable. Two strikes and you were out—of the church! Ambrose (340–397) wrote: "As one baptism, so one penance."[103] Tertullian (ca. 160–225) had said the same thing and called the major sins—idolatry, fornication, and shedding blood—"irremissible."[104] Likewise, in the third century, moral puritans (Montanists) went over the edge denying "the Church's ability to forgive the gravest sins."[105] Even among the moderates, "a mood of condescension gave aid to the fallen but then often regarded the one-time penitent as a second-class citizen of the Church."[106]

Forgiveness was a marathon. During the third and fourth centuries, penitents were divided into four classes:

> (The) "weepers," who were in the first or lowest stage of penance, and whose station was outside the door of the church. The other three were within the building. The "hearers," were placed in the vestibule; they were dismissed after the lesson and sermon and before the Eucharist. The "kneelers," were stationed further forward, yet in the rear of the congregation. When others stood during prayer these were required to kneel. They came to church clothed in sackcloth and with ashes on their heads. Finally, the "co-standers," were mingled with the congregation although they were not yet permitted to communicate. [107]

God the Father's parallels to the superego are unmistakable. In fact, in Freudian circles the connection between God and human fathers is taken for granted:

> Psycho-analysis has made us familiar with the intimate connection between the father-complex and belief in God; it has been shown us that a personal God is, psychologically, nothing other than an exalted father.[108]

Especially in the early centuries of Christianity, and for many even to this day, God the Father was experienced as a divine superego punishing the rebellious with guilt and fear of hell. This explains why people were so passionate about the theological debate at Nicea. That God the Father and God the Son were *homoousia* and consubstantial would have an important psychological affect. This is Jekels's penultimate point.

> So, we arrive at the final survey of the main problem which we are considering. The members of the Christian congregation labored under a sense of guilt which the zeal of the still relatively young Church had fostered till it was very highly developed. In their unconscious minds, where they were identified with the Son Jesus, they seized upon the true tendency of the theological controversy. Undeceived by all the formulas with their attempts at compromise and by all the half-statements of the protagonists they penetrated to the true heart of the matter. For what it really amounted to was nothing less than an attempt to dethrone God, the collective Super-Ego, with which the super-ego of the individual had such close relations.[109]

From Jekels's point of view, after Nicea and the yearly celebration of Nativity, there is a more gracious sheriff in town, at least one commensurate in power to the superego-bound father. Anyone who reads a book, sees a movie, or watches a play naturally identifies with the protagonist. So, as each Christian unconsciously identifies with the Son who is now coequal with the Father, the sting of guilt is significantly reduced. Jekels concludes:

> If the Son be co-equal with the Father, be very God, then there is neither suprem-
> acy nor subordination: all is equality, i.e. unity and harmony, and therefore there
> is no more guilt.[110]

The populace's carefree excesses and frequent indulgences are choreographed into the season, revealing the ego's victory over the superego. The defeat of, or equilib-rium with, the punitive superego at Christmas brings an oasis of peace.

This may be an explanation for something I have long pondered. At Christmastime, a living tradition draws many to assemble in concert arenas, town halls, and churches to hear Handel's "Messiah," originally conceived for Easter. The part in which all participate with high-octane vigor is the "Hallelujah Chorus," which is really about the Resurrection of Jesus. It is remarkable to watch and hear the masses, some no fans of religion, sing unrestrained and repeatedly: "And he shall reign for ever and ever. King of Kings and Lords of Lords, Hallelujah, Hallelujah, Hallelujah."[111] (Revelations 11:15, 17:14). If Jekels is correct, a good part of this full-throated gusto is from their unconscious celebration that Jesus is equal to the Father, that we are equal to our father (parents), that we are equal to our superego.

But, the reprieve is never absolute.

> Thus, when she ordained the celebration of Christ's nativity, the Church ful-
> filled the wish of the people, yet only half fulfilled it, for God the Father still
> remained enthroned.[112]

In other words, while laxity and merriment predominate, "you better be good, I'm telling you why" lingers round the corner.

Notes

1 C.G. Jung, "Psychology and Literature" (1950), in *The Spirit in Man, Art, and Literature* 15, (Princeton University Press, 1975), 80.
2 Wayne G. Rollins, "Lecture Psychologique" (unpublished manuscript, 2005), 11.
3 Sigmund Freud and Oskar Pfister, *Psychoanalysis and Faith: The Letters of Sigmund Freud and Oskar Pfister* (Basic Books, 1963), 63, 103; Sigmund Freud, *A Religious Experience* (1928), 21 (Hogarth Press, 1961), 171.
4 Sigmund Freud, *The Future of an Illusion* (1927), 21 (Hogarth Press, 1961), 42, 30–31, 44, 43.
5 Sigmund Freud, *Civilization and Its Discontents* (1930), 21 (Hogarth Press, 1961), 81.
6 Sigmund Freud, *The Psychopathology of Everyday Life* (1901), 6 (Hogarth Press, 1960), 259.
7 Sigmund Freud, *Obsessive Actions and Religious Practices* (1907), 9 (Hogarth Press, 1959), 117–127.

8 Sigmund Freud, *Totem and Taboo and Other Works* (1913), 13 (Hogarth Press, 1975).

9 Freud, *The Future of an Illusion*, 43.

10 Freud, *Civilization and Its Discontents*, 74.

11 Edwin R. Wallace, *Freud and Anthropology: A History and Reappraisal* (International Universities Press, 1983), 271–280.

12 Edwin R. Wallace, "Freud and Religion: A History and Reappraisal," in *The Psychoanalytic Study of Society* 10, ed. Werner Muensterberger (Lawrence Erlbaum Associates, 1984), 150.

13 Freud, *Psychoanalysis and Faith*, 126.

14 C.G. Jung, *Memories, Dreams, Reflections*, ed. Aniela Jaffé (Vintage Books, 1963), 150.

15 Jung, *Memories, Dreams, Reflections*, 150–151.

16 In a letter to Pfister on November 25, 1934, Freud comments: "That you should be such a convinced analyst and at the same time a clerical gentleman is one of the contradictions that make life so interesting." Freud, *Psychoanalysis and Faith*, 142, 106–107.

17 Freud, *Psychoanalysis and Faith*, 115–116. This was Jung's observation as well: "Freud's attitude towards the spirit seemed to me highly questionable. Wherever, in a person or in a work of art, an expression of spirituality (in the intellectual, not the supernatural sense) came to light, he suspected it, and insinuated that it was repressed sexuality," 147.

18 Sigmund Freud, *The Future Prospects of Psycho-Analytic Therapy* (1910), 11, 140.

19 Sigmund Freud, *Group Psychology and the Analysis of the Ego* (Hogarth Press, 1921), 140.

20 Sigmund Freud, "Religious Origins" (1919), 5 (Hogarth Press, 1957), 94.

21 Sigmund Freud, "Formulations Regarding the Two Principles of Mental Functioning" (1911), 4 (Hogarth Press: 1957), 18.

22 This is the bold assessment of James Strachey, editor of *The Complete Psychological Work of Sigmund Freud*. Sigmund Freud, "From the History of an Infantile Neurosis" (1918), in *An Infantile Neurosis and Other Works*, 17 (Hogarth Press, 1955), 3.

23 Sergius Pankejeff, *The Wolf-Man by the Wolf-Man: The Double Story of Freud's Most Famous Case*, ed. Muriel Gardiner (Basic Books, 1971), 4.

24 Freud, "From the History of an Infantile Neurosis," 7–8.

25 Freud, "From the History of an Infantile Neurosis," 36.

26 Freud, "From the History of an Infantile Neurosis," 4.

27 Freud, "From the History of an Infantile Neurosis," 15.

28 Freud, "From the History of an Infantile Neurosis," 33.

29 Freud, "From the History of an Infantile Neurosis," 33.

30 Freud, "From the History of an Infantile Neurosis," 29.

31 Freud, "From the History of an Infantile Neurosis," 30.

32 Freud, "From the History of an Infantile Neurosis," 34.

33 Freud, "From the History of an Infantile Neurosis," 35.

34 Freud, "From the History of an Infantile Neurosis," 15.

35 Freud, "From the History of an Infantile Neurosis," 36.

36 Freud, "From the History of an Infantile Neurosis," 43.

37 Freud, "From the History of an Infantile Neurosis," 43.

38 Freud, "From the History of an Infantile Neurosis," 33.

39 Freud, "From the History of an Infantile Neurosis," 34, 43.

40 Freud, "From the History of an Infantile Neurosis," 35, 44.

41 Freud, "From the History of an Infantile Neurosis," 43.

42 Freud, "From the History of an Infantile Neurosis," 37. Later on Freud adds: "I have already hinted at an earlier point in my story [p. 38] that one portion of the content of

the primal scene has been kept back. I am now in a position to produce this missing portion. The child finally interrupted his parent's intercourse by passing a stool, which gave him an excuse for screaming," 80.

43   Freud, "From the History of an Infantile Neurosis," 43.

44   Karin Obholzer, *The Wolf-Man: Conversations with Freud's Patient—Sixty Years Later.*, trans. Michael Shaw, (Continuum, 1982), 36.

45   Freud, "From the History of an Infantile Neurosis," 5.

46   Freud, "From the History of an Infantile Neurosis," 9, 7.

47   Freud, "From the History of an Infantile Neurosis," 48, see also 53, 97.

48   Freud, "From the History of an Infantile Neurosis," 35. Freud says, "There is no danger at all in communicating constructions of this kind [castration complex] to the person under analysis; they never do any damage to the analysis if they are mistaken." But Freud does point out that he utilized the Wolf-Man's strong "attachment to myself" (transference), 11, 19. Suggestion then takes on a particular potency. And despite that: "It required a long education to induce him [the Wolf-Man] to take an independent share in the work," 11.

49   Barry Magid, "Self Psychology Meets the Wolf Man," in *Freud's Case Studies: Self-Psychological Perspectives*, ed. Barry Magid (Analytic Press, 1993), 162.

50   Interestingly, the index for Vol. 17 of the *Complete Psychological Works of Freud*, which includes "From the History of an Infantile Neurosis," does not reference Christmas. What kind of conscious or unconscious censorship is that?

51   Ernest Jones, "The Significance of Christmas," in *Essays in Applied Psycho-Analysis* (Hogarth Press, 1951), 212.

52   Jones, "The Significance of Christmas," 215.

53   Jones, "The Significance of Christmas," 218.

54   Jones, "The Significance of Christmas," 224.

55   Jones, "The Significance of Christmas," 223.

56   Jones, "The Significance of Christmas," 223.

57   Jule Eisenbud, "Negative Reactions to Christmas," *The Psychoanalytic Quarterly* 10, (1941), 639.

58   Eisenbud, "Negative Reactions to Christmas," 639.

59   Clement Miles, *Christmas in Ritual and Tradition, Christian and Pagan,* (T. Fisher Unwin, 1912), 169.

60   Reverend Theodore Ledyard Cuyler, temperance writer of the mid-19th century, in his essay, "A Merry Christmas to You," found in *Christmas in Prose and Verse: Its Origin, Celebration and Significance*, ed. Allison Putala (Platinum, 2006) 142.

61   Eisenbud, "Negative Reactions to Christmas," 639.

62   Eisenbud, "Negative Reactions to Christmas," 645.

63   Eisenbud, "Negative Reactions to Christmas," 642.

64   Richard Sterba, "On Christmas," *The Psychoanalytic Quarterly* 13 (1944), 79–80.

65   Sterba, "On Christmas," 80.

66   Florence J. Levy, "On the Significance of Christmas for the 'Wolf Man'," *Psychoanalytic Review* 55, no. 4 (1989), 616. In Italy, the gift bringer is "traditionally the witchy woman figure called Befana, a corruption of Epiphania." See also William Sansom, *A Book of Christmas* (McGraw Hill, 1968), 106.

67   Sterba, "On Christmas," 80–81.

68   Sterba, "On Christmas," 83.

69   L. Bryce Boyer, "Christmas Neurosis," *Journal of the American Psychoanalytic Association* 3, no. 3 (1955).

70   L. Bryce Boyer, "Christmas 'Neurosis' Reconsidered," in *Depressive States and Their Treatment*, ed. V.D. Volkan (Jason Aronson, 1985), 297–316.

71   Boyer, "Christmas 'Neurosis' Reconsidered," 467.

72   Boyer, "Christmas 'Neurosis' Reconsidered," 469.

73 We must for the moment address the issue of "penis envy" that both Eisenbud and Boyer note in their "Christmas cases." We cannot ignore the fact that the Christ Child in the manger is a boy. This does give a particular psychological hue to the holiday. The one who is most treasured, by God and populace, is male.
74 Boyer, "Christmas Neurosis," 470.
75 Boyer, "Christmas Neurosis," 471.
76 Vamik D. Volkan and Gabriele Ast, *Siblings in the Unconscious and Psychopathology* (International Universities Press, 1997), 69.
77 Volkan and Ast, *Siblings in the Unconscious and Psychopathology*, 71.
78 Volkan and Ast, *Siblings in the Unconscious and Psychopathology*, 83–84.
79 Boyer, "Christmas Neurosis," 484.
80 Boyer, "Christmas Neurosis."
81 Ludwig Jekels, "The Psychology of the Festival of Christmas." First published in English in *The International Journal of Psycho-analysis* 17, I (1936).
82 Sigmund Freud, *Totem and Taboo*. Here Freud suggests that religions are a manifestation of an attempt to resolve the Oedipus complex.
83 Jekels, "The Psychology of the Festival of Christmas," 144.
84 Jekels, "The Psychology of the Festival of Christmas," 145.
85 Jekels, "The Psychology of the Festival of Christmas," 146.
86 Jekels, "The Psychology of the Festival of Christmas," 147.
87 Jekels, "The Psychology of the Festival of Christmas," 151.
88 J.W.C. Wand, *The Four Great Heresies* (A.R. Mowbray, 1967), 38–62.
89 A tavern song promoted Arius's view:
    "Arius of Alexander, I'm the talk of the town,
    Friend of the saints, elect of heaven, filled with learning and renown;
    If you want the Logos doctrine, I can serve it hot and hot;
    God begat him and before he was begotten, He was not."
90 Jaroslav Pelikan, *Jesus through the Centuries: His Place in the History of Culture* (Yale University Press, 1985), 52. The scholar noted is Adolf von Harnack, *Grundriss der Dogmengeschichte*, 4th ed. (J.C.B. Mohr, 1905), 192.
91 Wand, *The Four Great Heresies*, 49.
92 Jock Elliot, *Inventing Christmas: How Our Holiday Came to Be* (Abrams, 2001), 34.
93 James W. Lenhart, *Pilgrim Hymnal*, 512.
94 Robert M. Grant, *Augustus to Constantine: The Emergence of Christianity in the Roman World* (Barnes & Noble Books, 1970), 241.
95 Jekels, "The Psychology of the Festival of Christmas," 152.
96 Jekels, "The Psychology of the Festival of Christmas," 154. It is fascinating to note that Erich Fromm understands the passion and the reason for it from a very different perspective in *The Dogma of Christ and other Essays on Religion, Psychology and Culture* (Holt, Rinehart and Winston, 1963). He observes that Christ's first followers were the outcasts and poor. They liked the adoptionist theory because Jesus, a poor carpenter, was thereby made co-regent with God and would overturn the established order. However, in the third century and onward, Christianity became mainstream, and those in political power exercised theological sway. From Fromm's perspective, this change of theology meant that Jesus was God from the beginning; therefore, there was no challenge to God and his favored position. "The decisive element was the change from the idea of man becoming God to that of God becoming man. Then the poor were without hope. There was no challenge to the Father. Therefore, the social status quo could remain and the masses be integrated into the absolutist system of the Roman Empire," 62.
97 Sigmund Freud, *The Ego and the Id* (1923), (Norton Library, 1960), 38.
98 Freud, *The Ego and the Id*, 27.

 99 Freud, *The Ego and the Id*, 42.
100 Jekels, "The Psychology of the Festival of Christmas," 155.
101 This humiliation, and the possible legal repercussions of such public declarations, had penitents running to monks to receive a private confession. The church opposed this practice, but the people demanded it. James Dallen, *The Reconciling Community: The Rite of Penance*, Vol. 3 (Liturgical Press, 1974), 100–20.
102 Dallen, *The Reconciling Community*, 33.
103 John T. McNeill and Helena M. Gamer, "Penance in the Ancient Church," in *Medieval Handbooks of Penance* (Columbia University Press, 1990), 14.
104 McNeill and Gamer, "Penance in the Ancient Church," 5. *De pudicitia* iii. The Apostolic Decree of Acts 15:29 was the basis for the list.
105 Dallen, *The Reconciling Community*, 31.
106 Dallen, *The Reconciling Community*, 51, 59. The Synod of Elvira (dated between 295 and 314) illustrates the severe stance the ecclesiastical institution took toward sin and repentance.
107 McNeill and Gamer, "Penance in the Ancient Church."
108 Sigmund Freud, *Leonardo Da Vinci and Memory of His Childhood* (1910), 11 (Hogarth Press, 1960), 123.
109 Jekels, "The Psychology of the Festival of Christmas," 156.
110 Jekels, "The Psychology of the Festival of Christmas," 157
111 G.F. Handel, *The Messiah* (1741) (G. Schirmer, 1912), viii.
112 Jekels, 157.

Chapter 6

Christmas and Mirroring
Kohut

In the play *The Long Christmas Dinner*, Genevieve is planning a distant trip but declares to her family, "I promise I will be back for Christmas. I wouldn't miss that."[1] Christmas and home are bound fast. John Killinger, professor of religion and culture, cites a survey's unsurprising finding that "Christmas is the one time of year when people most want to be home. It leads birthdays by three to one."[2] Similar studies from the United Kingdom concur.

> In England, Christmas Day is normally spent at home, with the family: and it is regarded as a celebration of the family and its continuity. ... The evidence from a sample survey in the past two decades is consistent and unequivocal. Asked in December 1969 with whom they would spend Christmas, 86 per cent of an adult British sample responded that they would spend it with their family. ... Twenty years later, the picture was very similar.[3]

Come late December, multitudes of humans become like spawning salmon, overcoming every obstacle to return to the family circle. The nostalgic "I'll Be Home for Christmas" is both a pledge and a fight song. This shared longing for home is revealed in some of the most touching moments of our cultural lore: No longer in Kansas, Dorothy tearfully acknowledges "There's no place like home"; Simon and Garfunkel plaintively harmonize their wish to be homeward bound; around the evening fire, campers sing "I'm five hundred miles away from home"; even E.T. is desperate to "phone home." Christmas is the epicenter of this collective yearning. Yet, how is it that Jesus' Nativity and our own hearth have become wedded?

This relationship is so taken for granted that we miss its absurdity. Scripture offers no such connection but rather a categorical contradiction. Jesus is born 90 miles from home. Mary labors on a donkey. With no room at the inn, Jesus is delivered in a rude barn with cow and ox as extended family. Swords at their back, the holy family is pushed 300 more miles from home. They must remain until King Herod dies. Jesus is a refugee.

So how did Christmas become inextricably linked to the stability, security, and warmth of our idealized home? That we fail to notice this blatant inconsistency points to a connection that lives inwardly, at a deep level, in the unconscious.

DOI: 10.4324/9781003568629-7

The pioneering theories of psychoanalyst Heinz Kohut, MD (1913–1981) help us understand how this coupling makes sense psychologically.

The Theory of Self Psychology

Kohut's psychoanalytic credentials are impeccable: A medical degree from the University of Vienna, professorships in neurology and psychiatry at the University of Chicago, and a practice and teaching of psychoanalysis so well recognized that he was elected president of the American Psychoanalytic Association, vice president of the International Psychoanalytical Association, and vice president of the Sigmund Freud Archives.[4]

Kohut, however, was not a standard-bearer of the old. His psychoanalytic pedigree enabled him to be an effective evolutionary, advancing the stalled psychoanalytic tradition. Psychoanalyst Arnold Goldberg captured this beautifully in his obituary for Kohut:

> Kohut urged traditional psychoanalysis from its preoccupation with sexual and aggressive drives along with the centrality of the Oedipus complex to a more open inquiry of the self, its goals and ambitions, and its interactions with others. Kohut's theme was the study of the self, and his writings came together into a separate area of psychoanalysis called self psychology.[5]

In the mid-1980s, 138 leading American psychiatrists responded to a survey asking for the most important publications in their field. Only 13 books and one journal article were judged essential. Of those highly prized psychological pearls, Kohut alone was the author of two: *The Analysis of the Self* (1971) and *The Restoration of the Self* (1977).[6]

For Kohut, more crucial than an analyst's well-timed interpretation was the "analyst's creation of a new kind of *experience* [italics added] for the patient within the transference relationship."[7] Through a potent partnership—conscious and unconscious—with the analyst, analysands benefit from "a corrective emotional experience" and learn what is "possible for them in human relationships."[8]

What are the conceptual kernels of Self Psychology? Foundational is the notion that "the self is the center of the individual's psychological universe," "cohesive in space and enduring in time, which is the center of initiative and a recipient of impressions."[9] Kohut's followers J.D. Lichtenberg and Ernest Wolf describe the Self as "being a more or less independent, more or less interdependent center for initiating, organizing, and integrating motivation and experience."[10] Michael Basch, one of Kohut's first disciples, understands the Self as "the uniqueness that separates the experiences of an individual from those of all others while at the same time conferring a sense of cohesion and continuity on the disparate experiences of that individual."[11]

Kohut believed that it is in the interplay between an infant's innate potentials and the responsiveness of his or her caretakers that the child's Self develops. The formation of this cohesive and vital Self requires consistent empathetic responses from the parents.[12] Kohut describes empathy as "vicarious introspection" and defines it as "the capacity to think and feel oneself into the inner life of another person."[13] He goes on to say: "Empathy, the accepting, confirming, and understanding human echo evoked by the Self, is a psychological nutriment without which human life as we know and cherish it could not be sustained."[14]

Fortunately, "we are born preadapted to respond to an empathically sensitive family life that reliably provides soothing, vitalizing, and need-fulfilling experiences."[15] Kohut determined that the core Self encompasses two poles.[16] The healthy Self develops as this bipartite structure is built. The first constituent of this nuclear Self is a grandiose-exhibitionistic aspect: "The terms 'grandiose' and 'exhibitionistic' refer to a broad spectrum of phenomena, ranging from the child's solipsistic world view and his undisguised pleasure in being admired."[17]

Young children are naturally self-centered. From their perspective, they are the sun around which people orbit. In their natural state, children want to be noticed and validated as wonderful and desirable. This sounds very much like L. Bryce Boyer's description of Mrs. W. as a child: "Her basic wish was to be ... a child so beautiful that the whole world would love her."[18] In a telling episode of the popular television show *The Simpsons*, Bart is being abjectly ignored—an impossible psychological reality for him to bear. In crisis, he responds by running out naked in front of everyone, yelling "Look at me! Look at me!" Mission accomplished. Required attention received. From Kohut's point of view, this aboriginal self-indulgent need of the child should not be broken, as often is suggested by stern pedagogues,[19] but rather acknowledged and welcomed. The child feels a grandiose, exhibitionist Self affirmed when seen and appreciated. Parents and other important people in the child's life convey this truth in what Kohut calls *mirroring*: "to be looked upon with joy and basic approval by a delighted parental selfobject."[20]

Because the concept of selfobject is so central to Kohut's theory, we pause to understand it. *Selfobject* is a technical word that belies the very intensity of human relationship it denotes. Compared with Martin Buber's notion of a synergetic "I/Thou relationship," the term *selfobject* seems cold, hard, and distant.[21] To the contrary, selfobject describes an exceptionally intimate and essential relationship. As Maria T. Miliora explains: "Selfobjects refer to our subjective experience of people who are important to us, for example, parents, spouses and close friends."[22] Selfobjects "are themselves experienced as part of the self" and meet the needs of the Self, particularly by "shoring" it up.[23] A selfobject is "experienced by the person as performing functions that are normally performed by himself."[24] Analogous to a mother breastfeeding in the biological realm, selfobjects provide fundamentally necessary sustenance in the psychological domain.

Mirroring is essential for the psychological health of children because it nurtures their natural grandiose fantasies and satisfies their exhibitionist requirements. Children look to find joy on their parents' faces, a response that positively impacts the affective lives of children: Adored children feel adorable. For this result, mirroring must be empathetic, genuine, and developmentally appropriate.[25] Without this positive acknowledgment, a child can feel invisible. Eventually, external suppliers of self-esteem and their repetitive message—"you are a pleasure and joy to me, capable and appealing"—become introjected into the psyche of the child.

Inevitably, for all children, it is only a matter of time before a parent's attentions are imperfect or delayed. If these experiences are "optimal frustrations"—that is, nontraumatic but tolerable empathetic failures of a child's selfobjects—their psychic organization deals with the disturbance of narcissistic equilibrium by gradually incorporating the necessary dynamics of the selfobject. In withdrawing some expectations from a selfobject, a child's Self gains some particle of inner structure that will now do for her functions that previously only the selfobject could. Kohut calls this process "transmuting internalization."[26] In regard to mirroring, transmuting internalization results in the creation of a reservoir of self-esteem and ambition.[27] When a child's natural grandiosity and exhibitionism are met with approval, then his emotional gas tank is filled with good feelings about himself. He can enjoy life. If this need for joyful mirroring is routinely denied or shamed, a child's development of self-structures can be sabotaged.

This brings us to the second selfneed in Kohut's theory. To form a strong core, a child also requires a selfobject to idealize, a competent caretaker to experience as omnipotent and omniscient.[28] It is the parents' stout-hearted task to keep children thriving by effectively meeting their physical and psychological needs. This enables children to be "safe, comfortable, and calm."[29] Naturally, the helpless child will perceive a persistent and present provider to be a god and imbues them with "absolute power and perfection."[30]

Importantly, parents must be empathic enough to allow children to experience and merge with their "greatness, strength and calmness"[31]—to permit and enjoy their idealization.[32] In the center, a child feels, "You are perfect, and I am part of you."[33] Ernest Wolf, one of Kohut's first disciples, explains the idealizing selfobject experience as:

> a need to experience oneself as being part of an admired and respected selfobject other; a need for the opportunity to be accepted by, and merged into, a stable, calm, nonanxious, powerful, wise, protective other who possess qualities the subject experiences as lacking in the self.[34]

This omnipotent adult who provides, shields, and soothes; this invulnerable adult who does not fall apart under the stresses of life that would fragment a child; this omniscient adult who encourages and becomes knowledgeable about the emerging idiosyncratic interests of the child; this ideal adult who is worthy of admiration, becomes "an emotionally sustaining parent imago" in the psyche of the child.[35]

As in the mirroring developmental process, through "transmuting internalization" of the idealized selfobject, the child develops their own emotional reservoir of strength and calmness:[36]

> In a slow, well-timed process called "optimal disillusionment," the child gradually disabuses himself of his notions of parental omnipotence and omniscience,

and comes to be able to do for himself what his parent must inevitably fail to be able to do for him. He learns to comfort himself when his parents are absent. He learns to believe in his own ability when his parents have not provided him with sufficient emotional support. These capacities are borrowed from the parents by means of "transmuting internalizations"; Self structures are transformed in response to optimal (non-traumatic) frustration. Thus, as the child slowly becomes disillusioned of his parent's omnipotence, he replaces it with his own competence.[37]

These idealized parental imagos gradually become internalized so children can soothe and uplift themselves. And, just as important, children begin to exhibit admired aspects of an idealized selfobject. They identify with and hope to become like the target of their idealism. One could say, and Kohut does in his earlier works, that this is like the ego ideal of the superego.[38] We internalize the values of our ideal selfobjects and are inwardly rewarded with feelings of pride for having achieved them for ourselves.

Adequate selfobject mirroring and adequate selfobject idealization create an energetic bipolar structure.[39] A "tension arc"—of basic ambitions on one hand and basic ideals on the other—is put into operation. Kohut describes it as follows:

I am referring to the abiding flow of actual psychological activity that establishes itself between the two poles of the self, i.e. a person's pursuits toward which he is "driven" by his ambitions and "led" by his ideals.[40]

The establishment of this dynamic self structure makes possible a creative, productive, fulfilling life.[41]

In the final years of his life, Kohut added a third foundational need of the Self: Alter ego selfobjects. Though this was peeking from the margins of Kohut's earlier writings as a subset of mirroring, his final book, *How Does Analysis Cure?*, gave clarity that twinship was a foundational selfneed of its own.

The twinship/alter ego selfneed awakens after mirroring and idealizing selfneeds are in full swing. As a child becomes increasingly conscious of her autonomy and separateness, the world grows alien. At this point, the child may feel an urgency to experience an essential likeness with a selfobject, to be with someone similar and recognized as an acceptable peer. [42] When a child steps outside of home on his own for the first time, he soon finds similarly aged neighborhood children who become a cohort of play and mutual validation. A twin is someone just like us but not us; someone who shares our experiences and confirms our feelings, opinions, and values.[43] The child needs "to be surrounded by the quietly sustaining presence of alter egos."[44] With a "twin," they feel enfolded and buttressed.

In speaking about a case, Kohut wrote: "Her [Miss F.'s] self was sustained simply by the presence of someone she knew was sufficiently like her to understand her and to be understood by her."[45] Some plan to meet this need. In the 1880s, three summer-home communities were founded in Greene County, New York, within ten miles of one another. A group of artists established Onteora Park in 1887. German American industrialists in a choral group founded Elka Park in 1889. Free speech enthusiasts in 1888 founded Twilight Park "to establish a community where their particular style of interaction could be continued during the summer."[46] In each of these communities, like-minded people wanted to be together, and in so doing maturely fed their alter ego selfneed.

After their volcanic break, Jung lost Freud as a multifold selfobject and psychologically decompensated. Fortunately, as things were falling apart with Freud, Jung found the much older Théodore Flournoy to provide him with "needed support" (idealizing selfobject) and as the only person "who shared my interests in these matters" (alter ego selfobject).[47]

Humans continually seek out friendships, gravitating to peers with shared skills, visions, values, and experiences. They become "strong and cohesive as members of a group of people whom they experience as being in essence like them, doing similar work, sharing similar biases and predilections, and the like."[48] Those with whom we share common competencies and enthusiasms, enable us to know that we are like unto others, that we belong, a human among humans. In midwinter, this desire exponentially intensifies and roams large as the extravagant welcoming of the seasons manifest in the shared bonhomie of wishes for a merry Christmas.

According to Kohut, we require a milieu of these three core selfobjects to constellate a well-working Self, brimming with purpose and joie de vivre. Such a Self empowers us to pursue our ambitions and ideals as we develop our idiosyncratic gifts among those with whom we feel a natural affinity. On the other hand, those who suffered wide-ranging empathetic failures in childhood feel a key piece of themselves missing.[49] Rather than whole, they feel depleted. Self-wounded people continue to be compulsively driven to find archaic mirroring, idealizing alter ego selfobjects. Because their selfneeds are infantile, desperate, and voracious, they end up, as the saying goes, "looking for love in the all the wrong places."

This explains why certain adults must always be the center of attention, acting as if they were children. If not in the spotlight, they are depressed or enraged. Many politicians, actors, clergy, incessant talkers, and "high-maintenance" individuals fit here. Their behavior cannot be explained by the typological concept of extroversion. Rather, they are trying to make up for poor mirroring selfobjects in childhood by constantly getting others to notice and admire them. Kohut calls such people "mirror-hungry."[50]

Likewise, "ideal-hungry" personalities out of psychological necessity gravitate to people of importance. They are only fulfilled when in a tight orbit around a superior, wrapped in the coat of arms of some dominant person, or if they become a fanatic for some grand cause. These individuals attach to what they perceive as competent, beautiful, or powerful others or ideals to feel capable, attractive, and strong. Psychologically, this is the exoskeletal bulwark for those without sufficient inner strength and confidence.

For others, alter ego needs can be dominant and excessive. Some adults are compelled to roam in a pack of their peers, reminiscent of adolescent behavior.

The dynamic behind such pairings—whether drinking pals or fellow elite scientists—is equivalent. Any marriage therapist has experience with men who put their marriages in jeopardy with an inordinate need to be with their buddies. Kohut says that these alter ego-hungry individuals desperately "need a relationship with a selfobject that by conforming to the self's appearance, opinions, and values confirms the existence, the reality of the self."[51]

The good news, according to Kohut, is that the Self, impaired from the inadequate meeting of the three basic selfneeds in childhood, can be mended. In an "actuating matrix of the psychoanalytic situation," the immature or maimed Self becomes mobilized to "complete its development."[52] This is possible in the ultra-charged phenomenon of transference, where an analyst becomes in the unconscious of the patient a primary selfobject, an efficacious stand-in for a parent. Depending on which selfobject need is most prominent, one of three primary transferences will develop: A mirror transference that elicits confirming-affirming responses of the analyst; an idealizing transference that hopes to merge with the power and competence of the analyst; or an alter ego transference that "seeks a self object that will make itself available for the reassuring experience of essential likeness."[53] Kohut adroitly summarizes:

> The essential therapeutic conclusion of all my contributions to the understanding of the self and its development can be formulated as follows: it is the defect in the self that brings about and maintains a patient's selfobject (narcissistic) transference, and it is the working through of this transference which, via transmuting internalization, that is, via a wholesome psychic activity that has been thwarted in childhood, lays down the structure needed to fill the defect in the self. Indeed, I take the emergence of this process, and especially its persistent engagement, as evidence that the treatment situation has reactivated the developmental potential of the defective self.[54]

We close this section by underlining two all-important points. All of us have been, at best, scratched and dented. No child escapes nonoptimal empathetic failures, so all adults suffer self-deficits to some degree. We manifest inordinate selfneeds behavior. As Self psychiatrist Allen M. Siegel puts it: "[T]he point of [Kohut's] work is that his observations are about *people*, regardless of what treatment they seek or of whether they are in treatment at all."[55] No person escapes the requirement of some level of remedial selfobject relationship; "it is not immature and contemptible to search for them and to elicit their empathic support."[56]

The second point follows close on this line of reasoning. One of Kohut's chief tenets was that an individual's imperative for selfobjects never ends. Of this he was absolutely convinced. We may think we are independent, autonomous, and self-sufficient, but according to Kohut, this is just a comforting illusion. As Self psychologist James S. Grostein reports: "Kohut eschews the traditional notion of the increasing independence of the Self from its objects."[57] According to Kohut, the continuing sustenance of the Self by others is a universal need "from the moment of birth to the moment of death."[58]

It may become judicious, but there is no age limit to wanting our specialness mirrored back to us! At every stage and age of life, we require a supporting matrix of selfobjects.

> Self psychology holds that self-selfobject relationships form the essence of psychological life from birth to death, that a move from dependence (symbiosis) to independence (autonomy) in the psychological sphere is no more possible, let alone desirable, than a corresponding move from a life dependent on oxygen to a life independent of it in the biological sphere.[59]

This truth is apparent to anyone in caring professions. The precipitous physical decline of an elder whose spouse and friends have recently died and whose family is dispersed across the country is inevitably the result of selfobject starvation. When the selfobject milieu is shattered, self-disintegration is rapid.

Reverend Robert Randall, in his book on what Self Psychology means for the life of the parish, sums up what it means for humans in general:

> Every pastor, spouse, and parish normally needs empathetic response to retain a feeling of well-being within the self. Some ... particularly need admiration and praise; that is, we need mirroring responses from others for what we do and say in order for us to maintain our self-esteem. Some ... particularly need calming and soothing responses; that is, we need idealized figures with whose strength we can merge in order to maintain our inner security and vitality. Others of us need reassurance that we belong, that we are normal, like others; that is, we need alterego responses in order to maintain our basic sense of being human and of being accepted. These self needs are not signs of weakness, nor are they sinful. They are part of our created existence.[60]

Though selfobject needs do not dissipate with time, they undergo "maturation, development, and change":[61]

> Throughout his life a person will experience himself as a cohesive harmonious firm unit in time and space, connected with his past and pointing meaningfully into a creative-productive future [but] only as long as, at each stage in his life, he experiences certain representatives of his human surroundings as joyfully responding to him, as available to him as sources of idealized strength and calmness, as being silently present but in essence like him.[62]

The selfobjects that undergird us as we move through life include parents, committed partners, friends, social peers, professional associates, and interest groups. In Kohut's expansive understanding of selfobject, there were also "cultural selfobjects," such as "writers, artists, and political leaders."[63] He also included religious figures, which is to our point. Jesus, as described biblically or imagined theologically, is a potent selfobject for many.

Self Psychology and Christmas

What does Kohut's Self Psychology have to do with the subterranean meanings of Christmas? Very much. All three selfneeds, but most demonstrably mirroring, are in play at yuletide. Here we use, in a psychological way, Tillich's philosophical/theological method of correlation.

> It makes an analysis of the human situation out of which existential questions arise, and it demonstrates that the symbols used in the Christian message are the answers to these questions.[64]

Christmas, with its evocative storyline and absorbing customs, is a magical time when the myth of Jesus is readily experienced as the answer to all three selfobject needs. This explains, in some part, the mysterious grip the day has on so many. To keep us on track, we will focus exclusively on the compelling mirroring connection with the Nativity. The twin selfobject and idealizing selfobject aspects of Jesus as portrayed in the New Testament can be found in this book's appendix.

Christmas and the Mirroring Selfobject

Christmas evokes the strongest feelings of home through the primary selfneed of mirroring. This book began when I was standing before *The Virgin and Child* by Dieric Bouts (ca. 1415–1475) at New York's Metropolitan Museum of Art (see Figure 6.1). An intuitive flash struck me: The psychological meaning of Christmas is Mary's exquisite mirroring of Jesus and our abiding desire to have that as well. Such idyllic Christmas images—and there are so many Madonna and Child paintings that show this striking mirroring motif—stir up this deep-seated desire. The essence of Christmas hope, from a Self Psychology perspective, is the unconscious anticipation and expectation that we will be wholeheartedly reflected as Mary warmly and flawlessly takes joy in the Christ Child. Look again at Bouts's painting and note how the connection between the Madonna and Child's eyes make them almost one:

> The sense of dual unity between mother and child is perhaps nowhere more apparent than in the moment when the child sees herself in the gleam of her mother's eye, the moment when she sees herself being seen, as it were.[65]

At an art show outside Assisi, I was moved to see the painting *Sacra Famiglia*, attributed to Antonio Balestra (1666–1740). The central focus was the absolute joy on Joseph's face as he made close eye contact with his newborn child. The biblical Nativity story, as great artists elegantly visualize it, builds upon the mirroring within the Holy Family and expands it exponentially. The shepherds come and adore the

Figure 6.1 Virgin and Child, by Dieric Bouts (ca. 1415–1475). Courtesy Metropolitan Museum of Art, New York; Theodore M. Davis Collection, Bequest of Theodore M. Davis, 1915.

Christ Child. The Magi arrive and adore the Christ Child. The heavenly chorus appears and sings his praise. In the Basilica di Santa Maria Novella (ca. 1350–1470) of Florence, a pulpit relief of the Nativity even has a horse broadly smiling at the Christ Child in his manger. He is adored! All express their delight in the baby Jesus and mirror to him his grandiosity, his divinity. It is a most extravagant welcome.

Psychologically speaking, every infant is analogous to that Christ Child. Like the whole cast of Christmas characters, everyone reflexively smiles at a baby. A child born into a healthy family feels like a royal child. The spontaneous adoration and joy that parents naturally feel at the birth of their child immediately reveal this to the child.[66] The parents' faces continue to brighten at the sight of the child and thus continue to convey: You are worthy, you are special, you are wonderful, you are enjoyable, you are the center of my attention. As Professor Louise Kaplan puts it: "From the baby's point of view he is an angel baby held in the sumptuous lap of a saintly Madonna." [67]

Lillian Smith recalls the perennial Christmas morning ritual at her home in the early 1900s:

> After the excitement of the unexpected gift subsided, our father took down the Bible and opened it at the second chapter of St. Luke. Nine pairs of eyes turned toward him as we waited to hear what we had heard every Christmas of our lives. ... As he read in his deep warm voice, we followed the words, knowing them by heart. We knew, too, that *to him it was not only the story of the Christ Child but of Every Child.* [68]

To be the royal child/Child of God is a psychological necessity for every child, not just for infants, but in more mature ways for adults. Deep in our souls dwell remembrances of contented glory days, and so our unconscious naturally resonates with the Christmas story, especially as represented by the grand masters' archetypal paintings of adoration. As these hypogean memories are roused, we identify with the Christ Child who was so heartily mirrored, and wish we could return to that archaic mother/infant symbiosis. Part of the mounting joy in singing "O Come Let Us Adore Him" is the dim, deep remembrance that it once applied to us.

"Without mirroring," says theologian Donald Capps, "there can be no self; the light of the self depends on the mirroring it receives from without."[69] C.G. Jung agrees: "Only when the self mirrors itself in so many mirrors does it really exist."[70] The desire to experience the original mirroring once more is our primary nostalgia. The dormant hope of having a Madonna mother wells at Christmas. However, for those with acutely deficient mirroring, the desire is more dramatic and the hope more desperate, leading to an unconscious expectation so great that it is no wonder many find Christmas strangely melancholic.

"Second-Level" Mirroring

A fuller exposition of mirroring is now needed. In Thornton Wilder's play *Our Town*, Emily (who has died) is given the opportunity to go back and live one day again. She chooses a happy one, her 12th birthday. But Emily becomes distressed because her mother, occupied by cooking breakfast, doesn't look at her. To Emily, from the vantage point of death, every gesture and word is something to be savored. To her mother, it's just another day. With a pressing single-mindedness, Emily says: "Oh Mama, just look at me as if you really saw me."[71] That's our unconscious Christmas hope.

Primary mirroring attests to an infant's stardom and global desirability. To be empathetic, mirroring must keep pace developmentally and take a step up. Emily's longing for her mother's attentive mirroring is now more sweeping. Here Emily wants to be appreciated for the individual she has become, for her mother to joyfully reflect her singularity and complexity. We call this "second-level mirroring."

Early on, children have no capacity to mirror themselves and are totally dependent upon caregivers to reflect their feelings, experiences, etc. Ideally, the mother and father are there to reflect their joys, struggles, and interests. They say, "I see you and I will be your mirror, so that you may discover who you are."[72] Mirroring back what the child is feeling, seeing, and doing gives her a firm trust in what is going on in her own inner life.

Alexander Newman, a chronicler of D.W. Winnicott, writes: "So here we are at the heart of it. What does the baby see when he or she looks at the mother's face?"[73] What the baby sees is himself. "In other words, the mother is looking at the baby and what she looks like is related to what she sees there."[74] Or as psychoanalyst Thomas Wolman put it: "Hence, when the baby looks into the mother's face, what he sees is himself, or rather his emotional effect on the mother reflected in her face."[75] That's why Kenneth Wright reports in his book *Vision and Separation* that the face of a child's mother (primary caretaker) is a "guiding light," "the cherished center of his world," and "the most loved object in the child's universe."[76]

We can make sense of our immediate resonance with Bouts's painting when we realize that this mirroring is originally accomplished through eye-to-eye contact. Kohut writes: "The most significant relevant basic interactions between mother and child lie usually in the visual area: the child's bodily display is responded to by the gleam in the mother's eye."[77]

Tiffany Field, a researcher in infant development, conducted an experiment as to how babies only 36 hours old respond to a woman model's facial expression. She found that when the woman looked happy, the baby made a joyful face. When the model looked sad, the baby looked sad; when the model expressed astonishment, so did the baby (see Figure 6.2).[78] Self psychologist Michael Basch did not believe this mere "imitation." Rather, he understood it through Daniel Stern's notion of "affect attunement."[79]

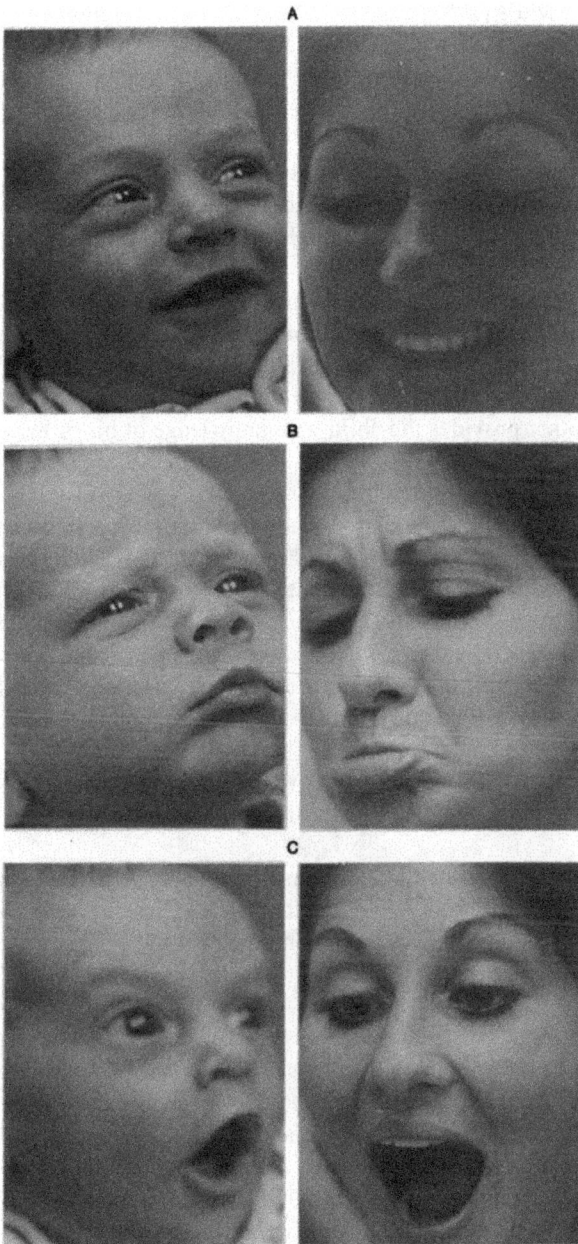

Figure 6.2 Images from Tiffany Field's study showing a model's happy, sad, and surprised expressions and an infant's corresponding expressions. From Tiffany M. Field et al., "Discrimination and Imitation of Facial Expression by Neonates," *Science* 218, 179-181 (1982). DOI: 10.1126/science.7123230. Reprinted with permission from AAAS.

As Tiffany Field's [1985] experiments have shown, the mother's facial expression calls forth in the baby's face the same expression, which is accompanied by bodily sensations associated with that particular affect—joy, anger, interest, and so on. In this way the baby experiences and "knows" what mother is feeling."[80]

Via "affect attunement," the infants were actually sharing the adult's inner affect state. As Kohut says, "the child experiences the feeling states of the self-object ... as if they were his own."[81] Or as Arnold H. Modell puts it:

Mirroring occurs through the medium of affective communication between mother and child. This communication must be authentic, for the child's cohesive sense of self is forged through the affective bond that is formed when the mother gazes at the child's face, reflecting the child's affects. In this fashion, the mother provides the child with knowledge of his or her own affective state.[82]

One follower of Winnicott writes: "What a child or baby will see when he looks in the mirror will have been determined by what he saw when he gazed into his mother's face."[83] If the child is happy but sees sorrow on the mother figure's face, he cannot help but be confused. *Why is she seeing me like that?* If parents are preoccupied or consumed by their own moods and anxieties, they become very faulty mirrors indeed. Accurate mirroring is essential for young children because, if given wrong signals, they will be quick to discount their own feelings and reorient them to reactions of the caretaker.

Taking exactly this tack, Alice Miller writes persuasively about how narcissistic parents can deform the emotional lives of their children.

But a mother who, as a child, was herself not taken seriously by her mother as the person she really was will crave the respect from her child as a substitute; and she will try to get it by training him to give it to her.[84]

She continues:

What happens if the mother not only is unable to take over the narcissistic functions for her child but also, as very often happens, is herself in need of narcissistic supplies? Quite unconsciously, and despite her own good intentions, the mother then tries to assuage her own narcissistic needs through her child, that is, she cathects him narcissistically. This does not rule out strong affection. On the contrary, the mother often loves her child as her selfobject, passionately, but not in the way he needs to be loved.[85]

In other words, although children need a mother to be the mirroring selfobject for them, the mother uses them to be *her* mirroring selfobject. How then can children know who they are? Because children are completely dependent upon parents for physical existence (food, water, warmth) and psychological existence (mirroring and idealization), their developing Self "will muster all his resources ... like a small plant that turns toward the sun in order to survive."[86]

In such a case, children learn not about who they are, but what their mother needs. And they will supply it; they have no other option if they want to live. Winnicott theorizes that the not "good-enough mother" repeatedly misses gestures rising from a child's true Self but instead substitutes her own gestures. This leads to the development of a false Self in the infant, a compliant Self that takes precedence over the genuine Self impulses of the child.[87] For Kohut, such severe mirroring deprivation prevents the development of a cohesive Self so that one becomes a mirror-hungry personality prone to depression and/or outbursts of rage.[88]

Case in Point: Mirroring Selfobject Damage and Repair

In Freud's case of the Wolf-Man, as well as in such literary works as Mary Shelley's *Frankenstein* and Eugene O'Neill's *A Long Day's Journey Into Night*, we see the theory of Self Psychology in clear operation.

The Wolf-Man Revisited

With the concepts of Self Psychology in hand, we turn again to Sergei Pankejeff, the Wolf-Man. A number of facts about his early childhood lead us to hypothesize that—rather than Freud's speculation that the Wolf-Man witnessed the primal scene of his parents when he was an infant—his psychic distress and unrest resulted from the inadequate quantity and inferior quality of mirroring from his mother and father. His "Recollections of my Childhood," from the memoir he wrote at 83, reveal substantial evidence to suggest a home atmosphere lacking in good mirroring. He recalls these experiences all happening before the age of five.

1. According to his nurse, when he was only a few months old, he suffered pneumonia that doctors believed terminal. He also had severe attacks of malaria. Such illnesses make mirroring difficult for children to receive.
2. As a child of parents with substantial wealth, Wolf-Man was attended by a nurse (Nanya), governesses, tutors, and servants.[89] Contact with his parents was minimized, at best, with their mirroring ability highly diluted.
3. "As our parents were often away, my sister and I were left mostly under the supervision of strangers, and even when our parents were home we had little contact with them."[90] Absent parents cannot mirror.
4. "From hearsay I know that I had, as an infant, Titian red hair. After my first haircut, however, my hair turned dark brown, something my mother deeply regretted. She kept a little lock of the cut-off Titian-red hair, as a sort of 'relic,' her entire life."[91] Her "deep regret" at her son's hair changing from the unusual red to common brown may indicate a narcissistic mother incapable of healthy mirroring, or at least disappointment in the older child's appearance.

5. When the Wolf-Man's parents traveled abroad, his maternal grandmother supervised the two nurses for him and his sister, Anna. He writes "unfortunately [she] did not really assume this responsibility."[92] This led to some emotional abuse and indicates a family system where children were not a priority.

6. "Since my mother, as a young woman, was so concerned about her health, she did not have much time left for us."[93] Preoccupied with her own problems, she could not mirror her children.

7. "But if my sister or I was ill, she became an exemplary nurse. She stayed with us almost all the time and saw to it that our temperature was taken regularly and our medicine given us at the right time. I can remember that as a child I sometimes wished I would be sick, to be able to enjoy my mother's being with me and looking after me."[94] Here is the clear connection that to be sick is to get enjoyable attention from a mother who is not normally available.

8. Likewise, the father probably lacked a capacity for adequate mirroring. The Wolf-Man was given a small accordion when he was four. He wrote, "I was literally in love with it." In the evenings he loved to improvise alone in his room. "I imagined a lonely winter landscape with a sleigh drawn by a horse toiling through the snow. I tried to produce the sounds on my accordion which would match the mood of this fantasy." His father had overheard and the next day asked him to repeat the playing in front of an unknown gentleman to whom his father had been enthusiastically telling about his son's accomplishment. When the Wolf-Man could not repeat the improvisation "on command," his father "angrily dismissed" him. This experience was so painful that he never touched his beloved instrument again.[95] This episode reveals a narcissistic parent looking for a child's performance to mirror his own importance.

9. In addition, the Wolf-Man says that as a child his father "had hardly taken notice of me" and "paid little attention to me."[96] Being noticed, being at the center of attention, is the beginning of mirroring.

The Wolf-Man gives ample documentation to suggest that he was starved for attentive and accurate mirroring as a child. Freud is on the mark when he says, "But [the Wolf-Man] has preserved the essential connection between his unsatisfied love, his rage, and Christmas."[97] Unfortunately, Freud passes this by to focus on the Wolf-Man's supposed trauma of witnessing his parents' primal scene. More likely, the deprivation of mirroring resulted in deficits in his Self structure that made psychological suffering inevitable.

One final point. Remember the Wolf-Man's dream took place at Christmas/ his birthday, both special days when children are the center of attention, when he would expect special notice and consideration. His natural hope was that it should have been a time of double specialness. But the dream reveals the cruel truth. Looking at the dream picture (see Figure 5.1), he sees not smiling faces but five carnivorous beasts staring intently at him.[98] The ravenous beasts focus on him, but not the kind of attention he needs: "In great terror, evidently of being eaten up by the wolves, I screamed and woke up."[99] Unlike Jesus in the manger who experienced domesticated animals smiling at him, welcoming him, adoring him, the Wolf-Man's experience was of those who would consume him. That is what absent/narcissistic parents do to their children. From a Self Psychology point of view, his dream represents the family that would consume him for their own narcissistic needs rather than acknowledge his specialness on his twofold special day.

Frankenstein's Monster

The so-called "monster" in Mary Shelley's *Frankenstein* is another case in point. How did he become a ghoul? The story is quite clear that the fault lies not in his nature but in his nurture. He was a hybrid. As are we all, biologically, psychologically, metaphorically. The most beautiful features of different people had been selected for this special son. Yet these handsome parts in composite, as a whole being now alive, were appalling to his creator. Victor Frankenstein is the real culprit. This father/creator rejects and abandons his son, seeing him as "the wretch— the miserable monster."[100] Exiled from his father, the creature had to endure what Kohut calls the "deeper and even more dreadful experience—the experience of the faceless mother, that is, the mother whose face does not light up at the sight of her child."[101] According to the story, this titanic initial insult, a traumatic lack of mirroring, was not sufficient to collapse his decidedly kind and empathetic disposition.

After the cruelest eviction, the creature takes refuge in a hovel adjacent to a cottage inhabited by a distressingly poor family. He watches in secret and understands their heavy load and suffering. He reacts with empathy and love:

> I found that the youth spent a great part of each day in collecting wood for the family fire; and, during the night, I often took his tools, the use of which I quickly discovered, and brought home firing sufficient for the consumption of several days. ... When I returned, as often as it was necessary, I cleared the path from the snow, and performed those offices that I had seen done by Felix. I afterwards found that these labours, performed by an invisible hand, greatly astonished them; and once or twice I heard them, on these occasions, utter the words, *good spirit, wonderful*; but I did not understand the signification of these terms.[102]

However, when Frankenstein physically reveals himself to those he has taken under his wing, Felix beats him furiously, simply because of his uncomely appearance. Frankenstein's orphan says: "I could have torn him limb from limb, as the lion rends the antelope. But my heart sunk within me as with bitter sickness, and I refrained."[103] No matter where he goes, regardless of good deeds done, he is met with fright and abuse.

It takes two years of absent mirroring from his father and constant negative mirroring from his fellows to turn this kindhearted spirit into a fiend that now reflects our nighttime fears of unmitigated rage. Mary Shelley has presented a casebook example of how worse-case scenario mirroring can turn one into a monster. Few are subjected to this kind of catastrophically failed parental/peer/societal response, just as few receive perfectly empathic mirroring. Most receive an admixture of adequate and inadequate mirroring and live in the upper portions of the bell curve, with varying degrees of self-cohesion and mirror hunger.

A Potential for Healing: A Long Day's Journey into Night

Inadequate or warped mirroring can be redeemed through transference in an analytical relationship. Such healing is also possible with a primary selfobject, such as a life partner or devoted friend, with whom we share a vital, primitive connection flowing with authentic mirroring, and common understandings. Eugene O'Neill's autobiographical play, *A Long Day's Journey Into Night*, is most instructive of our point. The story represents a family—mother (Mary), father (Tyrone), and two sons (James and Edmund, who represents the young O'Neill)—where no one feels at home at home. Mary, addicted to some opiate, wants to live alone in the fog where "No one can find or touch you any more."[104] To the servant, she says of the three men in her life: "I doubt if they'll come back for dinner. They have too good an excuse to remain in the barrooms where they feel at home."[105] They are all drunks.

Yes, this is a disturbingly dysfunctional family. But why? As Alice Miller has shown us, narcissistically injured parents—and in this play, the father's and mother's powerful addictions show them as such—cannot empathically mirror their children. Rather, they use their children to meet their own needs. Furthermore, addictive parents can hardly be idealized selfobjects. With failed primary mirroring and idealizing selfobjects in their lives, James's and Edmund's selves are fragmented, and they fall into the same addictive pattern as their parents. They too become self-absorbed, with all four bickering and blaming each other for their misery.

Mother Mary addresses the hopeless downward spiral they all suffer. Speaking of her eldest son Jamie, she says:

> But I suppose life has made him like that, and he can't help it. None of us can help the things life has done to us. They're done before you realize it, and once they're done they make you do other things until at last everything comes between you and what you'd like to be, and you've lost your true self forever.[106]

Speaking to Edmund, she says, "It's wrong to blame your brother. He can't help being what the past made him. Any more than your father can. Or you. Or I."[107] And finally, Mary speaks to Tyrone: "The past is the present, isn't it? It's the future, too. We all try to lie out of that but life won't let us."[108] Mirror-starved children grow into mirror-hungry adults who cannot empathetically mirror and thereby produce mirror-hungry children who will grow into mirror-hungry adults who cannot empathetically mirror and so on and on.

On the other hand, "good-enough parents" produce "good-enough parents." Domenico Ghirlandaio (1448–1494) pictures mother Anne mirroring infant Mary, just as Mary will one day mirror Jesus. Leonardo Da Vinci, in his 1510 *Virgin and Child and Saint Anne*, shows three happy generations together (see Figure 6.3). Good mirroring has worked its magic, visiting goodness from one generation to

Figure 6.3 Virgin and Child with Saint Anne (1510), by Leonardo da Vinci. GL Archive/Alamy
        Stock Photo

the next. If we look at Gentile da Fabriano's painting *Flight into Egypt* (see Figure
6.4), we see that mother Mary holds eye contact with Jesus even during the great
rush and anxiety of the moment. To the baby Jesus' psyche, her calm is more
important than the real outer threat.

Figure 6.4 *Flight into Egypt,* by Gentile da Fabriano (1370–1427). Smith Archive/Alamy Stock Photo

What is remarkable about *A Long Day's Journey Into Night* is the unexpected note of hope found on the dedication page.

> For Carlotta, on our 12th Wedding Anniversary
> Dearest: I give you the original script of this play of old sorrow, written in tears and blood. A sadly inappropriate gift, it would seem, for a day celebrating happiness. But you will understand. I mean it as a tribute to your love and tenderness which gave me the faith in love that enabled me to face my dead at last and write this play—write it with deep pity and understanding and forgiveness for all the four haunted Tyrones.
> These twelve years, Beloved One, have been a Journey into Light—into love. You know my gratitude. And my love! Gene[109]

O'Neill is saying that Carlotta's love has somehow healed parts of him, permitting him to experience something he never experienced with his parents. I take that to mean that in daily doses over more than two decades, Carlotta, as his intimate partner, became a precious selfobject for O'Neill and, in so doing, facilitated significant psychic mending.

Imago Relationship Theory

Harville Hendrix and Helen LaKelly Hunt, the constructors of imago relationship couples therapy, believe that multilevel mirroring is healing and the very essence of the intimate relationship. Kohut writes:

> I used to quip for many years that "a good marriage is one in which only one partner is crazy at any given time." ... It is only now, however, with the aid of self psychological understanding, that I can grasp the meaning of my own joke. The truth to which it alludes is that a good marriage is one in which one or the other partner rises to the challenge of providing the selfobject function that the other's temporarily impaired self needs at a particular moment. And who can potentially respond with more accurate empathic resonance to a person's needs than his or her marital partner.[110]

In some relationships, the task is not simply a matter of periodically getting each partner back into equilibrium but of healing parental damage that has caused and continues to cause relationship distress. In doing this for Eugene O'Neill, Carlotta—in her own broken way—became a manifestation of what is claimed for the Christ Child: "The light [that] shines in the darkness, and the darkness did not overcome it" (John 1:5).

This is the hope that Hendrix and Hunt's approach holds out for troubled couples. According to them, healing "childhood wounds" (the selfobject failures of childhood) can take place in committed intimate relationships because the partner becomes imbued (to use Kohut's term, which Hendrix/Hunt do not use, but imply) with paramount (archaic-parent-level) selfobject status. In other words, profoundly cathected, deeply committed relationships function as a double-sided transference. This gives partners enormous psychological power, for weal or woe, to repair or to repeat the original wounding.

Hendrix/Hunt's theory of imago relationship therapy rests on the foundational belief that each person in a close, personal bond—spouse, partner, child, friend— has a bedrock need to be known and understood, that is, mirrored well. Pastoral theologian Amy Allenby writes:

> But even when purged of infantile remnants the fundamental urge remains, the urge to feel confirmed and acknowledged as a person, as the person one really is.
>
> It has always struck me as significant that the Bible uses one particular word to express the combination of those various impulses and tendencies that make for relationship between man and woman, and this word is "to know." "And Adam knew his wife, and she conceived." It seems to be fully related to or to love another person is to "know" him, with a knowledge in which heart and mind and instinct are joined together. This "knowledge" is ... a recognition of another person's uniqueness.[111]

If such second-level mirroring is lacking, resentments build, fissures open, and rage or abandonment ensue. When second-level mirroring is present with the super-charged selfobject, it packs the capacity to considerably heal the Self of old paren-tal wounds and restore love, energy, and joy. With dysfunctional couples bound in narcissism and a long history of power struggles, such mirroring no longer happens naturally. Hendrix offers the prescription of his "couples dialogue," a system of intensive mirroring that, from my clinical experience, can yield miraculous results.

To help us understand the comprehensiveness of good second-level mirroring and how it relates to the psychological pull of Christmas, it behooves us to describe in detail the "couples dialogue."

As a precious gift to the other, one person agrees to actively listen to the other, with no commentary of his or her own. This happens in three stages. The first step is called "mirroring." However, this is a far more comprehensive mirroring than in many marriage therapy techniques. Initially, the sender tells the receiver the gen-eral nature of the problem. The receiver, to the best of his or her ability, says back in his or her own words what was heard and then asks, "Did I get that right?" The sender must be absolutely honest about their response to this because if they are not, they will not be understood and known. There is a strong inclination to settle for less than is needed.

If the answer to the question, "Did I get that right?" is no, the message is re-sent until the receiver gets it correct. If the answer is yes, then the receiver asks, "Is there more about that?" That's probably something they've never heard before and, again, may need encouragement to answer honestly. This process of sending a message, asking "Did I get it right?" and "Is there more?," continues until there is nothing further to be spoken about the issue. That is the end of stage one.

The second stage is based on the understanding that, unless the sender is psy-chotic, the gist of what they have said is based on premises that are linked in a logical way. The receiver may not agree with the premises, but this is no longer a battleground but the sacred ground of understanding. So, the receiver must try to discern the logic of the sender, in essence beginning to see the issue from their point of view, reflect that back, and then ask, "Did I get that right?" If the answer is an honest yes, they move on; if not, they continue dialoguing until the receiver understands and validates the logic of the sender.

The final step is to try to understand the emotions and feelings of the sender. The receiver says, "I imagine that all this makes you feel ... Did I get that right?" If the answer is no, the sender tells the receiver what was right or wrong or missed completely. When the answer is yes, the sender expresses gratitude for being lis-tened to.[112]

By the time this exercise is completed, the sender feels, perhaps for the first time in a long time, heard and understood. How could one not when the content, logic, emotions associated with the issue have all been mirrored. It is a miracu-lous gift because the sender does in fact become and feel known by the receiver. This process takes place quite naturally and directly in the interchange between the mirror selfobject needy child and an empathic mother. The couples dialogue thus functions as remedial work for each party, fundamental to overcoming past mirroring shortcomings. As time goes by, the couple no longer needs such a formalized protocol, but grows to organically communicate with each other to the same effect. Or to put it another way, this "couples dialogue" happens as a matter of course in already healthy relationships. What is amazing is how being and feeling truly understood often dissolves outer complaints.

Mirroring is the basic nutriment of psychic life. Psychologically speaking, to be known or not to be known is almost the equivalent of "to be or not to be." At an unconscious level, this deep crucial need to be understood and known is what is hoped for at each Christmas. We're longing for a substantial mirroring experience. This is also why Christmas is often such a disappointment. If we knew what each other's real Christmas expectations were, we could more effectively prepare a good Christmas for one another.

Gifts

We turn to a most misunderstood aspect of Christmas: Presents. Has materialism conquered the originally religious celebration? Yes, in one breath the child sings "Away in the Manger," and in the next rips apart wrapping paper like a starving pauper. Yet, these two acts are more connected than we at first realize. The hymn conjures a picture of the vital connection between mother and child, and a Christmas gift—a toy fire truck or butterfly pillowcases—can be as the Madonna's smile upon the royal child.

Marriage therapist Gary Chapman's best-selling book *The Five Love Languages* is required reading for all my wedding couples. I mention this because it has won their universal endorsement. Chapman claims there are five things that each person in an intimate relationship needs: quality time, words of affirmation, acts of service, physical touch, and gifts. Certainly, words of affirmation—"You are the best," "You can be counted on," "Your meatloaf is beyond compare," "Your eyes are reflecting pools of mystery"—mirror the positive qualities of the other and show them they are special. We all need such recognition. But gifts? Absolutely. A good gift not only incorporates but magnifies mirroring. It says, "You are special enough that I am thinking of you, exceptional enough that this thought passes through the threshold of inertia to procurement, and known enough that the gift reflects who you are, what you value, and/or your potential."

We easily trace the origin of Christmas presents back to the Magi and their largesse: Gold, frankincense, and myrrh. Early Christians quickly recognized these gifts as not only magnanimous but sagacious, indicating the Magi knew Jesus beyond his infant innocence and peasant poverty. Gold is the symbol of royalty. The Queen of Sheba brought "twenty talents of gold" as an offering to King Solomon (1 Kings 10:10).[113] The Nativity narratives say Jesus is a king. Frankincense, sweet when burned, is used to worship God (cf. Exodus 30:34–36; Leviticus 2:1, 15–16, 16:12). The Nativity narratives claim Jesus is God. Myrrh, bitter and with sedative and preserving qualities, anticipates his Passion. Jesus, according to Scripture, was given, but refused, wine mixed with myrrh during his Crucifixion (Mark 15:23; Matthew 27:34). Nicodemus brought a hundred pounds of myrrh and aloes to embalm Jesus' body (John 19:39). The Magi's gifts of gold, frankincense, and myrrh are thus not only chosen because they are exorbitant but because they reflected his purported nature and task.

We think of gifts as something you can hold in your hand and see with your eyes. Yet, they are so much more. Good gifts are outward manifestations of inward knowledge about us from those who are important to us, our selfobjects. Wilder's Emily, who is disappointed in her mother's overall inability to really look at her, is more than mollified when her mother gives her a gift that has taken considerable planning and thought: "And this is from you. Why, Mama, it's just lovely and it's just what I wanted. It's beautiful!'"[114]

Good gifts bring the double happiness of the thing itself and good mirroring. They can meet the receiver's first-level mirroring needs, when the number, size, and/or expense of the gift(s) resonate with the receiver's need to feel and be recognized as special. Just as important, good gifts can meet secondary mirroring needs: We open the box and its contents convey that we are intimately known by the giver. The Magi covered both bases.

Our deep human need for these dual aspects of mirroring are as much a psychological necessity as food, water, and air are physical necessities. Gifts are visual symbols of love.[115] That is why so much hangs on them. Wanting a present is unconsciously wanting to be positively mirrored through the gift—and when we are not, we feel profound disappointment, as the Wolf-Man experienced. To receive divine grace in a human face—mirrored and adored, known and delighted in—is the essential Christmas gift. This understanding dissolves the apparent paradox of Christmas being "at once the greatest religious holy day and the greatest commercial holiday in the Christian world."[116]

Conclusion

The symbol of the baby Jesus/Christ Child has for many been a capable twinship, idealizing and/or mirroring selfobject for Christians. The works of art inspired by the Nativity narratives reveal that mirroring, that ambrosia of being seen, known, and adored, is the primary selfneed activated by Christmas. The sway of the season invites believers as well as observers to press their hearts up against Christmas magic, hoping that a selfobject face will shine upon them, reflecting their specialness and applauding their complexity. The absolute delight in the eyes of Mary and Joseph, the adoration by Magi and shepherds, and the applause of angels for the baby we unconsciously identify with comforts and thrills us. To experience oneself as the baby Jesus, to be treated like a holy child, is the unconscious hope of Christmas.

Christmas is powerfully linked with the idealization of home because it was at home as an infant and child that we were, to one extent or another, loved, adored, mirrored, and warmly held, just as the baby Jesus was. Mirror-hungry personalities have towering expectations for Christmas, but this desire inevitably affects all because no one outgrows their selfobject needs. What about that "Christmassy"

Figure 6.5 The Adoration of the Shepherds, by Guido Reni (1575–1641), detail. IanDagnall Computing / Alamy Stock Photo

feeling? When adults experience the self-sustaining effects of a suitable selfobject, the selfobject experiences of the preceding stages of life reverberate unconsciously. They echo strongly at Christmas, at the storyline, images, and anticipation of mirroring gifts from a mirroring family. Part of the psychological meaning of Christmas is that we want to feel at home and, as Winnicott strongly suggests, the Self is only truly at home when lost in the mother's face. For most, family and close friends become that countenance of blessing (see Figure 6.5).

Notes

1 Thornton Wilder, *The Collected Short Plays of Thornton Wilder* 1 (Theater Communications Group, 1997), 13, 16.
2 John Killinger, "Home for Christmas," Preaching.com, November/December, 1989; preaching.com/sermons/christmas-home-for-christmas-text-luke-2/, accessed May 11, 2025.
3 Adam Kuper, "The English Christmas and the Family: Time Out and Alternative Realities," in *Unwrapping Christmas*, ed. Daniel Miller (Clarendon, 1993), 157.
4 For a complete biography of Kohut, see Charles B. Strozier, *Heinz Kohut: The Making of a Psychoanalyst* (Farrar, Straus and Giroux, 2001).
5 Arnold Goldberg, "Heinz Kohut, 1913–1981," *American Journal of Psychiatry* 160, no. 4 (2003), 670.

6 Gordon D. Strauss, et al., "The Cutting Edge in Psychiatry," *American Journal of Psychiatry* 141, no. 1 (1984), 42.

7 Arnold M. Cooper, "The Place of Self Psychology in the History of Depth Psychology," in *The Future of Psychoanalysis: Essays in Honor of Heinz Kohut*, ed. Arnold Goldberg (International Universities Press, 1983), 5.

8 Michael Franz Basch, *Practicing Psychotherapy* (Basic Books, 1992), 90. See also Heinz Kohut, *How Does Analysis Cure?* (University of Chicago Press, 1984), 78.

9 Heinz Kohut, *The Restoration of the Self* (International Universities Press, 1977), 311, 99, xv.

10 Joseph D. Lichtenberg and Ernest Wolf, "General Principles of Self Psychology: A Position Statement," *Journal of the American Psychoanalytic Association* 45, no. 2 (1997), 533.

11 Michael Franz Basch, "The Concept of the 'Self': An Operational Definition," in *Developmental Approaches to the Self*, ed. Benjamin Lee and Gil G. Noam (Plenum, 1983), 53.

12 Heinz Kohut, *The Analysis of the Self: A Systematic Approach to the Psychoanalytic Treatment of Narcissistic Personality Disorders* (International Universities Press, 1971), 136.

13 Kohut, *How Does Analysis Cure?*, 82.

14 Heinz Kohut, "The Psychoanalyst in the Community of Scholars," in *The Search for the Self: Selected Writings of Heinz Kohut: 1950–1978*, vol. 1, ed. Paul H. Ornstein (International Universities Press, 1978), 705.

15 Lichtenberg and Wolf, "General Principles of Self Psychology," 536.

16 Kohut, *The Restoration of the Self*, 171–219.

17 Kohut, *The Analysis of the Self*, 25.

18 L. Bryce Boyer, "Christmas 'Neurosis'," *Journal of the American Psychoanalytic Association* 3, no. 3 (1955), 470.

19 Here we do not just mean some Christians who try to overcome the devil in the child. An ancient proverb illustrates the pandemic demeaning of selfneeds: "Praise to the face is open disgrace."

20 Kohut, *How Does Analysis Cure?*, 142.

21 For Buber, engaging in I and Thou relationships is how we become fully human. When one meets another as Thou, rather than an It, the uniqueness and separateness of the other is recognized, as is our common humanness. Martin Buber, *I and Thou* (Free Press, 2023).

22 Maria T. Miliora, "Heinz Kohut and Eugene O'Neill: An Essay on the Application of Self Psychology to O'Neill's Dramas," *The Annual of Psychoanalysis* 28 (2000), 250.

23 Kohut, *The Analysis of the Self*, xiv. Kohut, *How Does Analysis Cure?*, 49.

24 Heinz Kohut, *Self Psychology and the Humanities: Reflections on a New Psychoanalytic Approach* (Norton, 1985), 217

25 Howard S. Baker and Margaret N. Baker, "Heinz Kohut's Self Psychology: An Overview," *American Journal of Psychology* 144, no. 1 (1987), 3.

26 Kohut, *The Restoration of the Self*, xiii, 4, 30–32, 123, 263.

27 Allen M. Siegel, *Heinz Kohut and the Psychology of the Self* (Routledge, 1966), 61–62.

28 Kohut, *The Analysis of the Self*, 164.

29 Baker and Baker, "Heinz Kohut's Self Psychology," 4.

30 Heinz Kohut, "Forms and Transformation of Narcissism," *Journal of the American Psychoanalytic Association* 14 (1966), 246.

31 Kohut, *How Does Analysis Cure?*, 194.

32 Kohut, *The Restoration of the Self*, 185.

33 Kohut, *The Analysis of the Self*, 27.

34 Ernest S. Wolf, "Selfobject Experiences: Development, Psychopathology, Treatment," in *Mahler and Kohut: Perspectives on Development, Psychopathology, and Technique*, ed. Selma Kramer and Salman Akhtar (Jason Aronson, 1994), 73.

35 Kohut, *The Analysis of the Self*, 8.

36 Kohut, *How Does Analysis Cure?*, 186.

37 Estelle Shane, "Self-Psychology: A New Conceptualization for the Understanding of Learning-Disabled Children," in *Kohut's Legacy: Contributions to Self Psychology*, ed. Paul E. Stepansky and Arnold Goldberg (Analytic Press, 1984), 193.

38 Kohut, *The Analysis of the Self*, 40, 54, 74, 79, 84, 96, 105.

39 This has nothing to do with the psychiatric diagnosis of "bipolar disorder," commonly referred to as manic depression.

40 Kohut, *The Restoration of the Self*, 180.

41 Kohut, *How Does Analysis Cure?*, 4–5.

42 Wolf, "Selfobject Experiences: Development, Psychopathology, Treatment," 73.

43 Kohut, *How Does Analysis Cure?*, 196.

44 Kohut, *How Does Analysis Cure?* 23. There are some similarities here with the developmental importance of childhood friends and then a special chum in Harry Stack Sullivan, *The Interpersonal Theory of Psychiatry* (Norton, 1953).

45 Kohut, *How Does Analysis Cure?*, 196. Jung presaged Kohut: "Kinship libido—which could still engender a satisfying feeling of belonging together, as for instance in the early Christian communities—has long been deprived of its object. But, being an instinct, it is not satisfied by any mere substitution such as creed, party, nation or state. It wants the human connection. That is the core of the whole transference phenomenon, and it is impossible to argue it away, because relationship to the self is at once a relationship to our fellow man, and no one can be related to the latter until he is related to himself." C.G. Jung, *The Psychology of the Transference* (1946) Vol. 16 (Princeton University Press, 1975), 233–234. Also Martin Buber: "Man wishes to be confirmed in his being by man, and wishes to have a presence in the being of the other. ... Secretly and bashfully he watches for a YES which allows him to be and which can come to him only from one human person to another." Martin Buber, *The Knowledge of Man* (Humanities Press International, 1988), 61.

46 John MacGahan, *Twilight Park: The First Hundred Years* (Allen D. Bragdon, 1988), 7.

47 Theodore Flournoy, *From India to the Planet Mars: A Case of Multiple Personality with Imaginary Languages* (1899) (Princeton University Press, 1994), forward by C.G. Jung. See also J. S. Witzig, "Theodore Flournoy—A Friend Indeed," *The Journal of Analytical Psychology* 27, no. 2 (1982), 131–148.

48 Kohut, *How Does Analysis Cure?*, 203. This reminds us of Edward Wallace's theory that Freud saw those bound together through psychoanalysis as such a community.

49 This is wonderfully depicted in Shel Silverstein's popular children's book, *The Missing Piece* (Harper Collins, 1976), with an anthropomorphized circle unhappily missing a segment searching for the piece that will make him complete—whole and happy.

50 Heinz Kohut and Ernest S. Wolf, "The Disorders of the Self and Their Treatment: An Outline," in *Essential Papers on Narcissism*, ed. Andrew P. Morrison (New York University Press, 1986), 190.

51 Kohut and Wolf, "The Disorders of the Self and Their Treatment," 190.

52 Kohut, *How Does Analysis Cure?*, 4.

53 Kohut, *How Does Analysis Cure?* 192–193. Transference is an amazing gift, miraculously allowing us to, in a sense, be born again. Such a felicitous dynamic did not have to be present in the created order, but God incorporated It for our hope and healing. Therefore, I have called it "the grace of transference." Kendrick Norris, "Projection and the Parish" (DMin, Andover Newton Theological School, 1984), 120.

54 Kohut, *How Does Analysis Cure?*, 4.

55 Siegel, *Heinz Kohut and the Psychology of the Self*, 1.

56 Heinz Kohut, "Reflections on Advances in Self Psychology," in *Advances in Self Psychology*, ed. Arnold Goldberg (International Universities Press, 1980), 494–495.

57 James S. Grotstein, "Some Perspectives on Self Psychology," in *The Future of Psychoanalysis: Essays in Honor of Heinz Kohut*, ed. Arnold Goldberg (International Universities Press, 1983), 176.

58 Kohut, *How Does Analysis Cure?*, 194.

59 Kohut, *How Does Analysis Cure?* 47.

60 Robert L. Randall, *The Eternal Triangle: Pastor, Spouse, and Congregation* (Fortress Press, 1992), 18.

61 Kohut, *How Does Analysis Cure?*, 193. Wolf concurs: "Similarly, experiences with idealized selfobject and alter-ego selfobjects are also needed over a lifetime. As the individual grows and matures from birth to death the original archaic form of the selfobject needs of infancy gradually change into other forms of selfobject needs—sometimes represented symbolically—that are appropriate to the level of maturity reached." Wolf, "Selfobject Experiences: Development, Psychopathology, Treatment," 82.

62 Kohut, *How Does Analysis Cure?*, 52.

63 Kohut, *How Does Analysis Cure?*, 220, note 11; Kohut, *Self Psychology and the Humanities*, 224–223.

64 Paul Tillich, *Systematic Theology: Three Volumes in One* (University of Chicago Press, 1967), I, 62.

65 Thomas Wolman, "Contrasting Roles of Narcissistic Mirroring in Self Psychology and Separation-Individuation Theory," in *Mahler and Kohut,* 143.

66 For most parents, the surging combination of oxytocin and dopamine makes this so. From an ideal selfobject perspective, infants experience their parents as omnipotent, omnipresent, and omniscient—as God. Therefore, before children know better, they feel a child of God.

67 Louise J. Kaplan, *Oneness and Separateness: From Infant to Individual* (Simon and Schuster, 1978), 116.

68 Lillian Smith, *Memory of a Large Christmas* (Norton, 1961), 51.

69 Donald Capps, *The Depleted Self: Sin in a Narcissistic Age* (Fortress Press, 1993), 21.

70 C.G. Jung, *Nietzsche's Zarathustra: Notes on the Seminar Given in 1934–1939*, ed. J.L. Jarrett (Princeton University Press, 1988), 805 or 795; see also 73.

71 Thornton Wilder, *Our Town* (1938) (Harper Colophon Books, 1964), 99.

72 As the child grows older, good mirroring gets more complicated and may include such words as "I may sometimes say no, but that will not be to what you are feeling, but what you are doing. No, you can't hit your baby brother, but I see that you would like to."

73 I concur with Alice Miller when she says: "By 'mother' I here understand the person closest to the child during the first years of life. This need not be the biological mother nor even a woman. In the course of the past twenty years quite often fathers have assumed this mothering function." Alice Miller, *The Drama of the Gifted Child: How Narcissistic Parents Form and Deform the Emotional Lives of Their Talented Children* (Basic Books, 1981), 8.

74 Alexander Newman, *Non-Compliance in Winnicott's Words: A Companion to the Writings and Work of D.W. Winnicott* (New York University Press, 1995), 286.

75 Wolman, "Contrasting Roles of Narcissistic Mirroring," 145.

76 Kenneth Wright, *Vision and Separation: Between Mother and Baby* (J. Aronson, 1991), 12, 335.

77 Kohut, *How Does Analysis Cure?*, 117.

78 I am indebted to Michael Franz Basch, "Self Psychology" (paper presented at the Albert Einstein College of Medicine: Michael Basch and Otto Kernberg, Cape Cod, July

1992). Part of his presentation can be found in Michael Franz Basch, *Understanding Psychotherapy: The Science Behind the Art* (Basic Books, 1988), 71–79. See also T.M. Field et al., "Discrimination and Imitation of Facial Expressions of Neonates," *Science* 218 (1982). Original research appears to have been done by A.N. Meltsoff and R.W. Borton, "Imitation of Facial and Manual Gestures by Human Neonates," *Science,* 198 (1977), 75–88. This showed correspondence of facial expressions of neonates to modeled expression. Field's experiment confirmed their results. She writes: "For example, eye widening occurred more frequently during eye-widening, surprise expression than other expressions. Similarly, lip protrusion occurred more frequently during the lip-protruding, sad expression, mouth opening during the mouth-opening, surprised expression. In addition, a relaxed brow occurred more frequently during the happy expression, a knit brow during the sad expression, and a raised brow during the surprise expression. Finally, the coder, who was blind to the expression being modeled, guessed the modeled expression at greater than chance probability simply by observing the face of the neonate. The data suggest, then, that neonates not only discriminate particular features of different facial expression but also respond differently to them with imitative behaviors or behaviors of similar appearance to those of the model." Tiffany M. Field, "Social Perception and Responsivity in Early Infancy," in *Review of Human Development* (Wiley, 1982), 25.

79 D.N. Stern, et al., "Affect Attunement: The Sharing of Feeling States Between Mother and Infant by Means of Inter-Modal Fluency," in *Social Perception in Infants,* ed. T.M. Field and N.A. Fox (Ablex Publishing, 1985). See also Daniel N. Stern, *The Interpersonal World of the Infant* (Basic Books, 1985), 138–161.
80 Basch, *Practicing Psychotherapy,* 142–143.
81 Kohut, *The Restoration of the Self,* 86.
82 Arnold H. Modell, "Comments on the Rise of Narcissism," in *The Future of Psychoanalysis,* ed. Arnold Goldberg (International Universities Press, 1983), 114.
83 Lawrence Sterling, "Winnicott and the Mother States," *The Journal of the Squiggle Foundation* 6 (1991), 21.
84 Miller, *The Drama of the Gifted Child,* viii.
85 Miller, *The Drama of the Gifted Child,* 34.
86 Miller, *The Drama of the Gifted Child,* 8.
87 D.W. Winnicott, "Ego Distortion in Terms of True and False Self," in *The Maturational Processes and the Facilitating Environment* (International Universities Press, 1960), 145.
88 Kohut, *The Analysis of the Self,* 65. Kohut, *The Restoration of the Self,* 123. Kohut, *How Does Analysis Cure?,* 5, 53.
89 Sergius Pankejeff, *The Wolf: The Double Story of Freud's Most Famous Case,* Muriel Gardiner, ed. (Basic Books, 1971), 3. See also Barry Magid, "Self Psychology Meets the Wolf Man," in *Freud's Case Studies: Self-Psychological Perspectives,* ed. Barry Magid (Analytic Press, 1993).
90 Pankejeff, *The Wolf-Man by the Wolf-Man,* 8.
91 Pankejeff, *The Wolf-Man by the Wolf-Man,* 5.
92 Pankejeff, *The Wolf-Man by the Wolf-Man.* Freud speaks of the "conspicuously neuropathic heredity in her [the Wolf-Man's mother's] family." Sigmund Freud, "From the History of an Infantile Neurosis," in An Infantile Neurosis and Other Works, 17 (Hogarth Press, 1955), 21.
93 Pankejeff, *The Wolf-Man by the Wolf-Man,* 9. Freud concurs that because of the ill health of Wolf-Man's mother, which began with abdominal disorders, that "she had relatively little to do with the children." Freud further points out that the Wolf-Man became for his Nanya a "substitute for a son of her own who had died young." Was she

able to see him for who he really was? See Freud, "From the History of an Infantile Neurosis," 13, 14.

94 Pankejeff, *The Wolf-Man by the Wolf-Man*, 9.

95 Pankejeff, *The Wolf-Man by the Wolf-Man*, 10.

96 Pankejeff, *The Wolf-Man by the Wolf-Man*, 25, 38. Freud corroborates that the Wolf-Man's father, from early on in the Wolf-Man's childhood "was disturbed by repeated attacks of severe depression." Freud also notes that the Wolf-Man's "father had an unmistakable preference for his sister, and he felt very much slighted by this." Freud, "From the History of an Infantile Neurosis," 8, 17.

97 Freud, "From the History of an Infantile Neurosis," 36.

98 C.G. Jung says that symbolically the wolf "is the typical destroyer." C.G. Jung, *Symbols of Transformation*, 5 (Princeton University Press, 1976), 438.

99 Freud, "From the History of an Infantile Neurosis," 29.

100 Mary Shelley, *Frankenstein; or, the Modern Prometheus* (1818) (Norton, 1996), 35.

101 Kohut, *How Does Analysis Cure?*, 21.

102 Shelley, *Frankenstein*, 74, 76.

103 Shelley, *Frankenstein*, 91.

104 Eugene O'Neill, *Long Day's Journey Into Night* (Yale University Press, 1956), 98. For a more complete analysis, see also Miliora, "Heinz Kohut and Eugene O'Neill," 245.

105 O'Neill, *Long Day's Journey Into Night*, 100.

106 O'Neill, *Long Day's Journey Into Night*, 61.

107 O'Neill, *Long Day's Journey Into Night*, 64.

108 O'Neill, *Long Day's Journey Into Night*, 87.

109 O'Neill, *Long Day's Journey Into Night*, Dedication page.

110 Kohut, *How Does Analysis Cure?*, 211, no. 11.

111 Amy I. Allenby, *Relationship and Healing*, no. 84 (Guild of Pastoral Psychology, 1954), 7. This is a crucial point in the Judeo-Christian tradition. Psalm 139 expounds on how God searches and knows individuals from before birth to after death. The Apostle Paul (I Corinthians 13:12b) reiterates: "Now I know only in part; then I will know fully, even as I have been fully known." To feel comprehensively known is a universal human desire. The scriptural assurance that God knows them to their depths is substantially comforting to a person of faith. Nevertheless, a deep hunger remains to know that we are understood by those closest to us. This is only possible through second-level mirroring.

112 Harville Hendrix, *Getting the Love You Want: A Guide for Couples* (Home Video Workshop Workbook) (Institute for Relationship Therapy, 1993), 49–50, 78.

113 A gold talent weighed 75 pounds. *New Revised Standard Vision of the Bible*, ed. Bruce M. Metzger and Roland E. Murphy (Oxford University Press, 1991), 440.

114 Wilder, *Our Town*, 99.

115 Gary Chapman, *The Five Love Languages: How to Express Heartfelt Commitment to Your Mate* (Northfield Publishing, 1995), 74–75.

116 Russell W. Belk, "Materialism and the Making of the Modern American Christmas," in *Unwrapping Christmas*, 75.

Chapter 7

Christmas and Regressive Peace / Progressing Wholeness

Jung

Carl Gustav Jung (1875–1961) was an inspired cartographer of the soul. While Freud made preliminary explorations into this realm, Jung was the first to conceive the unconscious as a whole world populated with indigenous personalities and powers. Aniela Jaffé, recorder and editor of Jung's autobiography, *Memories, Dreams, Reflections*, picked the perfect quote to begin her introduction:

> He looked at his own Soul
> with a Telescope. What seemed
> all irregular, he saw and
> shewed to be beautiful
> Constellations; and he added
> to the Consciousness hidden
> worlds within worlds.[1]

Surveying the psyche was Jung's calling: "From the beginning I had a sense of destiny, as though my life was assigned to me by fate and had to be fulfilled."[2] Jung's calling was to become an unyielding and tenacious seeker after the soul, a major prophet of interiority.

Jung's writings are generously laden with scriptural references of every kind. His knowledge of biblical personalities, stories, images, and theological arguments is comprehensive.[3] Jung spoke occasionally about the meaning of the Christmas tree, and revealed that Christmas is "the only Christian festival I could celebrate with fervor."[4] Regrettably, he never grants us an analysis of the birth of Jesus and all that has come to surround it. Nonetheless, the genius of Jung's psychological insights is most advantageous in understanding our deep attraction to and high hopes for Christmas.

In the Nativity narratives and deep-rooted Christmas traditions, peace is a dominant focus. From a Jungian perspective, Christmas evokes a desire for and holds the symbols to gain, no matter how briefly, psychic repose. This chapter's seven sections establish why this is so. We begin by detailing the grand multiplicity of the human soul, moving on to discuss how these psychic entities are often at odds with one another, causing distressful ambivalence and disharmony. We then introduce

DOI: 10.4324/9781003568629-8

the Jungian concept of the Self as producer, director, and integrator of the psyche. And that psychically, according to Jung, Christ as infant and adult is a symbol of the Self.[5] Next, we present biblical images and personal witnesses of the Christ Child as the bringer of peace. The chapter's final sections argue that the very symbolism of Christmas as well as the Christ Child narrative mediate peace in two opposing ways: First, as a regressive peace, a return to the uroboric oneness of mother and child, the psychic golden age; second, as a progressive peace, as the psyche pursues an integrated wholeness.

Jung's Notion of the Psyche

We continue our conversation by briefly explaining the multifaceted makeup of the psyche as Jung came to know it. Freud's brilliant discovery of the psychic troika of id, ego, and superego is well known and helpful. Jung's encounters with himself and in his work with analysands enabled him to map multiple levels of the psyche and introduce us to the powers and players who impact us with stealth and might. For Jung, the psyche is a village: Ego, persona, the *ectopsychic* functions and attitudes (typology), the personal unconscious that includes the shadow and complexes, the anima/animus as bridge to the collective unconscious percolating with core energies, images, and archetypes.

Ego

The ego is the "I" of the psyche, the agency of awareness, "the seat of individual identity,"[6] the "continuous center of consciousness."[7] It "comprises the empirical personality,"[8] and as such, is itself a conglomerate.

> [The ego] is not a simple or elementary factor but a complex one which, as such cannot be described exhaustively. Experience shows that it rests on two seemingly different bases: the somatic and the psychic.[9]

So, on the one hand, the ego is the "psychological expression of the firmly associated combination of all body sensations,"[10] and on the other hand, it includes memory, will, reason, and affect.

Jung understands free will as "the certain amount of energy that is at the disposal of the ego."[11] Yet, he is quick to note that free choice clashes with the necessities of the outside world and the exigencies of the inner world.[12] Therefore, Marie-Louise Von Franz calls the ego a "central office" and a "central bureau of decision" that regulates the impinging "powers and principalities" of our outer and inner worlds.[13] What is important for our line of inquiry is that the feeling of "me" is built up by this conflict. As Jung says:

> It [the ego] seems to arise in the first place from the collision between the somatic factor and the environment, and, once established as a subject, it goes on developing from further collisions with the outer world and the inner.[14]

The ego can cause psychic disturbance if it is too porous or impervious. Individuals with weak egos get pushed around in the outer world and are equally victimized by inner forces. Individuals with overpowering egos often overwhelm others and become unreceptive to their inner life. The "golden mean" of a secure and welcoming ego—confident, curious, and resilient—is most fortuitous.

Persona

The persona is, according to analyst Edward Whitmont, "the expression of the archetypal drive toward an adaption to external reality and collectivity."[15] Analyst Jolande Jacobi offers that it is "the mediating function between the ego and the outer world."[16] The persona, Jung said, is our "mask" worn according to one's role.[17] It is our outer appearance and approach to our present circumstance, allowing the individual to make a variety of psychological presentations to the world. The persona is the psychological function that allows us to confidently navigate cultural expectations according to the part we are playing at the time. It stands as a buffer between the ego and the external environment. In the same way that we wear different clothes to the lake, to work, a sporting event, or a funeral, so the persona enables us to react appropriately to any given situation. A surgeon's commanding demeanor is lifesaving in the operating room but off-putting at a neighborhood picnic. A fluid persona allows us a variety of expressions of self that winningly meet the given circumstance. While our sense of identity remains strong and unified, the persona permits us to modulate our responses to the key— major or minor—of the moment. It enables us to be winsome with friends, pious at church, competitive at work, and forceful with the car dealer. The persona works in service of the ego to help it accomplish its desired goals. Analyst Frances Wickes writes:

> Since the Persona is engrossed with its appearance in the world, it registers the reactions of the person by whom it is surrounded, noting what is *considered* respectable, worthy and desirable in the chosen circle in which it moves.[18]

A common pathology of the persona occurs when the ego identifies with one aspect of the personality, that is, with one's office, title, credentials, or career. This is a sad state of affairs. If, for instance, a physician, psychologically speaking, wears his white coat and stethoscope everywhere he goes, he has lost his individuality and simply thinks of himself as "the doctor." The whole person "may disappear in his social role," "become a semblance, a two-dimensional reality."[19] Jung says:

> In vain would one look for a personality behind the husk. Underneath all the padding one would find a very pitiable little creature. That's why the office—or whatever this outer husk may be—is so attractive: it offers easy compensation for personal deficiencies.[20]

Training analyst Alane Sauder MacGuire remarked that in today's world, we are just as likely to see the opposite problem.[21] Whitmont agrees:

> At the opposite end of the spectrum, when persona formation is inadequate because of poor social training or rejection of the social forms as a result of feeling excluded in some way, one cannot play or refuses to play the assigned role successfully. Such a person will suffer from lack of poise, unnecessary defiance and overdefensiveness.[22]

As Jung points out, the persona "is a compromise between the individual and society."[23] In this age of indulgent parents and stark individualism, compromise is not a welcome notion and people are reluctant to don any social costume. Analysts now often assist individuals to develop a persona that can enable them to achieve their way in the world. And so it is that an overly powerful or an underdeveloped persona are equally pernicious.

Typology: Attitudes and Functions

Why, Jung wondered, did he, Freud, and Adler have such different theories when faced with the same case studies? The easy answer—today's kneejerk answer—would be "I am right, they are ignorant or evil, or both." But Jung's way was to hold the question to his breast and explore without guile. Not only is his approach a needful lesson for our age, but, in this case, it yielded a bountiful harvest. His method of investigation, pursued with clear-eyed scrutiny, led Jung to his understanding of typology.

> Each investigator most readily sees that factor in the neurosis which corresponds to his peculiarity. ... each sees things from a different angle, and thus they evolve fundamentally different views and theories. ... This difference can hardly be anything else but a difference in temperament, a contrast between two different types of human mentality, one of which finds the determining agent pre-eminently in the subject, and the other in the object. ... The spectacle of this dilemma made me ponder the question: are there at least two different types, one of them more interested in the object, the other more interested in himself? ... I have ... finally, on the basis of numerous observations and experiences, come to postulate two fundamental attitudes, namely introversion and extraversion.[24]

His newly coined terms for these groundbreaking concepts, *introversion* and *extraversion*, are now part of everyday speech, and the attitudes they denote are well known. Attitude in this context is a habitual "readiness of the psyche to act or react in a certain way," "an essential bias which conditions the whole psychic process."[25] Jung gives this description:

The first attitude is normally characterized by a hesitant, reflective, retiring nature that keeps itself to itself, shrinks from objects, is always slightly on the defensive and prefers to hide behind mistrustful scrutiny. The second is normally characterized by an outgoing, candid, and accommodating nature that adapts easily to a given situation, quickly forms attachments, and, setting aside any misgivings, will often venture forth with careless confidence into unknown situations. In the first case obviously the subject, and in the second the object, is all-important.[26]

The reason for such a discrepancy of conscious activity can be found in analyzing the flow of energy.[27] For Jung, extraversion is an outward turning of psychic energy (or libido), while introversion is a habitual flow of libido inward.[28] Or we could say that the extravert is motivated by the object and reacts directly to it, while the introvert interposes a subjective view between the perception of object and his own response to it.[29] For Jung, this attitude is biologically determined, inborn, hereditary.[30] Jung compares his notions of attitude to two modes of adaption by animals:

> The one consists in a high rate of fertility with low powers of defense and short duration of life for the single individual; the other consists in equipping the individual with numerous means of self-preservation plus a low fertility rate.
>
> It is sufficient to note that the peculiar nature of the extravert constantly urges him to expend and propagate himself in every way, while the tendency of the introvert is to defend himself against all demands from the outside, to conserve his energy by withdrawing it from objects, thereby consolidating his own position.[31]

As opposite ways of relating to the world, "they cannot exist side by side but at best successively."[32] And this they do with varying degrees of regularity, because no one is a pure introvert or extravert.[33]

There is a second half to typology. According to Jung, we orient ourselves to the world with one of four "functions." Though attitude has to do with the direction of the libido, function indicates the way the "material is apprehended and formed."[34] Our four modes of organizing and perceiving reality are thinking, feeling, sensation, and intuition.[35] All four of the functions can be used in an extraverted or introverted fashion, making a total of eight different possible types.

Jung calls two of these functions—thinking and feeling—*rational* types because they are characterized by the "supremacy of reasoning and judging."[36] *Thinking* tells us what something is by "the linking up of ideas by means of a concept."[37] *Feeling* enables us to evaluate, to determine what is good/bad, pleasant/unpleasant, beautiful/ugly. Through this discrimination, we come to appreciate or dislike the situation, the person, the object, the moment. Jung writes: "Hence feeling is a kind of judgment, differing from intellectual judgment, in that its aim is not to establish conceptual relations but to set up a subjective criterion of acceptance or rejection."[38]

James Hillman says feeling also gives us a "sense of timing and tact."[39]

> It [the feeling function] balances value, compares tones and qualities, weighs importance and decides upon the values it discovers. The feeling function on a more primitive level is mainly a reaction of yes and no, like and dislike, acceptance and rejection. As it develops, there forms in us a subtle appreciation of values, and even of value systems, and our judgments of feeling then rest more and more on a rational hierarchy, whether it be in the realm of aesthetic taste, ethical goods, or social forms and human relationships. ... The developed feeling function is the reason of the heart which the reason of the mind does not quite understand. ... feeling provides the logic and order for love.[40]

Jung says: "One can only feel 'correctly' only when feeling is not disturbed by anything else. Nothing disturbs feelings so much as thinking."[41] Both are judging functions so "they cannot be employed at the same time for one cannot simultaneously apply two systems of measurement to the same thing."[42]

If rational types try to coerce the "untidiness and fortuitousness of life into a definite pattern," there are two other types that do not.[43] Jung labels sensation and intuition as "irrational" types because they simply report things as they are. They do not derive something the way feeling and thinking do. They simply acknowledge a given.[44] *Sensation* is that psychological function that mediates the perception of physical stimuli.

> By sensation I understand ... the sum total of my awareness of eternal facts given me through the function of my sense. Sensation tells me that something is: it does not tell me what it is and it does not tell me other things about that something; it only tells me that something is.[45]

This brings us to *intuition*, the fourth, final, and most mysterious of all the functions.

> Intuition is a function by which you see round corners, which you cannot really do; yet the fellow will do it for you and you trust him. . . People who live exposed to natural conditions use intuition a great deal, and people who risk something in an unknown field, who are pioneers of some sort, will use intuition. I say that intuition is a sort of perception which does not exactly go by sense, but it goes via the unconscious, and at that I leave it and say, "I don't know how it works."[46]

One thing is clear. Sensation and intuition are as mutually exclusive as thinking and feeling. They cannot operate at the same time, for how can one observe physical facts as they are and see around corners at the same time? These then are the four functions:

> Sensation (i.e., sense perception) tell us that something exists; thinking tells you what it is; feeling tells you whether it is agreeable or not; and intuition tells you whence it comes and where it is going.[47]

Individuals tend, sometimes excessively, toward introversion or extraversion. Likewise, individuals are prone to use one of the four functions predominantly and supplement it with a secondary one. One may be an extraverted intuitive feeling type or an introverted sensate thinker, etc. Typology is one more way that there can be intra-psychic strife.

Personal Unconscious

Jung calls the first layer of the unconscious the *personal unconscious*. Its contents "are acquired during the individual's lifetime."[48] This stratum includes "all the psychic material that lies below the threshold of consciousness,"[49] with our *shadow* and our *complexes* being the most dynamic. The shadow is "our 'dark twin', our 'other side', who is an invisible and estranged yet inseparable part of our psychic totality."[50] Or, as Esther Harding explains: "It embodies all those qualities that the individual most dislikes and fears in himself."[51] It is made up of our unwanted parts: That which we think is evil and inferior or unworthy. In other words, it is the still-living compilation of what our ego considers rubbish. Jung sees the shadow as "the 'negative' side of the personality, the sum of all those unpleasant qualities we like to hide, together with the insufficiently developed functions."[52] We are shown this in Fyodor Dostoevsky's nightmarish novel *The Double*, where the protagonist, Mr. Golyadkin, encounters a man who is physically his twin but is also the personification of all the dimly perceived, hated aspects of himself.

> The one who was now sitting opposite Mr. Golyadkin was Mr. Golyadkin's terror, was Mr. Golyadkin's shame, was Mr. Golyadkin's nightmare of the day before, in a word, was Mr. Golyadkin himself, not the Mr. Golyadkin who was now sitting on his chair with his mouth wide open and his pen frozen in his hand; not the one who served as assistant to his head of section; not the one who liked to efface himself and fade into the crowd; not the one, finally, whose gait clearly said: "Don't touch me, and I won't touch you" … no, this was a different Mr. Golyadkin, completely different but at the same time absolutely identical."[53]

Just as everyone casts a physical shadow, so too does everyone have a psychic shadow. It is inescapable—the inevitable dark side of the ego—and it is problematic. First, it haunts our dreams.

> The Shadow is the personification or representative of the personal unconscious and often figures in dreams as a rather shadowy other of the same sex as the dreamer. This shadow may accompany the dreamer in much of his dream activity. As it represents the unacceptable part of the personality, it frequently has a negative or even a sinister quality.[54]

Second, the shadow is often at the root of us doing something "out of character."

When an outburst of rage comes over us, when suddenly we begin to curse or behave crudely, when quite against our will we act antisocially, when we are stingy, petty, or choleric, cowardly, frivolous, or hypocritical, so displaying qualities which under ordinary circumstances we carefully hide or repress and of whose existence we ourselves are unaware. When emergence of such traits of character can no longer be overlooked, we ask ourselves in amazement: how was it possible? Is it really true that things like this are me?[55]

There is a third way to come to know our shadow. Concealed from our consciousness, we project our own troublesome, odious, and inferior elements onto others.[56] The recipients of our unconscious shadow projections become the scapegoats we love to loathe.[57] Unfortunately, we can only too easily imagine the consequences: Witch trials, lynchings, and their abundant analogs. Today, our shadows sow malice and cause harm. Those trying to understand their damaging self-righteousness can become suspicious of their own shadow projections at work when a particular person arouses a high level of dread, annoyance, or hatred.[58] As M. Esther Harding puts it: "the first step towards a greater consciousness is to make these unknown qualities clear—to bring them out of the shadowed land where they have been hiding and look them squarely in the eyes."[59] In this way, ethical people try to re-collect and integrate what belongs to them, rather than blame, undermine, or persecute the other.

Related but not identical to the shadow are our *complexes*. Everyone has them and no one escapes their compelling influence. The discovery of these complexes was the result of Jung's first major clinical research (ca. 1903–1907): word association experiments.[60] They led him to conclude early on that the individual "is not the master in his own house."[61] The complex is autonomous, "leading a life of its own in the psychic non-ego."[62] Complexes have significant "affect intensity."[63] These emotionally charged "intruders" have the power to plague individuals with "uncontrollable affects and neurotic states that their wills and their whole philosophy of life fail them miserably."[64] Because of trauma or irreducible conflict, a splinter personality breaks off from consciousness while retaining its power to assert itself against our will. Psychoanalyst Elie Humbert says that these split-off personalities "impose their emotions, images, and orientation upon consciousness."[65] Jung says:

They are "vulnerable points" which we do not like to remember and still less like to be reminded of by others, but which frequently come back to mind unbidden and in the most unwelcome fashion. They always contain memories, wishes, fears, duties, needs, or views, with which we have never really come to terms, and for this reason they constantly interfere with our conscious life in a disturbing and usually harmful way.[66]

Complexes have not only an obsessive, but very often a possessive, character, behaving like imps and giving rise to all sorts of annoying, ridiculous, and revealing actions, slips of the tongue, and falsifications of memory and judgment. They cut across the adapted performance of consciousness.[67]

Jung's discovery was so true to the mark that talk of complexes, such as "inferiority complex" or "mother complex," abounds today, even in casual conversation.

Anima/Animus

Jung also introduced the concepts of *anima* and *animus*, "the soul-images of man and woman."[68] Harding explains these complementary, contrasexual parts of the psyche:

> Every human being is constituted of elements derived from ancestors of both sexes. In a man the male elements are dominant and the female elements recessive, while the reverse hold in the case of a woman. The duality obtains in both biological and in the psychological sphere. Thus a complete man must be both masculine and feminine. The totality of the elements of the opposite sex resting in the individual makes up the soul. Jung, following the classical formulation, has given the name anima to this soul complex in man.[69]

The anima derives from a man's personal experience with his mother conjoined with the nonpersonal "eternal feminine." The animus is similarly constituted for a woman. This combination of elements makes the anima/animus highly autonomous, potent, and irresistible.

Von Franz gives a basic explanation of the anima, the Eve in every man.

> The anima is a personification of all feminine psychological tendencies in a man's psyche, such as vague feelings and moods, prophetic hunches, receptiveness to the irrational, capacity for personal love, feeling for nature, and—last but not least—his relation to the unconscious.[70]

Jung speaks about the Adam in every woman, the animus.

> Woman is compensated by a masculine element and therefore her unconscious has, so to speak, a masculine imprint. ... The animus corresponds to the paternal Logos just as the anima corresponds to the maternal Eros. ... Whereas, the cloud of "animosity" surrounding the man is composed chiefly of sentimentality and resentment, in woman it expressed itself in the form of opinioned views, interpretations, insinuations, and misconstruction, which all have the purpose (sometimes attained) of severing the relation between two human beings. ... Like the anima, the animus too has a positive aspect. Through the figure of the father he expresses not only conventional opinion but—equally—what we call "spirit," philosophical or religious ideas in particular, or rather the attitude resulting from them. Thus, the animus is a psychopomp, a mediator between the conscious and the unconscious and a personification of the latter.[71]

Just as the persona is the mediating function ("the outer face") between ego and the external world, so the anima/animus are the mediating functions ("the inner face") between the ego and the unconscious.[72] They are the "bridge" or "door" leading to the images of the collective unconscious.[73] In addition to working in a similar fashion, the persona and anima are also related in a compensatory way: "The more rigidly the mask, the persona, cuts off the individual from his natural, instinctive life, the more archaic, undifferentiated, and powerful becomes the soul image."[74]

So, men have a recessive female component and women a recessive male component: "Indeed," says Jung, "it seems a very natural state of affairs for men to have irrational moods and women irrational opinions."[75] But it goes beyond that. Jung gives the example of "the 'spotless' man of honour and public benefactor, whose tantrums and explosive moodiness terrify his wife and children. What is the anima doing here?"[76] Too often, the individual's contrasexual side is raw, immature, and compulsive, causing the person to act as a blatant caricature of a man or woman.

In much the same ways that we experience our shadow, so we experience our anima/animus: The diverse casting of masculine and feminine images in dreams; strange feelings and behaviors, such as "brooding withdrawal"[77] or sentimentality in a man and bickering or ex cathedra judgments from a woman; and spellbinding projections onto members of the opposite sex. In our individuation—that is coming to know, understand, honor, and appropriately accept, moderate, or constrain all the inner thoughts and feelings from our anima/animus—the spell is broken. When we realize that our inner world requires just as much attention as the outer world—that the former is just as blatant, nuanced, or complicated as the latter and so must be addressed with aplomb, empathy, and ego strength—then we have come to very different place indeed.

One becomes loosed from possession of the anima/animus by becoming conscious of it and relating it to the ego. Once this happens, they transform into life-giving and maturing forces of the psyche.

> Just as the anima becomes, through integration, the Eros of consciousness, so the animus becomes a Logos; and in the same way that the anima gives relationship and relatedness to a man's consciousness, the animus gives to woman's consciousness a capacity for reflection, deliberation, and self-knowledge.[78]

In other words, when the soul "accrues" to ego consciousness, its healthy purpose is released: "his anima wants to reconcile and unite; her animus tries to discern and discriminate."[79]

The notions of anima/animus first appeared in 1921. In that era, gender roles were rigid and unquestioned. So Jung, declaring there was a woman in every man and a man in every woman, was revolutionary and immensely helpful in letting individuals imagine their sweeping wholeness. A hundred-plus years later, with gender roles more fluid, there is no neat formula. Today, we would say that both men and women have unknown masculine and feminine traits. There is no longer consensus about what is masculine or feminine, but rather we label certain corresponding traits such as active/passive, penetrating/receiving, logos/eros, rational/irrational. As Jungian analyst Murray Stein says, "Structurally, however, there is no essential difference between animas and animus. Moreover, the content of both is highly variable and dependent on cultural factors."[80]

Collective Unconscious/Archetype

For Jung, the deepest layer of the psyche is transpersonal—universal and common to all. This *collective unconscious* is inhabited by *archetypes* that are foundational for human existence and are the underlying universal patterns of human behavior. These concepts are addressed in the last section of Chapter One, but I add a few thoughts here. Mircea Eliade writes:

> Every historical man carries on, within himself, a great deal of prehistoric humanity. That, indeed, is a point that was never quite forgotten even in the most inclement days of positivism; for who knows better than a positivist that man is an "animal," defined and ruled by the same instincts as his brothers, the animals? That correct but incomplete description served as an exclusive frame of reference. But today we are beginning to see that the nonhistorical portion of every human being does not simply merge into the animal kingdom, as in the nineteenth century so many thought it did, nor ultimately into "Life"; but that, on the contrary, it bifurcates and rises right above Life. This non-historical part of the human wears, like a medal, the imprinted memory of a richer, a more complete and almost beatific existence.[81]

Jung echoes Eliade:

> No biologist would ever dream of assuming that each individual acquires his general mode of behaviour afresh each time. It is much more probable that the young weaver-bird builds his characteristic nest, because he is a weaver-bird and not a rabbit. Similarly, it is more probable that man is born with a specifically human mode of behaviour and not with that of a hippopotamus or with none at all. Integral to his characteristic behaviour is his psychic phenomenology, which differs from that of a bird or quadruped.[82]

These still-living primordial images and powers are manifest in two types of archetypes. Some are anthropomorphized and appear as active personalities:

> The psychologist of the unconscious proceeds no differently in regard to the psychic figures which appear in dreams, fantasies, visions, and manic ideas, as in legends, fairytales, myth, and religion. Over the whole of this psychic realm there reign certain motifs, certain typical figures which we can follow far back into history, and even into prehistory, and which may therefore legitimately be described as "archetypes." They seem to me to be built into the very structure of man's unconscious, for in no other way can I explain why it is that they occur universally and in identical form.[83]

And so, we have such archetypes as the great mother, the wise old man, the hero, the divine child, the trickster, and so on.

Jung also notes a second class of archetypes that he calls the "archetypes of transformation." He says further that "They are not personalities, but are typical situations, places, ways and means, that symbolize the kind of transformation in question."[84] These would include such images as a circle, a bridge, fire, water, music, the ouroboros, the mandala.

All the archetypes—the preexistent, innate patterns of behavior living within every human psyche "for whose origin no individual experience can be made responsible"[85]—possess two qualities. First, they "can easily produce in the most widely differing individuals' ideas or combinations of ideas that are practically identical."[86] Second, they can and will assert themselves "without the co-operation of the conscious personality."[87]

In this section, we have shown that though central and critical to human functioning, ego consciousness is a relatively small part of the entire psyche, which encompasses a bristling personal unconscious and a collective unconscious brimming with potent, foundational archetypes. According to Analytical Psychology, multiple powers are at play in the human psyche: ego, persona, typology, shadow, complexes, anima/animus, and the archetypes. Each psyche is therefore a family—nuclear, extended, and ancestral—rich in diversity, steeped in tradition, more or less harmonious.

The Divided Self

The human condition is afflicted by psychic multiplicity and disunion. When the manifold psychic forces Jung identified cross paths, there is bound to be friction, even discord. This cacophony creates apprehension. "It has become a commonplace observation that we live in a time of particular anxiety."[88]

In his 1993 book, *The Protean Self: Human Resilience in an Age of Fragmentation*, professor of psychiatry Robert Jay Lifton argues that the sheer quantity of powers and points of view that regularly confront us wear us down, stimulate apprehension, incite confusion, and promote alienation.[89] He sees three sets of dynamics at work. The first he calls "sequential."

A changing series of involvements with people, ideals, and activities, as was especially vivid during the late 1960s and early 1970s, but has continued to occur more quietly (and as a sustained pattern) in much of American culture.

The second he labels "social."

In any given environment—office, school, or neighborhood—one may encounter highly varied norms of self-presentation: everything from conventional, buttoned-down demeanor, to jeans and male beads and earrings, to the "blissed-out" states of members of religious cults, to any conceivable in-between.[90]

Indeed, we are all aware of how outer events and pressures can affect us for weal or woe. In some instances, they can cause psychic suffering so severe that its effects cross over to our bodies.[91] For instance, in the 60 days following September 11, 2001, New York Methodist Hospital, just a few miles from ground zero, documented a 35 percent increase in heart attack patients.[92] We should never minimize the psychic cost involved in adjusting to the ever blowing vagaries and vicissitudes of life.

Lifton's third dynamic of proteanism directly addresses our point.

Proteanism can also be simultaneous, in the multiplicity of varied, even antithetical images and ideas held at any one time by the self, each of which it may be more or less ready to act upon—a condition sometimes referred to as "multimind."[93]

We've all experienced "monkey mind." Given Jung's revelation of the multilayered, generously populated psyche, how could we not? At its most basic, we see the common divisiveness of our wills as an everyday occurrence. For instance, at a tennis finals tournament on a blistering sunny day, I find the venue allows no escape from the unbearable heat and humidity. Yet the match is immensely engaging. Though I desperately want to cool down, I remain to watch. We cannot help but laugh at ourselves when in *Fiddler on the Roof*, Tevye the milkman goes into his strikingly accurate soliloquy: "On the one hand … but on the other hand."

Yet, noting that we are often of "two minds" just scratches the surface of the great divide within the human psyche. The initial verses of the Judeo-Christian creation myth describe humans as hybrids: Dust of the ground animated by the breath of God (Genesis 2:7); a creature yet in the likeness of God (2:26). According to this origin story, we are more than animal but less than God. Humans then have a unique place, but it is an uneasy one.

Jungian Analyst Marie-Louise Von Franz reveals that many creation myths around the world tell the same story: "human reality, that is, the reality of human consciousness—is in creation myths described as a middle phenomenon between two poles."[94] We are a bifurcated creature, pulled from above and yanked from below. We are an animal who knows past and future and, therefore, guilt and anxiety. Inwardly, we bear the gnawing cleft of these opposites. It's almost as if we're built for angst.

As an elementary school-aged child, Jung knew "the tormenting sense of being at odds with myself."[95]

Then to my intense confusion, it occurred to me that I was actually two different persons. … The play and counterplay between personalities No. 1 and No. 2, which has run through my whole life, has nothing to do with a "split" or dissociation in the ordinary medical sense. On the contrary, it is played out in every individual.[96]

So began an unflinching examination of his own inner life. In one of his first lectures (May 1897), while still a medical student, he stated:

> The new empirical psychology furnishes us with data ideally designed to expand our knowledge of organic life and to deepen our views of the world. They enable us to glimpse nature's abyss, to gaze into an intelligible world where the eyes seek in vain for any shore or any limit. Nowhere do we feel as keenly as here that we are living at the boundary between two worlds. Our body formed of matter, our soul gazing toward the heights, are joined into a single living organism. We see our lives coming in contact with a higher order of being. The laws governing our mental universe grow pale before that light, emanating from the metaphysical order, which it is granted us to dimly divine. Man lives at the boundary between two worlds. He steps forth from the darkness of metaphysical being, shoots like a blazing meteor through the phenomenal world, and then leaves it again to pursue his course into infinity.[97]

Later in his clinical work, Jung came to understand the human as "that personality which is split into partial aspects, that bundle of odds and ends which also calls itself 'man.'"[98] Indeed, for Jung, the individual is a "dangerous plurality": "Man's instincts are not harmoniously arranged, they are perpetually jostling each other out of the way."[99] Not only does this cause customary psychic suffering, but it may also lead to psychic illness, neuroticism, and psychosis. Jung writes:

> Disunity with oneself is the hall-mark of civilized man … The neurotic is only a special instance of the disunited man who ought to harmonize nature and culture within himself.[100]

Again, he writes:

> Neurosis is an inner cleavage—the state of being at war with oneself. … What drives people to war with themselves is the suspicion or the knowledge that they consist of two persons in opposition to one another. The conflict may be between the sensual and the spiritual man, or between the ego and the shadow. It is what Faust means when he says: "Two souls, alas, are housed within my breast." [101]

According to Jung, many people prefer to avoid the inner problem by making it an outer conflict.

> Again, the view that good and evil are spiritual forces outside us, and that man is caught in the conflict between them, is more bearable by far than the insight that the opposites are ineradicable and indispensable preconditions of all psychic life, so much so that life itself is guilt.[102]

In *The Red Book*, Jung revealed, in print and paint, the continental cleft of the psyche: The Spirit of the Times and Spirit of the Depths.[103] On his gravestone is the inscription: PRIMUS HOMO DE TERRA TERRENUS SECUNDUS HOMO DE CAELO CAELESTIS (1 Corinthians 15:47)[104] ("The first man being made of earth, is earthly by nature; the second man is from heaven.") From childhood to epitaph, Jung wrestled bare-chested with his entrenched psychic divide.

The rippling manifestations of this split, so meticulously catalogued by Jung, are also well documented in Western theology, the arts, and psychology. The Apostle Paul describes us all when he writes to the Romans (7:19): "I do not understand my own actions. ... For I do not do the good I want, but the evil I do not want is what I do." Augustine of Hippo (354–430 CE) bemoaned: "So my two wills, one old, one new, one carnal, the other spiritual, were in conflict, and they wasted my soul by their discord" (VIII, 5).[105] Where the soul is disturbed, there is no peace.

Similarly, the Puritans often spoke of the fissure and viscerally felt, "I am not a man, I am a civil war." Roger Brereley published a tract in 1677 (London) entitled "Self Civil War." And George Goodwin's poem of 1607, *Automachia*, was received with great popularity:

I sing my SELF; my *Civil Warrs* within;
The *Victories* I howrely loose and win
The dayly *Duel*, the continuall Strife,
The *Warr* that ends not, till I end my life.[106]

Paul Tillich, one of the most important and popular theologians of the 20th century, was keenly aware that the conditions of man's existence inevitably meant estrangement, ambiguity, and anxiety. He understood humanity's "disruptive drives which cannot be brought into unity."[107] Like Jung, Tillich knew the supraordinate powers in man.

The truth of the doctrine of angelic and demonic powers is that there are supra-individual structures of goodness and supra-individual structures of evil. Angels and demons are mythological names for constructive and destructive powers of being, which are ambiguously interwoven and which fight with each other in the same person.[108]

New Testament professor Frank Stagg aptly titled his book *Polarities of Man's Existence in Biblical Perspective*. The human position, he writes, "is unique. It is a polar situation: man is like God but not God, created but more than creature," is "body and spirit."[109] Stagg notes seven derivative polarities: (1) we are aspective yet holistic, (2) individual yet corporate, (3) made to become ("already but not yet"), (4) free yet bound (the "limited freedom" of Tillich and Sartre), (5) saint yet sinner, (6) know salvation as gift and demand, and finally (7) have our Self denied yet affirmed. Whatever value, purpose, or meaning these antinomies hold, they habitually conflict with one another and do not make for a life of peace.

We turn now to other psychologists' thoughts about the fissures and conglomerates of the psyche. Philosophers were the earliest psychologists. Plato allegorically describes the soul as a chariot driven by a charioteer, symbolizing the soul's rationality, who must deftly manage two opposing winged steads. The white horse is noble and wants to soar to heaven. The black horse is motivated by base passions and will not yield.[110] Presaging Freud by 2.3 millennium, Plato proposes that the soul is a tripartite composite. Von Franz gives us a quick analysis of early philosophical psychology:

> Already in Greek philosophy and again in Gnosticism and in medieval tradition, the human psyche has been attributed a middle place between the opposites. For instance, the psyche was looked upon as an intermediary phenomenon between spirit and body, between heaven and earth.[111]

America's foremost psychologist, William James (1842–1910) in *Psychology: The Briefer Course*, continues the argument that the Self is a multiplicity.[112]

> "Homo duplex, homo duplex!" writes Alphonses Daudet. "The first time I perceived that I was two was at the death of my brother Henri, when my father cried out so dramatically, 'He is dead, he is dead!' While my first self wept, my second self thought "How truly given was that cry, how fine it would be at the theatre.' I was then fourteen years old.
>
> "This horrible duality has often given me matter for self reflection. Oh, this terrible second me, always seated whilst the other is on foot, acting, living, suffering, bestirring itself. This second me that I have never been able to intoxicate, to make shed tears, or put to sleep. And how it sees into things, and how it mocks!"[113]

But, according to James, that is just the beginning. Self A, the me, is itself a composite including "the material me," "the social me," and "the spiritual me." In turn, these sub-selves are further divisible so that "a man has as many social selves as there are individuals who recognize him," and the *soul me* includes the "entire collection of my states of consciousness."[114] This leads to the "rivalry and conflict of the different mes."[115]

Another well-known American psychologist, Karl Menninger (1893–1990) wrote an entire book, *Man Against Himself*, based on Freud's observation that humans suffer an inner war between Eros (life instinct) and Thanatos (death instinct).[116] Professor of psychology Philip Zimbardo in a PBS series on psychology offered this assessment:

> The brain and mind can turn against themselves. Because we can love we can be jealous. Because we can remember the good, we can recall the bad and dwell on it. Because we can think about the future we can fear its uncertainties. It's

as if the coin of the psychological realm has one side that mocks and demeans the other.[117]

Finally, a 2024 science-based book by Yale professor of psychiatry, Samuel T. Wilkinson. *Purpose: What Evolution and Human Nature Imply About the Meaning of Our Existence* exhibits how "nature seems to have created in us competing dispositions."[118] Inherent in the evolutionary process is the push and pull of opposites: selfishness and altruism, aggression and cooperation, cruelty and kindness.

All the arts underscore our predicament. One has only to listen to popular music to hear that "the conflict between the opposites can strain our psyche to the breaking point."[119] Lou Christie in 1963 and Bruce Springsteen in 1987 wrote two different songs with the same theme—opposites in conflict—and similar titles proclaiming "Two Faces Have I."

Mary Wells (1943–1992), "founder of the world famous 'Motown Sound,'" recorded the song "Two Lovers."[120] One lover is generous and tender and the other selfish and hard. The slightly hidden surprise is that they are one and the same man. In 1962, "Two Lovers" became a top ten hit, as it resonated with the general populace then and still does today on oldies radio stations. In 2000, P!nk highlighted the duality of her psyche in her song "Split Personality." All these songs speak to the multitudes who are not pleased that their self-cohesiveness is easily disturbed by strong moods and unpredictable reactions.

In viewing modern art, Kohut conjectured that this sort of psychic fragmentation is worsening.

My hypothesis that the artist anticipates the dominant psychological problem of his era does not, of course, imply the absence of individual motivation. ... The work of such creators as Henry Moore, O'Neil, Picasso, Stravinsky, Pound, Kafka, would have been unintelligible even a hundred years ago—but now it is daring, profound, and beautiful for those of us who are open to their message, and we feel that they are in touch with the deepest problems of our age.[121]

Just as it is the understimulated child, the insufficiently responded-to child, the daughter deprived of an idealizable mother, the son deprived of an idealizable father, that has now become paradigmatic for man's central problem in our Western world, so it is the crumbling, decomposing, fragmenting, enfeebled self of the child and, later, the fragile, vulnerable, empty self of the adult that the great artists of the day described—through tone and word, on canvas and in stone—and that they try to heal. The musician of disordered sound, the poet of decomposed language, the painter and sculptor of the fragmented visual and tactile world: they all portray the breakup of the self and, through reassemblage and rearrangement of the fragments, try to create new structures that possess wholeness, perfection, new meaning.[122]

Robert Louis Stevenson (1850–1894), in authoring *The Strange Case of Dr. Jekyll and Mr. Hyde*, makes plain the suffering and destruction of inner powers fighting for dominance.[123] Likewise, W.B. Yeats (1865–1939) warned that the center might not hold.[124]

Perhaps, all this is best said in the plaintive poem of Nobel laureate Pablo Neruda (1904–1973) entitled "We Are Many."

> Of the many men who I am, who we are,
> I can't find a single one;
> they disappear among my clothes,
> they've left for another city.
>
> But when I call for a hero,
> out comes my lazy old self;
> so I never know who I am,
> nor how many I am, or will be.[125]

We are all over the place; it's disconcerting and painful.

Our literature, our music, our theology and psychology report the same truth: We are by nature fragmented into opposites. We are a creature wed to the image of God; we are psyche and soma, introverted and extraverted, altruist and hedonist; we are subject to nature and culture, inertia and compulsion, individuality and collectivity, Venus and Mars, Eros and Thanatos, limbic system and cerebral cortex, heart and mind, physical facts and visionary intuition. Simply put: We are a box store of bundled opposites. We want to do one thing, but we do another. We screw up our courage, muster our will, but there is no liftoff. We are a house divided. This is a universal human predicament.

At times, our intrapsychic components are so congruent and cooperative that we easily excel. We become an ensemble generating a harmonious ballad, a symphony achieving majesty. When the psyche works together, it's sublime. But when our heterogeneity billows and rages, we suffer significantly, as Tillich describes, from estrangement, anxiety and ambiguity. All of us at least some of the time—though some more than others—have a base yearning for psychic reconciliation, a home united, inner peace.

This "state of bondage and disunion, of disintegration, and of being torn in different directions" is an "agonizing unredeemed state which longs for union, reconciliation, redemption, and wholeness."[126] Jung was unequivocal that "No previous age has ever needed wholeness so much."[127] No wonder then that at Christmas, when the birth of the "Prince of Peace" (Isaiah 9:6) is celebrated, there is a charged, if unconscious, hope for intrapsychic concord. Let's see how this yuletide longing makes sense from a Jungian perspective.

Christ as Symbol of the Unifying Center of the Psyche in Analytical Psychology

Analytical psychology explicates Christmas peace. Sometimes we feel like Humpty-Dumpty—shattered—but a sovereign puts us back together again. Apart from any theology but rather from clinical observation, Jung maintained that the symbol of "Christ—means nothing less than the integration of those parts of the personality which are still outside ego-consciousness."[128] For a psychologist to claim that a religious figure can be a unifying agent of the psyche seems outrageous and unsupportable, yet Jung's assertion turns out to be reasonable.

We have postponed speaking about one critical component of the psyche until now—Jung's concept of the *Self*. As we sketch it, we will see the sense of Jung's astonishing assertion about the Christ archetype. On numerous occasions, Jung presents the same basic definition of the Self:

> The self is not only the center but also the whole circumference which embraces both conscious and unconscious; it is the center of this totality, just as the ego is the center of the conscious mind.[129]

We cannot miss the paradox: The Self is both the headquarters and the aggregate of the psyche.[130] To understand this enigma, we will examine each contention, beginning with the notion of the Self as psychic totality. Many live as if consciousness were the extent of their being. Jung writes:

> Most people confuse "self-knowledge" with knowledge of their conscious ego-personalities. Anyone who has any ego-consciousness at all takes it for granted that he knows himself. But the ego knows only its own contents, not the unconscious and its contents. People measure their self-knowledge by what the average person in their social environment knows of himself, but not by the real psychic facts which are for the most part hidden from them.[131]

He goes on to warn:

> Man thinks of himself as holding the psyche in the hollow of his hand. He dreams even of making a science of her. But in reality she is the mother and the maker ... reaches so far beyond the boundary line of consciousness that the latter could be easily compared to an island in the ocean, while the island is small and narrow, the ocean is immensely wide and deep.[132]

To say the Self is a sum total of the psyche means that the Self includes all the aspects of the human psyche that Jung unearthed: Persona, ego, shadow, complexes, anima/animus, and the archetypes. Taking a slightly different angle, Jung says: "The self is both ego and non-ego, subjective and objective, individual and collective."[133] Ego consciousness is imperative and substantial but, nonetheless, a part. In contradistinction, the Self is broader, deeper, fuller—the entire psychic house we inhabit.

Though unconscious parts of the Self can become conscious, the Self *qua* totality necessarily transcends the ego, our agency of consciousness, and therefore is unknowable.[134] The Self, however, can be represented and experienced in symbols.

Such symbols can be supraordinate personalities such as king, hero, or savior, or the Self can manifest in abstract symbols such as a circle, square, mandala, or cross.[135] "The symbols of the self," Jung notes, "coincide with God-images."[136]

To say that the Self is the center of the entire psyche is revolutionary. Similar to how Ptolemy and all the world for many years believed the sun circled Earth, it was commonly taken as indisputable that the psyche revolves around the ego. Copernicus discovered that Earth orbited the sun, and Jung revealed that the Self, not the ego, was the center of the psychic solar system. Such a notion inevitably deflates the ego's hegemony. The ego is absolutely critical, but our center of gravity is the Self. In "Paracelsus," Robert Browning (1812–1889) states, "There is an inmost center in us all, where truth abides in fullness."[137] Harding writes:

> The governor of a circle is of course its center, around which everything revolves. In the psyche, likewise, the center is the ruler of the entire man. In the conscious realm the ego is master, but in this larger sphere the ego is only one voice among many. The ruler here must transcend ego. It must be a supra personal value that can command the allegiance and obedience of the ego ... This ruler Jung has called the Self.[138] ... What this means is that the psyche can only attain wholeness "through the sacrifice of ego dominance and replacement of it by a new center of control, the Self."[139]

Jan Wiener writes:

> One of the central beliefs that bring us together as analytical psychologists is in the self as an organizing and unifying centre of the psyche—an archetypal impulse to bring together and mediate the tensions of the opposites.[140]

In summary, we could say with Edinger that the Self is "the totality of the psyche which manifests itself as a unitary entity."[141] Or as Neumann says, "Structural wholeness, with the self as center of the psyche, is symbolized by the mandala ... by the circle with a center."[142] (See Figure 7.1).

What is most germane to the flow of our argument is to understand that Jung throughout his writings claims that Christ is a symbol par excellence for the Self: "Christ *exemplifies the archetype of the self.*"[143] He elucidates:

> The Christ-symbol is of the greatest importance for psychology in so far as it is perhaps the most highly developed and differentiated symbol of the self, apart from the figure of Buddha.[144]
>
> Christ, as a hero and god-man, signifies psychologically the self; that is, he represents that projection of this most important and most central of archetypes. The archetype of the self has, functionally, the significance of a ruler of the inner world, i.e. of the collective unconscious.[145]

Figure 7.1 Detail of ceiling fresco by Gusto de Menabuoi (1363–1370), Padua Baptistery. Godong / Alamy Stock Photo

I have called the mediating or "uniting" symbol which necessarily proceeds from a sufficiently great tension of the opposite the "self" … . Living in the West I would have to say Christ instead of the "self" [146]

As a "uniting symbol," "Christ proves to be a mediator."

He holds an important position midway between the two extremes, man and God, which are so difficult to unite. Clearly the focus of the divine drama shifts to the mediating God-man. He is lacking neither in humanity nor in divinity, and for this reason he was long ago characterized by totality symbols, because he was understood to be all-embracing and to unite all opposites.[147]

Here, Jung is not concerned with Christ as a "historical figure and a metaphysical entity" but as "an inner, psychic fact," "the Christ within us" that functions as a "psychic center."[148] As the psychic center the Christ/Self "is the 'uniting symbol' which epitomizes the total union of opposites."[149] The Christ/Self is thus able to bring peace to a psyche hypertensive with conflict, shalom to a soul percolating with discord. As a symbol of the Self, the Christ Child is often found at the center of mandalas. In Notre-Dame Cathedral, we find a magnificent mandala—representing wholeness—in the form of stained glass windows with Mother and Christ Child in the center (see Figure 7.2).[150]

Jung claims this to be a psychological fact and expounds upon it by invoking a beloved Christmas prophesy:

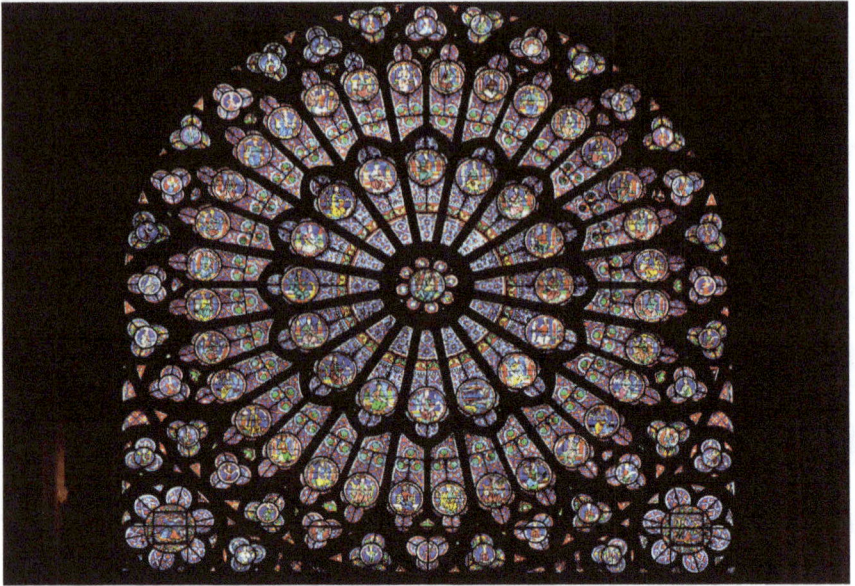

Figure 7.2 A Christian mandala, the Rose Window of the Cathedral of Notre Dame, Paris.
JOHN KELLERMAN/Alamy Stock Photo

The coming of the Saviour signifies a union of opposites: "The wolf also shall dwell with the lamb, and the leopard shall lie down with the kid; and the calf and the young lion and the fattling together; and a little child shall lead them. ... For unto us a child is born, unto us a son is given; and the government shall be on his shoulder; and his name shall be called Wonderful Counselor, the Mighty God, the Everlasting Father, the Prince of Peace."[151]

So important for Jung is this notion of the Christ Child as the bringer of inner harmony that twice he quotes Philalethe (from the "Introitus apertus"), who describes the Christ Child as "the most serene King."[152] Jacoby elucidates the inner workings:

Jung has also referred to the self as the *coincidentia oppositorum*, the uniting of opposites. Consciousness is inconceivable without polarities, though these also rend us and plunge us into conflict. When the polarities are united there is harmony and peace, the soul becomes a single entity which embraces and unites all opposites.[153]

Or as Jung says:

As opposites never unite at their own level (tertium non datur!), a supraordinate "third" is always required, in which the two parts can come together. And since the symbol derives as much from the conscious as from the unconscious, it is able to unite them both, reconciling their conceptual polarity through this form and their emotional polarity through its numinosity.[154]

The Christ Child as symbol of the Self, the serene monarch, actualizes periods of inner repose. To this point, Jung says plainly that we can experience "the reality represented in the sacred legend."[155] Though Jung says this about the Crucifixion, we argue that it is also true for Christ's Nativity. Christmas then constellates the archetype of the Christ Child/Self, activates its powerfully uniting function, and bestows a psychic peace.

The Biblical Picture and Christian Experience of the Christ Child as Bringer of Peace

Jung's understanding of the psychic functioning of the Christ Child/Self fits with the prophetic and Nativity narrative portraits of the Christ Child as well as the personal testimony of individual Christians.

According to Luke 2:1, Jesus was born in the time of Caesar Augustus, who brought to reality Pax Romana. To an extraordinary degree, the world—the empire—was at peace, though through the brutality of sword and spear. The longed-for Golden Age of Saturn anticipated in every Saturnalia had, in a manner though at its lowest level, been restored. How ironic that at this very time of civil peace, the Christ Child—the "Prince of Peace" (Isaiah 9:6)—is born. The question then is, what kind of peace will he bring?

The persistent longing of Christmas is for a comprehensive peace, including concord between nations, reconciliation among family, and, to our point, psychic consonance. This promise runs through Nativity narratives. Zachariah, priest and father of John the Baptist, became filled with the Holy Spirit and prophesied:

> God's Sunrise will break in upon us,
> Shining on those in the darkness,
> those sitting in the shadow of death,
> Then showing us the way, one foot at a time,
> down the path of peace.
>
> (Luke 1:78-79)

This declaration of God's dawn to the enduring shadows and God's peace to perennial discord is immediately followed by the heart of the Christmas story.

> In that region there were shepherds living in the fields, keeping watch over their flock by night. Then an angel of the Lord stood before them, and the glory of the Lord shone around them, and they were terrified. But the angel said to them, "Do not be afraid; for see—I am bringing you good news of great joy for all the people: to you is born this day in the city of David a Savior, who is the Messiah, the Lord. This will be a sign for you: you will find a child wrapped in bands of cloth and lying in a manger." And suddenly there was with the angel a multitude

of the heavenly host, praising God and saying, "Glory to God in the highest, and on earth peace, good will to men."

(Luke 2:1–14)

There is no missing link here. The claim is unmistakable. God's "good news of great joy for all the people" is the Christ Child who will bring peace. This is further confirmed when "righteous and devout" Simeon saw the newborn Jesus in the Temple, took him in his arms, and spoke directly to God, saying:

Master, now you are dismissing your servant in peace,
according to your word;
for my eyes have seen your salvation.

(Luke 2:29–30)

Clearly, Simeon experiences an interior peace as he embraces the Christ Child. Eugen Drewerman points out that "the fact that it was 'night' when the Christ Child came into the world (Luke 2:8) meant more than a mere indication of time. Rather, it described a state of soul."[156] The Christ Child brings peace to the dark night of the soul, a soul anxious and fractious.

The Christ Child becomes the father of the man. The tradition of the adult Jesus as a soul healer is unassailable. The Gospel of Mark, lacking a Nativity narrative, tells us that Jesus' first act of ministry was an exorcism on a man possessed by a menacing rogue spirit (Mark 1:25; Luke 4:35). The grown Christ later cast out a demon from the daughter of the Syrophoenician woman (Matthew 8:16, 15:28), a debilitating spirit from a boy (Matthew 17:18; Mark 9:25; Luke 9:42), and a disabling spirit from a mute man (Matthew 9:33). He released the Gerasene demoniac from a legion of inner tormentors (Mark 5:8; Matthew 8:32; Luke 8:33). He cast out seven demons from Mary Magdalene (Luke 8:2; Mark 16:9). Matthew provides us with the general picture: "That evening they brought to him many who were possessed by demons; and he cast out the spirits with a word, and cured all who were sick" (Matthew 8:16). The grown Christ Child saved many from evil spirits. Today, thanks to the pioneering work of Jung, we call these demons splinter personalities or complexes.

Furthermore, Luke records that Jesus greeted and healed people and then sent them on their way saying, "Go in peace" (Luke 7:50, 8:48); when he sent out the 70, he instructed them: "Whatever house you enter, first say, 'Peace to this house!'" (Luke 10:5; Acts 10:36). In his post-Resurrection appearance to the disciples, Jesus blessed them with his signature phrase, "Peace be with you" (Luke 24:36; John 20:21). In the Gospel of John, we find two of Jesus' most famous sayings in his farewell address: "Peace I leave with you; my peace I give to you" (14:27) and "These things I have spoken to you that in me you might find peace" (16:33). This was ever so much more than a conventional salutation. From the mouth of Jesus, according to his story, the word *peace* was efficacious, accomplishing its purpose. According to New Testament scholar C.L. Mitton, "With the word of peace went the actual bestowal of peace."[157] So according to the story, from his Nativity to his ascension, Christ's mission is one of peace, particularly an inner peace of the psyche/soul.

Given all this, it is interesting to discover how—when viewed from the soul's perspective—two of the major Christmas symbols picture just such a peace. First is the ubiquitous and compelling crèche scene. From the time of Francis of Assisi to today, the grouping within the crèche remains a most central and beloved part of Christmas. In his Christmas message of 1941, Methodist pastor Edward F. Randolph wrote:

> Now each of these individuals seems to come from a caste, either of race, culture, age, or finance. The Magi are classified as Gentiles, scholars, and wealthy men; the shepherds are Jews, illiterate and poor; Simeon and Anna represent the two sexes; and the age of Anna is stressed in contrast to the baby boy.
>
> Yet, the unusual happens when the Son of God is born: the Hebrew shepherds and certain Gentile from the East travel far to adore the new-born King. The wise Men of the astronomical schools and the illiterate herdsmen of the field bow at the same altar. The three rich men with their camels and the three poor men with their crooks find a common tie in the same cradle. The aged Simeon and the youthful boy embrace each other. While Simeon and Anna are revealed as equally prophetic, regardless of sex. In short antipathies, prejudices and divisional lines all fade away at the first Christmas."[158]

Randolph has, of course, forgotten to mention mother Mary and father Joseph, the angel Gabriel accompanied by the heavenly host, and the animal contingency, sheep, cattle, ox and ass (though not biblical are an ancient part of Christmas symbolism). But he is right: The divisional lines all fade away at that first Christmas—within our psyche as well! The crèche scene symbolizes a unity of the opposites, all come together around the Christ Child. On that holy night, the disparate parts become a beautiful mosaic of wholeness, the grand diversity an elegant tapestry of unconflicted oneness. The song of the heavenly host and the sounds of the menagerie should have been a jarring dissonance, but on that holy night, it became the sweetest of all sounds as "heaven and nature sing." The great attractiveness of the Christmas crèche unconsciously symbolizes a psyche, in its glorious but contentious diversity, at peace around the Christ Child.

Analogous to the Christmas manger scene is the vision of the Peaceable Kingdom. Isaiah (11) foretells, "A shoot shall come out from the stump of Jesse [house of David] and a branch shall grow out of his roots." This text is part of the Advent lectionary cycle because Christians have long assumed that this prophecy speaks about the Christ Child. Isaiah paints a picture of an Eden-like peace where ferocious beasts, defenseless domesticated animals, and innocent children live side by side in safety and harmony—all led by "a little child."

> The wolf shall live with the lamb,
> the leopard shall lie down with the kid,
> the calf and the lion and the fatling together,

and a little child shall lead them.
The cow and the bear shall graze,
their young shall lie down together;
and the lion shall eat straw like the ox.
The nursing child shall play over the hole of the asp,
and the weaned child shall put its hand on the adder's den.
They will not hurt or destroy
on all my holy mountain;
for the earth will be full of the knowledge of the LORD
as the waters cover the sea.

(Isaiah 6–9)

The Peaceable Kingdom is a secondary crèche scene, also representing psychic tranquility. We could just as easily imagine one's conscious and unconscious becoming a unified whole: the shadow lying down with the persona, the ego and archetypes grazing together, the anima/animus no longer afflicting but sustaining the ego's purpose, the primary function and the inferior function living side by side in mutual understanding and appreciation. They are led to do this by a little child, just as the angels, animals, and every sort of person is brought together around the manger of the Christ Child. Christmas is a time when we hope for such a relished peace of psychic harmony.

There is substantial precedent for such an interpretation. Edward Hicks (1780–1849), a Quaker preacher from Bucks County, Pennsylvania, is well known for having painted as many as a hundred versions of the Peaceable Kingdom (see Figure 7.3).[159] In one of his earliest renditions, the child is actually holding the "Branch out of the root of Jesse." Hicks was passionately concerned about the influence of the "inward light" of the "Christ within" upon the human soul. Understanding ancient animal symbolism, Hicks's animals represented aspects of the human personality. In a 1837 sermon, "Hicks described the nature of man in terms of the animals of Isaiah's prophecy, identifying them with the four humors, or temperaments, of medieval medicine: melancholy, sanguine, phlegmatic and choleric."[160] He saw the wolf as melancholy, bear as phlegmatic (sluggish and greedy), leopard as sanguine (buoyant), lion as choleric (angry and willful). Human personality traits are pictured theriomorphically, with each beast carrying other associated features; for instance, the leopard has a seductive sensuality prone to intemperance.[161] In his memoirs Hicks himself writes: "The leopard is the most subtle, cruel, restless creature, and at the same time the most beautiful of all the carnivorous animals of the cat kind."[162]

"Redeemed by the Inner Light," the "wild" animals become at home with their "domestic opposites: the lamb, the kid, the cow, and the ox."[163] For Hicks, there was no doubt that the little child was the Christ Child and the Peaceable Kingdom was a soul no longer discordant but led by Christ. His paintings are psychospiritual pictures, outward and visible presentations of the inward and spiritual peace of Christmas.

Figure 7.3 Peaceable Kingdom, by Edward Hicks (ca. 1834). Courtesy National Gallery of Art, Washington; Gift of Edgar William and Bernice Chrysler Garbisch, 1980.62.15

This reminds us of Sol Invictus. Marcel Metzger writes:

What seems clear is that his cult of *Sol Invictus* was promulgated, in the words of Henry Chadwick, "as a comprehensive monotheism which could embrace all the cults of the empire," a religious component of the program for the restoration of the unity of the empire that earned Aurelian the epithet "Restorer of the World."[164]

What Aurelian intended for Sol to accomplish in the fragmented outer world, Christ enables in the fractious, contentious psyche: unity. Aurelian is lauded as "restorer of the world." Symbolically, Christ is the "restorer of the soul."

Those who knew Christ best attested this ataraxia. Apostle Paul, who never physically met Jesus but dramatically experienced his spiritual presence on the road to Damascus, emphatically proclaimed that "he is our peace" (Ephesians 2:14), [165] and "In Christ all things hold together" (Colossians 1:17). In our era, Susan Howatch writes:

"No demon can withstand the power of Christ," said my father, repeating the words he had used long ago, and what he meant was that no dissociated mind can withstand the integrating power of the Living God whose spark lies deep in the core of the unconscious mind and who can not only heal the shattered ego but unify the entire personality.[166]

Describing a sublime experience that could be a direct commentary on W.H. Auden's (1907–1973) line from "Christmas Oratorio"—"Remembering the stable where for once in our lives Everything became a You and nothing was an It"[167]— Marcus Borg says:

> I saw the same world as I always see, except that it looked radically different. They were moments in which all of our categories (beautiful/ugly, ordinary/ extraordinary, familiar/novel, interesting/boring) fell away. Everything looked exquisite. Everything looked dear. I felt like I was seeing things as they actually are, apart from the domestication and valuation generated by the grid of culture. It seemed like an experience of God.[168]

Here, heaven and earth meet. We've all occasionally experienced these instances of mystical oneness that could be called "Christ moments." Nothing outwardly has actually changed—the smelly man still smells and the annoying woman still annoys—but in this holy time, we perceive it not. Such experiences are the outer projection of inner tranquility. For a brief, sacred moment, Christ has held every-thing together.

Tillich—who saw our lot as estrangement, ambiguity, and anxiety—claimed that in these Christ moments, we can know reconciliation, certainty, and peace. This is what he thought Paul meant when he said that anyone "in Christ ... is a new creation" (2 Corinthians 5:17). In his sermon, "The New Being," Tillich writes:

> Being reconciled—that is the first mark of the New Reality. And being reunited is its second mark. Reconciliation makes reunion possible. The New Creation is the reality in which the separated is united. The New Being is manifest in the Christ because in Him the separation never overcame the unity between Him and God, between Him and mankind, between Him and Himself. This gives His pic-ture in the Gospels its overwhelming and inexhaustible power. In Him we look at a human life that maintained the union in spite of everything that drove Him into separation. He represents and mediates the power of the New Being because he represents and mediates the power of an undisrupted union. ... real healing is not where only a part of body or mind is reunited with the whole, but where the whole itself, our whole being, our whole personality is united with itself.[169]

According to Tillich, we experience Christ as the "reconciling will of God."

> To experience the New Being in Jesus as the Christ means to experience the power in him which conquered existential estrangement in himself and every-one who participates in him ...

For it is Christ who brings the New Being, who saves men from the old being, that is, from existential estrangement and its self-destructive consequences ...

Estrangement [is] the main characteristic of existence. In this sense, healing means reuniting that which is estranged, giving center to what is split, overcoming the split between God and man, man and his world, man and himself.[170]

In this earthly life, the "New Being" is a free bird that graces us only from time to time, removing for the moment the Old Being of anguished separation. Nonetheless, the bottom line, as contemporary Australian Aboriginal Christian Khumo Nthla claims, is that Christ can "integrate the opposites that conspire to pull us apart."[171] This is precisely the experience we so long for on Christmas day. The unity of Self is always fleeting, but the image of the Christ Child in a manger surrounded by family and strangers, animals, and angels ever evokes that unconscious hope. As Phillips Brooks wrote in the hymn "O Little Town of Bethlehem," "How silently, how silently, the wondrous gift is given! So God imparts to human hearts the blessings of his heaven." The blessings of soul peace. And what touches us more deeply than singing or hearing:

Silent night, holy night
All is calm, all is bright.
Round yon Virgin mother and child,
Holy infant so tender and mild
Sleep in heavenly peace,
Sleep in heavenly peace.

Here, both image and music evoke an undisturbed oneness. If only for the season, a day, a moment, it is as though psychically we are the Peaceable Kingdom, our soul the crèche.

From a Jungian perspective, this peace has two poles: One regressive and the other teleological.

Christmas as Preconscious Peace/Uroboric Bliss

The epicenter of Christmas is the peaceful baby Jesus/Self sleeping in a manger. The focus is on Mother Mary holding her newborn in a seamless unity, the two as one. Enduring our inner splits, we embrace these symbols that pull us back to a time of innocence, of original wholeness, a time before fragmentation. No wonder Christmas is ineluctably linked with images of home! Regardless of our chronological age, we desire a return to our original peace, to our golden age, "to a paradisal state just as it was at the birth of Christ."[172] The living symbol of the Christ Child/Self in the Christmas story has the capacity to evoke a reprieve of stillness, as the peace before the expulsion from Eden.

Eliade reports that "The nostalgia for Paradise is universal."[173] Mario Jacoby seconds the obvious: "The longing for freedom from conflict, suffering and deprivation is an eternal dream of great emotional power. It is the dream of total happiness, embodied in almost all cultures in the myth of Paradise."[174] Tillich joins the chorus: "every individual, since he is separated from the whole, desires union with the whole."[175]

Jacoby argues that "depth psychology links ideas of Paradise, the Golden Age or the 'intact world' with the pre-conscious state of infancy, when the ego as the center of human consciousness has not yet been activated."[176] Erich Neumann, analytical psychology's expert in the development of human consciousness, says that, "An embryonic and still undeveloped germ of ego consciousness ... slumbers in the perfect round."[177] This is the uroboric state, represented by the snake that eats its tail, with no beginning or end.[178] In various writings, Neumann continues:

Because the early, uroboric phase of child development is characterized by a minimum of discomfort and tension, and a maximum of well-being and security, as well as by the unity of I and thou, Self and world, it is known to myth as paradisiacal. ... in the uroboric situation of the pre-ego period, in which the ego still lies dormant or emerges only for isolated moments, these oppositions and tensions do not exist. ... In the post-uterine as well as the uterine situation the child is sheltered in the contained round of maternal existence [Mary and Child], because for the child the mother is Self, thou and world in one.[179]

The paradisal pre-ego time is also characterized as "existence in unitary reality," because in it there is not yet any polarization between inner and outer, subject and object, ego and Self. The state of total exteriorization, in which the child has not yet separated itself from the mother and from the world, may be regarded as existence in total participation mystique, a universal existence of being, which constitutes the psychic amniotic fluid in which everything is still "suspended" and out of which the polarities of ego and Self, subject and object, person and world, have yet to be crystallized.[180]

The phase in which the ego germ is contained in the unconsciousness, like the embryo in the womb, when the ego has not yet appeared as a conscious complex and there is no tension between the ego system and the unconscious, is the phase we have designated as uroboric and pleromatic. Uroboric, because it is dominated by the symbol of the circular snake, standing for total nondifferentiation, everything issuing from everything and again entering into everything, depending on everything, and connecting with everything; pleromatic, because the ego germ still dwells in the pleroma, in the "fullness" of the unformed God, and, as consciousness unborn, slumbers in the primordial egg, in the bliss of paradise. The later ego deems this pleromatic existence to be man's first felicity, for at this stage there is no suffering; suffering only comes into the world with the advent of the ego and ego experience.[181]

Only slowly does the ego develop, like an emerging atoll buffeted by the sea. Paradise is lost.

Supporting Neumann's theory are the first drawings of young children (two to five years of age). Rhoda Kellogg, a nursery school teacher who studied more than a million children's drawings over 20 years, tells us that mandalas and their analogs such as suns and radials are among the first on the paper.[182] Furthermore, when young children draw themselves or other people, their representations remain looking very much like mandalas, suns, and radials (see Figure 7.4). Kellogg writes:

Figure 7.4 Child's drawing of Self at two years, three months.

The favorite subject of people is people. And so it is with children and their art. As soon as they are able, at about the age of four, children begin to draw the human figure. Interestingly, this follows in art soon after the children can make mandalas and draw the sun which shines so brightly in his work and on his days. From the sun in his drawings comes the human face, at first huge in its relationship to arms and legs. The first people drawings naturally seem pretty inhuman. Rays of the sun become arms and legs, ears, hair, and head decorations. A child may take away some of the sun's rays and lengthen others, add scribbles for facial features, use small suns for hands and rays for fingers. In the first drawings of humans, the arms are attached to the head, and there are markings on top—not of hair, really, but to balance the legs.[183]

Mandalas, as a representation of the Self, are symbols of unity, totality, and wholeness.[184] Therefore, it is easy to conclude that these first childhood drawings represent uroboric roundness, wholeness, oneness.

The uroboric state may hold the answer to why we are yearly "dreaming of a white Christmas." This zeal for snow cover is not just about an aesthetic scene, but rather about psychological release. On days of great snows, our world covered with "white nothingness,"[185] we are discharged from the outer demands upon us—school is canceled and work optional—and consciousness becomes sleepy, ego vigilance relaxes, and self-judgments rest. Neumann writes:

It is in dreams that we most readily regress to the uroboric stage of the psyche, which like all other bygone stages continues to exist in us and can at any moment be reactivated, provided that the level of consciousness falls, as during sleep, or as the result of some debility or illness or a lowering of consciousness otherwise induced.[186]

On snow days we relish a lowering of consciousness to uroboric stages into a psychic shalom that parallels Christmas peace.

A slightly different way to entertain this notion is to understand that much of our exhaustion at the end of the day is not simply the result of physical exertion but also due to holding ourselves psychically together. A good night's sleep is not just about rejuvenating the body; it is also about putting our psyche back into a cohesive whole after a day of fragmentation. Christmas is a magical day when this integration holds and is felt while we are conscious.

Henri Nouwen (1932–1996), beloved for his sensitivity to the weathers of the human soul, once wrote:

When I first saw [Rembrandt's] the *Prodigal Son*, I had just finished an exhausting six-week lecturing trip through the United States ... I was anxious, lonely, restless and very needy. ... I felt like a vulnerable little child who wanted to crawl onto its mother's lap and cry.[187]

Given the pressures and exigencies of our outer and inner lives, we all know the urge to regress, the "striving back to childhood and mother."[188] Given individual circumstances, this desire may press on any particular day, but Christmas, with its symbols of preconsciousness and oneness, naturally evokes such hopes of psychic peace for many. Christmas, to borrow Jung's words, holds the "inner longing for the stillness and profound peace"[189] of a waking dream, "childhood's golden dreams,"[190] a hypnagogic uroboric moment. Tillich calls this "dreaming innocence."[191] Jacoby says "the target or goal-image of nostalgic longing is the elimination of suffering, conflict, and malaise in an ultimate 'unitary reality.'"[192] Surrounded by the many living symbols of the season, it is possible for us to magically fall back into our original preconscious position of equanimity. Mature and awake, we nonetheless experience profound serenity, as if we were Jesus lying in the manger.

Progressive Aspects of the Christ Child

This regressive Christmas peace is a longed-for oasis from the estrangement, anxiety, and ambiguity of existence. Yet, it can only be a passing respite. It is not sustainable for the long term. To "sleep in heavenly peace" for more than a moment, hour, or season is not to live. It is a death state. In his "Christmas Oratorio," Auden puts these words into the shepherds' and Magi's mouths:

> Our arrogant longing to attain the tomb,
> Our sullen wish to go back to the womb,
> To have no past.
> No future.[193]

It's interesting that the Beatles' song "Golden Slumbers" bleeds into "Carry That Weight." The return to Eden is fiercely guarded and for good reason. We cannot long escape our birthright as a fragmented coalition, suffering a multitude of splits. This is not just a curse but also blessing. It is axiomatic for Jung that "life is born only of the spark of opposites."[194] Our affliction is also our boon.

How so? We turn to a cardinal Christmas symbol: Light. Once the feast of the Nativity began being celebrated, people immediately linked it to the birthday of Sol Invictus—the Invincible Sun. At Christmastime, around the world and across cultures, lights festoon the public squares while at home candles burn and fires blaze. The Great Star is a sign of Jesus' birth. Prophet Isaiah looks into the future and proclaims:

> The people who walked in darkness,
> have seen a great light;
> those who dwell in a land of deep darkness,
> on them has light shined.

(9:2)

John, in his Gospel, identifies the incarnate Christ as "the light of people. The light shines in the darkness, and the darkness has not overcome it" (1:4b, 5). In art, the Christ Child is consistently pictured with a nimbus, representing holy light. Most dramatically, in a number of paintings the Christ Child, who is born in the darkest night, radiates light, becoming the sole source of illumination. It is displayed in so many ways during the Christmas season as to leave no doubt that the Christ Child is the bearer of light, the one who "takes the role of Sol."[195]

The personal associations of our analysands should never be discounted, but when it comes to archetypal amplifications for Jung, "Light always refers to consciousness."[196] "'Light' is the symbolical equivalent of consciousness, and the nature of consciousness is expressed by analogies with light."[197] Jung notes that the child god "distinguishes itself by deeds that point to the conquest of the dark;"[198] therefore, he calls Christ "the archetype of consciousness."[199]

> Christ was primarily a light-bringer, who went forth from the Father in order to illuminate the stupidity, darkness, and unconsciousness of mankind and to lead the individual back to his origins through self-knowledge.[200]

The Christ Child, the manger babe, then is a bipolar symbol. Most obviously, he represents a time before ego, the uroboric oneness we prize. As Jacoby claims and we know, "Humankind has never accepted the loss of Paradise."[201] In direct opposition, the Christ Child vigorously represents the newborn sun, the coming of the light, a growing consciousness. Its aim is not regression to the original, unfragmented oneness but progression to an ever-widening integration and awareness of one's psychic totality. Jung writes: "The current flows backward to its source; the inner man wants something which the visible man does not want, and we are at war with ourselves. Only then in this distress, do we discover the psyche."[202] Similarly, theologian Stagg cautions us that "Salvation is not an escape from the tensions of our polar situation. Salvation is in the making to the extent that we properly see, understand, accept, and cultivate these polarities of our human existence."[203] Paradoxically, except for brief dispensations, there is no peace unless we are in the battle for greater self-awareness. Humans have a drive to individuate.

When Bartlett Giamatti resigned as president of Yale University to take on the task of commissioner for Major League Baseball, his decision was startling. Asked by a reporter why he would trade the prestige of Yale for the grit of baseball, Giamatti's answer was even more surprising: "Why, baseball is our greatest expression of what it is to be human!"

> As a player in this game, you … step up to the plate, a tiny box one foot square from which you mustn't move. You have a bat in your hand, and the odds are nine to one against you. There's a judge yelling things behind you, and nine opponents out in the field who want to see you lose the game. Someone throws a ball; it comes at a speed of 100 miles per hour at your head, and you're supposed

to hit it and run for your life. Along the way, as you run, you may be asked to steal, to slide through the dirt, and to somehow avoid the nine people who are trying to throw you out. You will be asked to sacrifice. And the only reason you endure all these hardships is in order to return home.[204]

While the regressive aspect of Christmas talks about returning home sleepy-eyed to the conflict-free psychic golden age, Giamatti is speaking about a repetitive coming home that takes place only after honest engagement with life's struggles and conflicts, where one returns hopefully wiser and more knowledgeable about one's soul. The Christ Child also symbolizes this increasing consciousness.

Analyst Michael Fordham argues "that the self divides up (deintegrates) to originate development in infancy."[205] He further postulates that as consciousness enlarges throughout life, "integration and deintegration have a rhythmic relation to each other." He sees the Self (for our purposes symbolized by the Christ Child) as the central archetype that organizes the unconscious, integrates unconscious material into developing ego consciousness, and "transcends and unites opposites."[206] The result is "the general tendency towards wholeness, towards an integration in which the conscious mind and the unconscious mind become united."[207] This is not the undifferentiated wholeness of uroboric infancy but an advancing process of psychic wholeness that enlarges by continually integrating unfamiliar parts of one's unconscious into awareness. The Christ Child points to this equally powerful desire, orchestrated by the Self. In his essay "On the Psychology of the Child Archetype," Jung makes this point and equates the archetype of the "child god" with "the still living 'Christ-child'."[208]

> One of the essential features of the child motif is its futurity. The child is potential future. Here the occurrence of the child motif in the psychology of the individual signifies as a rule an anticipation of future developments, even though at first sight it may seem like a retrospective configuration. Life is a flux, a flowing into the future, and not a stoppage or a backwash. It is therefore not surprising that so many of the mythological saviors are child gods. This agrees exactly with our experience of the psychology of the individual, which shows that the "child" paves the way for a future change of personality. In the individual process, it anticipates the figure that comes from the synthesis of conscious and unconscious elements in the personality. It is therefore a symbol which unites the opposites; a mediator, bringer of healing, that is, one who makes whole. Because it has this meaning, the child motif is capable of the numerous transformations mentioned above: it can be expressed by roundness, the circle or sphere, or else by the quaternity as another form of wholeness.[209]

The fear and desire of this progressive aspect of the archetypal "child god"/Christ Child is shown in multiple facets of our Christmas story and celebration. We look first to Matthew's account. The Magi, royalty in their own right, are nonetheless searchers looking for a power greater than themselves. So great is their desire that no sacrifice is too large. They take on a sacred quest, following a gloriously radiant star to the newborn king they will worship. In direct contrast is King Herod, who hearing a new king is born, feels threatened and becomes afraid, and commands all children of his kingdom be destroyed. No one likes this part of the Christmas story, and we wonder why it must be there. But given what we now know, it makes perfect sense.

Psychologically, Herod represents the ego, the king of consciousness. With the birth of the Christ Child (representing the Self, the whole psyche), a whole new state of affairs comes into being. Herod/ego must relinquish its place as the supreme center/king of the psyche to the Christ Child/Self who is the king of the entire psyche, the conscious and unconscious. Most of us are like Herod, until some intrusion of the unconscious—a life-compromising neuroses, a vexing complex, a dream that shakes us to the core—forces us to reconsider if consciousness is the circumference of our psyche, if the ego is king. When this happens, we too become Magi who search for something greater than ourselves. The ego, satisfied to be the governor of consciousness, abdicates being emperor of the entire psychic realm. Looking at it this way, Christmas invites us to "bow down and worship" the authentic sovereign of our psyche: The Self/Christ Child (see Figure 7.5). Rather than fearing dethronement by the child as Herod instinctively did, we lavish extraordinary gifts and well-wishes upon those who symbolize the continued development of our own psyches.

Secondly, as already noted, Christ is light, a child hero whose "main feat is to overcome the monster of darkness."[210] About the influence of the incarnation upon the psyche, Jung claims: "Thus the unconscious wholeness penetrated into the psychic realm of inner experience, and man was made aware of all that entered into his true configuration."[211] The ego rarely wants to know about the whole makeup of its personality, so as the innkeeper, it barks, "No room. No room in the inn!" The uprising content of the unconscious that hopes to find ego hospitality is turned away as the ego locks the door and goes back to business as usual.

Jung describes this psychologically.

It is in the nature of the conscious mind to concentrate on relatively few contents and to raise them to the highest pitch of clarity. A necessary result and precondition is the exclusion of other potential contents of consciousness, the exclusion is bound to bring about a certain one-sidedness of the conscious contents.[212]

Frequently, the archetypal drive to individuate forces the issue with dreams, complexes, and neuroses relentlessly knocking at our door. We see this in Dickens's ageless classic, *A Christmas Carol in Prose, Being a Ghost Story of Christmas*. The miserable, miserly Ebenezer Scrooge is blessed with an almost unbearable nightmare in which Christmas apparitions expose the monumental cost, to himself and others, of his tunnel vision. Three scenes crack him open, enabling him to evolve. Scrooge is subsequently enlarged, learning generosity, empathy, and

Figure 7.5 Adoration of the Magi, mandala by Fra Angelico and Fillipo Lippi (c. 1440–1460). Courtesy, National Gallery of Art, Washington; Samuel H. Kress Collection 1952.2.2

kindness. He finds joy and peace, a true Christmas miracle. Better late than never, he individuates.[213]

Jacobi reminds us, "Jung's method is finalistic, his eyes are always turned toward the totality of the psyche ... and within the psychic totality the unconscious ... is also the 'ever-creative mother of consciousness.'"[214] Christmas is a time to welcome psychic newcomers to consciousness. Nowhere in the Bible is there a greater concentration of dreams, angel communiqués, and mysterious inspirations than in the two Nativity narratives (Luke 1:11, 26; 2:9, 27; Matthew 1:20, 2:13). This darkest time of the year may naturally bring us closer to our unconsciousness and allow us an opening to pay greater attention to our dreams, to follow the inspiration of our fantasies, to consider projections that may have their origin in an unknown part of our Self. No wonder the fantastic story of "The Nutcracker," written by German E.T.A. Hoffman (1776–1822) and first published in 1816, became a perennial Christmas favorite.[215] Onstage, it brings to light unknown but fabulous sights from around the world; psychologically, it presents the ego with a carnival of the soul.

In an extraverted way, this extravagant welcome of every mood and behavior has always been part of the Christmas celebration. Christmas sermons and revelries, gifts to the poor, and excess for oneself all seem like irreconcilable opposites, but at Christmas no one minds or even notices the discrepancy. Unexpected reversals occur that any other time would make the ego take umbrage, like how slaves and strangers were welcomed at the family table during Saturnalia.

William Walsh in 1898 writes about the Christmas experience in Lima.

> Music of guitars, clattering castanets, and pebbles rattling in gourds fill the air with mild discordant sounds. No door is closed. There is music and dancing and the distribution of gifts in every house, all are welcome to enter. Strangers are sure of a hearty welcome, and to be a foreigner is to have a double claim on hospitality and to receive a double welcome.[216]

Dickens, the master of understanding Christmas, says all this best.

> Time was with most of us, when Christmas Day, encircling all of our limited world like a magic ring, left nothing out for us to miss or seek; bound together all our home enjoyments, affections, and hopes; grouped everything and everyone round the Christmas fire, and made the little picture shining in our bright young, complete.
>
> Welcome, everything! Welcome, alike what has been, and what never was, and what we hope may be, to your shelter underneath the holly, to your place round the Christmas fire, where what is sits open-hearted! ... On Christmas Day, we shall shut out from our fireside, Nothing.[217]

For Jung Christmas, under the sway of the integrating Christ Child, can become a time when we open the door of the ego and offer hospitality to unknown contents of the unconscious that want to be known and embraced—to become part of our enlarging consciousness. Harding writes:

> [Jesus] lived his own heritage, he lived *it into the future*. This is the most significant meaning of the child archetype. Inevitably the child grows and changes, and we cannot know beforehand what its destiny may be. So when we embark on the quest for individuation (for wholeness), of one thing we may be certain that we do *not* know where the quest will lead us.[218]

The Christ Child symbolizes the "life-urge which subjects every growing thing to the laws of maximum self-fulfillment."[219] The Christ Child became so dearly and permanently associated with the winter solstice because with him comes the growing light that symbolizes new contents of the unconscious coming to light, becoming conscious. As Jung concludes, with "a renewal of the light" comes "a rebirth of consciousness."[220]

Conclusion

A substantial part of the enduring appeal of Christmas is the unconscious yearning for the effortless pre-ego state of the uroborus symbolized by the holy infant in a manger. Psychoanalyst L. Bryce Boyer writes:

> One must wonder whether Christianity has succeeded in becoming the popular religion of the Western world at least partially because of the unconscious dream in all of us to retain the early belief in the unity of mother and child.[221]

We have shown this to be correct. Such episodes of pre-split consciousness are desired but necessarily fleeting. The Christ Child/Self represents not just original wholeness, the effortless golden age, but also hard-won integration into the ego of psychic strangers, a growing, maturing, individuated wholeness.

With this understanding, the crèche and the Peaceable Kingdom are no longer just sentimental images, but robust symbols of disparate elements achieving a higher level of integration, life-giving self-consonance. Jung quotes philosopher Karl Jöel:

> It is not the old, mindless unity that the artist strives for, but a felt reunion; not empty unity, but full unity; not the oneness of indifference, but the oneness attained through differentiation. ... All life is a loss of balance and a struggling back into balance. We find this return home in religion and art.[222]

The Christ Child foreshadows a burgeoning oneness. Indeed, Jung tells us that the appearance of the child god in a dream anticipates "an individuation process which is approaching wholeness."[223] It is only fitting that in one of Jung's last dreams, we might say his Christmas dream, "he saw a large round stone which bore the inscription: 'As a sign unto you of Wholeness and Oneness.'"[224] At Christmas, nearly every threshold bears witness to both our original and ever hoped-for oneness. Large and small, simple and ornate, on barn or apartment door, the Christmas wreath—circular, uroboric, evergreen—symbolizing the Self, our wholeness— past, present, and future.

Notes

1 C.G. Jung, *Memories, Dreams, Reflections* (1961), Aniela Jaffe, ed. (Vintage Books, 1989), v. From Coleridge, *Notebooks*.
2 Jung, *Memories, Dreams, Reflections*, 48.
3 Wayne Rollins, *Soul and Psyche: The Bible in Psychological Perspective* (Fortress Press, 1999), 49–52.

4 Jung, *Memories, Dreams, Reflections*, 19. The virgin or supernatural conception: "psychologically it tells us that a content of the unconscious ('child') has come into existence without the natural help of a human father (i.e., consciousness). It tells us, on the contrary, that some god has begotten a son and further that the son is identical with the father, which in psychological language means that a central archetype, the God-image, has renewed itself ('been reborn') and become 'incarnate' in a way perceptible to consciousness. The 'mother' corresponds to the 'virgin animas,' who is not turned toward the outer world and is therefore not corrupted by it. She is turned rather toward the 'inner sun,' the archetype of transcendent wholeness—the self." C.G. Jung, *The Symbols of Transformation*, 5 (Princeton University Press, 1975), 323.

5 William McGuire and R.F.C. Hull, eds., *C.G. Jung Speaking: Interviews and Encounters* (Princeton University Press, 1977), 401.

6 Edward F. Edinger, "An Outline of Analytical Psychology," *Quadrant* no. 1 (1968), 4.

7 C.G. Jung, "The Transcendent Function," in *The Structure and Dynamics of the Psyche*, 8 (Princeton University Press, 1975), 87.

8 C.G. Jung, *Aion: Researches into the Phenomenology of the Self*, 9ii (Princeton University Press, 1973), 3.

9 Jung, *Aion*, 3.

10 C.G. Jung, "The Psychology of Dementia Praecox" (1907) in *The Psychogenesis of Mental Disease*, 3 (Princeton University Press, 1975), 40.

11 Marie-Louise Von Franz, *Creation Myths*, rev. ed. (Shambhala, 1995), 166, 167.

12 Jung, *Aion*, 5.

13 Von Franz, *Creation Myths*, 166, 168.

14 Jung, *Aion*, 5.

15 Edward C. Whitmont, *The Symbolic Quest: Basic Concepts of Analytical Psychology* (Princeton University Press, 1991), 156.

16 Jolande Jacobi, *The Psychology of C.G. Jung* (Yale University Press, 1973), 18.

17 C.G. Jung, "Women in Europe" (1927) in *Civilization in Transition*, 10 (Princeton University Press, 1975), 127.

18 Frances G. Wickes, *The Inner World of Man* (Henry Holt, 1948), 65.

19 C.G. Jung, "The Relations Between the Ego and the Unconscious" (1917, 1943) in *Two Essays in Analytical Psychology*, 7 (Princeton University Press, 1975), 146, 158.

20 Jung, "The Relations Between the Ego and the Unconscious", 145.

21 Alane Sauder MacGuire, Course: *Two Essays on Analytical Psychology* (C.G. Jung Institute, 2004).

22 Whitmont, *The Symbolic Quest*, 158.

23 Jung, "The Relations Between the Ego and the Unconscious," 158, 302.

24 C.G. Jung, "On the Psychology of the Unconscious" (1917), in *Two Essays in Analytical Psychology*, 7 (Princeton University Press, 1975), 41–44.

25 C.G. Jung, *Psychological Types* (1921), 6 (Princeton University Press, 1976), 414 (687); *Modern Man in Search of a Soul,* Trans. W. S. Dell and Cary F. Baynes (Harcourt, Brace & World, 1933), 86.

26 Jung "On the Psychology of the Unconscious," 44.

27 Jacobi, *The Psychology of C.G. Jung*, 19.

28 Jung, *Psychological Types*, Vol. 6, 427, 330; Marie-Louise Von Franz, "The Inferior Function," in *Lectures on Jung's Typology* (Spring Publications, 1986), 1.

29 Jung, *Psychological Types*, 333–334, 374.

30 Jacobi, *The Psychology of C.G. Jung*, 19.

31 Jung, *Psychological Types*, 331–332.

32 Jung, *Psychological Types*, 392. In more detail, Jung writes: "In extraversion and introversion it is clearly a matter of two antithetical, natural attitudes or trends which Goethe once referred to as diastole and systole. They ought, in their harmonious alternation,

to give life a rhythm, but it seems to require a high degree of art to achieve such a rhythm." Jung, "On the Psychology of the Unconscious," 59.

33 A complete introvert would be depressed because all his energy would be kept inside. A complete extravert would have no substance because all his energy would continually flow out.

34 Jacobi, *The Psychology of C.G. Jung*, 19.

35 Jung, *Psychological Types*, 6.

36 Jung, *Psychological Types*, 359.

37 Jung, *Psychological Types*, 481.

38 Jung, *Psychological Types*, 434.

39 James Hillman, "The Feeling Function." In *Lectures on Jung's Typology* (Spring Publications, 1971), 92.

40 Hillman, "The Feeling Function," 91–92.

41 Jung, *Psychological Types*, 357.

42 Jacobi, *The Psychology of C.G. Jung*, 13.

43 Jung, *Psychological Types*, 360.

44 Jacobi, *The Psychology of C.G. Jung*, 12.

45 C.G. Jung, *Analytical Psychology: Its Theory & Practice* (Pantheon Books, 1968), 11.

46 Jung, *Analytical Psychology*, 14.

47 Marie-Louise Von Franz, *Man and His Symbols*, C.G. Jung, ed. (A Windfall Book, 1983), 49.

48 Jung, *Aion*, 8.

49 C.G. Jung, *Two Essays in Analytical Psychology*, 127.

50 Jacobi, *The Psychology of C.G. Jung*, 109.

51 Esther M. Harding, *Psychic Energy: Its Source and Transformation* (Princeton University Press, 1973), 295.

52 Jung, *Two Essays in Analytical Psychology*, 66; see also 54.

53 Fyodor Dostoevsky, *The Double*, trans. Evelyn Harden (Ardis, 1985), 64.

54 Harding, *Psychic Energy*, 295, note 27.

55 Jacobi, *The Psychology of C.G. Jung*, 111.

56 "It is a general rule that every unknown content of our unconscious is projected to other human beings or even objects." Gerhard Adler, *Studies in Analytical Psychology* (C.G. Jung Foundation for Analytical Psychology, 1966), 16.

57 Jung, *Analytical Psychology: Its Theory and Practice,* 179–180. This is a major point throughout Jung's work and analytical concern. See also Jung, *Modern Man in Search of a Soul*, 142; C.G. Jung, *The Undiscovered Self* (Mentor Book, 1958) 109, 114; Edward Edinger, *Ego and Archetype* (Shambhala, 1972), 85–91; Harding, *Psychic Energy*, 116.

58 The shadow also includes substantially positive elements that have been forced to our nether regions because of a trauma or because they were rejected by our parents, community, or society. In this case, we may encounter strong affect around people who strongly embody those traits.

59 Harding, *Psychic Energy*, 297. Jung says, "With a little self-criticism one can see through the shadow—so far as its nature is personal," *Aion*, 10.

60 See C.G. Jung, *Experimental Researches*, 2 (Princeton University Press, 1973). Jung writes: "When I took up the cudgels for Freud in public, I already had a scientific position that was widely known on account of my association experiments, conducted independently of Freud, and the theory of complexes based upon them." C.G. Jung, "A Rejoinder to Dr. Bally" (1934) in *Civilization in Transition*, 10 (Princeton University Press, 1975), 544 (note).

61 C.G. Jung, *Psychology and Religion*, (Yale University Press, 1963), 13.

62 C.G. Jung, *Psychology and Alchemy (1943)*, 12 (Princeton University Press, 1974), 301.
63 C.G. Jung, "On the Doctrine of the Complexes" (1911), in *Experimental Researches* 2 (Princeton University Press, 1973), 601.
64 C.G. Jung, "Commentary on 'The Secret of the Golden Flower,'" in *Alchemical Studies* 13, (Princeton University Press, 1976), 50.
65 Elie G. Humbert, *C.G. Jung: The Fundamentals of Theory and Practice* (Chiron, 1988), 4.
66 Jung, *Modern Man in Search of a Soul*, 79.
67 Jolande Jacobi, *Complex, Archetype, Symbol in the Psychology of C.G. Jung* (Princeton University Press, 1974), ix (foreword by Jung).
68 Aniela Jaffé, *C.G. Jung: Word and Image* (Princeton University Press, 1979), 6.
69 Harding, *Psychic Energy*, 135.
70 Marie-Louise Von Franz, "The Process of Individuation," in *Man and His Symbols*, ed. C.G. Jung (A Windfall Book, 1983), 177.
71 Jung, *Aion*, 14–16.
72 Jung, *Two Essays in Analytical Psychology*, 304; Jung, *Psychological Types*, 467.
73 Jung, *Memories, Dreams, Reflections*, 392; Edinger, *Ego and Archetype*, 100.
74 Jacobi, *The Psychology of C.G. Jung*, 120.
75 Jung, *Axion*, 17.
76 Jung, "The Relations Between the Ego and the Unconscious," 198.
77 Whitmont, *The Symbolic Quest*, 194.
78 Jung, *Aion*, 16.
79 C.G. Jung, *The Psychology of the Transference* (1946), 16 (Princeton University Press, 1975), 304.
80 Murray Stein, *The Bible as Dream: A Jungian Interpretation* (Chiron, 2018), 76.
81 Mircea Eliade, *Images and Symbols: Studies in Religious Symbolism*, trans. Philip Mairet (Sheed & Ward, 1961), 13.
82 C.G. Jung, "Synchronicity: An Acausal Connecting Principle" (1952) in *The Structure and Dynamics of the Psyche*, 8 (Princeton University Press, 1975), 226–227.
83 C.G. Jung, "Fundamental Questions of Psychotherapy" (1951), in *The Practice of Psychotherapy*, 16 (Princeton University Press, 1975), 124.
84 C.G. Jung, "Archetypes of the Collective Unconscious" (1954), In *Archetypes of the Collective Unconscious*, 9i, (Princeton University Press, 1975), 38.
85 Jung, *Symbols of Transformation*, 313.
86 Jung, *Symbols of Transformation*, 313.
87 Jung, *Symbols of Transformation*, 309.
88 Betram J. Cohler and David deBoer, "Maintaining a Sense of Coherence in a Troubled World," *Contemporary Psychology* 40, no. 10 (1995), 941.
89 Robert Jay Lifton, *The Protean Self: Human Resilience in an Age of Fragmentation* (University of Chicago Press, 1993).
90 Lifton, *The Protean Self*, 8.
91 "A psychic reaction can influence a physical one and a physical reaction a psychic condition." Von Franz, *Creation Myths*, 5.
92 William Whitney, "Heart Attacks Increase After 9/11," *Psychology Today*, November 14, 2003. psychologytoday.com/us/articles/200311/heart-attacks-increase-after-911, accessed May 13, 2025.
93 Lifton, *The Protean Self*, 8. In Greek mythology, Proteus was able to change himself into any shape. According to Lifton, such an open, fluid, and supple Self is needed for the individual to remain vital in the midst of fragmenting change and multiplicity.
94 Von Franz, *Creation Myths*, 65–66.
95 Jung, *Memories, Dreams, Reflections*, 21.
96 Jung, *Memories, Dreams, Reflections*, 33, 45.

97   C.G. Jung, *The Zofingia Lectures*, Supp. A (Princeton University Press, 1983), 47.

98   Jung, *Psychology and Alchemy*, 81.

99   Jung, *The Psychology of the Transference*, 262.

100 Jung, "On the Psychology of the Unconscious," 19.

101 Jung, *Modern Man in Search of a Soul*, 236–237.

102 C.G. Jung, *Mysterium Coniunctionis* (1954), 14 (Princeton University Press, 1976), 169–170.

103 C.G. Jung, *The Red Book* (Norton, 2011). In a way, psychiatrist, neuroscience researcher, and philosopher Iain McGilchrist, in his eBook, *The Divided Brain and the Search for Meaning: Why We Are so Unhappy* (Yale University Press, 2012) envisions this human predicament as the result of the two hemispheres of the brain not being given equal respect and privilege.

104 Jaffé, *C.G. Jung: Word and Image*, 217.

105 Augustine, *The Confessions*, trans. Rex Warner (Mentor, 1963), 168.

106 Sacvan Bercovitch, *The Puritan Origins of the American Self* (Yale University Press, 1975), 19.

107 Paul Tillich, *Systematic Theology: Three Volumes in One* (Chicago University Press, 1967), II, 34, 44, 61.

108 Tillich, *Systematic Theology*, II, 40.

109 Frank Stagg, *Polarities of Man's Existence in Biblical Perspective* (Westminster Press, 1973), 43. (1 Corinthians 7:34; cf. 2 Corinthians 7:1).

110 B. Jowett, trans., "The Phaedrus," *The Works of Plato* (Tudor Publishing, nd), 365, 403–404.

111 Von Franz, *Creation Myths*, 58.

112 William James, *Psychology: The Briefer Course* (Harper & Brothers, 1961), 43.

113 William James, *The Varieties of Religious Experience* (Collier, 1961), 144.

114 James, *Psychology: The Briefer Course*, 44–48.

115 James, *Psychology*, 53.

116 Karl Menninger, *Man Against Himself* (Harcourt Brace Jovanovich, 1938).

117 Philip Zimbardo, *Psychopathology: Biological and Social Factors of Mental Illness*, "Discovering Psychology" television series (Annenberg/Corporation for Public Broadcasting, 2001).

118 Samuel T. Wilkinson, *Purpose: What Evolution and Human Nature Imply About the Meaning of Our Existence* (Pegasus Books, 2024), 13–14.

119 Jung, *Memories, Dreams, Reflections,* 335.

120 "Mary Wells Biography," cmgww.com/music/wells/ [accessed 11/9/24].

121 Heinz Kohut, *The Restoration of the Self* (International Universities Press, 1977), 288.

122 Kohut, *The Restoration of the Self*, 286.

123 Robert Louis Stevenson, *The Strange Case of Dr. Jekyll and Mr. Hyde* (Charles Scribners' Sons, 1886).

124 W.B. Yeats, "The Second Coming," in *The Collected Poems of W.B. Yeats* (Macmillan, 1959), 184.

125 Pablo Neruda, excerpts from "We Are Many," from *Extravagaria* by Pablo Neruda, translated by Alastair Reid. (Farrar, Straus & Giroux, 1974), 98-101. Translation copyright © 1974 by Alastair Reid. Reprinted by permission of Farrar, Straus and Giroux. All Rights Reserved. Pablo Neruda "Muchos somos," *Estravagario* © Pablo Neruda, 1958, y Fundación Pablo Neruda.

126 Jung, *The Psychology of the Transference*, 208. The unconscious suffering of the opposites may well be revealed in the epidemic proportions of human addictions. Drugs, alcohol, tobacco, gambling, perfectionism, overeating, or compulsive buying—almost everyone is afflicted. Do these obsessions medicate the anxiety of our fragmentation?

127 Jung, *The Psychology of the Transference*, 281.

128   Jung, *Mysterium Coniunctionis*, 364.

129   Jung, *Psychology and Alchemy*, 41.

130   C.G. Jung, "Psychology and Religion" (Yale University Press, 1963), 82.

131   C.G. Jung, *The Undiscovered Self* (Mentor Book, 1958), 14–15.

132   Jung, *Psychology and Religion*, 102.

133   Jung, *The Psychology of the Transference*, 265.

134   Jung, *Psychology and Alchemy*, 182.

135   Jung, *Psychological Types*, 460.

136   C.G. Jung, "Flying Saucers: A Modern Myth of Things Seen in the Skies," in *Civilization in Transition* 10 (Princeton University Press, 1975), 424.

137   Robert Browning, *The Complete Poetic and Dramatic Works of Robert Browning* (Houghton Mifflin, 1895), 18.

138   Harding, *Psychic Energy*, 361.

139   Harding, *Psychic Energy*, 411.

140   Jan Wiener, "Transference and Countertransference: Contemporary Perspectives," in *Analytical Psychology: Contemporary Perspectives in Jungian Analysis*, eds. J. Cambray and L. Carter (Brunner-Routledge, 2004), 150.

141   Edward Edinger, *The Aion Lectures: Exploring the Self in C.G. Jung's Aion* (Inner City Books, 1996), 34.

142   Erich Neumann, *The Origins and History of Consciousness* (Princeton University Press, 1970), 417.

143   Jung, *Aion*, 36; see also 44, 68.

144   Jung, *Psychology and Alchemy*, 12; see also 355, and "A Psychological Approach to the Dogma of the Trinity," in *Psychology and Religion: West and East*, 11, 194.

145   Jung, *Symbols of Transformation*, 368, 392.

146   Jung, *Flying Saucers*, 410; see also *Mysterium Coniunctionis*, note 246; "Jung and Religious Belief," in *The Symbolic Life*, 18 (Princeton University Press, 1976), 730–731, 737, 738. Though the main force of Jung's contention is that Christ equals the Self, we acknowledge that on some occasions he qualifies this assertion. For instance: "Yet, although the attributes of Christ … undoubtedly mark him out as an embodiment of the self, looked at from the psychological angle he corresponds to only one half of the archetype. The other half appears in the Antichrist. The latter is just as much a manifestation of the self, except, that he consists of its dark aspect." Jung, *Aion*, 44. Again: "Even the Christ-figure is not a totality, for it lacks the nocturnal side of the psyche's nature, the darkness of the spirit, and is also without sin. Without the integration of evil there is no totality." "Psychological Approach to the Trinity," 156. To this I would ask: "How do we know that Christ did not integrate evil?" Furthermore, Jung qualifies the qualification: "It has been objected that Christ cannot have been a valid symbol of the self, or was only an illusory substitute for it. I can agree with this view only if it refers strictly to the present time, when psychological criticism has become possible, but not if it pretends to judge the pre-psychological age. Christ did not merely *symbolize* wholeness, but, as a psychic phenomenon, he *was* wholeness. This is proved by the symbolism as well as by the phenomenology of the past, for which—be it noted—evil was a *privatio boni*. The idea of totality is, at any given time, as total as one is oneself. Who can guarantee that our conception of totality is not equally in need of completion?" *Aion*, 62, note, 75.

147   Jung, "Answer to Job," 439, 430.

148   C.G. Jung, "Transformation Symbolism in the Mass (1954)," in *Psychology and Religion: West and East* 11 (Princeton University Press, 1975) 293. "As early as the period of primitive Christianity, the idea of the incarnation had been refined to include the intuition of 'Christ within us.'" Jung, *Memories, Dreams and Reflections*, 328.

149 Jung, *The Psychology of the Transference*, 265.
150 "There are also medieval mandalas with Christ at the center, surrounded by the four Evangelists." Mario A. Jacoby, *Longing for Paradise: Psychological Perspectives on an Archetype* (Sigo Press, 1985), 199. Jung writes: "the unconscious produces a natural symbol, technically termed a mandala, which has the functional significance of a union of the opposites," "Psychology and Religion," 90.
151 Jung, *Psychological Types*, 262.
152 Jung, *Aion*, 132; Jung, *Mysterium Coniunctionis*, 328.
153 Jacoby, *Longing for Paradise*, 198.
154 Jung, *Aion*, 180.
155 Jung, *Mysterium Coniunctionis*, 349.
156 Eugen Drewermann, *Discovering the God Child Within: A Spiritual Psychology of the Infancy of Jesus* (Crossroad Publishing, 1994), 18.
157 C.L. Mitton, "Peace in the New Testament," in *The Interpreter's Dictionary of the Bible*, Vol. 3, K–Q (Abingdon Press, 1962), 706.
158 Edward F. Randolph, "The Christmas Message for 1941 A.D.," *Pennsylvania Co-Op Review* 9 no. 1 (1941), 17.
159 Mariann Smith, *Edward Hicks*, exhibition notes, Albright-Knox Art Gallery, https://buffaloakg.org/artworks/194018-peaceable-kingdom [accessed November 9, 2024].
160 Eleanor Price Mather, *Edward Hicks Primitive Quaker: His Religion In Relation to His Art* (Pendle Hill Publications, 1970), 28–29.
161 John Brzostoski, "Hicks's Peaceable Kingdom," *Friends Journal*, February 2000, 3.
162 Mather, *Edward Hicks Primitive Quaker*, 30.
163 Smith, *Edward Hicks*.
164 Marcel Metzger, *History of the Liturgy: The Major Stages*, trans. Madeleine M. Beaumont (Liturgical Press, 1997), 89.
165 Paul says that Christ's message is a "gospel of peace" (Ephesians 6:15) and encourages us to "let the peace of Christ rule in our hearts" (Colossians 3:5). As a greeting, Paul often says: "Grace to you and peace" (Romans 1:7; 1 Corinthians 1:3; 2 Corinthians 1:2; Galatians 1:3; Philippians 1:1; 2 Thessalonians 1:21).
166 Susan Howatch, *Mystical Paths* (Fawcett Crest, 1992), 75.
167 W.H. Auden, "For the Time Being: A Christmas Oratorio," in *Collected Poems by W.H. Auden,* edited by Edward Mendelson. (Vintage International/Random House, 1991), 399. "For the Time Being," copyright 1944 and © renewed 1972 by W.H. Auden; from *Collected Poems by W.H. Auden,* edited by Edward Mendelson. Used by permission of Random House, an imprint and division of Penguin Random House LLC. All rights reserved. Copyright © 1944 by The Estate of W.H. Auden. Reprinted by permission of Curtis Brown, Ltd. All rights reserved.
168 Marcus Borg, "When Heaven and Earth Meet," *The Living Pulpit* 5, no. 4 (1996): 4.
169 Paul Tillich, *The New Being* (Charles Scribner's Sons, 1955), 22–23.
170 Tillich, *Systematic Theology*, II, 125, 150, 166, 169.
171 Khumo Nthla, "Community" in *The Living Pulpit* 3, no. 4 (1994), 13.
172 Jung, *Psychological Types*, 259.
173 Mircea Eliade, "Nostalgia for Paradise," *Parabola: Myth and the Quest for Meaning* 1, no. 1 (1976), 6.
174 Jacoby, *Longing for Paradise*, vii.
175 Tillich, *Systematic Theology*, II, 52.
176 Jacoby, *Longing for Paradise*, 7.
177 Neumann, *The Origins and History of Consciousness*, 12.
178 We note the uroboric parallel with Christ who declares: "I am the Alpha and the Omega, the beginning and the end" (Revelations 21:6, also 1:8).

179 Erich Neumann, *The Child: Structures and Dynamics of the Nascent Personality* (G.P. Putnam's Sons, 1973), 14.
180 Erich Neumann, "Narcissism, Normal Self-Formation and the Primary Relation to the Mother," in *Spring* (Analytical Psychology Club of New York, 1966), 108.
181 Neumann, *The Origins and History of Consciousness*, 276.
182 Rhoda Kellogg, *Analyzing Children's Art* (Mayfield Publishing, 1970), 64–113, 193.
183 Rhoda Kellogg, *The Psychology of Children's Art* (CRM Publishers, 1967), 65–66.
184 Jung, *Aion*, 31, 424.
185 Ad de Vries, *Dictionary of Symbols and Imagery* (North-Holland Publishing, 1976), 430.
186 Neumann, *The Origins and History of Consciousness*, 276.
187 Henri J.M. Nouwen, *The Return of the Prodigal Son* (Image Books, 1992), 4.
188 Jung, *Symbols of Transformation*, 367.
189 Jung, *Symbols of Transformation*, 346.
190 Jung, *Symbols of Transformation*, 403.
191 Tillich, *Systematic Theology*, II, 36.
192 Jacoby, *Longing for Paradise*, 13. "The striving for the experience of Paradise as containment within the 'Great Round,' the 'unitary reality,' is based on an archetypal pattern necessary to human development. As an inner image or expectation it lives on within us, creating a nostalgia the intensity of which is in inverse proportion to the amount of external fulfillment encountered in the earliest phase of life. Despite all the illusions and regressive tendencies it may entail, from the psychotherapeutic standpoint it is important that the longing for the positive aspect of the Maternal remains alive in the face of all experience to the contrary. For that longing harbors within it the yearning for confidence in some solid, nourishing ground. And, at least in part, this yearning can be temporarily transferred to the analyst in a therapeutically effective manner," 8.
193 Auden, *Christmas Oratorio*, 444. "For the Time Being," copyright 1944 and © renewed 1972 by W.H. Auden; from *Collected Poems by W.H. Auden*, edited by Edward Mendelson. Used by permission of Random House, an imprint and division of Penguin Random House LLC. All rights reserved. Copyright © 1944 by The Estate of W.H. Auden. Reprinted by permission of Curtis Brown, Ltd. All rights reserved.
194 Jung, "On the Psychology of the Unconscious," 54.
195 Jung, *The Psychology of the Transference*, 169.
196 Jung, *Psychology and Alchemy*, 186.
197 Jung, "Commentary on 'The Secret of the Golden Flower'," 20.
198 Jung, *The Archetypes of the Collective Unconscious*, 167.
199 C.G. Jung, "The Spirit Mercurius" (1948), in *Alchemical Studies*, 13 (Princeton University Press, 1976), 247.
200 C.G. Jung, "Address at the Presentation of the Jung Codex" (1953), in *The Symbolic Life: Miscellaneous Writings*, 18 (Princeton University Press, 1976), 827; see also an earlier version, 671.
201 Jacoby, *Longing for Paradise*, 199.
202 Jung, *Modern Man in Search of a Soul*, 202.
203 Stagg, *Polarities Of Man's Existence in Biblical Perspective*, 42.
204 Anna Carter Florence, "To Return Home" (sermon at First Church, Guilford, CT), 1994.
205 Michael Fordham, "The Empirical Foundation and Theories of the Self in Jung's Works," *Journal of Analytical Psychology* 8, no. 1 (1963), 19.
206 Fordham, "The Empirical Foundation and Theories of the Self in Jung's Works," 20.
207 Michael Fordham, "Some Observations on the Self in Childhood," *British Journal of Medical Psychology* 24, no. 2 (1951), 6.

208 C.G. Jung, "On the Psychology of the Child Archetype," *The Archetypes and the Collective Unconscious*, 9i (Princeton University Press, 1977), 159.

209 Jung, "On the Psychology of the Child Archetype," 164. In *The Red Book*, Jung says, "But I had to recognize and accept that my soul is a child and that my God in my soul is a child," 234.

210 Jung, "On the Psychology of the Child Archetype," 167.

211 Jung, *Memories, Dreams, and Reflections*, 328.

212 Jung, *On the Psychology of the Child Archetype*, 162.

213 Lionel Corbett well describes Scrooge as afflicted with narcissistic pathology. With the ghost of Christmas past showing him "the intense pathos of his childhood deprivations," Scrooge could have been a good candidate for Kohut's brand of psychoanalysis, but here a traumatic dream condenses the process. *The Religious Function of the Psyche* (Brunner-Routledge, 1996), 31.

214 Jacobi, *The Psychology of C.G. Jung*, 101.

215 E.T.A. Hoffman, *The Nutcracker*, trans. Ralph Manheim (Crown, 1989).

216 William Walsh, *Curiosities of Popular Custom and of Rites, Ceremonies, Observances, and Miscellaneous Antiquities* (Gibbings & Co., 1898), 237.

217 Charles Dickens, *A Christmas Tree (1850) & What Christmas Is as We Grow Older (1851)*, (Rimington and Hooper, 1927), 41, 45. Here there are strong resonances with the Buddha's and Rumi's *Guest House* writings.

218 Harding, "The Christmas Message from the Point of View of Analytical Psychology," *Concern* (December 1970), 20.

219 C.G. Jung, 166. "The individual human being must, through moral effort, bring this multiplicity together into *one* personality," Marie-Louise von Franz, *Projection and Re-collection in Jungian Psychology: Reflections of the Soul* (Open Court, 1980), 174.

220 Jung, *Symbols of Transformation*, 339.

221 L. Bryce Boyer, "Christmas 'Neurosis,'" *Journal of American Psychoanalytic Association* 3, no. 3 (1955), 481.

222 Jung, *Symbols of Transformation*, 324, note 31.

223 Jung, *The Archetypes and the Collective Unconscious*, 166.

224 Jaffé, *Word and Image*, 7.

Conclusion

Charles Dickens understood that Christmas was "King of the Seasons all!"[1] It began with two divergent prequels, the Nativity narratives of Luke and Matthew. Initially, they made little impact because the accounts of Jesus's passion and resurrection consumed the attention of early Christians. This changed dramatically in the fourth century, as is indicated by the great preacher John Chrysostom's Feast of the Nativity Sermon of 386: "This day … [which] has now been brought to us, not many years ago, has developed so quickly and borne such fruit."[2]

As Christianity became the official religion of the Roman Empire (380 CE), Jesus's birth became linked with Sol Invictus and the Saturnalia, making it a popular celebration of sacred and profane elements. Over the centuries, syncretism brought more and more pagan customs into the Christian playbook. This was particularly true of the Feast of the Nativity, which by the turn of the millennia was being called Christmas. Historian Philip Kopper sums it up succinctly: "Our Christmas celebrations combine Aramaic episode and Roman rite, Druid decoration and German fir, a Dutch saint's bounty and astronomical accident, Hebrew prophesy and Greek hearsay."[3] Christmas is a jingle-jangle amalgam.

After many years of putting this book together, it is most welcome to recognize that when the great writers talk about Christmas, so many of the motifs we have examined swim like a school of fish just beneath the surface of their words. They have known so much of this all along. For example, in *A Christmas Memory*, inspired by his early years with distant relatives subsisting in rural Alabama, Truman Capote deftly employs the image of rich, heavy, dense, whiskey-soaked fruitcakes, over-stuffed with the best ingredients—thirty-one to be exact. Made with love and from scratch to be shared and thoughtfully gifted, they symbolize the extravagance, complexity, community, absorption, willfulness, and generosity that is Christmas.[4]

Joseph Brodsky, 1987 Nobel Laureate in Literature, was so drawn to the nativity narratives that he felt compelled to pen a Christmas poem every year: "I liked that concentration in one place—which is what you have in the cave scene."[5] Like a Socratic dialogue, the yearly journey to Bethlehem reminds us of what we already know but have almost forgotten after another year of living, awakening what

DOI: 10.4324/9781003568629-9

Dickens called our "dormant sympathies."[6] The brimming, star-bright, remarkably inclusive manger scene brings us back to our essential self.

Upon hearing that I was researching the meaning of Christmas, one of my church members sent me a lengthy letter, here abbreviated:

> As a jeweler, Christmas can be an arduous time. Many hours at the workbench being an "elf," ... threatens to dampen my own Christmas spirit ... But there is something else that I want to tell you about. It always happens, and now I wait for it like a child waiting for the morning to see what's in the stocking. It is a turning point. Amidst all the rushing, fatigue and hyper-drive activity, and usually when I think I just can't take anymore, the tide turns. Everything becomes magical in an instant. Sometimes it hits me at the pageant, watching the children act out the Christmas story. One year it was returning home from shopping to find my toddler asleep under the Christmas tree in the middle of the afternoon. When it happens, it renders all the materialistic "stuff" superfluous. It is truly the wonder of the season, and it serves as a guidepost, to observe what is truly important about Christmas and what is not, and what is important about life and what is not. And yet it's not a conscious decision on my part. Maybe it is there all the time and I'm too busy to be aware of it, but it always comes to me as an inspirational realization, every year. And for the rest of that Christmas season, I bask in the magic. It is the most wonderful gift.[7]

Rilke conveys similar feelings in an evocative Christmas letter to his wife Clara as their daughter, Ruth, turned five. Repeatedly, he returns to the images of light, the Christmas tree, and his daughter's and wife's faces:

> And when I ... thought that then Christmas was coming, only the hall which was so big and so shadowy up to the bright, big tree to which you drew near for a while, quickly, with an uncertainty that was quite girlish again, more girlish than anything, holding the tiny head [Ruth] against your lovely face and together with it into the radiance which neither of you could see, each filled with her own life and the other's. Then only did I notice that for me that Christmas was still there and not like one that once was and has passed, but rather like an everlasting, eternal Christmas celebration to which one's inner eye can turn as often as it needs.[8]

The symbol-laden nativity narratives and traditions have abundant life and evoke that Christmas feeling because they have deep roots in the psyche. Some of the primary aspects of Christmas enchantment are unearthed by what we have learned from our look at depth psychology. The strongest case, among several, made by the followers of Freud is that Christmas is about the unconquerable wish of a son's (child's) equality with their father (parent). Read: The desire for the ego's equality with the super-ego as seen in Jesus's equality with his Father. There is little question that during Yuletide the super-ego is largely banished so that excess and extravagance, as well as feelings of equality and self-efficacy, take the helm.

The theories of Self psychology reveal why Christmas and home are so tightly woven together. It was at home as an infant and child that we were, to one extent or another, loved and warmly held, mirrored and adored, just as the baby Jesus was by parents, animals, angels, shepherds, and Magi at the manger. At Christmas, we hope for some miracle of mirroring—to be deeply known, valued, and enjoyed. As Kohut maintains, "The child needs the gleam in the mother's eye."[9] That need matures but never dissipates, so that as adults we seek the extravagant welcome from family and kin communities. In the classic Christmas movie, *It's a Wonderful Life*,[10] a crushed George Bailey bemoans: "I wish I'd never been born." Yet, thanks to the genius of novice angel Clarence, George discovers his own preciousness, allowing himself to be held and to hold close those in his circle of love. Mary Chapin Carpenter's heartrending song "Jubilee" speaks exquisitely to this foundational imperative for unrestrained hospitality for our idiosyncratic, motley, multiple being. That's why on Christmas Eve, so many intone with moist eyes the carol "Silent Night:" "Radiant beams from thy holy face, with the dawn of redeeming grace. Sleep in heavenly peace." This is the crowning gift of the Nativity, the *sine qua non* of Christmas.

Christmas, through the lens of Analytical psychology, finds two fundamental meanings, seemingly diametrically opposed. First, the universal Christmas theme of peace, combined with the compelling images of Mother Mary and Christ Child, nearly merged as one, reveals our unconscious yearning for the effortless, paradisiacal pre-ego state of original oneness. Given the richly composite nature of our psyche, we ache, as people of all times have, for the peaceful Golden Age of wholeness before fragmentation. This is the enchantingly regressive aspect of Christmas. Yule offers up such fleeting experiences.

Christmas also holds a progressive, heroic side. Yuletide celebrations have always included the stranger. The Christ Child is linked to light and celebrated by displays of luminaries of every description. From a Jungian point of view, light equals consciousness. Therefore, Christmas is also the courageous introduction to and integration of psychic strangers. It's like Rumi's "The Guest House." Dickens' reformed Scrooge confesses: "I will live in the Past, the Present, and the Future. The Spirits of all Three shall strive within me. I will not shut out the lessons they teach."[11] Neuman, presaging and enlarging upon the *New York Times*' editorial (see Chapter 4), calls for "*a magic circle (of) all contents* [italics mine] whether of the world or the unconscious, outside or inside."[12] The Christ Child is a symbol of the Self that pushes for an ever-widening embrace of psychic totality, a prospering individuated wholeness.

All three depth psychological perspectives have merit. No doubt there is much we have left unnamed that is responsible for the magic and the wonder of Christmas. Poet Sir Laurence Whistler (1912–2000) beckons us to marvel at its potency and then to explore further: "Christmas lives! Loses one habit, acquires another, sometimes falls back into ancient ways—but lives."[13]

Notes

1 Charles Dickens, *The Pickwick Papers* (J.M. Dent, 1998), 386.
2 James F. White, *Introduction to Christian Worship*, 3 (Abingdon, 2000), 62.
3 Philip Kopper, *A Christmas Testament* (Stewart, Tabori & Chang, 1982), 16.
4 Truman Capote, *A Christmas Memory* (Modern Library, 2007), 3–29.
5 Joseph Brodsky, *Nativity Poems* (Farrar, Straus and Giroux, 2001), 108, 103.
6 Dickens, *The Pickwick Papers*, 366.
7 Rebecca Bunting, Personal Letter, March 2, 2002.
8 Rainer Maria Rilke, *Letters of Rainer Maria Rilke: 1892–1910* (Norton, 1945), 251.
9 Heinz Kohut, "Forms and Transformation of Narcissism" (1966), in *The Search for the Self: Selected Writings of Heinz Kohut: 1950–1978*, Vol. 1, edited by Paul H. Ornstein (International Universities Press, 1978), 252.
10 Philip Van Doren Stern, *The Greatest Gift* (Penguin, 1996).
11 Charles Dickens, *A Christmas Carol (1843)* (Stewart, Tabori & Chang, 1990), 136.
12 Neumann, *The Origins and History of Consciousness* (Princeton University Press, 1970), 417.
13 "'A Critique of Ben Johnson's Masque of Christmas,'" found in Hubert, *Christmas in Shakespeare's England* (Sutton Publishing, 1998), 123.

Appendix

The Biblical Description of Jesus as Twin Selfobject and Idealized Selfobject

Christmas and the Twin Selfobject

It is not our first thought when Jesus comes to mind, but Scripture presents him as a suitable and robust alter ego selfobject. The Gospels are clear. Jesus is one of us (Philippians 2:7). He is "the Son of Man" (some 80 references in the Gospels). Jesus is living flesh (John 1:14) that casts a shadow and leaves footprints, even making trouble for his parents as an inconsiderate adolescent (Luke 2:48). Like us, Jesus gets thirsty and hungry (Mark 11:12; John 4:7, 19:28), angry (Mark 3:5; Matthew 12:34, 23:33; John 2:15), and anxious (Mark 14:33, 34; John 13:21). Like us, Jesus has compassion (Luke 7:13; Mark 6:34, 8:2), gets tired (Mark 6:31), welcomes touch (Luke 7:37; John 12:3), and enjoys male and female companionship (Mark 3:14; Luke 22:15, 23:55, 24:22; Matthew 27:55, 56; John 13:34). Like us, he sometimes needs to be alone (Matthew 14:23; Luke 4:42; Mark 6:46, 7:24). He sometimes parties and often prays (John 2:2; Luke 5:29, 6:12, 9:28, 11:1). Like us, he knows temptation (Mark 1:13, 8:33), and can feel forsaken (Matthew 27:46). He is lauded and hated (John 7:7, 12, 12:13; Mark 15:13); he grieves and weeps (Mark 3:5; Matthew 23:37; Luke 19:41; John 11:35); he calls those close to him friends (John 15:15). Like us, he experiences physical pain (Mark 15:15), suffers betrayal (Mark 14:17), and knows he will die (Luke 18:32–33). He embraces children (Mark 10:14). He loves (John 11:5, 20:2). What human experience or feeling is unknown to him? As the United Church of Christ Statement of Faith declares, Jesus "shared our common lot."[1]

At Christmas, we are poignantly reminded of our kinship with Jesus. As we have established, the Feast of the Nativity did not begin until the fourth century CE. Raymond Brown noted that its institution had the effect, if not the intention, of countering the Docetists,[2] those who believed "that the humanity of Jesus Christ was an appearance or illusion."[3] It would be hard to discount that such concerns were not a reason for the eruption of the newfound interest in Jesus' birth.

The earliest known Christmas hymn (fourth century CE) begins in a clearly anti-Docetist fashion:

> He was born at Bethlehem,
> He was raised at Nazareth,
> He lived in Galilee.[4]

DOI: 10.4324/9781003568629-10

This fixes Jesus in time and space, a real human neonate. More explicit is the third verse of "Once in Royal David's City," the opening hymn of the traditional and ever popular Service of Lessons and Carols:

For he is our childhood's pattern, day by day like us he grew.
He was little, weak and helpless, tears and smiles like us he knew;
And he feeleth for our sadness, and he shareth in our gladness.

On Christmas Eve, those who believe the story are fascinated and find their hearts strangely warmed by this tiny fellow sojourner who is nurtured in Mary's womb (Luke 1:31), born in a stable and placed in a manger (Luke 2:17), and protected by loving parents. This all-so-human infant knows the same existential vulnerability and potential that we all experience. For Christians, Jesus is a strong alter ego selfobject. This stress on Jesus' humanity begins and is prominently noted at the Feast of the Nativity.

Christmas and the Idealized Selfobject

As we mature, our circle of idealized selfobjects enlarges and may include a charismatic leader, a prototypical historical figure, or a personified god. Kohut, as far as I can determine, never directly wrote about Christmas. However, in one of the rare occurrences in which he mentions Jesus, Kohut pronounces that "the divine figure of Christ" is an "omnipotent selfobject."[5]

The stories about Jesus show him as an engaging and upbuilding sage who provides ideals to emulate. He speaks with authority (Mark 1:22, 2:10), heals (Matthew 4:23, 8:16, 12:22), welcomes the outcasts (Luke 8:2, 19:5), and calls the interested to become followers (Matthew 4:19; John 15:17). His Sermon on the Mount and Beatitudes are ambitious moral ideals. Viewed as the Risen Christ, who has conquered death (1 Corinthians 15:54) and sits at the right hand of God (1 Peter 3:22). For those who hold the story dear, Jesus takes center stage as the leading ideal selfobject.

Extraordinarily, even as an infant, Jesus is depicted as the preeminent sovereign. With Kohut's notion of the idealizing selfobject in mind, we look afresh at the familiar Christmas narratives and hymns.

An angel of the Lord comes in a dream to Joseph:

Joseph, son of David, do not be afraid to take Mary as your wife, for the child conceived in her is from the Holy Spirit. She will bear a son, and you are to name him Jesus, for he will save his people from their sins.

(Matthew 1:20–21)

Shepherds, "keeping watch over their flock by night," are astonished by a visit from a heavenly chorus:

Do not be afraid; for see—I am bringing you good news of great joy for all the people: to you is born this day in the city of David a Savior, who is the Messiah, the Lord. This will be a sign for you: you will find a child wrapped in bands of clothe and lying in a manger.

(Luke 2:10–12)

In both episodes, the baby Jesus is identified as a savior, a suitable synonym for an idealizing selfobject.

The angel Gabriel announces to Mary:

You will conceive in your womb and bear a son, and you will name him Jesus. He will be great, and will be called the Son of the Most High, and the Lord God will give to him the throne of his ancestor David. He will reign over the house of Jacob forever, and of his kingdom there shall be no end.

(Luke 1:31–33)

The Magi corroborate this as they undauntedly journey to find "the child who has been born king of the Jews."[6] The image of these royal soul searchers bowing humbly before the newborn king is yearly projected onto the Western collective psyche. After all the years of corrupt, weak, selfish kings, here at last is a good king, peasant-born, one for all the people. Who could be more powerful?

Devout and aged, Simeon has been waiting all his life "for the consolation of Israel." Holding baby Jesus in his arms, Simeon realizes he has found it. Praising God, he says:

You are dismissing your servant in peace according to your word; for my eyes have seen your salvation, which you have prepared in the presence of all peoples, a light for revelation to the Gentiles and for glory to your people Israel.

(Luke 2:29–32)

There is no doubt, the babe in swaddling clothes becomes the consummate idealizing selfobject for Simeon, so much so that just the sight of him allows Simeon to die in peace. Matthew seconds this Lukan account and claims that Jesus is the confirmation of Isaiah's prophecy (7:14): "Look, the virgin shall conceive and bear a son, and they shall name him Emmanuel" (Isaiah 7:14), which means, "God is with us."

Who could better fulfill Kohut's notion of the idealizing selfobject than the Child God who is with us?

These Nativity story lines inspired unnumbered Christmas carols that flow easily and ebulliently from the mouths of Christmas worshippers. Those roused by the season soak up this message, at least unconsciously, during a monthlong barrage of Christmas music filling the air. In "Angels, From the Realms of Glory," the visceral refrain is: "Come and worship, come and worship, Worship Christ, the new-born King." In "Angels We Have Heard on High," it is "Come, adore on bended knee, Christ the Lord, the new-born King." It is "Hark! The herald angels sing, 'Glory to the new-born King!'" And, emphatically:

> Joy to the World! The Lord is come;
> Let earth receive her King;
> Let every heart prepare him room.

In Handel's *Messiah*, the majestic, full-throated refrain is "King of Kings and Lord of Lords." In "What Child Is This?" the mood is tender but the message is just as penetrating: "This, this is Christ the King, Whom shepherds guard and angels sing: Haste, haste to bring him laud, the babe, the son of Mary."

At Christmastime, whether his story is fact or fiction, the Christ Child functions subjectively, symbolically, and psychologically as an idealizing selfobject. As humans, we all need the continuing support of idealizing selfobjects, and being reminded of Jesus in this way at Christmastime is for some a felicitous addition. And, for those who have been significantly failed by their original, self-forming ideal selfobjects, Jesus, the newborn king, has added healing potential, filling a gnawing void and becoming an essential and sustaining support to their self. For Christians, the manger child is an idealized selfobject without equal.

Notes

1 *Book of Worship: United Church of Christ* (United Church of Christ, 1986), 512.
2 Raymond E. Brown, *The Birth of the Messiah: A Commentary on the Infancy Narratives in the Gospels of Matthew and Luke* (Doubleday, 1977), 26.
3 *The Dictionary of Historical Theology*, edited by Trevor A. Hart (Paternoster Press, 2000), 163. "Irenaeus and Clement of Alexandria repeatedly criticize those who hold that Christ's birth and body were only 'in appearance,' a view which they attribute to such heretics as Marcion and various Gnostics."
4 Lucien Deiss, *Springtime of the Liturgy: Liturgical Texts of the First Four Centuries*, translated by Matthew J. O'Connell (Liturgical Press, 1967), 257.
5 Heinz Kohut, *Self Psychology and the Humanities: Reflections on a New Psychoanalytic Approach* (Norton, 1985), 128.
6 When self-injured King Herod hears this he is so frightened that he will lose his subjects mirroring of him as the king that he goes into a psychological tailspin. The dark fear of such a catastrophic loss leads him to commit mass infanticide, the slaughter of the innocents.

Bibliography

Achtemeier, P.J. *Harper's Bible Dictionary*. Harper & Row, 1985.

Adler, Alfred. *Studies in Analytical Psychology*. C.G. Jung Foundation for Analytical Psychology, 1966.

Alcott, Louisa May. *Little Women*. Running Press, 1995.

Allenby, Amy I. *Relationship and Healing*. No. 84. Guild of Pastoral Psychology, 1954.

Alvear, Michael. "The Christmas That Comes to the Door." *New York Times*, December 25 2000, 33.

Anderson, Chester G. *Growing up in Minnesota: Ten Writers Remember Their Childhoods*. University of Minneapolis Press, 1976.

Antonelli, Judith S. *In the Image of God: A Feminist Commentary on the Torah*. Jason Aronson, 1997.

Aries, Philippe. *Centuries of Children: A Social History of Family Life*. Translated by Robert Baldick. Vintage Books, 1962.

Armstrong, Neil. "England and German Christmas Festlichkeit, c. 1800–1914." *German History* 26, no. 4: 486–503.

Arnold, Eberhard. *The Early Christians after the Death of the Apostles*. Plough Publishing House, 1972.

Auden, W.H. "For the Time Being: A Christmas Oratorio." In *The Collected Poetry of W.H. Auden*. Edited by Edward Mendelson. Vintage International/Random House, 1991.

Augustin: On the Holy Trinity, Doctrinal Treatises, Moral Treatises. Edited by Philip Schaff. Vol. 3, *Nicene and Post-Nicene Fathers*. T&T Clark, 1993.

Augustine. *The Confessions*. Translated by Rex Warner. Mentor, 1963.

Auld, William Muir. *Christmas Traditions*. MacMillan, 1931.

Baier, Marjorie. "The 'Holiday Blues' as a Stress Reaction." *Perspectives in Psychiatric Care* 24, no. 2 (1987): 64–8.

Baker, Howard S. and Margaret N. Baker. "Heinz Kohut's Self Psychology: An Overview." *American Journal of Psychology* 144, no. 1 (1987): 1–8.

Ballard, Clive G., Carol Bannister, Rachel Davis, Sumithra Handy, et al. "Christmas Census at a District General Hospital Psychiatric Unit." *Irish Journal of Psychological Medicine* 8, no. 1 (1991): 46–7.

Barr, Stringfellow. *The Mask of Jove: A History of the Roman-Greco Civilization from the Death of Alexander to the Death of Constantine*. J.B. Lippincott, 1966.

Barron, Caroline M. *Medieval London: Collected Papers of Caroline M. Barron*. Medieval Institute Publications, 2017.

Barton, Arnold H. *Letters from the Promised Land: Swedes in America, 1840–1914*. University of Minnesota Press, 1975.

Basch, Michael Franz. "The Concept of the 'Self': An Operational Definition." In *Developmental Approaches to the Self*, edited by Benjamin Lee and Gil G. Noam, 7–58. Plenum, 1983.

Basch, Michael Franz. *Practicing Psychotherapy*. Basic Books, 1992.

Basch, Michael Franz. "Self Psychology." Paper presented at the Albert Einstein School of Medicine: Michael Basch and Otto Kernberg, Cape Cod, July 1992.

Basch, Michael Franz. *Understanding Psychotherapy: The Science Behind the Art*. Basic Books, 1988.

Beit-Hallahmi, Benjamin. "Sacrifice, Fire, and the Victory of the Sun: A Search for the Origins of Hanukkah." *Psychoanalytic Review* 63, no. 4 (1976): 497–509.

Belk, Russell W. "Materialism and the Making of the Modern Christmas." In *Unwrapping Christmas*, edited by Daniel Miller, 75–104. Clarendon Press, 1993.

Bercovitch, Sacvan. *The Puritan Origins of the American Self*. Yale University Press, 1975.

Book of Worship: United Church of Christ. United Church of Christ, 1986.

Borg, Marcus. "When Heaven and Earth Meet." *The Living Pulpit* 5, no. 4 (1996): 4–5.

Boring, M. Eugene. *New Testament Articles, Matthew, Mark*. Edited by Leander E. Keck. 12 vols. Vol. 8, *The New Interpreter's Bible*. Abingdon Press, 1995.

Boyer, L. Bryce. "Christmas Neurosis." *Journal of the American Psychoanalytic Association* 3, no. 3 (1955): 467–88.

Boyer, L. Bryce. "Christmas 'Neurosis' Reconsidered." In *Depressive States and Their Treatment*, edited by V.D. Volkan. Jason Aronson, 1985, 297–316.

Bowler, Gerry. *The World Encyclopedia of Christmas*. McClelland & Stewart, 2000.

Bradshaw, Paul. *Early Christian Worship: A Basic Introduction to Ideas and Practice*. The Liturgical Press, 1996.

Bradshaw, Paul F. *The Search for the Origins of Christian Worship: Sources and Methods for the Study of Early Liturgy*. Oxford University Press, 1992.

Bragg, Rick. "A Cajun Christmas Tradition Won't Die Down." *New York Times*, December 24, 1995, 10.

Brand, John. *Observations on the Popular Antiquities of Great Britain (1795)*. Edited by Sir Henry Ellis. Henry G. Bohn, 1849.

Brandon, Reiko Mochinaga and Barbara B. Stephan. *Spirit and Symbol: The Japanese New Year*. Honolulu Academy of Arts, 1994.

Brodsky, Joseph. *Nativity Poems*. Farrar, Straus and Giroux, 2001.

Bronte, Emily. *Wuthering Heights (1847)*. Bantam Books, 1981.

Brooks, Phillips. *Christmas Carols*. E.P. Dutton, 1877.

Brown, Malcome and Shirley Seaton. *Christmas Truce: The Western Front December 1914*. Papermac, 1984.

Brown, Raymond E. *The Birth of the Messiah: A Commentary on the Infancy Narratives in the Gospels of Matthew and Luke*. Doubleday, 1977.

Browning, Robert. "Paracelsus." In *The Complete Poetic and Dramatic Works of Robert Browning*, edited by Horace Scudder. Houghton Mifflin, 1895.

Bryson, Megan. "Japan's Laughing Buddha Hotei is merging into Santa Claus." The Conversation, published December 12, 2022. theconversation.com/japans-laughing

-buddha-hotei-is-merging-into-santa-claus-both-are-roly-poly-sacred-figures-with-a-bag-of-gifts-195090.

Brzostoski, John. "Hick's Peaceable Kingdom." *Friends Journal* February (2000): 1–7.

Buber, Martin. *I and Thou*. Free Press, 2023.

Buber, Martin. *The Knowledge of Man*. Humanities Press International, 1988.

Bulfinch, Thomas. *Myths of Greece and Rome*. Penguin Books, 1983.

Bunting, Rebecca. Personal letter, March 2, 2002.

Burgoyne, Carole B. and Stephen E.G Lea. "The Psychology of Christmas." *The Psychologist*, December (1995): 549–53.

Byers, Bryand and Richard A. Zeller. "Christmas Mortality: Death Dip, No; Death Rise, Yes." *Professional Psychology: Research and Practice* 18, no. 4 (1987): 394–6.

Cagner, Ewert, ed. *Swedish Christmas*. Tre Tryckare, 1955.

Cann, D.L. *Saint Nicholas, Bishop of Myra: The Life and Times of the Original Father Christmas*. Novalis, 2002.

Capps, Donald. *The Depleted Self: Sin in a Narcissistic Age*. Fortress Press, 1993.

Carson, R.A.G. *Principal Coins of the Romans: The Republic C. 290-31 BC*. Vol. 1. British Museum Publications, 1978.

Cary, Phillip. *Augustine's Invention of the Inner Self: The Legacy of a Christian Platonist*. Oxford University Press, 2000.

Catholic Encyclopedia. Edited by Catholic University of America. Vol. 10. McGraw Hill, 1967.

Celano, Thomas of. *St. Francis of Assisi: First and Second Life of St. Francis*. Translated by Placid Hermann. Franciscan Herald Press, 1988.

Center for Interfaith Dialogue Yadev, Amy. "Celebrating Christmas as a non-Christian Sikh," by Amy Yadev. December 17, 2020. interfaith.wisc.edu/2020/12/17/celebrating-christmas-as-a-non-christian-sikh-amy-yadev/.

Chadwick, Owen. *A History of Christianity*. St. Martin's Press, 1995.

Chapman, Gary. *The Five Love Languages: How to Express Heartfelt Commitment to Your Mate*. Northfield Publishing, 1995.

Charles Rivers Editors. *Saint Nicholas and Krampus: The History of the Popular Companions Who Rewards and Punish Children During the Christmas Season*. Published by author, 2024.

Christmas Tree Association. "Deck the Halls and Embrace Christmas Tree Care and Maintenance This Holiday Season." November 27, 2023. christmastreeassociation.org/press-releases/deck-the-halls-and-embrace-christmas-tree-care-and-maintenance-this-holiday-season.

Church, Francis Pharcellus. "Yes Virginia, There Is a Santa Claus." *New York Sun*, September 21, 1897, Editorial Page.

Clauss, Manfred. *The Roman Cult of Mithras: The God and His Mysteries*. Translated by Richard Gordon. Routledge, 2000.

Cohler, Betran J. and David deBoer. "Maintaining a Sense of Coherence in a Troubled World." *Contemporary Psychology* 40, no. 10 (1995): 941–3.

Cole, Joanna. *A Gift from Saint Francis: The First Creche*. William Morrow, 1989.

Collins, Ace. *Stories Behind the Great Traditions of Christmas*. Zondervan, 2003.

Cooper, Arnold M. "The Place of Self Psychology in the History of Depth Psychology." In *The Future of Psychoanalysis: Essays in Honor of Heinz Kohut*, edited by Arnold Goldberg. International Universities Press, 1983.

Corbett, Lionel. *The Religious Function of the Psyche*. Brunner-Routledge, 1996.

Count, Earl W. and Alice Lawson Count. *4000 Years of Christmas: A Gift from the Ages*. Seastone, 2000.

Crashaw, Richard. *The Poems, English, Latin and Greek, of Richard Crashaw*. Oxford University Press, 1957.

Crossan, John Dominic. "Perspectives and Methods in Contemporary Biblical Criticism." *Biblical Research* 22 (1977): 39–49.

Crouch, James E. "How Early Christians Viewed the Birth of Jesus." *Bible Review,* October (1991): 34–8.

Cullum, Sarah J., Jose Catalan, Kaye Berelowitz, Stephanie O'Brien, et al. "Deliberate Self-Harm and Public Holidays: Is There a Link." *Crisis: Journal of Crisis Intervention and Suicide* 14, no. 1 (1993): 39–42.

Culpepper, R. Alan. *Luke, John*. Edited by Leander E. Keck. 12 vols. Vol. 9, *The New Interpreter's Bible*. Abingdon Press, 1995.

Cunningham, Hugh. *Children and Childhood in Western Society Since 1500*. Routledge, 2021.

Dallen, James. *The Reconciling Community: The Rite of Penance*. Vol. 3 of series "Studies in the Reformed Rites of the Catholic Church." A Pueblo Book/The Liturgical Press, 1974.

Davies, W.D. *Invitation to the New Testament: A Guide to Its Main Witnesses*. Doubleday, 1969.

De Groot, Adriaan D. *Saint Nicholas: A Psychoanalytic Study of His History and Myth*. Moutin & Co., 1965.

de Vries, Ad. *Dictionary of Symbols and Imagery*. North-Holland Publishing, 1976.

Deiss, Lucien. *Springtime of the Liturgy: Liturgical Texts of the First Four Centuries*. Translated by Matthew J. O'Connell. Liturgical Press, 1967.

Delitzsch, Franz. *A System of Biblical Psychology*. Translated by Robert Ernest Wallis. Baker Book House, 1977.

Deming, Jr., Frank S. "Christmas Tree-Cosmic Tree: Archetypal Dimensions in Contemporary Interviews on the Tree at Christmas." Doctor of Ministry, Princeton Theological Seminary, 1999.

Di Giampaolo, Mario and Andrea Muzzi. *Correggio Catalogo Completo Dei Dipinti*. Cantini, 1993.

Dickens, Charles. *A Christmas Carol (1843)*. Stewart, Tabori & Chang, 1990.

Dickens, Charles. *A Christmas Tree (1850) & What Christmas Is as We Grow Older (1851)*. Rimington and Hooper, 1927.

The Dictionary of Historical Theology. Edited by Trevor A. Hart. Paternoster Press, 2000.

Dodd, C.H. *The Apostolic Preaching and Its Developments*. Harper and Row, 1964.

Dolinska, Barbara, Jakub Jarzabek, and Dariusz Dolinski. "I like You even Less at Christmas Dinner." *Basic and Applied Social Psychology* 42, no. 2 (2020): 88.

Dostoevsky, Fyodor. *The Double*. Translated by Evelyn Harden. Ardis, 1985.

Dostoevsky, Fyodor. "The Wedding and the Christmas Tree." In *The Best Short Stories of Dostoevsky*. Translated by David Magarshack. Modern Library, 1992.

Dourley, John P. *The Illness That We Are: A Jungian Critique of Christianity*. Inner City Books, 1984.

Drewermann, Eugen. *Discovering the God Child Within: A Spiritual Psychology of the Infancy of Jesus*. Crossroad Publishing, 1994.

Duchesne, L. *Christian Worship: Its Origin and Evolution: A Study of Latin Liturgy up to the Time of Charlemagne*. 5th ed. Society for Promoting Christian Knowledge, 1923.

Dumezil, Georges. *Archaic Roman Religion*. Volumes 1 and 2. University of Chicago Press, 1966.

Dunn, E.W., L.B. Aknin, and M.I. Norton. "Spending Money on Others Promotes Happiness." *Science* 319 (2008): 1687–1688.

Dyble, Mark, Abram van Leeuwen, and R.I.M Dunbar. "Gender Difference in Christmas Gift Giving." *Evolutionary Behavioral Sciences* 9, no. 2 (2014): 140.

Edinger, Edward. *The Aion Lectures: Exploring the Self in C.G. Jung's Aion*. Inner City Books, 1996.

Edinger, Edward. *The Bible and the Psyche: Individuation Symbolism in the Old Testament*. Inner City Books, 1986.

Edinger, Edward. "An Outline of Analytical Psychology." *Quadrant*, no. 1 (Spring, 1968): 1–12.

Ehrman, Bart D. *The New Testament: A Historical Introduction to the Early Christian Writings*. 2nd ed. Oxford University Press, 2000.

Eisenbud, Jule. "Negative Reactions to Christmas." *The Psychoanalytic Quarterly* 10 (1941): 639–45.

Eliade, Mircea. *Images & Symbols: Studies in Religious Symbolism*. Translated by Philip Mairet. Sheed & Ward, 1961.

Eliade, Mircea. "Nostalgia for Paradise." *Parabola: Myth and the Quest for Meaning* 1, no. 1 (1976): 6–15.

Ellens, J. Harold. "The Bible and Psychology: An Interdisciplinary Pilgrimage." *Pastoral Psychology* 45, no. 3 (1997): 193–208.

Elliott, Jock. *Inventing Christmas: How Our Holiday Came to Be*. Abrams, 2001.

Engels, Stephen E. and Theresa Rice. *An Illinois Christmas Anthology*. Partridge Press, 1991.

Enjoy Strasbourg. "The Great Christmas Tree of Strasbourg's Christmas Market." October 18, 2023. enjoystrasbourg.com/great-christmas-tree-strasbourg/.

Eusebius. *The Church History: A New Translation with Commentary*. Translated by Paul L. Maier. Kregel Publications, 1999.

Exum, Cheryl J. and David J.A. Clines, eds. *The New Literary Criticism and the Hebrew Bible*. Sheffield Academic Press, 1993.

Ferguson, John. *The Religions of the Roman Empire*. Cornell University Press, 1982.

Ferrari, Joseph R. "Christmas and Procrastination: Explaining Lack of Diligence at a 'Real World' Task Deadline." *Personality and Individual Differences* 14, no. 1 (1993): 25–33.

Ferris, Theordore Parker. *Theological and Ethical*. Vol. 2. Trinity Church, 1983.

Field, T.M., R. Woodson, R. Greenberg, and D. Cohen. "Discrimination and Imitation of Facial Expressions by Neonates." *Science* 218 (1982): 179–81.

Field, Tiffany M. "Social Perception and Responsivity in Early Infancy." In *Review of Human Development*, edited by Tiffany M. Field, Aletha Huston, Herbert C. Quay, Lillian Troll, and Gordon E. Finley. Wiley, 1982.

Fingerman, Karen L. and Patricia C. Griffiths. "Season's Greetings: Adults' Social Contacts at the Holiday Season." *Psychology and Aging* 14, no. 2 (1999): 192–205.

Fischer, Eileen and Stephen J. Arnold. "More Than a Labor of Love: Gender Roles and Christmas Gift Shopping." *Journal of Consumer Research* 17, no. 3 (1990): 333–45.

Fitzmyer, Joseph A. *Luke the Theologian: Aspects of His Teaching*. Paulist Press, 1989.

Fitzmyer, Joseph A. *Pauline Theology: A Brief Sketch.* Prentice-Hall, 1967.

Fitzmyer, Joseph A. *Scripture, the Soul of Theology.* Paulist Press, 1994.

Florence, Anna Carter. "To Return Home." Sermon preached at First Church, Guilford, CT, 1994.

Flournoy, Theodore. *From India to the Planet Mars: A Case of Multiple Personality with Imaginary Languages (1899).* Princeton University Press, 1994.

Fordham, Michael. "The Empirical Foundation and Theories of the Self in Jung's Works." *Journal of Analytical Psychology* 8, no. 1 (1963).

Fordham, Michael. "Some Observations on the Self in Childhood." *The British Journal of Medical Psychology* 24, no. 2 (1951).

Foster, Genevieve. *Augustus Caesar's World: A Story of Ideas and Events from BC 44 to 14 AD.* Charles Scribner's Sons, 1947.

Freud, Sigmund. *"Civilization and Its Discontents (1930)."* Vol. 21, In *The Standard Edition of the Complete Psychological Works of Sigmund Freud*, edited by J. Strachey. Hogarth Press, 1961.

Freud, Sigmund. *The Ego and the Id (1923).* Translated by Joan Riviere. Edited by James Strachey. Norton Library, 1960.

Freud, Sigmund. "Formulations Regarding the Two Principles of Mental Functioning (1911)." Vol. 4, In *Collected Papers,* edited by J.D. Sutherland. Hogarth Press, 1957.

Freud, Sigmund. "From the History of an Infantile Neurosis (1918)." Vol. 17, *The Standard Edition of the Complete Works of Sigmund Freud,* edited by J. Strachey. Hogarth Press, 1955.

Freud, Sigmund. "The Future of an Illusion (1927)." Vol. 21, *The Standard Edition of the Complete Psychological Works of Sigmund Freud,* edited by J. Strachey. Hogarth Press, 1961.

Freud, Sigmund. "The Future Prospects of Psycho-Analytic Therapy (1910)." Vol. 11, *The Standard Edition of the Complete Psychological Works of Sigmund Freud,* edited by J. Strachey. Hogarth Press, 1960.

Freud, Sigmund. "Group Psychology and the Analysis of the Ego (1921)." Vol. 18, *The Standard Edition of the Complete Psychological Words of Sigmund Freud,* edited by J. Strachey. Hogarth Press, 1961.

Freud, Sigmund. "Leonardo Da Vinci and Memory of His Childhood (1910)." Vol. 11, *The Standard Edition of the Complete Psychological Works of Sigmund Freud,* edited by J. Strachey. Hogarth, 1960.

Freud, Sigmund. "Obsessive Actions and Religious Practices (1907)." Vol. 9, *The Standard Edition of the Complete Psychological Works of Sigmund Freud,* edited by J. Strachey. Hogarth Press, 1959.

Freud, Sigmund. *An Outline of Psychoanalysis (1938/1940).* Translated by James Strachey. Norton, 1949.

Freud, Sigmund. "The Psychopathology of Everyday Life (1901)." Vol. 6, *The Standard Edition of the Complete Psychological Words of Sigmund Freud,* edited by J. Strachey. Hogarth Press, 1960.

Freud, Sigmund. "Religious Origins (1919)." Vol. 5, *Collected Papers,* edited by J.D. Sutherland. Hogarth Press, 1957.

Freud, Sigmund. "A Religious Experience (1928)." Vol. 21, *The Standard Edition of the Complete Psychological Works of Sigmund Freud,* edited by J. Strachey. Hogarth Press, 1961.

Freud, Sigmund. "Totem and Taboo and Other Works (1913)." Vol. 13, *The Standard Edition of the Complete Psychological Works of Sigmund Freud,* edited by J. Strachey. Hogarth Press, 1975.

Freud, Sigmund and Oskar Pfister. *Psychoanalysis and Faith: The Letters of Sigmund Freud and Oskar Pfister.* Translated by Eric Mosbacher. Edited by Heinrich Meng and Ernst L. Freud. Basic Books, 1963.

Friedberg, Robert D. "Holidays and Emotional Distress: Not the Villains They Are Perceived to Be." *Psychology: A Quarterly Journal of Human Behavior* 27, no. 1 (1990): 59–61.

Fromm, Erich. *The Dogma of Christ and Other Essays on Religion, Psychology and Culture.* Holt, Rinehart and Winston, 1963.

Fromm, Erich. *Psychoanalysis and Religion.* Yale University Press, 1950.

Gallup. "More Americans Celebrating a Secular Christmas," by Zach Hrynowski, December 20, 2019. news.gallup.com/poll/272378/americans-celebrating-secular-christmas.aspx (accessed November 15, 2024).

Gardiner, Muriel, ed. *The Wolf-Man and Sigmund Freud.* Hogarth Press, 1973.

"The Ghost of Christmas Depression." *The New York Times,* December 15, 1996, E12.

Giorgi, Rosa. *Saints in Art.* Translated by Thomas Michael Hartmann. Edited by Stefano Zuffi. J. Paul Getty Museum, 2003.

Girdlestone, R.B. *Synonyms of the Old Testament: Their Bearing on Christian Doctrine.* Logos Research Systems, 1998.

Gockerell, Nina. *Nativity Scenes.* Taschen, 1998.

Golby, J.M. and A.W. Purdue. *The Making of the Modern Christmas.* University of Georgia Press, 1986.

Goldberg, Arnold. "Heinz Kohut, 1913–1981." *American Journal of Psychiatry* 160, no. 4 (2003): 670.

Goodenough, Erwin R. *Jewish Symbols in the Greco-Roman Period.* Edited by Jacob Neusner. Princeton University Press, 1988.

Goodenough, Erwin R. *Toward a Mature Faith.* Prentice-Hall, 1955.

Grant, Frederick C. *An Introduction to New Testament Thought.* Abingdon-Cokesbury Press, 1950.

Grant, Frederick C. "Psychological Study of the Bible." In *Religions in Antiquity: Essays in Memory of Erwin Ramsdell Goodenough,* edited by Jacob Neusner. Studies in the History of Religion vol XIV. E.J. Brill, 1968.

Grant, Michael. *History of Rome.* Prentice Hall, 1978.

Grant, Robert M. *Augustus to Constantine: The Emergence of Christianity in the Roman World.* Barnes & Noble Books, 1970.

Greenberg Quinlan Rosner Research. "Holiday Stress Survey," December 12 , 2006. apa.org/news/press/releases/2006/12/holiday-stress.pdf.

Grimal, Pierre, ed. *The Dictionary of Classical Mythology.* Translated by A.R. Maxwell-Hyslop. Basil Blackwell, 1986.

Grimal, Pierre, ed. *Larousse World Mythology.* Translated by Patricia Beardsworth. Chartwell Books, 1976.

Grisbrooke, W. Jardine. *The Liturgical Portions of the Apostolic Constitution.* Grove Books, 1990.

Grisham, John. *Skipping Christmas.* Doubleday, 2001.

Grotstein, James S. "Some Perspectives on Self Psychology." In *The Future of Psychoanalysis: Essays in Honor of Heinz Kohut*, edited by Arnold Goldberg, 165–201. International Universities Press, 1983.

Hadlaczky, Gergö and Sebastian Hokby. "Increased Suicides During New Year, But Not During Christmas in Sweden: Analysis of Cause of Death Data 2006–2015." *Nordic Journal of Psychiatry* 72, no. 1 (2018): 72–4.

Halsberghe, Gaston H. *The Cult of Sol Invictus*. E.J. Brill, 1972.

Hammond, N.G.L. and H.H. Scullard, eds. *The Oxford Classical Dictionary*. Oxford University Press, 1970.

Handel, G.F. *The Messiah (1741)*. G. Schirmer, 1912.

Harding, Esther M. "The Christmas Message from the Point of View of Analytical Psychology." *Concern* vol. 12, no. 10 (December 1970): 15–20.

Harding, Esther M. *Psychic Energy: Its Source and Transformation*. Princeton University Press, 1973.

Hatic, Dana and Hillary Dixler Canavan. "The King Cake Tradition, Explained." *Eater.com*, February 2, 2024.

Helander, E.E., B. Wansink, and A. Chieh. "Weight Gain over the Holidays in Three Countries." *New England Journal of Medicine* 375, no. 12 (2016): 1200–2.

Hendrickx, Herman. *The Infancy Narratives: Studies in the Synoptic Gospels*. Geoffrey Chapman, 1984.

Hendrix, Harville. *Getting the Love You Want: A Guide for Couples*. Harper Perennial, 1990.

Hendrix, Harville. *Getting the Love You Want: A Guide for Couples*. Home Video Workshop Workbook. Institute for Relationship Therapy, 1993.

Henry, O. *The Gift of the Magi*. Hawthorn Books, 1972.

Hesiod. *The Works and Days, Theology, the Shield of Herakles*. Translated by Richmond Lattimore. University of Michigan Press, 1959.

Hifler, Joyce Sequichie. *A Cherokee Feast of Days*, vol. 3. Council Oak Books, 2002.

Hill, R.A. and R.I.M. Dunbar. "Social Network Size in Humans." *Human Nature: An Interdisciplinary Biosocial Perspective* 14, no. 1 (2003): 53–72.

Hillman, James. "The Feeling Function." In *Lectures on Jung's Typology*. Spring Publications, 1971: 75–148.

Hobe, Phyllis, ed. *The Meaning of Christmas*. A.J. Holman, 1975.

Hoffman, E.T.A. *The Nutcracker*. Translated by Ralph Manheim. Crown, 1989.

"Holiday Blues, Depression, Stress, Anxiety & Tips for Adults." In, www.brownielocks.com/holidayblues.html (accessed December 7, 2005).

Hone, William. *Ancient Mysteries Described*. Spring Tree Press, reissue 1969 from 1823.

Hoole, Charles H. trans. *The Didache*. Athenaeum of Christian Antiquity, 1994.

Hornung, Erik. *Akhenaten and the Religion of Light*. Translated by David Lorton. Cornell University Press, 1999.

Hougaard, A., U. Lindberg, N. Arngrim, H.B. Larsson, J. Olesen, F.M. Amin, H. Ashina, and B.T. Haddock. "Evidence of a Christmas Spirit in the Brain: Functional MRI Study." *BMJ* 351, h6266 (2015).

Howatch, Susan. *Mystical Paths*. Fawcett Crest, 1992.

Hubert, Maria. *Christmas in Shakespeare's England*. Sutton Publishing, 1998.

Hubert, Maria. *The Great British Christmas*. Sutton Publishing, 1999.

Hubert, Maria and Andrew Hubert. *A Monmouthshire Christmas*. Sutton Publishing, 1995.

Hubert, Maria and Andrew Hubert. *A Wartime Christmas*. Sutton Publishing, 1999.

Hugo, Victor. *Les Misérables*. Translated by Lee Fabnestock and Norman MacAfee. New American Library, 1987.

Humbert, Elie G. *C.G. Jung: The Fundamentals of Theory and Practice*. Chiron, 1988.

Irving, Washington. *Old Christmas in Merrie England*. Peter Pauper Press, ND.

Jacobi, Jolande. *Complex/Archetype/Symbol in the Psychology of C.G. Jung*. Princeton University Press, 1974.

Jacobi, Jolande. *The Psychology of C.G. Jung*. Yale University Press, 1973.

Jacoby, Mario A. *Longing for Paradise: Psychological Perspectives on an Archetype*. Sigo Press, 1985.

Jaffe, Aniela. *C.G. Jung: Word and Image*. Princeton University Press, 1978.

Jaffe, Aniela. *The Myth of Meaning in the Work of C.G. Jung*. Daimon, 1984.

Jaffe, Aniela. *Reflections on the Life and Dreams of C.G. Jung: From Conversations with Jung*. Daimon, 2023.

James, William. *Psychology: The Briefer Course*. Edited by Gordon Allport. Harper & Brothers, 1961.

James, William. *The Varieties of Religious Experience: A Study in Human Nature*. Collier, 1961.

Jekels, Ludwig. "The Psychology of the Festival of Christmas." In *Selected Papers*, 142–158. International Universities Press, 1952.

Jessen, G., B.F Jensen, E. Arensman, V. Bille-Brahe, P. Crepet, D. Deleo, K. Hawton, C. Haring, H. Hjelmeland, K. Michel, A. Ostamo, E. Salander-Renberg, A. Schmidtke, B. Temesuary, and D. Wasserman. "Attempted Suicide and Major Public Holidays in Europe: Findings from the WHO/EURO Multicenter Study on Parasuicide." *ACTA Psychiatrica Scandivavica* 99, no. 6 (1999): 412–18.

Jones, Charles W. *Saint Nicholas of Myra, Bari, and Manhattan: Biography of a Legend*. University of Chicago Press, 1978.

Jones, Ernest. "The Significance of Christmas." In *Essays in Applied Psycho-Analysis* Vol. 2, in series "Essays In Folklore, Anthropology and Religion." Hogarth Press, 1951: 212–224.

Jones, Prudence and Nigel Pennick. *A History of Pagan Europe*. Routledge, 1995.

Jordan, Michael. *Encyclopedia of the Gods*. Facts on File, 1993.

Jowett, B., trans. "The Phaedrus." *The Works of Plato*. Tudor Publishing Company, n.d.

Jung, C.G. "Address at the Presentation of the Jung Codex (1953)." In *The Symbolic Life: Miscellaneous Writings*, vol. 18 *Collected Works*, 826–830. Princeton University Press, 1976.

Jung, C.G. *Aion: Researches into the Phenomenology of the Self*, vol. 9ii, *Collected Works*. Princeton University Press, 1975.

Jung, C.G. "Analytical Psychology and Education (1946)." In *The Development of Personality*, vol. 17, *Collected Works*. Princeton University Press, 1974.

Jung, C.G. *Analytical Psychology: Its Theory and Practice*. Pantheon Books, 1968.

Jung, C.G. "Answer to Job (1952)." In *Psychology and Religion: West and East*, vol. 11, *Collected Works*. Princeton University Press, 1975.

Jung, C.G. "Archetypes of the Collective Unconscious (1954)." In *The Archetypes of the Collective Unconscious*, vol. 9i, *Collected Works*. Princeton University Press, 1975.

Jung, C.G. "Commentary on 'The Secret of the Golden Flower' (1957)." In *Alchemical Studies*, vol. 13, *Collected Works*. Princeton University Press, 1976.

Jung, C.G. *Experimental Researches*. Vol 2, Collected Works. Edited by Gerhard Adler. Princeton University Press, 1973.

Jung, C.G. "Flying Saucers: A Modern Myth of Things Seen (1958)." In *Civilization in Transition,* vol. 10, *Collected Works*. Princeton University Press, 1975.

Jung, C.G. "Fundamental Questions of Psychotherapy (1951)." In *The Practice of Psychotherapy,* vol. 16, *Collected Works*. Princeton University Press, 1975.

Jung, C.G. "Jung and Religious Belief." In *The Symbolic Life: Miscellaneous Writings,* vol. 18, *Collected Works*. Princeton University Press, 1976.

Jung, C.G. "The Meaning of Psychology for Modern Man (1934)." *Civilization in Transition,* vol. 10, *Collected Works.* Princeton University Press, 1975.

Jung, C.G. *Memories, Dreams, Reflections (1961)*. Edited by Aniela Jaffe. Vintage Books, 1989.

Jung, C.G. *Modern Man in Search of a Soul*. Translated by W.S. Dell and Cary F. Baynes. Harcourt, Brace & World, 1933.

Jung, C.G. *Mysterium Coniunctionis (1954)*, vol. 14, *Collected Works*. Princeton University Press, 1976.

Jung, C.G. *Nietzsche's Zarathustra: Notes on the seminar given in 1934–1939*. Edited by J.L. Jarrett. Princeton University Press, 1988.

Jung, C.G. "On the Doctrine of Complexes 1911." In *Experimental Researches,* vol. 2, *Collected Works*. Princeton University Press, 1973.

Jung, C.G. "On the Nature of the Psyche." In *Structure and Dynamics of the Psyche,* edited and translated by Gerhard Adler and R.F.C. Hull, vol. 8, *Collected Works*. Princeton University Press, 1975

Jung, C.G. "On the Psychology of the Child Archetype." In *The Archetypes of the Collective Unconscious,* vol. 9i, *Collected Works*. Princeton University Press, 1977.

Jung, C.G. "On the Psychology of the Unconscious (1917)." In *Two Essays in Analytical Psychology,* vol. 7, *Collected Works*. Princeton University Press, 1975.

Jung, C.G. "On the Relation of Analytical Psychology to Poetry (1931)." In *The Spirit in Man, Art, and Literature,* vol. 15, *Collected Works*. Princeton University Press, 1975.

Jung, C.G. *The Portable Jung.* Edited by Joseph Campbell. Viking, 1973.

Jung, C.G. "Principles of Practical Psychotherapy (1935)." In *The Practice of Psychotherapy,* vol. 16, *Collected Works*. Princeton University Press, 1975.

Jung, C.G. "A Psychological Approach to the Dogma of the Trinity." In *Psychology and Religion: West and East,* vol. 11, *Collected Works*. Princeton University Press, 1975.

Jung, C.G. "The Psychological Aspects of the Kore (1951)." In *The Archetypes of the Collective Unconscious,* vol 9i, *Collected Works.* Princeton University Press, 1975.

Jung, C.G. "The Psychological Foundations of Belief in Spirits (1948)." In *Structure and Dynamics of The Psyche,* vol. 8, *Collected Works.* Princeton University Press, 1975.

Jung, C.G. *Psychological Types (1921)*, vol. 6, *Collected Works*. Princeton University Press, 1976.

Jung, C.G. *Psychology and Alchemy (1943)*, vol. 12, *Collected Works.* Princeton University Press, 1974.

Jung, C.G. "The Psychology of Dementia Praecox (1907)." In *The Psychogenesis of Mental Disease,* vol. 3 *Collected Works*. Princeton University Press, 1975.

Jung, C.G. "Psychology and Literature (1950)." In *The Spirit of Man, Art, and Literature,* vol. 15 *Collected Works*. Princeton University Press, 1975.

Jung, C.G. *Psychology and Religion*. Yale University Press, 1963.

Jung, C.G. "The Psychology of the Transference (1946)." In *The Practice of Psychotherapy*, vol. 16 *Collected Works*. Princeton University Press, 1975.

Jung, C.G. *The Red Book*. Norton, 2009.

Jung, C.G. "A Rejoinder to Dr. Bally (1934)." In *Civilization in Transition*, vol. 10, *Collected Works*. Princeton University Press, 1975.

Jung, C.G. "The Relations between the Ego and the Unconscious (1917, 1943)." In *Two Essays in Analytical Psychology*, vol. 7, *Collected Works*. Princeton University Press, 1975.

Jung, C.G. "Schizophrenia (1958)." In *The Psychogenesis of Mental Illness*, vol. 3, *Collected Works*. Princeton University Press, 1972.

Jung, C.G. "The Significance of Constitution and Heredity in Psychology (1929)." In *The Structure and Dynamics of the Psyche*, vol. 8, *Collected Works*. Princeton University Press, 1975.

Jung, C.G. "The Spirit Mercurius." In *Alchemical Studies*, vol. 13, *Collected Works*. Princeton University Press, 1976.

Jung, C.G. "The State of Psychotherapy Today." In *Civilization in Transition*, vol. 10, *Collected Works*. Princeton University Press, 1970.

Jung, C.G. *Symbols of Transformation*, vol. 5, *Collected Works*. Princeton University Press, 1975.

Jung, C.G. "Synchronicity: An Acausal Connecting Principle (1952)." In *The Structure and Dynamics of the Psyche*, vol. 8, *Collected Works*. Princeton University Press, 1975.

Jung, C.G. "The Transcendent Function (1916)." In *The Structure and Dynamics of the Psyche*, vol. 8, *Collected Works*. Princeton University Press, 1975.

Jung, C.G. "Transformation Symbolism in the Mass (1954)." In *Psychology and Religion: West and East*, vol. 11, *Collected Works*. Princeton University Press, 1975.

Jung, C.G. *The Undiscovered Self*. Mentor Book, 1958.

Jung, C.G. "Women in Europe (1927)." In *Civilization in Transition*, vol. 10, *Collected Works*. Princeton University Press, 1975.

Jung, C.G. *The Zofingia Lectures*. Vol. Supplementary A, *Collected Works*. Princeton University Press, 1983.

Kadhim, Nada, Catherine E. Amiot, and Winnifred R. Louis. "The Buffering Role of Social Norms for Unhealthy Easting Before, During and After the Christmas Holidays: A Longitudinal Study." *Group Dynamics: Theory, Research, and Practice* 27, no. 2 (2023): 133–50.

Kaplan, Louise J. *Oneness and Separateness: From Infant to Individual*. Simon and Schuster, 1978.

Karas, Sheryl Ann. *The Solstice Evergreen: The History, Folklore and Origins of the Christmas Tree*. Aslan Publishing, 1991.

Kasser, Tim and Kennon M. Sheddon. "What Makes for a Merry Christmas?" *Journal of Happiness Studies* 3, no. 4 (2002): 313–29.

Kellogg, Rhoda. *Analyzing Children's Art*. Mayfield Publishing, 1970.

Kellogg, Rhoda. *The Psychology of Children's Art*. CRM Inc., 1967.

Kennedy, Benjamin Hall. *P. Vergili Maronis, Bucolica, Georgica, Aeneis: The Works of Virgil with Commentary and Appendix*. Longmans, Green, and Co., 1876.

Kerferd, G.B. "Psyche." In *The Encyclopedia of Philosophy*, edited by Paul Edwards. Macmillan, 1967.

Keyte, Hugh and Andrew Parrott. "Psychology and the Bible: Three Worlds of the Text." *Pastoral Psychology* 51 (2002): 125–34.

Keyte, Hugh and Andrew Parrott, eds. *The Shorter New Oxford Book of Carols*. Oxford University Press, 1993.

Killinger, John. "Home for Christmas." *Preaching*, no. November/December 1989. preaching. com/sermons/christmas-home-for-christmas-text-luke-2/.

Kinukawa, Hisako. "The Christian Church in Japan." First Congregational Church, Guilford, CT, November 30, 2003.

Kinzer, Stephen. "Strange, That's Santa in the Seat of the Sultans." *The New York Times*, December 21, 1996, 4.

Knickerbocker, Diedrich. *A History of New York from the Beginning of the World to the End of the Dutch Dynasty (1809)*. John R. Alden, 1884.

Kohut, Heinz. *The Analysis of the Self: A Systematic Approach to the Psychoanalytic Treatment of Narcissistic Personality Disorders*. International Universities Press, 1971.

Kohut, Heinz. "Forms and Transformation of Narcissism." *Journal of the American Psychoanalytic Association* 14 (1966).

Kohut, Heinz. *How Does Analysis Cure*. University of Chicago Press, 1984.

Kohut, Heinz. "The Psychoanalyst in the Community of Scholars." In *The Search for the Self: Selected Writings of Heinz Kohut: 1950–1978*, vol. 1, edited by Paul H. Ornstein, 685–724. International Universities Press, 1978.

Kohut, Heinz. "Reflections on Advances in Self Psychology." In *Advances in Self Psychology*, edited by Arnold Goldberg, 473–554. International Universities Press, 1980.

Kohut, Heinz. *The Restoration of the Self*. International Universities Press, 1977.

Kohut, Heinz. *Self Psychology and the Humanities: Reflections on a New Psychoanalytic Approach*. Norton, 1985.

Kohut, Heinz and Wolf, Ernest S. "The Disorders of the Self and Their Treatment: An Outline." In *Essential Papers on Narcissism*, edited by Andrew P. Morrison. New York University Press, 1986.

Kopper, Philip. *A Christmas Testament*. Stewart, Tabori & Chang, 1982.

Kuper, Adam. "The English Christmas and the Family: Time Out and Alternative Realities." In *Unwrapping Christmas*, edited by Daniel Miller, 157–75. Clarendon, 1993.

Lachmann, F.M. and M. Lachmann. "Mary Tyrone's Long Day's Journey into Night." *The Annal of Psychoanalysis* 20 (1992): 235–44.

Lapointe, Francois H. "Origin and Evolution of the Term 'Psychology'." In *American Psychologist* 25, no. 7 (1970): 640–6.

Latourette, Kenneth Scott. *The First Five Centuries: A History of the Expansion of Christianity*, vol. 1. Harper & Brothers, 1937.

Leary, Lewis. *Washington Irving*. University of Minnesota Press, 1963.

Legendre, M. and A. Hartmann. *Domenikos Theotokopoulos Called El Greco*. Commodore Press, 1937.

Lenhart, James W., et. al. *Pilgrim Hymnal*. The Pilgrim Press, 1931, 1935, 1958; renewed 1986. 28th printing, 1988.

Leo, Pope. *Sermons*. Edited by Philip Schaff. Vol. 12, *Nicene and Post-Nicene Father of the Christian Church: Second Series*. Eerdmans, 1979.

Lesley, Adkins and Roy A. Adkins. *Dictionary of Roman Religion*. Oxford University Press, 1996.

Lester, David. "Suicide and Homicide Rates on National Holidays." *Psychological Reports* 60, no. 2 (1987): 414.

Levi-Strauss, Claude. "Father Christmas Executed." In *Unwrapping Christmas*, edited by Daniel Miller, 38–51. Clarendon Press, 1993.

Levy, Florence J. "On the Significance of Christmas for the 'Wolf Man.'" *Psychoanalytic Review* 55, no. 4 (1989): 615–22.

Lichtenberg, Joseph D. and Ernest Wolf. "General Principles of Self Psychology: A Position Statement." *Journal of the American Psychoanalytic Association* 45, no. 2 (1997).

Lifton, Robert Jay. *The Protean Self: Human Resilience in an Age of Fragmentation.* University of Chicago Press, 1993.

Lossky, Andrew. *Louis XIV and the French Monarchy.* Rutgers University Press, 1994.

Ludwig, M. "Christmas: An Event Driven by Our Hormones?" *Journal of Neuroendocrinology* 23, no. 12 (2011): 1191–3.

Mabie, Hamilton W., ed. *The Book of Christmas.* Macmillan, 1909.

MacGahan. *Twilight Park: The First Hundred Years.* Allen D. Bragdon, 1988.

MacGuire, Alane Sauder. *Course: Two Essays on Analytical Psychology.* C.G. Jung Institute, Fall 2005.

MacMullen. *Christianity & Paganism in the Fourth to Eighth Centuries.* Yale University Press, 1997.

Macrobius. *The Saturnalia.* Translated by Percival Vaughan Davies. Columbia University Press, 1969.

McGilchrist, Iain. *The Divided Brain and the Search for Meaning: Why We Are So Unhappy.* eBook: Yale University Press, 2012.

"The Magic Circle." Editorial, *The New York Times*, December 25, 1985, 30.

Magid, Barry. "Self Psychology Meets the Wolf Man." In *Freud's Case Studies: Self-Psychological Perspectives*, edited by Barry Magid. Analytic Press, 1993.

Maier, Paul L. *In the Fullness of Time: A Historian Looks at Christmas, Easter, and the Early Church.* Kregel Publications, 1997.

Martin, Ralph P. *Worship in the Early Church.* William B. Eerdmans, 1976.

Martyr, St. Justin. *The First and Second Apologies.* Translated by Leslie William Barnard. Edited by Walter J. Burghardt. Vol. 56, *Ancient Christian Writers: The Words of the Fathers in Translation.* Paulist Press, 1997.

Mather, Eleanore Price. *Edward Hicks Primitive Quaker: His Religion in Relation to His Art.* Pendle Hill Publications, 1970.

Matthews, John. *The Winter Solstice: The Sacred Traditions of Christmas.* Quest Books, 1998.

May, Robert E. *Yuletide in Dixie: Slavery, Christmas, and Southern Memory.* University of Virginia Press, 2019.

McGuire, William and R.F.C. Hull, eds. *C.G. Jung Speaking: Interviews and Encounters.* Princeton University Press, 1977.

McKinion, Steven A., ed. *Ancient Christian Commentary on Scripture: Isaiah 1–39.* Vol. 10. InterVarsity Press, 2004.

McNeill, John T. and Helena M. Gamer. "Penance in the Ancient Church." In *Medieval Handbooks of Penance.* Columbia University Press, 1990.

Meir, Brian. "Bah Humbug: Unexpected Christmas Cards and the Reciprocity Norm." *The Journal of Social Psychology* 156, no. 4 (2016): 449.

Meir, Brian. *The World's Great Madonnas: An Anthology of Pictures, Poetry, Music and Stories Centering in the Life of the Madonna and Her Son.* Harper and Brothers, 1947.

Meltsoff, A.N. and R.W. Borton. "Imitation of Facial and Manual Gestures by Human Neonates." *Science* 198 (1977): 75–88.

Mencken, H.L. *Christmas Story*. Knopf, 1946.

Menninger, Karl. *Man against Himself*. Harcourt Brace Jovanovich, 1938.

Meter, David Van. *Roman Imperial Coins: A Complete Guide to the History, Types and Values of Roman Imperial Coinage*. Laurion Press, 1991.

Metzger, Bruce M. *The Bible in Translation: Ancient and English Versions*. Baker Academic, 2001.

Metzger, Bruce M. and Roland E. Murphy, eds. *New Revised Standard Version of the Bible*. Oxford University Press, 1991.

Metzger, Marcel. *History of the Liturgy: The Major Stages*. Translated by Madeleine M. Beaumont. Liturgical Press, 1997.

Meyer, Marvin W. *The Secret Teachings of Jesus: Four Gnostic Gospels*. Random House, 1984.

Miles, Clement A. *Christmas in Ritual and Tradition, Christian and Pagan,* 2nd ed. T. Fisher Unwin, 1913.

Miles, Jack. "Jesus before He Could Talk." *New York Times Magazine*, December 24, 1995, 28–33.

Miliora, Maria T. "Heinz Kohut and Eugene O'Neill: An Essay on the Application of Self Psychology to O'Neill's Dramas." *The Annual of Psychoanalysis* 28 (2000): 244–58.

Miller, Alice. *The Drama of the Gifted Child: How Narcissistic Parents Form and Deform the Emotional Lives of Their Talented Children*. Basic Books, 1981.

Miller, John W. *Jesus at Thirty: A Psychological and Historical Portrait*. Fortress Press, 1997.

Minear, Paul S. *The Bible and the Historian: Breaking the Silence About God in Biblical Studies*. Abingdon Press, 2002.

Minear, Paul S. *Mark*. Edited by Balmer H. Kelly. 25 vols. Vol. 17, *The Layman's Bible Commentary*. John Knox Press, 1962.

Mish, Frederick C., ed. *Webster's Ninth New Collegiate Dictionary*. Merriam-Webster, 1988.

Mitton, C.L. "Peace in the New Testament." In *The Interpreters Dictionary of the Bible*, Vol. 3, K–Q. Abingdon Press, 1962.

Modell, Arnold H. "Comments on the Rise of Narcissism." In *The Future of Psychoanalysis*, edited by Arnold Goldberg. International Universities Press, 1983.

Moeran, Brian and Lise Skov. "Cinderella Christmas: Kitsch, Consumerism, and Youth in Japan." In *Unwrapping Christmas*, edited by Daniel Miller. Clarendon, 1993: 105–33.

Mohamed, Besheer. "Christmas Also Celebrated by Many non-Christians." *Pew Research Center*, December 23, 2013. pewresearch.org/short-reads/2013/12/23/christmas-also-celebrated-by-many-non-christians (accessed November 15, 2024).

Mowinckel, S. *He That Cometh*. Translated by G.W. Anderson. Abingdon Press, 1954.

Moynahan, Brian. *The Faith: A History of Christianity*. Doubleday, 2002.

Neruda, Pablo. "We Are Many." In *Extravagaria*, translated by Alastair Reid. Farrar, Straus and Giroux, 1974.

Neumann, Erich. *The Child: Structure and Dynamics of Nascent Personality*. G.P. Putnam's Sons, 1973.

Neumann, Erich. *Depth Psychology and a New Ethic*. Translated by Eugene Rolfe. Harper Torchbooks, 1973.

Neumann, Erich. "Narcissism: Normal Self-Formation and the Primary Relation to the Mother." *Spring.* Analytical Psychology Club of New York, 1966.

Neumann, Erich. *The Origins and History of Consciousness.* Princeton University Press, 1970.

Newman, Alexander. *Non-Compliance in Winnicott's Words: A Companion to the Word of D.W. Winnicott.* New York University Press, 1995.

Nichols, Christopher. "From Jól to Yule," *Scandinavian Archaeology,* December 23, 2021 (scandinavianarchaeology.com).

Nissenbaum, Stephen. *The Battle for Christmas: A Social and Cultural History of Christmas That Shows How It Was Transformed from an Unruly Carnival Season into the Quintessential American Family Holiday.* Knopf, 1996.

Norris, Kendrick. "Projection and the Parish." D.Min. Dissertation, Andover Newton Theological School, 1984.

Nouwen, Henri J.M. *The Return of the Prodigal Son.* Image Books, 1992.

Nthla, Khumo. "Community." *Living Pulpit* 3, no. 4 (1994).

O'Cass, Aron and Peter Clarke. "Dear Santa, Do You Have My Brand: A Study of Brand Requests, Awareness and Request Styles at Christmas Time." *Journal of Consumer Behavior* 2, no. 1 (2002): 37–53.

O'Dea, Thomas F. *"The Sociology of Religion."* In *Foundations of Modern Sociology,* edited by Alex Inkeles. Prentice-Hall, 1966.

O'Neill, Eugene. *Long Day's Journey into Night.* Yale University Press, 1956.

Obholzer, Karin. *The Wolf-Man: Conversations with Freud's Patient—Sixty Years Later.* Translated by Michael Shaw. Continuum, 1982.

Oleszkiewicz, Malgorzata. "Mother of God and Mother Earth: Religion, Gender, and Transformation in East-Central Europe." Hawaii International Conference on Arts and Humanities, San Antonio, 2003.

Pankejeff, Sergius. *The Wolf-Man: The Double Story of Freud's Most Famous Case.* Edited by Muriel Gardiner. Basic Books, 1971.

Partridge, Burgo. *A History of Orgies.* Bonanza Books, 1960.

Pelikan, Jaroslav. *Jesus through the Centuries: His Place in the History of Culture.* Yale University Press, 1985.

Peters, R.S. and C.A. Mace. "Psychology." In *The Encyclopedia of Philosophy,* edited by Peter Edwards. Macmillan, 1967.

Pew Research. "Americans Say Religious Aspects of Christmas Are Declining in Public Life," December 12, 2017. pewresearch.org/religion/2017/12/12/americans-say-religious-aspects-of-christmas-are-declining-in-public-life (accessed November 15, 2024).

Phillips, David P. and John S. Wills. "A Drop in Suicides around Major Holidays." *Suicide and Life-Threatening Behavior* 17, no. 1 (1987): 1–12.

Phillips, David P., Jason R. Jarvinen, Ian S. Abramson, Rosalie R. Phillips, "Cardiac Mortality is Higher Around Christmas and New Year's Than at Any Other Time: the Holidays as a Risk Factor for Death." *Circulation* 110, no. 25 (2004).

Pine, K.J. and A. Nash. "Dear Santa: The Effects of Television Advertising on Young Children." *International Journal of Behavioral Development* 26, no. 6 (2002): 529–39.

Pinchbeck, Daniel. *Breaking Open the Head: A Psychedelic Journey into the Heart of Contemporary Shamanism.* Broadway Books, 2002.

Pintard, John. *Letters from John Pintard to His Daughter Eliza Noel Pintard Davidson 1816–1820.* Vol. 1. New York Historical Society, 1940.

Pintard, John. *Letters from John Pintard to His Daughter Eliza Noel Pintard Davidson 1821 1827.* Vol. 2. New York Historical Society, 1940.

Pintard, John. *Letters from John Pintard to His Daughter Eliza Noel Pintard Davidson 1828–1831*. Vol. 3. New York Historical Society, 1941.

Plotinus. *The Essential Plotinus*. Translated by Elmer O'Brien. Hackett Publishing, 1964.

Plotinus. *The Six Enneads*. Translated by Stephen MacKenna and B.S. Page. William Benton, 1952.

Pot, Gaijin, "Ho, Ho, Hotei: The Japanese Santa Claus." *Japan Today*, December 7, 2021.

Powell, Matthew. *The Christmas Creche: Treasure of Faith, Art & Theater*. Pauline Books & Media, 1997.

Putala, Allison C. *Christmas in Prose and Verse: Its Origin, Celebration and Significance*. Platinum Press, 2000.

Randall, Robert L. *The Eternal Triangle: Pastor, Spouse and Congregation*. Fortress Press, 1992.

Randolph, Edward F. "The Christmas Message for 1941 A.D." *Pennsylvania Co-Op Review* 9, no. 1 (1941): 17–18.

Reade, Charles. *Put Yourself in His Place* (1870). Chatto & Windus, 1885.

Reagan, Michael, ed. *The Hand of God: Thoughts and Images Reflecting the Spirit of the Universe*. Andrews McMeel, 1999.

Records of the Governor and Company of Massachusetts Bay, vol. 4, part 1, 1853.

Reeves, Margaret. "'A Prospect of Flowers': Concepts of Childhood and Female Youth in Seventeenth-Century British Culture." In *The Youth of Early Modern Women*, edited by E.S. Cohen and M. Reeves, 36–37. Amsterdam University Press, 2018.

Restad, Penne L. *Christmas in America: A History*. Oxford University Press, 1995.

Rilke, Rainer Maria. *Letters of Rainer Maria Rilke: 1892–1910*. Norton, 1945.

Robinson, Herbert Spencer and Knox Wilson. *Myths and Legends of All Nations*. Bantam Books, 1961.

Rogers, William A. "Tillich and Depth Psychology." In *The Thought of Paul Tillich*, edited by James Luther Adams, Wilhelm Pauck, and Roger Lincoln Shinn, 102–18. Harper & Row, 1985.

Roll, Susan K. *Toward the Origins of Christmas*. Kok Pharos Publishing House, 1995.

Rollins, Wayne G. *Jung and the Bible*. John Knox Press, 1983.

Rollins, Wayne G. "Lecture *Psychologique*." Unpublished manuscript, 2005.

Rollins, Wayne G. "Psychology, Hermeneutics, and the Bible." In *Jung and the Interpretation of the Bible*, edited by David L. Miller. Continuum, 1995.

Rollins, Wayne G. *Soul and Psyche: The Bible in Psychological Perspective*. Fortress Press, 1999.

Ronander, Albert C. and Ethel K. Porter. *Guide to the Pilgrim Hymnal*. United Church Press, 1966.

Salmon, E. Togo. *Roman Coins and Public Life under the Empire*. University of Michigan Press, 1999.

Sandburg, Carl. *The Complete Poems of Carl Sandburg*. Harcourt Brace Jovanovich, 1970.

Sansom, William. *A Book of Christmas*. McGraw-Hill Book Company, 1968.

Sato, Wataru, Taknori Kochiyama, Shota Uono, Yasutaka Kubota, Reiko Sawada, Sayaka Yoshimura, Motomi Toichi . "The Structural Neural Substrate of Subjective Happiness." *Scientific* Reports 5.1 (2015): 15891

Schneider, Else, Timur Liwinski, Lukas Imfeld, Undine E. Lang, and Annette B. Bruhl. "Who is Afraid of Christmas? The Effect of Christmas and Easter Holidays on Psychiatric

Hospitalizations and Emergencies—Systematic Review and Single Center Experience From 2012 to 2021." *Front Psychiatry* 11, no. 13 (2023).

Scott, T. Kermit. *Augustine: His Thought in Context*. Paulist Press, 1995.

Sear, David R. *Roman Coins and Their Values*. Audley House, 1974.

Sedgwick, Elizabeth. "The Game of Jackstraws and The Christmas Box." In *The Pearl; or, Affection's Gift*. Thomas T. Ash, 1834.

Seymour, Robert. *A Survey of the Cities of London and Weftminfter*. T. Read, 1733.

Shakespeare, William. *The Tragedy of Hamlet, Prince of Denmark*. Washington Square Press, 1992.

Shane, Estelle. "Self-Psychology: A New Conceptualization for the Understanding of Learning Disabled Children." In *Kohut's Legacy: Contributions to Self Psychology*, edited by Paul E. Stepansky and Arnold Goldberg. Analytic Press, 1984.

Sheen, Fulton J. *From the Angel's Blackboard: The Best of Fulton J. Sheen*. Triumph Books, 1995.

Shelley, Mary. *Frankenstein; or, the Modern Prometheus (1818)*. Norton, 1996.

Sherif, M. "Self Concept." In *International Encyclopedia of the Social Sciences*, vol. 14, edited by D.L. Sills, 150–9. Collier/Macmillan, 1968.

Siegel, Allen M. *Heinz Kohut and the Psychology of the Self*. Routledge, 1966.

Silverstein, Shel. *The Missing Piece*. Harper Collins, 1976.

Simek, Rudolph. *Dictionary of Northern Mythology*. Trans. Angela Hall. D.S. Brewer, 2007.

Smith, F. Hopkinson. *Colonel Carter's Christmas*. Charles Scribner's Sons, 1903.

Smith, Lillian. *Memory of a Large Christmas*. Norton, 1961.

Smith, Mariann. *Edward Hicks*. Exhibition notes. https://buffaloakg.org/artworks/194018 -peaceable-kingdom (accessed November 9, 2024).

Smith, William Cantwell. "The Study of Religion and the Study of the Bible." *Journal of the American Academy of Religion* 39, no. 2 (1971): 131–40.

Sobersides, Solomon. *Christmas Tales for the Amusement and Instruction of Young Ladies and Gentlemen in Winter Evening*. Isaiah Thomas, 1786.

"Songs and Rhymes from Sweden," Mama Lisa's World of International Music & Culture, mamalisa.com/?t=es&p=1302.

Sparhawk, Thomas G. "Traditional Holidays and Suicide." *Psychological Reports* 60, no. 1 (1987): 245–6.

Squire, Charles. *The Mythology of the British Islands*. Blackie and Son, 1905.

Stagg, Frank. *Polarities of Man's Existence in Biblical Perspective*. Westminster Press, 1973.

Staley, Jeffrey L. *Reading with a Passion: Rhetoric, Autobiography, and the American West in the Gospel of John*. Continuum, 1995.

Staley, Vernon. *The Liturgical Year: An Explanation of the Origin, History and Significance of the Festival and Fasting Days of the English Church*. A.R. Molwbray & Co., 1907.

Stark, Freya. *The Zodiac Arch*. Tauris Parke Paperbacks, 1968.

Stein, Murray. *The Bible as Dream: A Jungian Interpretation*. Chiron, 2018.

Sterba, Richard. "On Christmas." *The Psychoanalytic Quarterly* 13 (1944): 79–83.

Sterling, Lawrence. "Winnicott and the Mother States." *The Journal of the Squiggle Foundation* 6 (1991).

Stern, D.N., L. Hofer, W. Haft, and J. Dore. "Affect Attunement: The Sharing of Feeling States between Mother and Infant by Means of Inter-Modal Fluency." In *Social Perception in Infants*, edited by T.M Field and N.A. Fox, 249–68. Ablex Publishing, 1985.

Stern, Daniel N. *The Interpersonal World of the Infant*. Basic Books, 1985.

Stern, Philip Van Doren. *The Greatest Gift*. Penguin, 1996.

Stevenson, Robert Louis. *The Strange Case of Dr. Jekyll and Mr. Hyde*. Charles Scribners' Sons, 1886.

Strauss, Gordon D., Joel Yager, and Gayle E. Strauss. "The Cutting Edge in Psychiatry." *American Journal of Psychiatry* 141, no. 1 (1984): 38–43.

Stokker, Kathleen. *Keeping Christmas: Yuletide Traditions in Norway and the New Land*. Minnesota Historical Society Press, 2000.

Strozier, Charles B. *Heinz Kohut: The Making of a Psychoanalyst*. Farrar, Straus and Giroux, 2001.

Sturlson, Snorri. *Heimskringla or The Lives of the Norse Kings*. Dover, 2018.

Sullivan, Harry Stack. *The Interpersonal Theory of Psychiatry*. Norton, 1953.

Swarzenski, Hanns. *An 18th Century Creche*. Museum of Fine Arts, 1967.

Talley, Thomas J. *The Origins of the Liturgical Year*. Pueblo Publishing Company, 1986.

Telushkin, Rabbi Joseph. *Jewish Literacy: The Most Important Things to Know About the Jewish Religion, Its People, and Its History*. William Morrow, 1991.

Tertullian, De Anima. An English translation of Tertullian's *A Treatise on the Soul* can be found at www.newadvent.org/fathers/0310.htm.

Teusch, Rita. "Selections from Two German Journals." *The Psychoanalytic Quarterly* 83, no. 3 (2014).

Theissen, Gerd. *Psychological Aspects of Pauline Theology*. Translated by John P. Galvin. Fortress Press, 1987.

Thiery, Clément. "King Cake: A French Tradition Little Known in the U.S." *France-Amérique,* January 2, 2020.

Thomas, Dylan. *A Child's Christmas in Wales*. New Direction Books, 1954.

Thompson, Sue Ellen. *Holiday Symbols: A Guide to the Legend and Lore,* 2nd ed. Omnigraphics, 2000.

Thundy, Zacharias P. *Buddha and Christ: Nativity Stories and Indian Traditions*. E.J. Brill, 1993.

Thurman, Howard. *The Mood of Christmas & Other Celebrations*. Friends United, 1985.

Tille, Alexander. *Yule and Christmas: Their Place in the Germanic Year*. David Nutt, 1899.

Tillich, Paul. *Dynamics of Faith*. Harper Torchbooks, 1957.

Tillich, Paul. *The New Being*. Charles Scribner's Sons, 1955.

Tillich, Paul. *Systematic Theology: Three Volumes in One*. University of Chicago Press, 1967.

Tolkien, J.R.R. *The Father Christmas Letters*. Houghton Mifflin, 1976.

Todd, Margo. *The Culture of Protestantism in Early Modern Scotland*. Yale University Press, 2002.

Tozer, H.F. *Dante: La Divna Commedia: Notes on Inferno*. Clarendon Press, 1902.

Ueland, Brenda. *Me*. The Schubert Club, 1983.

Ulansey, David. *The Origins of the Mithraic Mysteries: Cosmology and Salvation in the Ancient World*. Oxford University Press, 1989.

Updike, John. *The Twelve Terrors of Christmas*. Pomegrante, 1993.

van Dyke, Henry. *The Story of the Other Wise Man*. Harper & Brothers, 1906.

Van Rensselaer, Mrs. Schuyler. *History of the City of New York in the Seventeenth Century*. Vol. 1. Macmillan, 1909.

Velamoor, Varadaraj R., Zach Z. Cernovsky, and Lakshmi P. Voruganti, "Psychiatric Emergency Rates During the Christmas Season in the Years 1991–1997." *Psychological Reports* 85 no. 2 (1999): 403–4.

Velamoor, Varadaraj R., Lakshmi P. Voruganti, and Neelesh K. Nadkarni. "Feelings About Christmas as Reported by Psychiatric Emergency Patients." *Social Behavior and Personality* 27, no. 3 (1999): 303–8.

Virgil. *The Pastoral Poems: A Translation of the Ecologues.* Translated by E.V. Rieu. Penguin Books, 1949.

Volk, A.A. and J.A. Atkinson. "Infant and Child Death in the Human Environment of Evolutionary Adaption." *Evolution and Human Behavior* 34, no. 3 (2013): 182–92.

Volkan, Vamik D. and Gabriele Ast. *Siblings in the Unconscious and Psychopathology.* International Universities Press, 1997.

Von Franz, Marie-Louise. *Creation Myths.* Revised ed. Shambhala, 1995.

Von Franz, Marie-Louise. "The Inferior Function." In *Lectures on Jung's Typology.* Dallas: Spring Publications, 1986.

Von Franz, Marie-Louise. "The Process of Individuation." In *Man and His Symbols*, edited by C.G. Jung. A Windfall Book, 1983.

Von Franz, Marie-Louise. *Projection and Re-collection in Jungian Psychology: Reflections of the Soul.* Open Court, 1980.

Wallace, Edwin R. *Freud and Anthropology: A History and Reappraisal.* International Universities Press, 1983.

Wallace, Edwin R. "Freud and Religion: A History and Reappraisal." In *The Psychoanalytic Study of Society,* Vol. 10, edited by Werner Muensterberger, 113–61. Lawrence Erlbaum Associates, 1984.

Walsh, William S. *Curiosities of Popular Customs and of Rites, Ceremonies, Observations, and Miscellaneous Antiquities.* Gibbings & Co., 1898.

Wand, J.W.C. *The Four Great Heresies.* A.R. Mowbray, 1967.

Weigall, Arthur. *The Paganism in Our Christianity.* G.P. Putnam's Sons, 1928.

White, James F. *Documents of Christian Worship: Descriptive and Interpretive Sources.* Westminster John Knox Press, 1992.

White, James F. *Introduction to Christian Worship,* 3rd ed. Abingdon, 2000.

White, Victor. *Soul and Psyche: An Enquiry into the Relationship of Psychiatry and Religion.* Collins and Havill Press, 1960.

Whitmont, Edward C. *The Symbolic Quest: Basic Concepts of Analytical Psychology.* Princeton University Press, 1991.

Whitney, William. "Heart Attacks Increase after 9/11." In *Psychology Today Online,* Nov. 14, 2003. psychologytoday.com/us/articles/200311/heart-attacks-increase-after-911.

Whittier, George Greenleaf. *The Complete Poetical Works of Whittier.* Houghton Mifflin Company Boston, 1894.

Wickes, Frances G. *The Inner World of Man.* Henry Holt, 1948.

Wiener, Jan. "Transference and Countertransference: Contemporary Perspectives." In *Analytical Psychology: Contemporary Perspectives in Jungian Analysis*, edited by J. Cambay and L. Carter. Brunner-Routledge, 2004.

Wilder, Thorton. *The Collected Short Plays of Thorton Wilder,* vol.1. Theater Communications Group, 1997.

Wilder, Thorton. *Our Town (1938).* Harper Colophon Books, 1964.

Wilkinson, John. *Egeria's Travels to the Holy Land*, Revised ed. Ariel Publishing House, 1981.

Wilkinson, Samuel T. *Purpose: What Evolution and Human Nature Imply about the Meaning of our Existence.* Pegasus Books, 2024.

Wink, Paul. "Freud, Truth, and the Wolf Man." *Psychoanalysis and Contemporary Thought* 13, no. 3 (1990): 365–416.

Winnicott, D.W. "Ego Distortion in Terms of True and False Self." In *The Maturational Process and the Facilitating Environment.* International Universities Press, 1960.

Wither, George. *Poems by George Wither.* George Routledge & Sons, 1891.

Witzig, J.S. "Theodore Flournoy—a friend indeed." *The Journal of Analytical Psychology* 27, no. 2 (1982): 131–48.

Wolf, Ernest S. "Selfobject Experiences: Development, Psychopathology, Treatment." In *Mahler and Kohut: Perspectives on Development, Psychopathology, and Technique,* edited by Selma Kramer and Salman Akhtar. Jason Aronson, 1994.

Wolman, Thomas. "Contrasting Roles of Narcissistic Mirroring." In *Mahler and Kohut: Perspectives on Development, Psychopathology, and Technique,* edited by Selma Kramer and Salman Akhtar. Jason Aronson, 1994.

Wright, Kenneth. *Vision and Separation.* J. Aronson, 1991.

WuDunn, Sherul. "A World of Christmas, Not Just for Christians." *The New York Times*, December 25, 1997, 6.

Yeats, W.B. *The Collected Poems of W.B. Yeats.* Macmillan, 1959.

Zimbardo, Philip. *Psychopathology: Biological and Social Factors of Mental Illness*, "Discovering Psychology" television series. Annenberg/Corporation for Public Broadcasting, 2001.

Index

For Product Safety Concerns and Information please contact our EU
representative GPSR@taylorandfrancis.com
Taylor & Francis Verlag GmbH, Kaufingerstraße 24, 80331 München, Germany

www.ingramcontent.com/pod-product-compliance
Lightning Source LLC
Chambersburg PA
CBHW050347270326
41926CB00016B/3639